D1180018

ANTON
CHEKHOV

PLAYS

ANTON
CHEKHOV

EIGHT
PLAYS

Translated by Elisaveta Fen

A LIMITED EDITION

THE FRANKLIN LIBRARY
Franklin Center, Pennsylvania
1976

CONTENTS

IVANOV

A DRAMA IN FOUR ACTS

THE
CHARACTERS

IVANOV, *Nikolai Alekseevich* (Kolya, Nikolàs, Nikolasha), *a permanent member of the County Council*

ANNA PETROVNA (Anya, Anyuta), *his wife; before her marriage and baptism called Sarah Abramson*

SHABELSKI, *Matvei Semënovich* (Count Matyusha), *Ivanov's maternal uncle*

LEBEDEV, *Pavel Kirillich* (Pasha), *the chairman of the County Council*

ZINAIDA SAVISHNA (Zyuzyushka), *his wife*

SASHA (Aleksandra Pavlovna, Sanichka, Shurka, Shurochka, Shura), *their daughter, aged twenty*

LVOV, *Yevgeni Konstantinovich, a young doctor*

BABAKINA, *Marfa Yegorovna* (Marfusha, Marfutka), *the young widow of a landowner and daughter of a rich merchant*

KOSYKH, *Dmitri Nikitich, excise officer*

BORKIN, *Mikhail Mikhailovich* (Misha, Michel), *a distant relative of Ivanov's and the steward of his estate*

AVDOTYA NAZAROVNA, *an old woman of no definite occupation*

YEGORUSHKA, *a dependent of the Lebedevs'*
FIRST GUEST
SECOND GUEST
THIRD GUEST
PËTR, *Ivanov's manservant*
GAVRILA, *Lebedev's manservant*
MAID
VISITORS *of both sexes*

The action takes place in one of the provinces of Central Russia

ACT ONE

The garden in Ivanov's estate. On the left, the front of the house with a terrace. One window is open. In front of the terrace a wide semicircular space from which, center and right, avenues lead into the more distant parts of the garden. On the right, garden seats and tables. A lamp on one of the tables is lit. The evening is drawing in. As the curtain rises, the sound of a cello and piano duet being practiced can be heard coming from indoors.

    Ivanov is sitting at the table, reading a book. Borkin, wearing shooting boots and carrying a gun, appears at the far end of the garden; he is rather drunk. On seeing Ivanov, he approaches him on tiptoe and, when quite near, aims the gun at his face.

IVANOV
Sees Borkin, starts, and jumps up
Misha, my God! What are . . . You frightened me.
I'm upset enough as it is, and now you, with your
stupid tricks.   *sits down*   You frightened me, and of
course you're only too pleased.
    BORKIN
Laughs heartily   There, there! I'm sorry, I'm sorry.
sits down beside him   I won't do it again, honestly I

won't. *takes off his peaked cap* It's hot. You won't believe me, old pal, but I've covered fifteen miles in less than three hours. I'm worn out. . . . Just feel my heart, see how it's thumping.

IVANOV

Continues reading All right, later on.

BORKIN

No, feel it now. *takes Ivanov's hand and puts it to his chest* Do you hear? Tum-tum-tum-tum-tum. That means I've got heart disease. I might die suddenly at any moment. Tell me, will you be sorry if I die?

IVANOV

I'm reading . . . Later on. . . .

BORKIN

No, seriously, will you be sorry if I die suddenly? Nikolai Alekseevich, will you be sorry if I die?

IVANOV

Don't pester me!

BORKIN

Tell me, my friend, will you be sorry?

IVANOV

I'm sorry that you smell of vodka. It's disgusting, Misha.

BORKIN

Laughs Do I really smell? Surprising. . . . Not that there's really anything surprising about it. At Plesniki I happened to meet the examining judge, and I must admit we both tossed down about eight glasses. Drinking is very harmful, generally speaking. Tell me, it is harmful, isn't it? Eh? Isn't it?

IVANOV

This is positively unbearable. I wish you'd understand how maddening it is.

BORKIN

Well, well. . . . I'm sorry, I'm sorry! Bless your heart!

Stay there; don't get up. *gets up and walks off* What
amazing people, you're not even allowed to talk to
them. *returns* Oh, yes. I'd almost forgotten. Please
let me have eighty-two rubles.

IVANOV

Why eighty-two rubles?

BORKIN

I must pay the workmen tomorrow.

IVANOV

I haven't got it.

BORKIN

Thanks very much! *mimics him* I haven't got it!
Can't you see that the workmen have got to be paid?
Haven't they?

IVANOV

I don't know. I haven't got anything today. Wait till
the first of the month; then I'll be getting my salary.

BORKIN

Oh, what's the use of discussing things with people
like you? The workmen won't come for their money
on the first of the month; they'll come tomorrow
morning!

IVANOV

Well, what can I do about it now? What's the good
of going on nagging and pestering me? And where
did you get this abominable habit of plaguing me
just when I'm busy reading or writing or . . .

BORKIN

What I want to know is: are the workmen to be paid
or aren't they? Oh, what's the use of talking to you!
waves his hand Call themselves landowners—the
devil take them! Rationalized farming! A thousand
acres of land—and not a kopeck in your pocket. It's
like owning a wine cellar without a corkscrew! See
if I don't sell the troika tomorrow. I will! I sold the

IVANOV

oats before they were harvested, and you see if I
don't go and sell the rye tomorrow too. *walks up
and down the stage* You don't think I'm going to
stand on ceremony about it—or do you? Well, I won't.
I'm not that sort of man.

*Shabelski's voice is heard through the window: "It's
quite impossible to play with you. You've no more ear
than a stuffed fish, and your touch is revolting!"*

ANNA PETROVNA
Appears at the open window
Who was that talking here just now? Was it you,
Misha? Why are you stamping around like that?

BORKIN
Anyone who had to deal with your *cher* Nicolàs
would stamp around!

ANNA PETROVNA
Listen, Misha, will you have some hay brought to
the croquet lawn?

BORKIN
Waves his hand
Leave me alone, please.

ANNA PETROVNA
Tut-tut, what a tone of voice! That tone of voice
doesn't suit you at all. If you want women to like you,
you must never be angry or high and mighty with
them. *to her husband* Nikolai, let's go and do
somersaults in the hay!

IVANOV
It's bad for you to stand at the open window, Anyuta.
Go in, please. *shouts* Uncle, will you shut the
window?

ANTON
CHEKHOV *The window is shut*

BORKIN

Another thing, don't forget that in two days' time
Lebedev will have to be paid the interest.

IVANOV

I know. I'll be at Lebedev's today and I'll ask him to
wait. *looks at his watch*

BORKIN

When will you be going to him?

IVANOV

Quite soon.

BORKIN

Eagerly Wait a minute! Isn't it Shurochka's birthday
today? Dear, dear, dear. . . . And I'd almost forgotten!
What a memory, eh? *skips around* I'll be off, I'll
be off. *chants* I'll be off. I'm going to have a swim
and chew some paper and take a few drops of wood
alcohol to get rid of the smell of this vodka—and
then I'll be ready to start the day all over again. My
dear Nikolai Alekseevich, what a fellow you are!
Always nervous and depressed and moaning about
yourself. And yet, you know, you and I could do great
things together. Heaven knows, I'd be prepared to do
anything for your sake. How would you like me to
marry Marfusha Babakina? I'd give you half the
dowry—no, not half—you could have it all!

IVANOV

I would stop talking nonsense if I were you.

BORKIN

No, I mean it seriously. Would you like me to marry
Marfusha? We'll share the dowry. . . . But why am I
talking to you like this? You don't understand, do you?
mimics him "I would stop talking nonsense!" You're
a good man and an intelligent man, but you haven't
got that touch of—you know what I mean—you   IVANOV

haven't got any drive. If only you could take a good smack at something, enough to make the sparks fly, I mean. You're a neurotic, a weakling. If you were a normal man, you'd be making a million a year. Take me, for instance. If I had two thousand, three hundred rubles now, I'd have twenty thousand in two weeks. You don't believe me? You think that's nonsense too? Well, it's not. You give me the two thousand, three hundred rubles, and in a week I'll show you twenty thousand. On the other side of the river, just opposite us, Ovsyanov is selling a strip of land for two thousand, three hundred rubles. If we buy that strip, both the banks will be ours. And if both the banks are ours, then—you see what I mean?—we'd have the right to dam the river, d'you see? That's so, isn't it? Then we'll start building a mill, and as soon as we announce that we want to make a dam, everybody living down the river will raise a hubbub. "All right," we'll say. "*Kommen Sie hier her,* if you don't want the dam, you must pay." You see what I'm driving at? The Zarevskaya factory will give us five thousand; Korolkov, three thousand; the monastery, five thousand.

IVANOV

That's all sharp practice, Misha. If you don't want to quarrel with me, keep it to yourself.

BORKIN

Sitting down at the table

Of course! I knew it! You don't do anything yourself, and you won't let me do anything.

SHABELSKI

Coming out of the house with Lvov

Doctors are just the same as lawyers; the only difference is that lawyers merely rob you, whereas doctors rob you and kill you too. I'm not speaking of present company.   *sits down on one of the seats*   Charlatans,

ANTON
CHEKHOV

exploiters. Perhaps in some paradise you might come
across an exception to the general rule, but . . . in the
course of a lifetime I've spent about twenty thousand
on medical treatment and I haven't met a single
doctor who didn't seem to me an obvious swindler.

BORKIN

To Ivanov   Yes, you do nothing yourself, and you
don't let me do anything either. That's why we
haven't any money.

SHABELSKI

As I say, I'm not speaking of present company. Possibly
there may be exceptions, but anyway . . .   *yawns*

IVANOV

Closing his book
Well, what have you got to say, Doctor?

LVOV

Glancing back at the window
The same as I said in the morning : she must leave for
the Crimea immediately.   *walks up and down the
stage*

SHABELSKI

Bursts out laughing
To the Crimea! Why aren't we doctors, Misha, both
of us? It's so simple. Some woman or other, say
Madame Angot or Ophelia, starts sneezing or coughing
out of sheer boredom. So you take a sheet of paper
and write out a prescription based on the most scientific
principles : to begin with, a young doctor, then a trip
to the Crimea, and when she gets to the Crimea, a
handsome Tartar guide.

IVANOV

To the count
Oh, will you stop driveling?   *to Lvov*   To go to the
Crimea you need money. But even suppose I do find
the money; she still flatly refuses to go.   IVANOV

LVOV

Yes, I know she does. . . .

BORKIN

After a pause

Listen, Doctor, is Anna Petrovna really so seriously ill that she must go to the Crimea?

LVOV

Glances back at the window

Yes, she's got tuberculosis.

BORKIN

Hm!. . . That's not so good. For a long time I've thought from the look on her face that she wouldn't last long.

LVOV

But . . . please speak more quietly. They can hear you in the house. . . .

BORKIN

After a pause, sighs

Such is life. . . . It's like a flower that blossoms gaily in a meadow: along comes a goat, eats it up, and— it's all over.

SHABELSKI

All this is just nonsense, nonsense, nonsense! *yawns* Nonsense and pretense. . . .

BORKIN

After a pause

Well, gentlemen, I've been trying yet once again to teach Nikolai Alekseevich how to make money. I've given him a marvelous idea, but, as usual, the seed fell on barren ground. You can't teach him anything. Just look at him—sour, depressed, gloomy, miserable.

SHABELSKI

Rises and stretches himself

You're so clever; you make plans for everybody and teach everybody what they ought to do—but you've

ANTON
CHEKHOV

never taught me anything, never once! Come on,
clever man, show me the way to get along!

BORKIN

Rises There are scores of ways of getting along. If I
were in your place, I'd have twenty thousand rubles
in a week's time. *walks off*

SHABELSKI

Following him What's that? Show me how then.

BORKIN

There's nothing to show. It's very simple. *returns*
Nikolai Alekseevich, give me a ruble!

Ivanov silently gives him the money

Merci. *to the count* You've still got plenty of
trumps in your hand.

SHABELSKI

Following him Well, what are they?

BORKIN

If I were in your place, I'd have thirty thousand in a
week, if not more.

Borkin and the count go out

IVANOV

After a pause
Useless people, useless talk, having to answer stupid
questions. . . . Doctor, all this has tired me to the
point of making me ill. I've become so irritable, bad-
tempered, rude, and petty that I don't recognize
myself. Every day I have a headache, I can't sleep,
there are noises in my ears. And there's simply
nowhere where I can get any peace. . . . Simply
nowhere.

LVOV

I must have a serious talk with you, Nikolai
Alekseevich.

IVANOV

IVANOV

Very well.

LVOV

It's about Anna Petrovna. *sits down* She hasn't agreed to go to the Crimea, but she would go with you.

IVANOV

After a moment's thought

It would take a lot of money for both of us to go. Besides, I won't be given a long leave. I've already had leave once this year.

LVOV

All right, let's accept that. The next point is this. The most effective medicine for tuberculosis is absolute rest. But your wife never gets any rest, not even for a minute. She's worrying continually about her relationship with you. Forgive me, I'm upset about it and I must speak frankly. Your conduct's killing her. *pause* Nikolai Alekseevich, I wish you'd let me think better of you!

IVANOV

All that is true, I know. I suppose I'm dreadfully to blame, but my mind is so confused. . . . I feel in the grip of a kind of indolence. I can't understand myself. I don't understand myself or other people. *glances at the window* Someone may hear us; let's take a stroll. *they rise* My friend, I would like to tell you the whole story from the beginning, but it's so long and complicated that I could hardly hope to finish it before the morning. *they start walking off* Anyuta is a remarkable, an extraordinary woman. She changed her religion for my sake, left her father and mother, gave up her money, and if I'd asked for a hundred more sacrifices, she would have made them without blinking an eyelid. As for me—well, there's nothing remarkable

ANTON
CHEKHOV

about me, and I've sacrificed nothing. However, it's a long story. . . . The gist of the matter, my dear Doctor, is that . . . that, to put it briefly, I was passionately in love with her when I got married and I swore I'd love her forever, but . . . Well, five years have passed, and she still loves me, but I . . . *makes a helpless gesture with his hands* Here you are, telling me that she's soon going to die, and I don't feel any love or pity but just a sort of indifference and lassitude. To anyone looking at me it must seem dreadful; I don't understand myself what's happening to me. *they walk off down the avenue*

Enter Shabelski and later Anna Petrovna

SHABELSKI
Laughs loudly as he comes in
Upon my word, he's not a fraud after all; he's a thinker, a brilliant fellow! They ought to put up a monument in his honor. He's a combination of every variety of up-to-date rottenness: lawyer, doctor, official, accountant. *sits down on the bottom step of the terrace* Apparently he never finished off a proper course of study anywhere—which only goes to prove that he would have been a perfect genius of a scoundrel if only he could have acquired some culture and a liberal education! "You could have twenty thousand in a week," he tells me. "You still have an ace of trumps in your hand," he says, "your title of count." *laughs uproariously* "Any girl with a dowry would marry you."

Anna Petrovna opens the window and looks down

"Would you like me to arrange a match between you and Marfusha?" he says. Who is this Marfusha, any-

way? Oh, of course, it's that woman Balabalkina . . .
Babakalkina . . . the one that looks like a washerwoman.

ANNA PETROVNA
Is that you, Count?

SHABELSKI
Who's that?

Anna Petrovna laughs

with a mock Jewish accent   What are you laughing at?

ANNA PETROVNA
I was thinking of something you said. Something you
said at dinner, do you remember? A repentant thief,
a horse . . . How did it go?

SHABELSKI
A baptized Jew, a repentant thief, and a horse that's
been ill and gotten over it—they're all worth the same
in the end.

ANNA PETROVNA
Laughs   You can't even make a simple joke without
bitterness. You're a malicious person.   *seriously*
Joking apart, Count, you really are very bitter and
spiteful, you know. Living with you is so depressing
and upsetting. You're always complaining and
grumbling; according to you everyone is some sort
of a cad or a scoundrel. Tell me frankly, Count, have
you ever said a good word for anybody?

SHABELSKI
What sort of a cross-examination is this?

ANNA PETROVNA
We've been living in the same house for five years now,
and I've never once heard you speak of other people
calmly, without bitterness or sneers. What harm have
they done you? Do you really think you're better than
everybody else?

ANTON
CHEKHOV

I don't think that at all. I'm just as much of a cad and
a scoundrel as anybody else. *Mauvais ton,* an old
washout, that's me. I'm always running myself down.
Who am I? What am I? For a while I was rich and
free and happy, but now . . . I'm just a parasite, a
hanger-on, a futile buffoon. I show my indignation and
contempt for them, and they laugh at me. I laugh,
and they shake their heads sadly and say, "The old
man's off his rocker." But most often they don't hear
me at all or notice me.

ANNA PETROVNA

Quietly It's screeching again.

SHABELSKI

What's screeching?

ANNA PETROVNA

The owl. It screeches every night.

SHABELSKI

Let it screech. Things can't get any worse than they
are already.   *stretches himself* Ah, my dear Sarah,
if only I'd won a hundred thousand or so, I'd have
shown you something to make you sit up! You
wouldn't have seen me again. I'd have run away from
this hole, away from all your blessed charity, and my
feet wouldn't have trod this dust again till the Last
Judgment.

ANNA PETROVNA

And what would you have done if you'd won the
money?

SHABELSKI

After a moment's thought
First of all I'd have gone to Moscow and listened to
the Gypsy choir. Then . . . then I'd have made a dash
for Paris. I'd have rented an apartment there and gone
to the Russian church regularly.   IVANOV

ANNA PETROVNA
And what else?

SHABELSKI
I'd have spent days sitting by my wife's grave, thinking. I'd have sat by her grave till I died. You see my wife is buried in Paris. . . .

ANNA PETROVNA
After a pause
How terribly depressing! Shall we play another duet or what?

SHABELSKI
Very well. Will you get the music ready?

Anna Petrovna moves away from the window.

IVANOV
Comes down the avenue with Lvov
You only qualified last year, my dear boy. You're young and full of energy, while I'm thirty-five. I'm entitled to offer you advice. Don't marry a Jew or a neurotic or a blue stocking, but choose someone ordinary and undistinguished, someone who doesn't sparkle, who doesn't make a lot of unnecessary noise. And, generally speaking, my friend, build your whole life according to an ordinary, commonplace pattern. The more flat and monotonous the background, the better. Don't try to battle with the multitude single-handed, don't go fighting with windmills, don't try to ram down walls with your head. And for heaven's sake avoid all this rationalized farming and new-fangled education for peasants and passionate speech making. Shut yourself up in your shell and do your small job, the job God gave you. It's more human and honest and healthy. As for my own life—how tiring it's been! Ah, how tiring! So many mistakes, faults, inconsistencies! *seeing the count, with irritation*

ANTON
CHEKHOV

You're always hanging around, uncle, you never give
me a chance to talk to anyone alone!

SHABELSKI

In a tearful voice
I might as well go and drown myself! There's no
place for me anywhere! *jumps up and goes into the
house*

IVANOV

Shouts after him
I'm sorry, I'm sorry! *to Lvov* Why did I hurt his
feelings like that? Really, I'm positively overwrought.
I must do something about myself. I must.

LVOV

Agitated Nikolai Alekseevich, I've heard you out,
and . . . and—forgive me—but I want to speak
frankly, without beating around the bush. In the way
you talk, in the very tone of your voice, to say nothing
about what you say, there's so much heartless egoism,
such cold inhumanity. Here there's someone near to
you, dying just because she's near to you; her very days
are numbered, and yet it's possible for you not to feel
any affection for her at all, to walk around, to give
advice, to show off. I can't express it very well; I'm
not clever at talking, but . . . Really you revolt me!

IVANOV

Perhaps, perhaps. You can see better from outside.
Maybe you can see through me. Probably I am very
much to blame. *listens* It sounds as if the horses
are ready. I must go and change. *walks toward the
house, then stops* You don't like me, Doctor, and
you don't conceal it. That does you credit. *enters
the house*

LVOV

Alone I could curse myself. I missed the chance again!
I didn't speak to him as I should have done. I can't

IVANOV

talk to him calmly. I've only got to open my mouth and say one word, and something here *points at his chest* begins to suffocate me and turns over inside me, and my tongue seems to stick to my palate. How I hate this Tartuffe, this pompous impostor! I hate him with all my heart. There he is, going out! His unhappy wife's only pleasure in life is having him near her; he's the breath of life to her. She implores him to spend at least one evening with her, but he . . . he can't! He finds his home too suffocating; there's not enough scope here! Just one evening at home and he'd have to shoot himself for sheer boredom! Poor fellow. He needs plenty of scope to think up some new bit of dirty work, I know. Oh, I know why you go to visit these Lebedev people every evening! I know!

SHABELSKI

Coming out of the house with Ivanov and Anna Petrovna

Really, Nicolàs, this is simply barbarous! You go out every night, and we're left here alone. We have to go to bed at eight o'clock from sheer boredom. It's a hideous existence. It's simply not life at all. How is it that you can go out, and we're not allowed to? Why?

ANNA PETROVNA

Leave him alone, Count! Let him go, let him.

IVANOV

To his wife

But where could you go, with your illness? You're ill; you're not allowed to go outside after sunset. Ask the doctor here. You're not a child, Anyuta; you must be reasonable. *to the count* And why should you want to go there?

SHABELSKI

I'd go to the devil, to hell itself, if only I could get

away from here! I'm bored. I've gone stupid with
boredom! Everybody's tired of me. You leave me at
home to keep her from getting bored, but I've almost
nagged her to death!

ANNA PETROVNA

Leave him alone, Count. Let him go if he finds it
amusing there.

IVANOV

Anya, why that tone of voice? You know I'm not going
there for amusement. I must see them about that
promissory note.

ANNA PETROVNA

I don't know why you should want to try to justify
yourself. Go along. Who's trying to stop you?

IVANOV

Let's not nag at one another. It's really so unnecessary.

SHABELSKI

In a tearful voice

Nicolàs, my dear boy, please take me along with you!
It might be amusing to see all those nitwits and bad
eggs. You know I haven't been out since Easter.

IVANOV

Irritated   All right then, come along! How tired I
am of you all!

SHABELSKI

Yes? Well, *merci, merci!   takes his arm gaily and leads
him aside*   May I wear your straw hat?

IVANOV

Yes, but hurry up, please.

The count runs into the house

How tired I am of you all! However . . . Lord! What
am I saying? I know, it's positively outrageous the
way I'm talking to you, Anya. It's never happened   IVANOV

like this to me before. Well, good-bye, Anya, I'll be
back by one o'clock.

ANNA PETROVNA

Kolya, dear, do stay at home!

IVANOV

Agitated My darling, my own, my poor unhappy
girl, I do implore you not to try to stop me from going
out in the evenings. I know it's cruel and selfish of me,
but you must allow me to be selfish. I find it so
unbearably oppressive at home. As soon as the sun
goes down, a sort of anguish begins to torment me.
And what anguish it is! Don't ask me why. I don't
know myself. Honestly, I don't know. I'm depressed
here, but when I go to the Lebedevs', it's even worse
there. I come home, and I'm still depressed, and so it
goes on all night. . . . I feel quite desperate.

ANNA PETROVNA

Kolya . . . but . . . why don't you stay at home? Let's
talk, like we used to. Let's have supper together, then
read. We've practiced lots of duets for you, the old
misery and I. *puts her arms around him* Do stay!
pause I don't understand you. This has been going
on for a whole year. Why have you changed?

IVANOV

I don't know, I don't know. . . .

ANNA PETROVNA

And why don't you want me to go out with you in the
evenings?

IVANOV

Oh, well, I suppose I might as well tell you if you
really want me to. It's a bit cruel to say it, but it's
better if I do. When I feel so tormented by this mental
pain, I . . . I begin not to love you. Then I run away
from you too. I have to get away from home, that's
all.

ANTON
CHEKHOV

Mental pain? I understand, I understand. Listen, Kolya!
Why don't you try to sing and laugh and get angry,
like you used to? Stay at home, and let's have a laugh
and a drink together, and your depression will be
gone in a minute. Would you like me to sing something? Or shall we go and sit in your study, in the dark,
like we used to, and you can tell me about your depression. . . . Your eyes look so tormented! I'll look
into them and cry, and we'll both feel better for it.
laughs and weeps   Or—can't we? How does the
song go, Kolya? "The flowers return in the spring,
but not the joy." . . . No? Well, go, go. . . .

IVANOV

Pray for me, Anya!   *starts off, then stops and thinks*
No, I can't!   *goes out*

ANNA PETROVNA

Go!   *sits down at the table*

LVOV

Walking about the stage
Anna Petrovna, you must make it a rule: as soon as it
strikes six o'clock, you must go indoors and stay in
until the morning. The evening dampness is bad for
you.

ANNA PETROVNA

Yours to command, sir.

LVOV

Why "yours to command"? I'm quite serious.

ANNA PETROVNA

But I don't want to be serious.   *coughs*

LVOV

You see—you're coughing already.

SHABELSKI

Comes out of the house wearing a hat and an overcoat
Where's Nikolai? Are the horses ready?   *walks*   IVANOV

quickly up to Anna Petrovna and kisses her hand
Good night, my charmer! *makes a grimace*
Gewalt![1] 'Shcuse me, please! *goes out quickly*

LVOV

What a clown!

The distant sound of an accordion is heard

ANNA PETROVNA

How depressing! You see, the coachmen and the
cooks are having a dance, while I . . . I'm left alone.
Yevgeni Konstantinovich, what are you walking around
for? Come here, sit down!

LVOV

I can't sit still. . . .

ANNA PETROVNA

After a pause

They're playing the "Starling" in the kitchen. *sings*
"Starling, starling, where have you been? Drinking
vodka down on the green." *pause* Doctor, have
you got a father and mother?

LVOV

My father's dead, but my mother's alive.

ANNA PETROVNA

Don't you miss having your mother living with you?

LVOV

I have no time to miss anybody.

ANNA PETROVNA

Laughs "The flowers return in the spring, but not
the joy." Who told me that? I wish I had a better
memory! I think Nikolai himself must have told me.
listens The owl's screeching again!

LVOV

Well, let it screech!

1. A Jewish exclamation, meaning "shouts," "uproar."

You know, Doctor, I'm beginning to think that fate's
cheated me. Lots of people who are probably no better
than me are happy, and yet they don't pay anything
for their happiness. But I've paid for everything,
absolutely for everything! And how dearly! Why
should I have to pay such terribly high interest? My
dear friend, you're always so considerate with me, so
delicate, so afraid to tell me the truth. But do you
think I don't know what my illness is? I know perfectly well. However, it's boring to talk about that.
with a Jewish accent   'Shcuse me, please! Can you
tell funny stories?

LVOV
No, I can't.

ANNA PETROVNA
Nikolai can. And now, you know, I'm beginning to
feel surprised at the unfairness of people: why don't
they respond to love with love? Why must they pay
back truth with falsehood? Tell me, how much longer
are my father and mother going to go on hating me?
They live about fifty miles away from here, but I can
feel their hatred day and night, even in my sleep. And
what am I to make of Nikolai's depression? He says
it's only in the evenings he doesn't love me, when he
feels depressed. I understand that, and I think it's
probably true. But suppose he's stopped loving me
altogether? Of course, that's impossible but—if he has?
No, no, I mustn't even think about it.   *sings*
"Starling, starling, where have you been?"   *starts*
What frightening thoughts I have! You haven't a
family of your own, Doctor, and there are lots of
things you can't understand.

LVOV
You are surprised.   *sits down beside her*   No, it's   IVANOV

I that am surprised—surprised at you! Explain this to
me, please: how did it happen that you, an intelligent,
honorable, in a way almost a saintly woman, allowed
yourself to be so impudently deceived, to be dragged
into this mire? Why are you here? What have you got
in common with that cold, heartless . . . But let's
leave your husband out of it. What have you in
common with these futile, vulgar people? Oh, my
God, oh Lord! That eternally grumbling, moldy old
lunatic count—and that scoundrel, that outrageous
impostor Misha with his disgusting face! Well, explain
it to me: what are you here for? How did you get here?

ANNA PETROVNA

Laughs He used to talk just like that. Exactly like
that. But he's got bigger eyes than you, and when he
began to talk with passion about anything, they used
to glow like burning coals. Go on talking.

LVOV

Gets up and waves his hand

What's the use of my talking? Please go indoors.

ANNA PETROVNA

You're saying all sorts of things about Nikolai. How
can you know him? Is it really possible to get to know
a man in six months? He's a remarkable man, Doctor,
and I'm sorry you didn't know him two or three years
ago. He's depressed now, he doesn't talk, he doesn't
do anything. But in the past . . . How fascinating he
was! I fell in love with him at first sight. *laughs* I
just looked at him and—bang went the mousetrap!
He said, "Come with me." . . . I cut all my connec-
tions, you know, just like cutting off dead leaves with
a pair of scissors—and I went. *pause* But now it's
different. Now he goes off to the Lebedevs' to amuse
ANTON   himself with other women, and I . . . sit in the garden
CHEKHOV and listen to the owl screeching.

Doctor, have you any brothers?

LVOV

No, I haven't.

Anna Petrovna sobs

Well, what is it now? What's the matter?

ANNA PETROVNA

I can't, Doctor. I'm going there.

LVOV

Where do you mean?

ANNA PETROVNA

To where he is. I'm going. Will you order the horses?
runs into the house

LVOV

I absolutely refuse to treat anybody in these conditions!
It's not merely that they don't pay me a kopeck, but
they upset me too. No, I've finished. Enough of it!
goes into the house

CURTAIN

---

1. In former days it was usual for a man to go around an estate, striking
a wooden board with a stick to frighten away potential thieves.

ACT TWO

*A reception room in the Lebedevs' house; doors left,
right, and center, the last leading into the garden.
Expensive antique furniture. Chandeliers, candlesticks,
and pictures, all under dust covers.*

*Zinaida Savishna, Kosykh, Avdotya Nazarovna,
Yegorushka, Gavrila, Babakina. Girls and elderly
ladies, visitors in the house. A maid.*

*Zinaida Savishna is on a sofa; on either side of her
sit elderly ladies in armchairs; the young people sit on
chairs. In the background, by the door leading into
the garden, several guests are playing cards; among
them are Kosykh, Avdotya Nazarovna, and
Yegorushka. Gavrila stands by the door on the right.
The maid hands around a tray of sweets and pastries.
Throughout the act the guests pass in and out of the
garden and through the door on the right. Babakina
enters through the door on the right and walks up to
Zinaida Savishna.*

ZINAIDA SAVISHNA
Joyfully Darling, Marfa Yegorovna!

ANTON
CHEKHOV

BABAKINA
How are you, Zinaida Savishna? Congratulations on

your daughter's birthday! *they embrace* God grant
that . . .

ZINAIDA SAVISHNA
Thank you, darling, I'm so glad to . . . And how are
you?

BABAKINA
Thank you, very well. *sits down on the sofa beside
her* Good evening, you young people!

The guests rise and bow

FIRST GUEST
Laughing "Young people" . . . as if you were so old
yourself!

BABAKINA
With a sigh
I feel out of place among young people.

FIRST GUEST
Laughs deferentially Good gracious, why . . . You
may be a widow, but you can outshine any girl you
like.

Gavrila serves Babakina tea

ZINAIDA SAVISHNA
To Gavrila Really, Gavrila, why do you serve the
tea like that? Why don't you bring some preserves?
Some gooseberry or something?

BABAKINA
Please don't trouble yourself, thank you so much. . . .

FIRST GUEST
After a pause
Did you come by Mushkino, Marfa Yegorovna?

BABAKINA
No, through Zaymeshche. The road's better that way.

FIRST GUEST
Yes, of course.   IVANOV

KOSYKH

Two spades.

YEGORUSHKA

Pass.

AVDOTYA NAZAROVNA

Pass.

BABAKINA

Lottery tickets are going up fast again, Zinaida
Savishna, my dear. Can you imagine it : tickets for the
first draw are two hundred and seventy already, and
for the second they're nearly two hundred and fifty.
It's never happened before.

ZINAIDA SAVISHNA

With a sigh

The people with a lot of tickets are in luck.

BABAKINA

Well, hardly, my dear. Even though their price is high,
they aren't really a profitable investment. The insurance alone is enough to ruin you.

ZINAIDA SAVISHNA

Maybe, my dear, but all the same one keeps on
hoping. *sighs* God is merciful.

THIRD GUEST

In my view, ladies, it isn't profitable to have capital
at all at the present time. Gilt-edged securities bring
in very little, and speculation is extremely risky. As
I see it, ladies, anyone with capital at the present time
is in a more tricky position than people who . . .

BABAKINA

Sighs That's quite true!

The first guest yawns

ANTON
CHEKHOV

You think it well mannered to yawn in the presence
of ladies?

I beg your pardon, I didn't mean to.

*Zinaida Savishna gets up and goes out through the
door on the right. A long silence follows*

YEGORUSHKA
Two diamonds.
AVDOTYA NAZAROVNA
Pass.
KOSYKH
Pass.
BABAKINA
Aside   Oh Lord, how boring all this is! Enough to
kill you!
ZINAIDA SAVISHNA
*Coming out of the door on the right with Lebedev, in a
subdued voice*
What's the idea—sitting out there by yourself? What
a prima donna you are! Sit in here with the guests!   *she
takes her former seat*
LEBEDEV
Yawns   Oh, what a life, for our sins!   *seeing
Babakina*   Goodness gracious, there's our little ray
of sunshine, our little lollipop!   *greets her*   How are
you, my sweetheart?
BABAKINA
Thank you, very well.
LEBEDEV
Thank God for that! Thank God!   *sits down in an
armchair*   Well, well. . . . Gavrila!

*Gavrila serves him a small glass of vodka and a glass
of water. He drinks the vodka first, then the water*   IVANOV

FIRST GUEST

Good health to you!

LEBEDEV

Health, indeed! I'm thankful to manage to keep alive.
to his wife Where's our little one, Zyuzyushka?

KOSYKH

Tearfully Now just tell me, how is it we didn't get a
single trick? *jumps up* Why the devil did we lose?

AVDOTYA NAZAROVNA

Also jumps up, angrily

I'll tell you why, my dear man: if you don't know how
to play, don't join in the game. What business have
you to go into somebody else's suit? So you held
back your ace and got left with it! *both run forward
from behind the table*

KOSYKH

Tearfully Just listen, my friends. I was holding the
ace, king, queen, jack, and eight down in diamonds;
ace of spades and one, you understand, just one little
heart. . . . And she, heaven forgive her, couldn't go a
small slam! I declared no trumps.

AVDOTYA NAZAROVNA

Interrupting I was the one who went no trumps!
You bid two no trumps.

KOSYKH

That's preposterous! Just let me . . . You had . . . I
had . . . You had . . . *to Lebedev* Now you be the
judge, Pavel Kirillich! I had the ace, king, queen,
jack, and eight down in diamonds.

LEBEDEV

Stopping his ears

Leave me alone . . . please, please. . . . Leave off.

ANTON
CHEKHOV

AVDOTYA NAZAROVNA

Shouts It was I who said no trumps!

KOSYKH

Fiercely I'll be damned if I ever sit down to play with
that old trout again! *goes rapidly out into the garden*

AVDOTYA NAZAROVNA

Ugh! He makes my blood boil! Trout! Trout yourself!

BABAKINA

Well, you're not so sweet-tempered yourself, grandma!

AVDOTYA NAZAROVNA

Seeing Babakina, throws up her hands
If that's not my precious Marfa Yegorovna! She's here
all the time and I'm such a blind old hen that I didn't
see her. My little darling! *kisses her shoulder and
sits down beside her* What a joy this is! Now let me
look at you, my precious! It can't do any harm to look
at you—I haven't got an evil eye!

LEBEDEV

There she goes! You'd do better to find her a husband.

AVDOTYA NAZAROVNA

Just see if I don't! Before I'm dead and buried, I'll have
her and Sanichka married. I'll be hanged if I don't.
Before I'm dead and buried, I say. *sighs* But where
are you to find them nowadays, these husbands? Here
they are, our future husbands, all sitting around,
huddled up like a lot of wet roosters!

THIRD GUEST

Not a very suitable comparison. In my view if modern
young men prefer a bachelor's existence, it's social
conditions that are responsible for that, so to speak.

LEBEDEV

There, there, please don't philosophize! I don't like it.

SASHA

Comes in and walks up to her father
Such marvelous weather we're having, yet here you're
all sitting in a stuffy room!

ZINAIDA SAVISHNA

Sanichka, don't you see that Marfa Yegorovna's here?

SASHA

I'm sorry. *goes up to Babakina and greets her*

BABAKINA

How standoffish you're getting, Sanichka. You haven't been to see me once lately. *they embrace* Congratulations, darling!

SASHA

Thank you. *sits down beside her father*

LEBEDEV

Yes, Avdotya Nazarovna, it's a difficult business getting husbands nowadays. And not only husbands— you can't even get a decent best man. Modern young men, if I may say so without offense, seem to me to be insipid, like food that's overdone. God help them! You can't dance or talk or drink with them properly.

AVDOTYA NAZAROVNA

They're all past masters at drinking—as long as you give them something to drink.

LEBEDEV

There isn't much in mere drinking—even a horse can drink. No, you must drink intelligently! In my days a young man would grind away at his studies all day long. But as soon as the evening came around, off he'd go straight to the first brightly lit place he could find, and dance like a top until morning. He'd dance and flirt with the ladies, and all that. *gives himself a flick on the throat* And he'd tell stories and philosophize until his tongue nearly dropped off. But the modern young men . . . *waves his hand* I can't understand them. No good to man or beast. In the whole district there's only one decent fellow, but he's married, *sighs* and it seems that he's beginning to run wild too.

BABAKINA

Who's that?

LEBEDEV

Nikolasha Ivanov.

BABAKINA

Yes, he's a nice man.   *with a grimace*   Only he's so
unhappy.

ZINAIDA SAVISHNA

You're right there, darling. Well, how could he be
happy?   *sighs*   What a mistake he made, poor man!
He married a Jew, and, of course, the poor fellow
calculated that her parents would give away a fortune
with her; but it turned out to be quite the reverse.
From the day she changed her religion, her father and
mother simply haven't recognized her; in fact, they've
put their parental curse on her. So he didn't get a
kopeck after all. He's regretting it now, but it's too
late.

SASHA

Mamma, it's not true.

BABAKINA

With animation   But how isn't it true, Shurochka?
You know that everybody knows it. If he didn't count
on that, why would he have married a Jew? Aren't
there enough Russian girls? He just made a mistake,
darling, he made a mistake!   *eagerly*   And, good
Lord! Doesn't she get it in the neck from him now! It's
quite laughable! Sometimes he comes home from
somewhere or other and goes straight to her and says,
"Your father and mother have swindled me! Get
out of my house!" But where can she go to? Her father
and mother won't take her back; she might do a
servant girl's job, but she hasn't been trained to work.
So he torments and torments her until the count takes

IVANOV

her side. If it weren't for the count, he'd soon send her to her grave.

AVDOTYA NAZAROVNA
And sometimes he locks her up in a cellar and tells her to eat garlic. "Come on, you so-and-so, swallow it," he says. So she goes on eating it until it blows her out terribly.

Laughter

SASHA
Papa, but this is all lies!

LEBEDEV
Well, what does it matter? Let them talk rubbish as much as they like. *shouts* Gavrila!

Gavrila serves him vodka and water

ZINAIDA SAVISHNA
So that's how it is the poor man's ruined, darling. His financial affairs are in a very bad way. If Borkin weren't looking after his estate, he and his Jew wouldn't have anything to eat. *sighs* As for us, darling, I can't tell you how we've suffered on his account. God alone knows how we've suffered! Would you believe it, my dear? He's owed us nine thousand for the last three years!

BABAKINA
Horrified Nine thousand!

ZINAIDA SAVISHNA
Yes. It was my dear husband Pashenka who arranged to lend him money. He can't tell a man you can lend money to from a man you can't. I'm not complaining about the capital—God be with it! But I wish he'd pay the interest regularly.

ANTON
CHEKHOV

Passionately Mamma, you've told us all this a
thousand times already!

ZINAIDA SAVISHNA

What's it got to do with you? Why are you defending
him?

SASHA

Rising But how have you the heart to say all that
about a man who hasn't done you any harm? Tell me,
what harm has he done you?

THIRD GUEST

If I may say so, Aleksandra Pavlovna, I respect Nikolai
Alekseevich, and I've always felt it an honor to know
him—though, speaking *entre nous,* he does seem to
me to be an adventurer.

SASHA

If that's how you feel, I congratulate you.

THIRD GUEST

Just as a proof of what I was saying, I'll tell you
something that was passed on to me by his *attaché* or,
if you like, his *chicherone,* Borkin. Two years ago
when there was a cattle epidemic, he bought a lot of
cows, insured them . . .

ZINAIDA SAVISHNA

Yes, yes, yes! I remember that. I've been told about
it too.

THIRD GUEST

He insured them and, do you know, then he infected
them with the plague and got the insurance money.

SASHA

Oh, but all this is sheer nonsense! Utter rubbish! No
one ever dreamed of buying cattle or infecting cattle!
Borkin invented the idea himself and went boasting
about it everywhere. When Ivanov found it out,

IVANOV

38 Borkin had to beg his forgiveness for a whole two weeks afterward. Ivanov's only fault is weakness of character, so that he hasn't the heart to turn that Borkin out. And then he trusts people too much! He's had everything stolen and plundered from him; anyone who felt inclined could make money out of his generosity.

LEBEDEV

Shura, don't get so heated about it. That's enough.

SASHA

But why do they talk such nonsense? And how boring it all is! Ivanov, Ivanov, Ivanov—there's no other topic of conversation. *goes toward the door, then returns* I'm simply astonished! *to the young guests* I'm simply astonished at your patience. Aren't you bored to be sitting here like this? The very air is stiff with boredom! Well, say something, try to entertain the young ladies, do something! If you've nothing else to talk about except Ivanov, can't you laugh or sing or dance or something?

LEBEDEV

Laughing That's right, tell them off! Tell them off properly!

SASHA

Listen then, just do me this favor. If you don't want to dance or sing or laugh, if all that bores you, then just for once in your life, as an exception, I mean, do try to make a tremendous effort and think of something witty and brilliant to say, something to amuse us. It doesn't matter if it's rude and impertinent, so long as it's funny and novel. Or if you could all *do* something, something quite small, hardly noticeable, but something a bit original and daring, so that we young ladies could look at you and say "oh" admiringly, for once in our lives! You do want to be popular with

ANTON
CHEKHOV

us, don't you? Then why don't you try to make us
admire you? Oh, you gentlemen! You're a poor lot, a
poor lot, all of you. It's enough to make a cat weep
just to look at you! I've told you a thousand times,
and I'll go on telling you too—you're a poor lot!

SHABELSKI
Comes in with Ivanov through the door on the right
Who's making a speech here? You, Shurochka?
laughs loudly and shakes hands with her   Congratulations on your birthday, my dear. May you live long
and never be born again.

ZINAIDA SAVISHNA
Joyfully   Nikolai Alekseevich, Count!

LEBEDEV
Well! Whom do I see. . . . Count!   *goes to meet him*

SHABELSKI
*Seeing Zinaida and Babakina and stretching his arms
toward them*
Two bankers on one sofa! Beautiful to behold!   *greets
them; to Zinaida*   How d'you do, Zyuzyushka?   *to
Babakina*   How d'you do, my precious?

ZINAIDA SAVISHNA
I'm so glad to see you. You're such a rare visitor here,
Count.   *shouts*   Gavrila, bring some tea! Do sit
down, please.   *gets up and goes out through the door
on the right, then returns immediately, looking extremely
preoccupied*

*Sasha takes her former seat. Ivanov greets everybody in
silence*

LEBEDEV
To Shabelski   Where have you come from? What's
brought you here? This really is a surprise.   *embraces
him*   Count, you're a wretch, you know! Decent
people don't behave the way you do.   *leads him to*   IVANOV

the front of the stage by his arm   Why don't you ever come to see us? Angry or what?

SHABELSKI

But how can I come to see you? Riding a broomstick? I haven't got any horses of my own, and Nikolai won't bring me with him. He tells me to stay at home with Sarah, so that she won't feel lonely. Send your horses to fetch me; then I'll come to see you.

LEBEDEV

Waves his hand

No fear! Zyuzyushka would sooner die than lend her horses. My dear fellow, my good old friend, don't you know that you're nearer and dearer to me than any-body else? You and I are the only ones left now out of all the old cronies! "In you I love my former griefs, and the days of my ruined youth." . . . Joking apart, I do feel I could almost weep.   *embraces the count*

SHABELSKI

Let me go! You smell like a wine cellar.

LEBEDEV

My dear fellow, you can't imagine how I miss my friends! Sometimes I could hang myself with boredom. *quietly*   Zyuzyushka has driven all the decent people away with her money lending, so that now we only have Zulus, as you see. . . . All these Doodkins and Boodkins. . . . Now, have some tea.

Gavrila serves the count tea

ZINAIDA SAVISHNA

Preoccupied, to Gavrila

Really, why will you serve tea in this way? Why don't you bring some preserves? Gooseberry or something?

SHABELSKI

Laughing loudly, to Ivanov

ANTON
CHEKHOV
Well, what did I tell you?   *to Lebedev*   I had a bet

with him on the way that when we arrived,
Zyuzyushka would immediately offer us gooseberry
preserves.

ZINAIDA SAVISHNA

You enjoy laughing at people, Count, just as you
used to.

LEBEDEV

They've made about twenty barrels of it, so what
can you do with it?

SHABELSKI

Sits down beside the table

You're still making money, Zyuzyushka? I suppose
you've got a million or so by now, eh?

ZINAIDA SAVISHNA

With a sigh

To an outsider we may appear to be richer than
anybody else, but where do they think the money
comes from? It's only talk.

SHABELSKI

Come on! We know! We know what a poor hand you
are at the game.   *to Lebedev*   Pasha, tell me on
your honor, have you saved a million?

LEBEDEV

I don't know. You ask Zyuzyushka.

SHABELSKI

To Babakina   And our plump little pigeon here will
soon have a million too! She gets prettier and plumper
every hour, let alone every day. That's what a lot
of money does to a woman!

BABAKINA

Thank you very much, Your Excellency, but I don't
like all this mockery.

SHABELSKI

But, my dear little banker, do you call this mockery?
It's simply a cry from the heart; I'm moved to speech   IVANOV

by excess of feeling. Really I love you and Zyuzyushka beyond words. *gaily* It's sheer rapture! It's ecstasy! I can't look at either of you unmoved.

ZINAIDA SAVISHNA

You're just as you used to be. *to Yegorushka* Yegorushka, blow out the candles. What's the point of keeping them lit if you're not playing?

Yegorushka starts, then blows out the candles and sits down

to Ivanov How's your wife keeping, Nikolai Alekseevich?

IVANOV

Not at all well. Today the doctor told me definitely that she has TB.

ZINAIDA SAVISHNA

Really? What a pity! *sighs* And we all are so fond of her.

SHABELSKI

Nonsense, nonsense, nonsense! She hasn't got TB at all. It's just a doctor's quackery, nothing but a trick. Aesculapius wants to come to the house, so he invents TB. A good thing that the husband's not jealous!

Ivanov makes an impatient movement

As for Sarah herself, I don't trust a single word or action of hers. All my life I've never trusted doctors or lawyers or women. Nonsense, nonsense! Quackery and tricks!

LEBEDEV

You are an astonishing fellow, Matvei! You've adopted a sort of misanthropic pose and carry it around with you like a child with a new toy. You're a man like any other, but as soon as you start talking,

ANTON
CHEKHOV

anyone would think you'd gotten a frog in your throat
or perpetual catarrh.

SHABELSKI

Well, you wouldn't expect me to embrace all these
impostors and cads, would you?

LEBEDEV

But where do you see these impostors and cads?

SHABELSKI

Well, present company excepted, of course, but . . .

LEBEDEV

There's your "but." All this is just a pose.

SHABELSKI

A pose? You're lucky not to have a philosophy of life
of any kind.

LEBEDEV

What's my philosophy of life? I just sit around and
wait for the moment when I can kick the bucket.
That's my philosophy of life. You and I, brother, are
past the age when one thinks of philosophies of life.
shouts Gavrila!

SHABELSKI

You've had enough of Gavrila already. Just look at
the color of your nose!

LEBEDEV

Never mind, my dear fellow. I'm not getting married
today.

ZINAIDA SAVISHNA

Doctor Lvov hasn't been to see us for a long time.
He's quite forgotten us.

SASHA

He's my pet aversion. A paragon of honesty! He can't
ask for a glass of water or light a cigarette without
letting you know how wonderfully honest he is.
Walking or talking, it's written all over his forehead:
"I'm an honest man!" He bores me.

IVANOV

SHABELSKI

He's a narrow-minded, bigoted leech!   *mimics*
"Make way for honest labor!" He lays down the law
at every step, like a parrot, and he's gotten it into
his head that he really is another Dobrolyubov.[1]
Anyone who doesn't lay down the law is a cad. His
opinions are quite astonishing in their profundity. If a
peasant is prosperous and lives like a human being,
it means he's a cad and a profiteer. If I wear a velvet
jacket and have a manservant to help me to dress, I'm
a cad and a serf owner. He's so honest, so wonderfully
honest, that he's bursting with it. He's all on edge with
it. I'm almost afraid of him. Really I am. I feel at
any moment he may, out of a sense of duty, punch me
in the face or call me a cad.

IVANOV

I find him terribly tiring, but all the same I like him.
He's very sincere.

SHABELSKI

And what sincerity! Last night he came up to me and
apropos of nothing said, "You are profoundly
repugnant to me, Count." Thank you very much! And
all this isn't just naïveté. It's done with a purpose:
his voice trembles, his eyes burn, his knees shake. The
devil take his pigheaded sincerity! Why, I may be
repulsive and vile to him, that's natural in a way. I'm
conscious of it myself, but why need he say so to my
face? I'm a worthless man, but when all's said and
done, I have got gray hair. This futile, ruthless
honesty!

LEBEDEV

Now, now, now! Surely, you've been young yourself;
you ought to understand.

ANTON
CHEKHOV

1. A Russian literary critic of the nineteenth century, well known for
his radical views.

Yes, I've been young and foolish, and I've fancied
myself as another Chatskiy[1] too, exposing the cads
and impostors. But never in all my life have I called
thieves thieves to their face or talked about a rope in
the house of a condemned man. I was properly brought
up. But your fat-headed leech would think he was on
top of the world, grappling with his life's problem, if
only fate would give him an opportunity, in the name
of principles and human ideals, to swipe me publicly
in the face.

LEBEDEV

All young men have their little foibles. I had an uncle
once, a follower of Hegel. He would fill up his house
with guests and, after a drink or two, he'd get up on
a chair and begin : "You are ignoramuses! You're the
power of darkness! The dawn of a new life . . ."
Etc., etc., etc. And so he'd go on lecturing them.

SASHA

And what did the guests do?

LEBEDEV

Nothing. They just listened and went on drinking.
However, once I challenged him to a duel . . . my own
uncle. It happened because of Lord Bacon. As far as I
remember—God help my poor memory—I was sitting
just as Matvei is sitting now, and my uncle, with
poor Gerasim Nilych, was just about where Nikolasha
is standing. . . . Well, Gerasim Nilych asked a
question.

*Borkin comes skipping and singing into the room
through the door on the right. He is smartly dressed
and carries a parcel. There is a hum of welcome*

1. The hero of a famous comedy by Griboyedov, *The Mischief of
Being Clever.*

YOUNG LADIES

Mikhail Mikhailovich!

LEBEDEV

Michel Michelich! I can hear him.

SHABELSKI

The life of the party!

BORKIN

Here I am! *runs up to Sasha* Most noble *signorina*, may I congratulate the universe on the birth of so noble a flower as yourself? As a testimony of my admiration, may I present you *hands her the parcel* with these fireworks and roman candles of my own manufacture? May they brighten the night just as you brighten the gloom of this dark realm. *bows theatrically*

SASHA

Thank you.

LEBEDEV

Laughing loudly, to Ivanov

Why don't you turn out this Judas?

BORKIN

To Lebedev Pavel Kirillich, my respects! *to Ivanov* My patron. *sings* Nicolàs *voilà,* hidy-ho! *goes around greeting everybody* The most estimable Zinaida Savishna. . . . The divine Marfa Yegorovna. . . . The most worthy Avdotya Nazarovna. . . . His Excellency the Count.

SHABELSKI

Laughing loudly The life of the party! As soon as he comes, the atmosphere gets brighter. D'you notice it?

BORKIN

Ugh, I'm tired. I've said "how d'you do" to everybody, haven't I? Well, what's the news, gentlemen? Isn't there something special, something with a strong smell? *earnestly, to Zinaida Savishna* Just listen

ANTON
CHEKHOV

to this, mamma dear. As I was on my way here . . . *to*
Gavrila Gavrila, bring me some tea, but no gooseberry preserves! *to Zinaida Savishna* As I was on
my way here, I saw some peasants stripping the bark
off your willow bushes by the river. Why don't you
lease out those willow bushes?

LEBEDEV

To Ivanov Why don't you turn out this Judas?

ZINAIDA SAVISHNA

Alarmed But that's quite true! It never entered my
head!

BORKIN

Moving his arms as if doing physical exercises
I can't manage without exercise. . . . Now, mamma
dear, isn't there some game we could play? Marfa
Yegorovna, I'm in such high spirits. . . . I feel quite
exalted! *sings* "Again I stand before you."

ZINAIDA SAVISHNA

Let's arrange something, please—everybody's feeling
bored.

BORKIN

Really, gentlemen, why are you all so downcast? You
sit there like a lot of jurymen in court! Let's arrange
something! What would you like? Forfeits, a game of
catch, dancing, or fireworks?

YOUNG LADIES

Clapping Fireworks, fireworks!

They run into the garden

SASHA

To Ivanov Why are you looking so sad today?

IVANOV

I've got a headache, Shurochka. Besides, I'm depressed.

SASHA

Come to the drawing room. IVANOV

They go out through the door on the right. All the others go out into the garden except Zinaida Savishna and Lebedev

ZINAIDA SAVISHNA

That's what I like—there's a young man for you. He hasn't been here a minute and he's cheered up everybody already. *turns down the large lamp* While they're in the garden there's no point in burning good candles. *blows out the candles*

LEBEDEV

Following her Zyuzyushka, we ought to offer our visitors some refreshments.

ZINAIDA SAVISHNA

There! Look at all these candles. . . . No wonder people think we're rich. *blows them out*

LEBEDEV

Following her Zyuzyushka, why don't you give these people something to eat? They're young; they must be hungry by now, poor things. Zyuzyushka . . .

ZINAIDA SAVISHNA

The count hasn't finished his glass. What a waste of sugar! *goes out through the door on the left*

LEBEDEV

Pshaw! *goes out into the garden*

SASHA

Entering with Ivanov through the door on the right Everyone's gone into the garden.

IVANOV

That's how things are, Shurochka. In the past I used to think a great deal and work a great deal, yet I never felt tired. Nowadays, I do nothing and think about nothing, but I feel exhausted in mind and body. My conscience worries me day and night. I feel I'm deeply at fault, yet how exactly I am at fault I can't make out.

ANTON
CHEKHOV

And in addition to that, there's my wife's illness, the
lack of money, the constant nagging, the scandal-
mongering, the futile talk, the stupid Borkin. . . . My
own home has become odious to me, and living there
is worse than torture. I tell you frankly, Shurochka,
even the company of my wife, who loves me, has
become unbearable to me. You're an old friend, and
you won't mind my frankness. I've come here to you
now just to amuse myself, but I feel bored even here,
and I'm longing to go home again. Forgive me,
please. I'll go back quietly now.

SASHA

Nikolai Alekseevich, I understand your trouble. Your
misfortune is that you're lonely. You need someone
with you whom you could love, someone who would
understand you. Only love can regenerate you.

IVANOV

Can it indeed, Shurochka! It would be the last straw
if an old washout like me started a new love affair!
God preserve me from any such misfortune! No, my
little clever-head, it isn't a love affair that I need. I tell
you, before God I tell you, I can bear anything:
anxiety, mental depression, financial ruin, the loss of
my wife, premature old age, and loneliness. But I just
can't bear the contempt I feel for myself. I'm dying
of shame at the thought that I, a healthy, strong man,
have somehow got transformed into a sort of Hamlet
or Manfred or one of those "superfluous" people, the
devil knows which! There are some pitiable people
who are flattered when you call them Hamlets or
superfluous, but to me it's a disgrace! It stirs up my
pride, a feeling of shame oppresses me, and I suffer.

SASHA

Jokingly, through tears

Nikolai Alekseevich, let us run away to America. IVANOV

I feel too lazy to walk to that door, and you talk of America! *they go toward the garden exit*   Really, Shura, you must find it terribly difficult living here. When I look at the sort of people who surround you, I feel quite afraid. Whom could you marry here? The only hope is for some passing lieutenant or student to take you away.

Zinaida Savishna enters through the door on the left with a jar of preserves

Excuse me, Shurochka, I'll catch up with you.

Sasha goes out into the garden

Zinaida Savishna, I have a request to make.

ZINAIDA SAVISHNA

What is it, Nikolai Alekseevich?

IVANOV

Hesitates   The fact is, you see, that my promissory note is due for payment the day after tomorrow. You would oblige me greatly by deferring it or by allowing me to add the interest to the capital. I have no money at all at present.

ZINAIDA SAVISHNA

Alarmed   But, Nikolai Alekseevich, how could I? What sort of arrangement would it be? No, no, please don't suggest it. For God's sake, don't torment an unfortunate woman!

IVANOV

I'm sorry, I'm sorry.   *goes out into the garden*

ZINAIDA SAVISHNA

Ugh, my goodness, how he frightened me! I'm trembling all over. . . . All over . . .   *goes out through the door on the right*

ANTON
CHEKHOV

*Enters through the door on the left and walks across
the stage*

I was holding ace, king, queen, jack, eight down in
diamonds, ace of spades, and one . . . one little heart;
and she, devil take her, couldn't go a small slam.   *goes
out*

AVDOTYA NAZAROVNA

Enters with the first guest from the garden

I'd like to tear her to pieces, the old miser. Tear her to
pieces, I would. It's really no joke. Here I am—I've
been in this house since five o'clock, and she hasn't
offered me a bit of stale herring! What a house! What a
household!

FIRST GUEST

I'm so bored, I could almost run and smash my head
against the wall! What people, God forgive them!
I feel I could start howling like a wolf and biting people
from sheer boredom and hunger!

AVDOTYA NAZAROVNA

I'd like to tear her to pieces, God forgive me!

FIRST GUEST

I think I'll have a drink and be off! Not even the brides
you offered to find me would keep me here. How
the devil can a fellow think of love when he hasn't had
a single glass of anything since dinner?

AVDOTYA NAZAROVNA

Shall we go and look or what?

FIRST GUEST

Sh-sh! Quietly! I think there's some schnapps in the
sideboard in the dining room. We'll tackle Yegorushka.
Sh-sh!

*They go out through the door on the left. Anna Petrovna
and Lvov enter through the door on the right*   IVANOV

Never mind; they'll be glad to see us. No one's in here.
I suppose they're in the garden.

LVOV

I wish you'd tell me why you've brought me here, to
this vultures' nest? This is no place for either of us.
Honest people can't breathe in this atmosphere!

ANNA PETROVNA

Now just listen to me, Mister Honest! It isn't good
manners to take a lady out and talk about nothing but
your own honesty all the time! It may be honest,
but it's also boring, to say the least. Never talk to
women about your virtues. Let them discover them on
their own. When my Nikolai was like you, he only
sang songs and told quaint stories when he was with
women; yet they all knew what sort of man he was.

LVOV

Ah, don't talk to me about your Nikolai; I know all
about him!

ANNA PETROVNA

You're a good man, Doctor, but you don't understand
anything. Let's go into the garden. He never used to
say, "I'm honest. I suffocate in this atmosphere!" He
never talked about "vultures" and "this owls' nest"
and "these crocodiles." He left the menagerie alone;
but when he felt indignant about something, all he'd
say was, "Oh, how unfair I've been today!" or
"Anyuta, I'm sorry for that man!" That's how it was
with him, but you . . .   *they go out*

FIRST GUEST

Entering through the door on the left

If there isn't any in the dining room, there must be
some in the pantry or somewhere. We ought to find
Yegorushka. Let's go through the drawing room.

ANTON
CHEKHOV

*Advotya Nazarovna and Guest go out through the door
on the right. Babakina and Borkin run in from the
garden, laughing. Shabelski trots in after them, also
laughing and rubbing his hands*

BABAKINA

Oh, how boring it is! *laughs loudly* How boring!
They all just walk around or sit as stiffly as if they'd
all swallowed pokers. My very bones are numb with
boredom. *jumps around* I must stretch my legs!

Borkin seizes her by the waist and kisses her cheek

SHABELSKI

Laughs and snaps his fingers
Well, I'll be damned! *grunts* In a way . . .

BABAKINA

Let go! Keep your hands off me, you shameless man!
Or God knows what the count here will be thinking!
Leave me alone!

BORKIN

My soul's delight, my heart's desire! *kisses her*
Lend me two thousand, three hundred rubles!

BABAKINA

No, no, no. It's all very well, but when it comes to
money . . . thank you very much. No, no, no! . . .
Please let go of my hands!

SHABELSKI

Trotting around them
Little pompon! She has her attractive points.

BORKIN

Seriously Well, that's enough of that. Let's talk
business. Let us discuss things straightforwardly, in a
businesslike way. Answer me honestly, without eva-
sions or beating about the bush—just yes or no.

IVANOV

Listen! *points at the count* He needs money, at least three thousand a year. You need a husband. Do you want to be a countess?

SHABELSKI

Laughing loudly What an amazing cynic!

BORKIN

Do you want to be a countess? Yes or no?

BABAKINA

Agitated You're making it all up, Misha, really. Besides such things aren't done like this, in such a rush. If the count wants to, he can talk about it himself, and . . . and anyway I don't know how it can . . . so suddenly, I mean, all at once.

BORKIN

Now, now do stop putting it on! It's a business matter. Yes or no?

SHABELSKI

Laughing and rubbing his hands
Well, I must say. . . . The devil take it, I'd better arrange this scandalous business for myself, eh? Little precious. *kisses Babakina's cheek* Charmer! You little duck!

BABAKINA

Stop, stop a moment. You've quite upset me. . . . Go away, go! . . . No, don't go yet!

BORKIN

Quickly! Yes or no? We've no time to waste.

BABAKINA

What do you say to this, Count? Come and stay at my house for a day or two. We have a gay time there; it's not like this place. Come tomorrow. *to Borkin* You were joking, weren't you?

BORKIN

Angrily Now who'd want to joke about serious matters like this?

BABAKINA

Stop, stop a moment. . . . Oh, I feel quite faint! I feel faint! A countess. . . . I'm going to faint. . . . I'm going to fall down.

Borkin and the count, laughing, take her by the arms and kiss her on the cheeks as they lead her out through the door on the right. Ivanov and Sasha run in from the garden

IVANOV

Clutching his head in despair
It can't be! Please don't, Shurochka, don't. . . . Oh, it mustn't be!

SASHA

With abandon I love you madly. You're all my joy. Without you my life has no meaning, no happiness! To me—you're everything.

IVANOV

But why, why? My God, I don't understand any-thing. . . . Shurochka, please don't go on like this!

SASHA

When I was a child you were the only joy in my life. I loved you; I loved you body and soul, more than I loved myself, and now. . . . Oh, I love you, Nikolai Alekseevich. I'll go anywhere with you, to the other end of the world, even beyond the grave. . . . Only for heaven's sake, let's go soon, otherwise I'll suffocate.

IVANOV

Bursts into happy laughter
What is all this? Can it mean beginning life all over again, from the beginning? Can it, Shurochka? Oh, my happiness! *draws her to himself* My youth, my freshness!

IVANOV

56   *Anna Petrovna enters from the gardens and, seeing her husband and Sasha, stops as if rooted to the spot*

It means—to live again? Yes? Work again?   *they kiss, then look around and see Anna Petrovna; he is horrified* Sarah!

CURTAIN

ACT THREE

*Ivanov's study. A desk, on which papers, books, official
envelopes, knickknacks, and revolvers are lying in
disorder; beside the papers a lamp, a bottle of water, a
plate with salt herring, slices of bread, and cucumbers.
On the walls are maps of the locality, pictures, shotguns,
pistols, sickles, riding whips, etc. It is midday.*

 *Shabelski, Lebedev, Borkin, and Pëtr. Shabelski and
Lebedev are sitting by the desk. Borkin is astride a
chair in the middle of the stage. Pëtr is standing by
the door.*

LEBEDEV

France has a clear-cut and definite policy. The French
know what they want. They just want to rip the guts
out of the sausage makers, and that's all. But
Germany's playing quite a different tune, my friend.
Germany has plenty of irons in the fire besides France.

SHABELSKI

Nonsense! In my view, the Germans are cowards,
and so are the French. They shake their fists at one
another but they keep their other hands in their pockets.
Believe me, the matter won't go beyond gestures.
They won't fight.

IVANOV

BORKIN

And what I say is, why should they? What's the use of
all these armaments and congresses and all the expense?
You know what I'd do? I'd collect all the dogs in
the country, inject them with a good dose of Pasteur's
poison, then let them loose at the enemy's country.
All my enemies would be mad in a month.

LEBEDEV

Laughing   His head's small to look at, but what great
ideas it contains—millions of them, like fish in the
sea.

SHABELSKI

Quite a virtuoso!

LEBEDEV

God bless you, Michel Michelich! Anyway, you make
us laugh!   *stops laughing*   Well, gentlemen, we
talk and talk, but what about some vodka? *Repetatur.*
fills three glasses   Our good health!   *they drink and
eat*   Salt herring makes a good snack, better than
anything I know.

SHABELSKI

Well, no, I don't think so. Cucumber's better.
Scientists have been puzzling their brains since the
world began, but they've never thought up anything
nicer than a salt cucumber.   *to Pëtr*   Pëtr, go and
fetch some more cucumbers, and tell them to bake us
four meat pies with some onions. And see that they
are hot.

Pëtr goes out

LEBEDEV

Caviar goes well with vodka too. Only you must
know how to serve it. You must use intelligence. Take
a quarter of pressed caviar, two heads of green onion,

ANTON
CHEKHOV

some olive oil, mix it all up, and then, you know . . .
just a little lemon juice on top. It's enough to bowl
you over! The smell alone makes you dizzy!

BORKIN

Another nice snack after vodka is fried gudgeons. Only
you must know how to fry them. First you clean them,
then roll them in crumbs, and fry until they're brown,
so that they crackle as you eat them. . . . Crackle-
crackle-crackle.

SHABELSKI

Yesterday Babakina had a nice hors d'oeuvre—white
mushrooms.

LEBEDEV

Ah, lovely!

SHABELSKI

Only they were prepared in a special way. You know,
with onion and bay leaf and all sorts of spices. When
they took the lid off the saucepan, the steam, the
fragrance that came out! It was a real joy!

LEBEDEV

Now then! *Repetatur*, gentlemen! *they drink* Our
good health. . . . *looks at his watch* It doesn't look
as if I'm going to see Nikolasha today. It's time for
me to be going. You say you've had mushrooms at
Babakina's, but in my house there's not a sign of a
mushroom yet. Tell me, Count, why the devil do you
go to Marfutka's so often?

SHABELSKI

Pointing at Borkin with a movement of his head
It's him. He wants me to marry her.

LEBEDEV

Marry? How old are you?

SHABELSKI

I'm sixty-two.   IVANOV

LEBEDEV

Just the right age to get married. And Marfutka is just the right woman for you.

BORKIN

Marfutka's not the point; it's Marfutka's money.

LEBEDEV

Is that what you want—Marfutka's money? Perhaps you'd like the moon too?

BORKIN

You won't talk about the moon when you see this fellow marry and fill his pockets. You'll be licking your lips with envy then.

SHABELSKI

He's serious, you know. Our great genius here is quite certain that I'm going to take his advice and get married.

BORKIN

Well, aren't I right then? Isn't it definite anymore?

SHABELSKI

What? You must be mad! When was it definite? Pshaw!

BORKIN

Thank you very much! I'm very grateful to you. Does this mean you're going to let me down? Now you say you will marry her, now you say you won't. The devil alone knows which. Yet you gave me your word of honor! So you won't marry her, then?

SHABELSKI

Shrugs his shoulders

He's really serious. What an amazing fellow!

BORKIN

Indignantly In that case what did you get an honest woman excited for? Now she's mad to be a countess; she can't sleep or eat. Is that the sort of thing to joke about? Is it honorable?

ANTON CHEKHOV

SHABELSKI

Snaps his fingers
All right then, supposing I do do this ignominious
thing? Eh? Just to spite them! I'll go and do it. My
word of honor, I will. That'll be quite a joke!

Enter Lvov

LEBEDEV

Aesculapius—our most humble respects.   *he shakes
Lvov's hand and sings*   "Doctor, little father, save
me, pray. I'm scared to death of my dying day."

LVOV

Hasn't Nikolai Alekseevich come back yet?

LEBEDEV

No, I've been waiting for him for more than an hour
myself.

Lvov paces the stage impatiently

Tell me, old man, how's Anna Petrovna?

LVOV

She's bad.

LEBEDEV

Sighs   May I go and say good morning to her?

LVOV

No, please don't. I think she's asleep. . . .

LEBEDEV

After a pause
A nice, likable woman.   *sighs*   When she fainted
on Shurochka's birthday around at our house, I
happened to glance at her face—and I knew then she
wouldn't live long, poor thing. I can't understand why
she fainted then. I ran into the room, and there she
was on the floor, quite pale, with Nikolasha kneeling
beside her. He was pale too, and Shurochka was there   IVANOV

62 crying. After that Shurochka and I just went around
for a whole week as if we were in a daze.

SHABELSKI

To Lvov Tell me, most talented priest of science,
who's the great scientist who discovered that frequent
visits from a young physician are beneficial to ladies
suffering from chest complaints? It's a great discovery!
A very great discovery indeed! Should one class it as
allopathy or homoeopathy?

*Lvov makes as if to answer him; then, with a
contemptuous gesture, goes out*

What a withering glance!

LEBEDEV

What's gnawing at you, Count? Why did you try to
hurt him?

SHABELSKI

With irritation Well, why does he tell lies, then?
TB, there's no hope, she's going to die. He's lying,
I say! I can't stand that.

LEBEDEV

But why do you think he's lying?

SHABELSKI

Gets up and walks to and fro
I can't conceive how a living being can suddenly die
for no reason at all! Let's drop the subject!

KOSYKH

Runs in, out of breath
Is Nikolai Alekseevich at home? How d'you do?
quickly shakes hands all around Is he at home?

BORKIN

He is not.

ANTON
CHEKHOV

KOSYKH

Sits down, then jumps up

In that case I'll be going.   *drinks a glass of vodka and*
quickly eats a snack   I must go. Business. . . . I'm
quite worn out. . . . Can hardly stand on my feet.

KOSYKH

Barabanov's. We played vint all night, and we've only
just finished. I lost all I had on me. That Barabanov
plays like a trooper.   *tearfully*   Just listen to this: I
was holding hearts all the time.   *he addresses Borkin,*
who retreats from him abruptly   He goes diamonds,
I go hearts again, he goes diamonds. Well, I don't get a
trick.   *to Lebedev*   We play four clubs. I hold ace,
queen, six in my hand; ace and ten, three of spades . . .

LEBEDEV
Stops his ears
Spare me, for Christ's sake, spare me!

KOSYKH
To the count
You do understand—ace, queen, six in clubs; ace, ten,
three of spades . . .

SHABELSKI
Pushing him away
Go away. I don't want to listen.

KOSYKH

And all at once—bad luck! My ace of spades taken
in the first round!

SHABELSKI
Snatching up a revolver from the desk
Go away or I'll shoot!

KOSYKH
Waving his hand
What the devil . . . Can't I even talk to anybody?
It's like living in Australia: no common interests, no

social life. Everyone living on his own. However,
I'd better go. It's time. *snatches up his cap* Time's
precious. *shakes hands with Lebedev* Pass!

*Laughter. Kosykh goes out and collides with Avdotya
Nazarovna in the doorway*

AVDOTYA NAZAROVNA
Gives a shriek
Curse you! You nearly knocked me off my feet!

ALL TOGETHER
Ah-ah! Here she is again!

AVDOTYA NAZAROVNA
Oh, there you are! And I've been looking all over the
house for you. How d'you do, my charming people?
Good appetite to you! *shakes hands*

LEBEDEV
What are you doing here?

AVDOTYA NAZAROVNA
I'm on business, my friend. *to the count* It concerns
you, Your Excellency. *bows* The lady told me to
give you her regards and inquire after your health.
And she also commanded—the pretty little darling—
she commanded me to tell you that if you don't come
to see her this evening, she'll cry her pretty eyes out.
"Take him aside and whisper it secretly into his ear,"
that's what the little darling said. But why secretly?
You're all friends here. Anyway, we're not stealing
chickens; this is a genuine love match, and we're
arranging it according to law and with mutual consent.
I never touch drink—old sinner that I am—but just
for this once I'll have one!

LEBEDEV
So will I. *pours it out* You know, old girl, you do
wear well! I've known you as an elderly woman for
the last thirty years.

ANTON
CHEKHOV

Well, I've lost count of my age. I've buried two
husbands, and I'd have married a third, but no one
would have me without a dowry. I've had about eight
children.   *takes her glass*   Well, we've begun a good
job; may God help us to finish it. They'd live happily
together, and we'd be able to look at them and rejoice.
We'd offer them good advice and wish them love and
happiness.   *drinks*   This vodka's strong!

SHABELSKI
Laughing loudly, to Lebedev
The curious thing is, you know, that they seriously
think that I . . . Amazing!   *rises*   But what if I
really decided to go through with this ignominious
thing? Eh, Pasha? Just out of spite. . . . There, you
old dog, down the hatch! Pasha, eh?

LEBEDEV
You're talking nonsense, Count. Your business is to
prepare to kick the bucket, brother—and mine too.
As for Marfutka's money, you've missed your chance
there long ago. Our time's over.

SHABELSKI
Yes, I'll do it! My word of honor, I will!

Enter Ivanov and Lvov

LVOV
I want you to give me just five minutes.

LEBEDEV
Nikolasha!   *goes to meet Ivanov and embraces him*
How are you, my friend? I've been waiting for you
a whole hour.

AVDOTYA NAZAROVNA
Bows   How d'you do, sir?

IVANOV
Bitterly   So you've turned my study into a public bar   IVANOV

again! I've asked you all a thousand times not to do this. *walks up to the table* There, you've spilled vodka over my papers. . . . Crumbs . . . Cucumbers . . . It's disgusting, you know!

LEBEDEV

My fault, Nikolasha, my fault. Forgive me. I must have a talk with you, my friend, about a very serious matter.

BORKIN

And I too.

LVOV

Nikolai Alekseevich, may I have a word with you?

IVANOV

Points at Lebedev

He wants me too. Will you wait? I'll see you afterward. *to Lebedev* What is it you want?

LEBEDEV

Gentlemen, I want to speak to him privately. Please.

The count goes out with Avdotya Nazarovna; Borkin, then Lvov follow

IVANOV

Pasha, you can drink as much as you like; it's your weakness. But I do entreat you not to make a drunkard of my uncle. He never used to drink before. It's bad for him.

LEBEDEV

Alarmed My dear fellow, I didn't know. I didn't even notice.

IVANOV

If that silly old baby dies—God forbid!—it is I who'd feel bad about it, not you. What is it you want?

ANTON
CHEKHOV

LEBEDEV

After a pause

You see, my dear friend . . . I don't know how to
begin, to make it seem less shocking. Nikolasha, I'm
ashamed, I know I'm blushing, and my tongue's
sticking in my throat. But, my dear fellow, do try to
put yourself in my place. Please understand that I'm
just a subordinate, a slave, a mere doormat. Do
forgive me.

IVANOV

What is it?

LEBEDEV

My wife's sent me. . . . Do me a favor. Be a good
friend; please pay her the interest! You'd hardly believe
it; she's almost nagged me to death. She keeps on
going for me. Settle up with her, for God's sake!

IVANOV

Pasha, you know that I haven't any money at present.

LEBEDEV

I know, I know, but what am I to do? She won't wait.
If she presents your promissory note, how will
Shurochka and I ever be able to look you in the face?

IVANOV

I'm ashamed myself, Pasha. I wish I could sink into
the earth, but . . . but where can I get money from?
Tell me : where? The only thing is to wait until the
autumn, when I sell the corn.

LEBEDEV

Shouts She doesn't want to wait!

IVANOV

After a pause

Your position is awkward and unpleasant, but mine
is far worse. *walks up and down, thinking* I can't
think of anything. . . . I've nothing to sell.

LEBEDEV

Why don't you go and ask Mülbach? You know he
owes you sixteen thousand.

IVANOV

I'll tell you what, Nikolasha. I know you'll be angry, but . . . do a favor for an old drunkard! As one friend to another. Do consider me as a friend. We've both been to the university, and liberals too. Community of ideas and interests. We both studied at Moscow University. *Alma Mater.*   *he takes out his wallet* Here, I've got some special money. Not a soul at home knows about it. Take it as a loan.   *takes out the money and puts it on the table*   Drop your pride and take it as from one friend to another. I'd accept it from you, my word of honor I would.   *pause*   There it is, on the table: one thousand, one hundred. You go and see her today and give it to her yourself. Say, "There, Zinaida Savishna, and may it choke you!" Mind, though, don't give a hint that you borrowed it from me—God help you! Or I'll get it in the neck from Madam Gooseberry Preserves!   *stares into Ivanov's face*   There, there, don't!   *quickly picks up the money from the table and puts it in his pocket*   Please, don't! I was joking. Forgive me, for Christ's sake!   *pause* You're fed up with it all?

Ivanov waves his hand

Yes, it's a bad business.   *sighs*   You're going through a bad spell, a sad time. You know, my friend, a man is like a samovar. He isn't always put away quietly on a shelf. Every now and again he gets some live charcoal pushed into him: psh . . . psh! . . . Of course, that's a rotten comparison, but I can't think of anything cleverer.   *sighs*   Misfortune hardens the soul. I don't pity you, Nikolasha. You'll land on your feet; things will come right. But I feel hurt and angry,

ANTON
CHEKHOV

my friend, when I hear what other people . . . Tell
me, where does all this gossip come from? The sort of
thing that's being said about you all over the district—
it's almost enough to make the public prosecutor's
assistant drop in on you. You're said to be a murderer,
a bloodsucker, a robber.

IVANOV

All that's nonsense. I don't care. . . . But I've got a
headache.

LEBEDEV

It's all because you think too much.

IVANOV

I'm not thinking anything.

LEBEDEV

Anyway, Nikolasha, don't take any notice of all that.
Just you come to see us. Shurochka is fond of you;
she understands and appreciates you. She's a good,
honest girl, Nikolasha. She doesn't take after her
father or mother. Perhaps it was a passing stranger!
Sometimes I look at her, my friend, and I can hardly
believe that a drunkard with a red nose like mine could
own such a treasure. Just come over and discuss something clever with her and—it'll cheer you up. She's
loyal and sincere. . . .

IVANOV

After a pause

Pasha, my dear friend, leave me alone.

LEBEDEV

I understand, I understand. *hurriedly looks at his
watch* I understand. *embraces Ivanov* Good-bye.
I've got to get to a consecration service at a school
they're opening. *walks to the door, then stops* She's
intelligent. Yesterday Shurochka and I began to talk
about gossip. *laughs* And she fired off an aphorism: IVANOV

"Papa," she said, "the glowworms only shine so that the birds can find them easier at night, and good men only shine so that gossip and rumor can prey on them." What do you think of that? Quite a genius! George Sand!

IVANOV

Pasha! *stops him* What's the matter with me?

LEBEDEV

I've been wanting to ask you that question myself, but I felt too shy to do it. I don't know, my friend. Sometimes it seems to me that bad luck has got you down, but on the other hand I know that you're not that sort, that you . . . you wouldn't be defeated by misfortune. It must be something else, Nikolasha; but what it is, I can't make out.

IVANOV

I can't grasp it myself. It seems to me or . . . Anyway it's not that! *pause* What I wanted to say is this. I used to have a workman, a fellow called Semën; you must remember him. Once, during the threshing, he wanted to show his strength off before the girls, so he hoisted two sacks of rye onto his back and strained himself. He died soon after. Well, it seems to me that I've strained myself too. The high school, then the university, then farming, schools for peasant children, all sorts of plans and projects. I had different ideas from all the other people, I married differently, I took risks, I threw my money around right and left, I got too excited, as you know. I've been happier and I've suffered more than anyone in the district. Those have been *my* sacks, Pasha. I hoisted a load on my back, but my back gave way. At twenty we're all heroes, we undertake anything, we can do anything; but at thirty we're tired already and good for nothing. Tell me, how do you explain the way one gets so tired? However,

ANTON
CHEKHOV

perhaps it isn't that. . . . Not that, not that! . . . Go
now, Pasha. God bless you. You must be tired of me.

LEBEDEV

Eagerly D'you know what? It's your surroundings
that are killing you.

IVANOV

That's silly, Pasha . . . and stale too. Be off with you!

LEBEDEV

True enough, it is silly. Now I see it myself. I'm
going, I'm going! *goes out*

IVANOV

Alone I'm a rotten, pitiful, contemptible creature.
You need to be a wretched, worn-out drunkard like
Pasha to be able to love and respect me still. Oh, God,
how I despise myself! I hate my voice, my footsteps,
my hands, these clothes, my thoughts. Isn't it ridiculous?
Isn't it infuriating? It's hardly a year since I was tough
and healthy, in good spirits too; energetic, enthusiastic
. . . Since I worked with my own hands and could
talk so well that even the commonest louts were moved
to tears. . . . Since I could weep when I saw grief and
feel indignation when I met with wickedness. I knew
what inspiration was then; I knew the charm and
poetry of those quiet nights when you sit at your desk
working from sunset till dawn, or just sit and muse
and dream. I had faith then; I could look into the
future as if it were my own mother's eyes. . . . And
now, oh, my God! I'm tired, I've no faith, I idle away
my days and nights. I can't make my brain or my
hands or my feet do what I want them to. The estate
goes to ruin. The forests are groaning under the ax.
weeps My land looks at me as an orphan looks at a
stranger. I expect nothing; I regret nothing. But my
soul trembles with fear at the thought of tomorrow.
. . . And this business with Sarah! I swore I'd love

IVANOV

her forever; said how happy we'd be. I painted a picture of a future life such as she'd never dreamed of! She believed me. During all these five years I've just seen her wasting away under a burden of self-sacrifice, exhausting herself in her struggle with her conscience, yet—God knows—with never a glance or a word of reproach to me. . . . And what happens then? I fall out of love with her. How? Why? What for? I can't understand it. Now she's ill and suffering. She's going to die . . . and I . . . I run away from her pale face, her sunken chest, her imploring eyes, like the mean coward I am. . . . I'm ashamed, ashamed! *pause* Sasha, a mere child, is touched by my troubles. She says she's in love with me—me, almost an old man—and I get drunk with it. I forget everything else in the world, like someone fascinated by music, and I start shouting, "A new life! Happiness!" But the next day I don't believe in the new life or the new happiness any more than I believe in ghosts. What is it that's the matter with me then? What is this precipice that I seem to be pushing myself over? Where does all this weakness come from? What's happened to my nerves? If my poor wife upsets my vanity or the servants annoy me or my gun doesn't go off, I immediately get boorish and bad-tempered, quite unlike myself. *pause* I don't understand it, I don't, I don't! . . . I feel like putting a bullet into my head!

LVOV
Comes in I must talk things over with you, Nikolai Alekseevich

IVANOV
If we both keep talking things over day after day, Doctor, it will be more than human strength can stand.

ANTON CHEKHOV

LVOV
Will you hear me out?

IVANOV

I hear you out every day, but I still can't make out
what it really is you want from me.

LVOV

I've said it clearly enough, and only someone completely heartless could fail to understand me.

IVANOV

My wife is about to die—I know that. I'm irreparably
guilty as far as she's concerned—I know that too.
You are an honest, sincere man—I know it! What
else do you want to say?

LVOV

I feel indignant when I see human cruelty! A woman
is dying. She has a father and a mother whom she
loves and whom she would like to see before she dies.
They are perfectly well aware that she's going to die
soon and that she still loves them, but—the damnable
cruelty of it!—they still go on cursing her, as if they
wanted to astound everybody by their own religious
strength of mind. You, the man for whom she's
sacrificed everything—her own home, her peace of
mind—you go off every day quite openly and with the
most obvious intentions to visit those Lebedev people!

IVANOV

Oh, I haven't been there for two weeks.

LVOV

Without listening to him
With people like you, you have to speak plainly,
without beating around the bush. But if you don't
want to listen to me, don't. I'm used to calling a
spade a spade. You want her to die, so you'll be free
for new adventures. All right, then, but couldn't you
wait? If you let her die naturally, without hammering
away at her all the time with your beastly cynicism,
do you think you'd lose the Lebedev girl and her

IVANOV

dowry? What of it? In a year's time, or maybe in two years, you'd succeed in turning some young girl's head and in getting hold of her dowry, just as you would now—you wonderful Tartuffe. So what are you in such a hurry for? Why is it so essential that your wife should die now, and not in a month or a year?

IVANOV

You're torturing me. You're a poor sort of doctor if you imagine that a man can go on controlling himself indefinitely. It's costing me a terrific effort not to answer back your insults.

LVOV

Oh, enough of that! Whom are you trying to fool? Drop this pretense!

IVANOV

Try to think clearly, if you're so clever. You seem to imagine it's the simplest thing in the world to understand me, don't you? I married Anya in order to get a fat dowry. I wasn't given the dowry. I lost the trick, so now I'm kicking the life out of her so that I can marry someone else and get another dowry. Is that right? How simple and uncomplicated! A man is such a simple, uncomplicated machine. No, Doctor, we all have too many wheels and screws and valves inside of us to be judged by first impressions or by a few external traits. I don't understand you, you don't understand me, and we don't understand ourselves. It's possible to be an excellent physician, and at the same time not to know anything about people. Admit that I'm right—and don't be so sure of yourself.

LVOV

But do you really think that you're so deep and I'm so lacking in intelligence that I can't distinguish between wickedness and honesty?

ANTON
CHEKHOV

It's obvious that you and I will never agree about these things. For the last time I ask you . . . and please answer me without beating around the bush : what exactly do you want from me? What are you driving at? *with irritation* And anyway with whom have I the honor to be talking : with the counsel for the prosecution or with my wife's doctor?

LVOV

I'm a doctor, and as a doctor, I demand that you behave differently. Your conduct is killing Anna Petrovna.

IVANOV

But what am I to do? What? If you understand me better than I understand myself, then answer me straight : what am I to do?

LVOV

At least don't do what you do so openly.

IVANOV

Oh, my God! Do you really understand yourself? *drinks water* Leave me. I'm at fault a thousand times. I'll answer for it before God . . . but no one has given you the right to torture me every day like this.

LVOV

And who's given you the right to offend against my idea of what's right! You've worn me out and poisoned my mind. Until I happened to come into this district, I used to be able to accept the existence of people who were stupid and mad and capable of being carried away by their feelings. But I never believed that there were actually criminal people who deliberately and consciously directed their activities toward evil ends. I used to respect and love human beings, but when I saw you . . .

IVANOV

IVANOV

I've already heard all about that!

LVOV

You have, have you?   *he catches sight of Sasha, who has just come in; she is wearing a riding habit*   Well, now I hope we understand each other perfectly! *shrugs his shoulders and walks out*

IVANOV

Alarmed   Sasha—you here?

SASHA

Yes, I'm here! How are you? Weren't you expecting me? Why haven't you been to see us for so long?

IVANOV

Shura, for God's sake, this is rash of you! This might have a dreadful effect on my wife.

SASHA

She won't see me. I came in through the back door. I'll go in a minute. I'm worried: are you well? Why haven't you been to see us for so long?

IVANOV

My wife is upset with me as it is. She's almost dying, and you come here! Shura, Shura, this is thoughtless and unfeeling of you!

SASHA

But what was I to do? You haven't been to see us for two weeks; you never answered my letters. I've been worn out with worry. I imagined you here, suffering unbearably, ill, dead. I haven't slept a single night in peace. I'll go in a minute. But do tell me at least: are you well?

IVANOV

No, I've worn myself out, and other people are tormenting me continually. I just can't bear it any longer. And now you! How unhealthy all this is! How unnatural! Shura, I'm so much to blame, so much!

ANTON
CHEKHOV

SASHA
How you do like saying frightening, gloomy things!
You to blame? You? To blame? Well, tell me what for,
then?

IVANOV
I don't know, I don't know. . . .

SASHA
That's not an answer. A sinner must know how he's
sinned. Have you been forging bank notes or what?

IVANOV
That's not funny.

SASHA
Are you to blame because you've stopped loving your
wife? Well, maybe, but a man isn't master of his
feelings; you didn't want to stop loving her. Are you to
blame because she saw me telling you I loved you?
No, you didn't want her to see it.

IVANOV
Interrupting Go on, go on. Fallen in love, fallen out
of love, not master of my feelings—what common-
places these are. Trite phrases which just don't help.

SASHA
It's tiring, talking to you. *looks at the pictures on the
walls* How well that dog's painted! Was it done
from life?

IVANOV
Yes, from life. And this love affair of ours is all just
something commonplace and trite: "He lost heart
and lost his grip on things. She appeared, cheerful and
strong in spirit, and held out a helping hand." It's
beautiful, but it's only like what happens in novels.
In real life you don't . . .

SASHA
In real life it's just the same.

IVANOV

I can see you've a very deep understanding of life! My
whining inspires you with a sort of reverent awe; you
seem to think that you've got hold of a second Hamlet
in me. . . . But in my opinion this neurotic state of
mine and all the symptoms that go with it are just
something to laugh at, and nothing else! People ought
to laugh till their sides split at all my affectations, but
you—what a wonderful fuss you make! You want
to save me, to do something heroic! . . . Oh, how
angry I am with myself today! I feel this state of tension
I'm in today will come to a crisis. Either I'll break
something or . . .

SASHA

That's it, that's it, that's just what you need. Do break
something, smash something, or start shouting. You're
angry with me; it was stupid of me to come here. All
right, then, show your indignation, shout at me, stamp
your feet. Well? Start being angry. *pause* Well?

IVANOV

Funny child!

SASHA

Splendid! We actually seem to have smiled! Now do
me a favor and agree to smile again!

IVANOV

Laughs I've noticed when you start trying to save
me and drive some sense into me, the expression on
your face gets quite naïve, and the pupils of your eyes
get bigger, as if you were staring at a comet or something. Just a minute, your shoulder's covered with
dust. *brushes the dust off her shoulder with his hand*
A man who's naïve is a fool. But you women somehow
contrive to be naïve in such a way that it's charming
and natural and comforting . . . and not as silly as it
appears to be. And then there's another queer thing

ANTON
CHEKHOV

about you. As long as a man is healthy and strong and
cheerful, you don't take any notice of him. But as
soon as he starts slithering downhill and playing the
poor Lazarus, you hang yourself around his neck. Is it
really worse to be the wife of a strong, courageous man
than a nurse to some tearful failure?

SASHA

It is worse.

IVANOV

But why? *laughs loudly* It's lucky Darwin didn't
hear you say that, or he would have told you what's
what. You're spoiling the human race. Thanks to
people like you, we will soon only have slobberers and
neurotics born into the world.

SASHA

There are a lot of things men don't understand. Every
girl is more attracted by a man who's a failure than
by one who's a success, because what she wants is
active love. Do you understand that? Active love. Men
are taken up with their work and so love has to take a
back seat with them. To have a talk with his wife,
to take a stroll with her in the garden, to pass time
pleasantly with her, to weep a little on her grave—
that's all. But for us, love is life. I love you, and that
means that I dream about how I'd cure you of your
depression, how I'd follow you to the end of the world.
If you went up a mountain, I'd follow you; if you fell
over a precipice, I'd follow you. For instance, it would
be sheer happiness for me to copy out your papers all
night long, or watch over you all night so that no
one woke you up, or just walk with you for miles—
a hundred miles! I remember once you came to our
house about three years ago at harvest time, and you
were all covered with dust and tired out, and you asked
for a drink of water. I went to get you a glass, but you   IVANOV

were lying on the sofa, sound asleep, when I came back with it. You slept the best part of the day in our house, and I stood outside the door all the time and guarded it, so that no one would come in. And I was so happy! The greater the effort, the greater the love. I mean one feels it more strongly.

IVANOV

Active love. Hm . . . It's infatuation, girlish muddle-headedness . . . or perhaps that's the way it ought to be. *shrugs his shoulders* God knows! *gaily* Shura, on my word of honor, I really am a decent fellow! You can judge for yourself. I know I've always been one for talking, but at least I've never in my life accused women of being depraved or said, "That woman's on the downward path!" I've merely been grateful, and nothing else. Nothing else! My sweet little girl, how good you are, and how entertaining too! And what a ridiculous fool I am! I go about upsetting honest people, playing the poor Lazarus day in, day out. *laughs* Boo-hoo! *walks quickly to one side* But do please go away, Sasha! We've been forgetting ourselves.

SASHA

Yes, it's time I went. Good-bye! I'm afraid your honest doctor may tell Anna Petrovna about my being here—just out of a sense of duty. Now listen to me: go to your wife now and stay with her, keep staying with her. If it's necessary to stay a year, then stay a year. If you have to stay ten years, stay ten years. Do your duty. Experience the grief of it, ask her forgiveness, weep—all that's just as it should be. But the main thing is—don't forget your work!

IVANOV

I've got this sensation again—as if I'd eaten an enormous meal of toadstools. Again!

SASHA

Well, God bless you, Nikolai! You don't have to
think about me at all! If you send me a line in about
two weeks, I'll be grateful for that. As for me, I'll
write to you.

Borkin pokes his head through the door

BORKIN

Nikolai Alekseevich, may I come in? *seeing Sasha*
I beg your pardon; I didn't notice. *comes in* *Bonjour!*
bows

SASHA

Embarrassed How d'you do?

BORKIN

You've grown plumper and prettier.

SASHA

To Ivanov Well, I'll be going now, Nikolai
Alekseevich. I'll go. *goes out*

BORKIN

What a wonderful vision! I came on a prosaic matter
but found poetry. *sings* "You came into my sight
as the bird flies to the light."

Ivanov paces back and forth in agitation

sits down You know, Nicolàs, she's got something,
something the others haven't got. Isn't that so? Something special, phantasmagoric. *sighs* As a matter
of fact, she's the wealthiest match in the whole district,
but her mamma's such a Tartar that no one wants
to hook up with her. After she's dead Shurochka will
get everything, but until she dies she'll only give her
ten thousand or so, and perhaps a few old pots, and
she'll expect gratitude even for that. *rummages
through his pockets* Have a smoke—*de los mejores.*   IVANOV

82 Would you like one? *offers his cigarette case*
They're good. Quite smokable.

IVANOV

Walks up to Borkin, almost speechless with rage
Get out this minute and don't ever dare cross my
threshold again! This very minute!

Borkin half-rises and drops a cigar

Out this very minute!

BORKIN

Nicolàs, what does this mean? Why are you angry?

IVANOV

Why? And where did you get those cigars? And do you
think I don't know where you take the old man every
day and what for?

BORKIN

Shrugs his shoulders
What do you want to worry about that for?

IVANOV

Cad that you are! You're giving me a bad name all over
the district with your vile scheming. We've nothing
in common, and I want you to leave my house now,
this very minute! *paces back and forth*

BORKIN

I know you're saying all this because you're irritated
about something, and for that reason I don't feel
angry with you. You may insult me as much as you
like. *picks up the cigar* As for this melancholy of
yours, it's time you dropped all that. You're not a
schoolboy.

IVANOV

What did I tell you? *trembling* Are you playing the
fool with me?

ANTON
CHEKHOV *Enter Anna Petrovna*

BORKIN

Well, now Anna Petrovna's come. I'll go. *goes out*

*Ivanov stops beside his desk and stands with his head
down*

ANNA PETROVNA

After a pause

Why was she here just now? *pause* Oh, so that's what
you are! Now I understand you. At last I see what sort of
a man you are. Dishonorable, base. . . . Do you remember how you came and lied to me and said you loved
me? I believed you and I left my father and mother.
I gave up my religion and I followed you. It was lies
you told me about goodness and truth, about your
high-minded plans, and I believed every word.

IVANOV

Anyuta, I have never lied to you.

ANNA PETROVNA

I've lived with you five years. I've been miserable and
I've fallen ill, but I've loved you and never left you
for a minute. You've been my idol. And what now?
All that time you were just deceiving me brazenly.

IVANOV

Anyuta, don't tell lies. I made mistakes, that's true.
But I've never lied once in my life. Don't you dare
reproach me with that.

ANNA PETROVNA

Everything's clear now. You married me thinking that
my parents would forgive me and give me money.
You thought that. . . .

IVANOV

Oh, my God! Anyuta, why must you try my patience
like this? *weeps*

ANNA PETROVNA

Be quiet! When you saw that there wouldn't be any   IVANOV money, you started a new game. . . . Now I remember everything; now I understand. *weeps* You've never loved me or been faithful to me. Never!

IVANOV

Sarah, that is a lie! Say what you like, but don't insult me by lying to me.

ANNA PETROVNA

Dishonorable and base. You owe money to Lebedev, and now to avoid paying your debt you're trying to turn his daughter's head, to deceive her just as you've deceived me. Isn't that true?

IVANOV

Suffocating Stop, for God's sake! I can't answer for myself like this! I feel absolutely suffocated with rage, and I . . . I might say something insulting to you.

ANNA PETROVNA

You've always deceived me scandalously, and not me alone. You've blamed all your wicked acts on Borkin, but now I know who was guilty.

IVANOV

Sarah, stop this, go away, or I'll lose control and say something! I can hardly stop myself from saying something horrible and insulting. *shouts* Be quiet, Jewess!

ANNA PETROVNA

I won't be quiet. You've deceived me too long for me to stay silent now.

IVANOV

So you won't be silent? *struggles with himself* For God's sake . . .

ANNA PETROVNA

Now go and deceive Lebedev.

IVANOV

Then you might just as well know that you . . . will die soon. The doctor told me that you'll die soon.

ANNA PETROVNA

Sits down, her voice failing her
When did he say that?

IVANOV

After a pause, clutching his head with his hands
How wicked I am! God, how wicked!   *sobs*

CURTAIN

*About a year passes between the Third
and Fourth Acts*

ACT FOUR

One of the drawing rooms at the Lebedevs' house. In the center of the stage there is an arch, separating the drawing room from the ballroom; there are doors right and left. Antique bronze, family portraits. Everything is ready for a reception. There is an upright piano with a violin on top of it and a cello beside it. During the entire act visitors pass to and fro through the ballroom. They are in evening dress.

LVOV
Comes in, looks at his watch
It's past four. I suppose the blessing will begin in a minute. The blessing, and then off to the wedding. So here's the triumph of virtue and righteousness. He didn't succeed in robbing Sarah, so he sent her to her grave, and now he's found another one! He'll play the honest man with this one too until he's robbed her. And after he's robbed her, he'll send her to the same place that poor Sarah's lying in now. It's the old money-grubbing story.   *pause*   So now he's in his seventh heaven, and he's going to live nicely to a ripe old age and then die with a clear conscience. . . . But

no, you won't, I'll show you up! When I tear off your
damned mask and everyone knows what sort of a cur
you are, you'll be chucked down from your seventh
heaven headfirst into such a pit that all the devils in
hell won't be able to get you out of it! I'm an honest
man; it's my duty to come forward and open their eyes.
I'll do my duty, and then tomorrow I'll get out of this
accursed district! *muses* But what am I to do?
Explain everything to Lebedev? Waste of breath!
Challenge Ivanov to a duel? Start a row? Oh, my God,
I feel as nervous as a schoolboy, and I've completely
lost the power to think things out. What am I to do?
A duel?

KOSYKH

Comes in gleefully to Lvov
Yesterday I went a small slam in clubs but got a grand
slam. This fellow Barabanov spoiled the whole game
for me again. We play. I go no trumps; he passes. Two
no trumps; he passes. I go two diamonds . . . three
clubs . . . and—would you believe it?—I bid slam, but
he doesn't show his ace. If the idiot had only shown
his ace, I would have declared grand slam in no
trumps.

LVOV

Excuse me, I don't play cards, and so I can't share your
feelings. Is the blessing to be soon?

KOSYKH

It must be soon. They're trying to bring Zyuzyushka
around. She's sobbing her heart out. So upset to lose
the dowry.

LVOV

But not her daughter?

KOSYKH

No, it's the dowry. She's annoyed too. Since he's
marrying her daughter, it means he won't pay his debt.   IVANOV

You can't very well produce your son-in-law's
promissory note as evidence.

*Babakina, overdressed, walks across the stage past Lvov
and Kosykh in an affectedly pompous manner. Kosykh
bursts out laughing, his hand over his mouth. She looks
around*

BABAKINA
Stupid!

*Kosykh touches her waist with his finger and laughs
loudly*

The oaf! *goes out*

KOSYKH
Laughing loudly That woman's gone quite off her
rocker! Until she began wanting to be an Excellency,
she was a woman like any other. But now you simply
can't go near her. *mimics her* The oaf!

LVOV
Agitated Listen, tell me honestly: what's your
opinion of Ivanov?

KOSYKH
He's no good. Plays cards like a cobbler. Just think, last
year about Easter time we sat down to play: I, the
count, Borkin, and Ivanov. I dealt . . .

LVOV
Interrupting him Is he a good man?

KOSYKH
What, Ivanov? A clever scoundrel! A cunning fellow!
He knows all the tricks of the trade. He and the count
are birds of a feather. They'll manage to sniff out
anything that's easy to pinch. He missed the mark with
the Jew, so now he's nosing his way into Zyuzyushka's

ANTON
CHEKHOV

moneybags. I'll bet you—and you can call me what you
like if I'm wrong—that in a year's time he'll send
Zyuzyushka begging in the streets. He'll be the
ruin of Zyuzyushka, and the count will be the ruin of
Babakina. They'll grab the money and then go on
living happily ever after, just getting richer and richer.
Doctor, why are you so pale today? You look like
nothing on earth.

LVOV

Nothing, nothing's the matter. I drank a bit too much
yesterday.

LEBEDEV

Comes in with Sasha
We'll have a talk here. *to Lvov and Kosykh* Go into
the ballroom, boys, and join the young ladies. We
want to talk privately here.

KOSYKH

Snaps his fingers in admiration as he passes Sasha
What a picture! A queen of trumps!

LEBEDEV

Out you go, caveman, pass along!

Lvov and Kosykh go out

Sit down, Shurochka, that's it. *sits down and glances
around* Now just listen to me attentively and with
proper respect. The fact is that your mother's ordered
me to give you a message. Is that clear? I'm not
speaking in my own name, but on orders from your
mother.

SASHA

Be quick about it, papa!

LEBEDEV

Fifteen thousand rubles in silver have been made over
to you as a dowry. So see there isn't any argument   IVANOV

about it later. Wait a moment, be quiet! That's only the blossom; the fruit will come afterward. Fifteen thousand are made over to you, but since Nikolai Alekseevich owes your mother nine thousand, a deduction is being made from your dowry. Then, in addition, besides that . . .

SASHA

Why are you telling me all this?

LEBEDEV

Your mother's orders.

SASHA

Leave me alone! If you had the slightest respect for me and yourself, you wouldn't allow yourself to talk to me like this. I don't want your dowry. I haven't asked for it, and I'm not asking for it!

LEBEDEV

What are you coming down on me for? The rats in Gogol's play at least smelled the thing first and then ran away. But you go for me without even sniffing at my offer, you independent creature!

SASHA

Leave me alone. Don't insult me with your petty sums and calculations!

LEBEDEV

Flying into a temper

Pshaw! You'll finish by making me stick a knife into myself or cutting somebody's throat, you and your mother! One sets up a hullabaloo all day long, nagging and pestering me and counting her kopecks, while the other's so clever and humane and emancipated that she can't understand her own father—devil take it! I insult her! Can't you see that before I came here to insult you, I was being hanged, drawn, and quartered in there? *points at the door* She can't understand!

You've made me dizzy; I'm losing my senses. I'll go!
goes to the door, then stops I don't like it. I dislike
everything about it!

SASHA

What is it you dislike?

LEBEDEV

I dislike everything! Everything!

SASHA

What do you mean by everything?

LEBEDEV

Do you expect me to sit down in front of you and tell
you all about it? I don't like anything, and I don't
want to see your wedding! *approaches Sasha and
continues affectionately* Do please forgive me,
Shurochka.... Perhaps your marriage is clever and
honest and high-minded and all according to the best
principles, but there's something wrong about it. It's
not the real thing! It isn't like other marriages. You're
young and fresh, clean as a pane of glass, good-looking
too; while he—he's a widower, and he's knocked
around a lot and is worn-out. I can't understand him
either—God help him! *kisses his daughter*
Shurochka, forgive me, but there's something not quite
right. People are talking too much. First that Sarah
woman died at his house; then for some reason or other
he suddenly decided to marry you. *with animation*
However, I'm just an old woman, an old woman. I've
turned womanish, like an old maid. Don't listen to
me. Don't listen to anybody; only listen to yourself.

SASHA

Papa, I've been feeling myself that something's wrong.
Not quite as it should be ... not ... not as it should
be. If you only knew how oppressed I feel! Unbearably!
I feel embarrassed and afraid to confess it. Dear papa,   IVANOV

do say something to cheer me up, for God's sake. . . .
Tell me what to do!

LEBEDEV

What's that? What are you saying?

SASHA

I'm more afraid than I've ever been! *looks around*
I feel as though I don't understand him and never will
understand him. During the whole time I've been
engaged to him, he's never once smiled, never once
looked me straight in the eyes. All the time complaining, repenting about something, hinting at some guilt
or other, trembling. . . . I'm tired of it. There are
even moments when it seems to me that I . . . that I
don't love him as much as I should. And when he
comes to see us or talks to me, I begin to feel bored.
What does it all mean, papa dear? I'm afraid!

LEBEDEV

My darling, my only child, listen to your old father!
Give him up!

SASHA

Alarmed   Don't, don't!

LEBEDEV

I mean it, Shurochka! There'll be a row; all the
neighbors will wag their tongues like a lot of church-
bells. But it's surely better to live through a row than
to ruin your whole life.

SASHA

Don't say that, don't, papa! I don't want to listen.
One must just struggle against all these gloomy
thoughts. He's a good, unhappy, misunderstood man.
I will love him, learn to understand him, put him on
his feet again. I'll fulfill my task. That's settled!

ANTON
CHEKHOV

LEBEDEV

That's not fulfilling a task—that's just madness!

SASHA

That's enough. I've confessed something to you which I didn't even want to confess to myself. Don't tell anybody. Let's forget it.

LEBEDEV

I don't understand anything. Either I've gotten dull with old age or you've all gotten too clever, but I'll eat my hat before I understand anything about it.

SHABELSKI

Coming in The devil take everybody, including myself! It's revolting!

LEBEDEV

What is it?

SHABELSKI

No, I mean it seriously. I'm going to have to do something so mean and base that everyone will be disgusted, including myself. But, whatever the cost, I'll do it. My word of honor! I've told Borkin to announce my engagement today. *laughs* Everyone's rotten, so I'll be rotten too.

LEBEDEV

I'm tired of you! Listen, Matvei, if you go on talking like that, it'll end by your being taken to the loony bin, excuse the expression.

SHABELSKI

And how's the loony bin worse than anywhere else? Do me a favor and take me there now. Yes, please do! Everyone's so low and small-minded and dull-witted. And I'm vile even to myself; I don't believe a single word I say.

LEBEDEV

I'll tell you what to do, my friend. Put some tallow into your mouth, light it up, and breathe fire at people. Or better still, take your hat and go home. There's a

IVANOV

wedding on here; everyone's enjoying himself, and you go around croaking like a crow. Yes, I mean it.

Shabelski leans on the piano and sobs

Good Heavens! . . . Matvei! . . . Count! . . . What's the matter with you? Matyusha, my dear man . . . my dearest fellow. Did I hurt you? You must forgive me, old fool that I am. Forgive an old drunkard. Have a drink of water.

SHABELSKI
I don't want it.   *raises his head*

LEBEDEV
Why are you crying?

SHABELSKI
It's nothing. . . . Just nothing.

LEBEDEV
No, Matyusha, don't tell lies. Now, why? What's the cause of it?

SHABELSKI
I happened to see this cello just now, and . . . that made me think of the little Jew!

LEBEDEV
Eh! What a time to think of her! May she rest in peace, poor soul, but this isn't the time to think of her.

SHABELSKI
We used to play duets together. . . . A wonderful, excellent woman!

Sasha sobs

LEBEDEV
What, now you? Do leave off! Oh, Lord, now they're both howling, while I . . . I . . . Why don't you go somewhere else where the guests won't see you?

SHABELSKI

Pasha, when the sun shines you can feel cheerful even in a cemetery. And when there's hope, you can be happy even in old age. But I haven't got a ray of hope, not a single ray!

LEBEDEV

Yes, it's true; you are in a pretty bad way. You haven't got any children or money or work. However, what can you do about it? *to Sasha* But why are you crying?

SHABELSKI

Pasha, let me have some money. I'll settle with you in the next world. I'll go to Paris and have a look at my wife's grave. I've given away a lot in my life. I've given away half my fortune, so I've a right to ask. Besides I'm asking it of a friend.

LEBEDEV

Bewildered My dear fellow, I haven't got a kopeck! However, all right, all right! That is, I don't promise, but you understand . . . of course, of course! *aside* They've worn me out!

BABAKINA

Comes in And where's my cavalier now? Count, how dare you leave me alone? Oo-oo, you naughty man! *strikes the count on the hand with her fan*

SHABELSKI

With revulsion Leave me alone! I hate you!

BABAKINA

Taken aback What? Eh?

SHABELSKI

Get away!

BABAKINA

Falls into an armchair
Oh! *weeps*

IVANOV

ZINAIDA SAVISHNA

Comes in, weeping
Someone's just arrived. I think it's the best man. It's
time for the blessing.   *sobs*

SASHA

Imploringly   Mamma!

LEBEDEV

There now, everyone's blubbering now. A quartet!
Do stop spreading all this wet weather around!
Matvei! Marfa Yegorovna! If you go on, I . . . I'll
start crying too.   *cries*   Oh, Lord!

ZINAIDA SAVISHNA

If you don't want your mother, if you're not an
obedient daughter . . . well, have your own way. I'll
give you my blessing.

Ivanov comes in, wearing a tailcoat and gloves

LEBEDEV

This is the last straw. What is it?

SASHA

What are you here for?

IVANOV

Forgive me, ladies and gentlemen. Please allow me to
have a word with Sasha alone.

LEBEDEV

It's not right to come to see your bride just before the
wedding! You ought to be going to the church!

IVANOV

Pasha, please. . . .

*Lebedev shrugs his shoulders; then he, Zinaida
Savishna, the count, and Babakina go out*

ANTON
CHEKHOV

SASHA

Sternly   What do you want?

I'm boiling over with anger, but I'll speak coolly.
Listen. Just now, as I was dressing for the wedding, I
glanced at myself in a mirror, and I saw . . . gray hair
on my temples. Shura, let us drop it! We must stop
this senseless comedy while it's still not too late.
You're young and pure. You have your life before you,
while I . . .

SASHA

All this isn't new; I've heard it a thousand times and
I'm tired of it! Go to the church and don't keep people
waiting!

IVANOV

I'll go home in a minute, and then you tell your people
that there won't be a wedding. Explain to them
somehow. It's time we came to our senses. I've acted
Hamlet and you've acted a high-minded young
woman—but we can't go on like that.

SASHA

Flushing What are you talking like this for? I'm not
listening.

IVANOV

But I'm speaking, and I'll go on speaking.

SASHA

What have you come for? Your whining's becoming
a sheer mockery.

IVANOV

No, I'm not whining any more. A mockery! Yes, I'm
mocking you! And if I could mock myself a thousand
times more bitterly and make the whole world jeer
at me, I'd do that too! I caught sight of myself in the
mirror—and it was like a shell exploding inside my
conscience. I laughed at myself and I nearly went out of
my mind with shame. *laughs* Melancholy! Noble
anguish! Inexplicable grief! Only one thing's lacking—   IVANOV

I ought to write poetry. Whining and playing the poor Lazarus and making everyone miserable with your anguish—no, no, no! To realize that your life's energy has gone forever, that you've gotten rusty and outlived your time, that you've given way to cowardice and gotten stuck up to your neck in a disgusting bog of melancholy. And all that when you can see the sun shining and even the ants dragging their burdens manfully and feeling pleased with themselves—no, no, no! To have some people take you for a charlatan and others feel sorry for you and stretch out a helping hand to you. And others—this is worst of all—others listen to your sighs with awe and look at you as though you were a second Mohammed about to reveal a new religion at any moment. No, thank God, I still have some pride and conscience left! As I was coming here, I laughed at myself, and it seemed that the birds were laughing at me, and the trees too.

SASHA

This isn't anger—it's madness!

IVANOV

You think so? No, I'm not mad. Now I see things in their true light, and my thoughts are as clear as your conscience is. We love each other, but our wedding won't take place! I'm entitled to rave and groan as much as I like, but I've no right to ruin other people! I poisoned the last year of my wife's life with my whining. Since we've been engaged, you've forgotten how to smile and you've grown five years older. Then your father—everything used to be clear and simple to him, but thanks to me he doesn't understand people anymore. It doesn't matter whether I go to a meeting or to a shooting party or to visit someone—wherever I

go, I produce boredom and dejection and discontent. Stop; don't interrupt me! I'm being rude and fierce

about it, but you must forgive me. The bitterness of it
is choking me, and I can't speak any differently. I've
never meant to lie; I've never deliberately spoken ill of
life. But I've developed into a grumbler and I curse it
against my will, without noticing it myself. I blame
fate; I complain. And everyone who listens to me is
infected with a sort of disgust toward life and begins
to curse it too. And what an attitude! As if I were doing
nature a favor by being alive! Oh, the devil take me!

SASHA

Just a minute! From what you've just been saying it
follows that you're tired of all your whining and it's
time to begin a new life! That's excellent!

IVANOV

I see nothing excellent in it. What new life is there?
I'm ruined irretrievably! It's time we both understood
that. A new life!

SASHA

Nikolai, pull yourself together! Where's the proof that
you're ruined? What's all this cynicism about? No, I
don't want to talk or listen. Go to the church!

IVANOV

I'm ruined!

SASHA

Don't shout like that; the guests will hear!

IVANOV

If an intelligent, educated, healthy man starts playing
the poor Lazarus without any obvious cause, if he
starts rolling downhill, he'll go on rolling without
stopping, and there's no salvation for him! Well,
where *is* my salvation? Where? I can't drink—wine
gives me a headache; I can't write bad poetry; I can't
enjoy spiritual idleness and see it as something noble
and lofty. Idleness is idleness, weakness is weakness—
I don't know any other names for them. I'm ruined,   IVANOV

ruined—that's beyond any argument! *glances around*
We may be interrupted here. Listen, if you really love
me, you must help me. Now, this very minute, you
must give me up! Now, quickly!

SASHA

Oh, Nikolai, if you knew how tired you make me!
You've worn my spirit down! You're a kind, intelligent
man. Ask yourself: is it fair to set me these problems?
Every day there is some problem, each one harder than
the last. I wanted active love, but this is martyred love!

IVANOV

When you're my wife the problems will be more
complicated still; so you'd better give me up now! I
wish you'd understand: you're not moved by love, but
just the stubbornness of your own honesty. You set
yourself a goal—to resurrect the man in me, to save
me at whatever cost—and the idea of doing a great
deed gratified you. Now you're ready to withdraw, but
there's a false emotion preventing you. I wish you'd
understand!

SASHA

What a queer, crazy logic! How can I give you up?
How? You haven't got a mother or a sister or a friend.
You're ruined, your estate's been pilfered away,
everyone slanders you.

IVANOV

I was a fool to come here. I should have done what
I wanted to.

Enter Lebedev

SASHA

Runs toward her father

Papa, for God's sake help me. He's come bursting in
here like a lunatic, and he's tormenting the life out
of me! He says I must give him up because he doesn't

want to ruin me. Tell him I don't want his
magnanimity! I know what I'm doing.

LEBEDEV

I don't understand anything about it. What
magnanimity?

IVANOV

There'll be no wedding.

SASHA

There will be a wedding! Papa, tell him that there will
be a wedding!

LEBEDEV

Wait, wait! Why don't you want the wedding to take
place?

IVANOV

I've explained to her why, but she doesn't want to
understand.

LEBEDEV

No, not to her, explain it to me, and explain it so that
I can understand it. Oh, Nikolai Alekseevich, may
God be your judge! You've brought so much fog into
our lives that I feel as if I were living in a chamber of
horrors. I look on and I don't understand anything.
It's simply dreadful. . . . Well, what do you expect me
to do? What do you want an old man to do about it?
Shall I challenge you to a duel or what?

IVANOV

There's no need for any duel. All that's needed is for
you to have a head on your shoulders and to understand
plain language.

SASHA

Paces the stage in agitation
This is dreadful, dreadful! He's just like a child!

LEBEDEV

There's nothing for it but just to shrug your shoulders,
that's all. Listen to me, Nikolai! You think you're

IVANOV

acting intelligently, subtly, according to all the rules of psychology. But I think this is all a scandal and disaster. Now hear an old man out for the last time. This is all I want to tell you: just calm your mind down! Look at things simply, like everybody else does! In this world everything is simple. The ceiling is white, the boots are black, sugar is sweet. You love Sasha, she loves you. If you love her, stay with her; if you don't love her, go. We won't bear you any malice. It's really as simple as that! You're both healthy, intelligent, and clean living; and you're well fed and clothed, thank God. What else do you want? You've no money? That doesn't really matter. Happiness doesn't depend on money. Of course, I understand. . . . Your estate's mortgaged; you haven't any money to pay the interest. But I—I'm her father, I understand. . . . Mother can do as she likes, God be with her. If she won't give you any money, she doesn't have to. Shurka says she doesn't need a dowry. Principles, Schopenhauer. All that's nonsense. I've got my special ten thousand in the bank. *looks around* Not a soul knows about it in the house. It's granny's. That'll be for you both. You can take it; only promise me one thing—give Matvei a thousand or two.

Visitors begin to assemble in the ballroom

IVANOV
Pasha, this is all useless talk. I'm acting according to my conscience.

SASHA
And I'm acting according to mine. You can say what you like; I won't release you. I'll go and call mamma. *goes out*

ANTON
CHEKHOV

LEBEDEV
I don't understand anything.

Listen, my poor old fellow. I won't try to explain to
you what sort of a person I am—whether I'm honest or
base, healthy or mentally sick. You wouldn't grasp it.
I used to be young, eager, sincere, and intelligent. I used
to love, hate, and believe in my own way, differently
from other people. I used to work like ten men and
hope like ten men too. I fought windmills; I tried to
ram down walls with my head. Without realizing my
strength or weakness, without reasoning, without
knowing anything about life, I took up a burden which
promptly tore my muscles and broke my back. I went
all out to spend myself, I got drunk, I got excited, I
worked madly, I did everything without moderation.
Well, what else could I do? There are so few of us;
there's so much work to be done, so much! God, how
much! And now how cruelly life, the life which I
fought against, is avenging itself on me. I've worn
myself out. At thirty-five I feel like a man after a
drunken bout. I'm old already; I've put on an old man's
dressing gown. I go about with a heavy head, with a
lazy soul, tired and broken, without faith, without
love, without aim. I wander about among my friends
like a shadow, and I don't know who I am or why I
live or what I want. Already it seems to me that love is
silly, that caresses and endearments are sugary nonsense,
that there isn't any meaning in work, that song and
impassioned words are trivial and old-fashioned. And
wherever I go, I bring misery, blank boredom, discontent, disgust with life. I'm ruined, hopelessly ruined!
Before you stands a man tired at thirty-five, disen-
chanted, crushed by his trivial efforts—burning with
shame and jeering at his own weakness. . . . Oh, how
my pride revolts. I feel suffocated with anger! *swaying
slightly*   You see how I've worn myself out. I can't   IVANOV

stand straight. I've gone weak. Where's Matvei? Tell
him to take me home.

VOICES IN THE BALLROOM
The best man's arrived!

SHABELSKI
Coming in Here I am. In a shabby old tailcoat, not
even my own . . . and no gloves. And so, of course,
they all sneer and leer and start making stupid jokes.
Disgusting, small-minded creatures!

BORKIN
*Comes in quickly, carrying a bouquet; he wears a tailcoat
and the best man's boutonniere*
Ugh! Where is he?   *to Ivanov*   They've been waiting
all this time for you in church, and you're still here,
talking philosophy. What a comical person you are!
You really are a joke! Don't you know you're not
supposed to drive with the bride? You're supposed to go
separately, with me, and then I have to come from
the church to fetch the bride. Can't you even understand that? Honestly, you're a joke!

LVOV
Comes in; to Ivanov
Oh, you're here?   *loudly*   Nikolai Alekseevich
Ivanov, I want to tell you publicly that you're a cad!

IVANOV
Coldly Thank you very much.

General astonishment

BORKIN
To Lvov Sir, this is contemptible conduct! I challenge
you to a duel!

LVOV
Monsieur Borkin, I regard it as a humiliation to have
to speak to you, let alone fight you. As for Monsieur

Ivanov, he can have satisfaction from me whenever he
wishes.

SHABELSKI

Then, sir, I'll fight you!

SASHA

To Lvov What did you do it for? What did you insult
him for? My friends, please make him tell me what
he did it for!

LVOV

Aleksandra Pavlovna, I didn't insult him without
reason. I came here as an honest man in order to open
your eyes to the truth, and I beg you to hear me out.

SASHA

Well, what do you want to say? That you're an honest
man? All the world knows that! I'd rather you told
me whether you understand yourself or whether you
don't. You just came in here now and hurled a shocking
insult at him which nearly killed me. You did that as
an honest man. Before that you'd been pursuing him
like a shadow and interfering with his life, and, of
course, you did that too in the certainty that you were
fulfilling your duty, that you were an honest man.
You meddled with his private life. You slandered and
ran him down whenever you could. You bombarded
me and all my friends with anonymous letters. And
all the time you were doing it you thought of yourself
as an honest man. Yes, Doctor, you thought it was
honest not even to spare his sick wife, to keep on
worrying her with your suspicions. And whatever you
may do in the future—acts of violence or cruelty or
meanness—you'll still think yourself an extraordinarily
honest and high-minded person!

IVANOV

Laughing This isn't a wedding—it's a parliament!
Bravo, bravo!

SASHA

To Lvov   So just think that over: do you understand
yourself or don't you? Stupid, heartless creature!
takes Ivanov's hand   Let us go from here, Nikolai!
Father, come!

IVANOV

Go? Where to? Just wait a moment; I'll put an end
to all this! I can feel youth waking up in me—the old
Ivanov speaks again!   *takes out a revolver*

SASHA

Shrieks   I know what he's going to do! Nikolai, for
God's sake!

IVANOV

I've been going downhill long enough. Now I'm
going to stop! There's a limit to everything! Stand
away! Thank you, Sasha!

SASHA

Shrieks   Nikolai, for God's sake! Stop him!

IVANOV

Leave me alone!   *runs aside and shoots himself*

CURTAIN

THE
SEAGULL

A DRAMA IN FOUR ACTS

THE
CHARACTERS

ARKADINA, *Irina Nikolaevna* (Madame Trepleva by marriage), *an actress*

TREPLEV, *Konstantin Gavriilovich* (Kostya), *her son, a young man*

SORIN, *Pëtr Nikolaevich* (Petrusha), *her brother*

ZARECHNAYA, *Nina Mikhailovna, a young girl, the daughter of a wealthy landowner*

SHAMRAYEV, *Ilya Afanasievich, a retired army lieutenant and Sorin's steward*

POLINA, *Andreyevna, his wife*

MASHA (Marya Ilyinichna, Mashenka), *his daughter*

TRIGORIN, *Boris Alekseevich, a writer*

MEDVEDENKO, *Semën Semënovich, a schoolmaster*

DORN, *Yevgeni Sergeevich, a doctor*

YAKOV, *a workman*

A CHEF

A HOUSEMAID

The action takes place in Sorin's house and garden.
Between the Third and Fourth Acts there is
an interval of two years

ACT ONE

*The park on Sorin's estate. A wide avenue leads toward
a lake in the background. A rough stage erected for an
amateur theatrical performance has been built across
the avenue and conceals the view of the lake. There
are bushes close to the stage, right and left, and in the
foreground, a few chairs and a small table.*

*The sun has just gone down. Yakov and some other
men are working on the stage behind the curtain; they
can be heard hammering and coughing. Masha and
Medvedenko, returning from a walk, enter from the left.*

MEDVEDENKO
Why do you always wear black?

MASHA
I am in mourning for my life. I'm unhappy.

MEDVEDENKO
But why? *meditatively* I can't understand it. You're
in good health. Your father isn't rich, but he's com-
fortably well-off. My life is much harder than yours.
I only get twenty-three rubles a month, and from that
my pension is deducted. Yet I don't wear mourning.

MASHA
It isn't money that matters. Even a pauper can be happy.

MEDVEDENKO

Yes, in theory he can, but in practice it works out like
this: there's myself, my mother, two sisters, and a
small brother; and there's my salary, twenty-three
rubles in all. We all have to eat and drink, don't we?
And then what about tea and sugar? What about
tobacco? You've got to scrape and save.

MASHA

Glancing back at the stage
They'll be starting the show soon.

MEDVEDENKO

Yes. Zarechnaya is going to act, and the play is by
Konstantin Gavriilovich. They are in love with one
another, and today their souls will be merged in an
attempt to create a single work of art. But your soul
and mine have no points of contact. I love you. I can't
stay at home because of my longing for you, and I
walk six miles here and six miles back every day; but
I get nothing from you except indifference. Oh, it's
quite understandable. I haven't any money, we are a
large family. . . . Who would want to marry a man
who hasn't even got enough to eat?

MASHA

Nonsense. *takes snuff* I feel touched by your love,
but I can't return it, that's all. *holds out the snuff box*
Have some snuff.

MEDVEDENKO

I don't feel like it now. . . .

MASHA

It's close. There'll be a thunderstorm tonight, I think.
You're always philosophizing or else talking about
money. You believe there is no greater misfortune than
poverty, but in my opinion it's a thousand times better
to go around in rags and be a beggar than . . . However,
that's something you wouldn't understand.

ANTON
CHEKHOV

SORIN
Leaning on a walking stick
Somehow country life doesn't suit me, my boy. It's
obvious that I will never get accustomed to it. Last
night I went to bed at ten, and this morning I woke up
at nine, feeling as though my brain was sticking to
the inside of my skull from sleeping too long.   *laughs*
Then after dinner I fell asleep again by mistake, and
now I feel sort of exhausted, as if I'd had a nightmare.

TREPLEV
You're right; you ought to live in town.   *seeing*
Masha and Medvedenko   Say there, you two, we'll
be calling you as soon as we begin, but you shouldn't
be here now. Please go away.

SORIN
To Masha   Marya Ilyinichna, I wish you'd ask your
father to have the dog let off his chain. It keeps howling.
My sister was kept awake again all night.

MASHA
Why don't you speak to my father yourself? I won't.
Please excuse me.   *to Medvedenko*   Come, let's go.

MEDVEDENKO
You will send someone to tell us when you're going
to begin, won't you?

Masha and Medvedenko go out

SORIN
That means that the dog will be howling all night
again. The strange thing is that I've never really lived
in the country in the way I wanted to. I used to take a
month's leave and come down here to have a rest,   THE
and all that sort of thing. But as soon as I got here,   SEAGULL

people started to plague me with all sorts of rubbish, and within a day I'd feel like running away again. *laughs* I was always pleased to leave this place. But there you are, I'm retired now; I've got nowhere to go. I've got to live here now, whether I want to or not.

YAKOV

Appears from behind the curtain

We're going to have a swim, Konstantin Gavriilovich.

TREPLEV

Very well then, but you must be sure to be back in your places in ten minutes. *looking at his watch* We're going to start soon.

YAKOV

Yes, sir. *goes out*

TREPLEV

Looking over the stage

There's a theater for you! Just the curtain and the two wings and beyond it—open space. No scenery. You have an unimpeded view of the lake and the horizon. We'll raise the curtain at half past nine when the moon comes up.

SORIN

Splendid!

TREPLEV

But if Zarechnaya is late, the whole effect will be lost, of course. It's time she were here now. Her father and stepmother always keep watch on her, and it's as hard for her to break out of the house as it would be if it were a prison. *adjusting his uncle's tie* Your hair and beard are all in a tangle. Shouldn't you have them cut or trimmed or something?

SORIN

Combing his hair

That's the tragedy of my life. My appearance. . . .

ANTON
CHEKHOV

Even in my young days I looked as if I were a secret

drinker, and all that sort of thing. The women never
loved me. *sits down* Why is my sister in such a
bad mood today?

TREPLEV

Why? She's bored. *sits down beside him* Jealous too.
She's down on me anyway, and she's down on this
show and on my play because Zarechnaya, and not
she, is acting in it. She hasn't read my play, but she
hates it all the same.

SORIN

Laughing Well, really! What an idea!

TREPLEV

It makes her angry to think that it won't be she, but
Zarechnaya, who's going to make a success of it on
this tiny stage! *glancing at his watch* A psychologi-
cal oddity—that's my mother. Oh, there is no doubt
about her being very gifted and intelligent: she's
capable of weeping bitterly over a book, of reciting the
whole of Nekrasov by heart, of nursing the sick with
the patience of an angel. But just try and give a word
of praise to Duse! Oh-ho-ho! You mustn't praise
anybody but her, you mustn't write about anybody but
her, you must acclaim her and go into raptures over
her wonderful acting in *The Lady with the Camellias*
or *The Fumes of Life*. But we can't offer her such
intoxicating praise here in the country; so she feels
bored and in a bad mood. And we all seem like enemies;
we are all to blame. And then she's superstitious: she's
afraid of having three candles lit, she's afraid of the
number thirteen. And she's tightfisted too. She has
seventy thousand in the bank, in Odessa—that I know
for certain. But you try to borrow money from her,
and she'll just burst into tears.

SORIN

You've somehow got it into your head that your

mother doesn't like your play, and so you're upset, and so on. Calm yourself; your mother adores you.

TREPLEV

Pulling off the petals of a flower, one by one
She loves me . . . she loves me not . . . she loves me . . . loves me not . . . loves me . . . loves me not.   *laughing*
You see, my mother doesn't love me. And why should she indeed? She wants to live, to have love affairs, to wear light-colored blouses, and here I am, twenty-five years old already. I'm always reminding her that she isn't young any longer. When I'm not around she's thirty-two, but when I'm with her she's forty-three, and she hates me for it. Moreover, she knows that I have no use for the theater. She loves the theater; she imagines that she's serving humanity. Whereas in my opinion the theater of today is in a rut and full of prejudices and conventions. When I see the curtain rise on a room with three walls; when I watch these great and talented people, these high priests of a sacred art depicting the way people eat, drink, make love, walk around, and wear their clothes, in the artificial light of the stage; when I hear them trying to squeeze a moral out of the tritest words and emptiest scenes— some petty little moral that's easy to understand and suitable for use in the home; when I'm presented with a thousand variations of the same old thing, the same thing again and again—well, I just have to escape. I run away as Maupassant ran away from the Eiffel Tower, which so oppressed him with its vulgarity.

SORIN

We can't do without the theater.

TREPLEV

We need new art forms. New forms are wanted, and if
they aren't available, we might as well have nothing at all. I'm fond of my mother, very fond of her, but

she leads such a fatuous life, forever fussing around
with this novelist of hers, her name always being
bandied about in the papers. I find it all so fatiguing.
And sometimes I simply regret, like the ordinary selfish
mortal I am, that I have a famous actress for a mother.
And I find myself imagining that if she were an ordinary woman I would have been happier. Uncle, can
you imagine a sillier, a more hopeless situation? Often
she'd have a roomful of visitors, all famous people—
writers and actors; and there I'd be among them,
alone—a nonentity, tolerated only because I was her
son. Who am I? What am I? I left the university in my
third year, owing to "circumstances over which we
have no control," as the editors sometimes say. I have
no special gifts, not a kopeck of my own, and in my
passport I'm described as a member of the lower
middle class, born in Kiev. Well, my father was a
member of the petty bourgeoisie, as you know—
although he was a well-known actor too—and his
native town was Kiev. So when all these artists and
writers who were gathered together in my mother's
drawing room condescended to pay a little attention to
me, I used to feel that they were sizing me up as they
looked at me standing there in all my insignificance.
I read their thoughts, and I suffered with the humiliation of it all.

SORIN

By the way, you might tell me, what sort of a person
is this writer? He's hard to understand. Always so
silent.

TREPLEV

He's intelligent, unaffected, a bit on the melancholy
side, I think. Really a very decent fellow. He's still a
long way from forty, but he's famous already and he's
had his fill of the good things of life. As for his

THE
SEAGULL

writing . . . Well, how shall I put it? It's very clever and charming, but . . . if you've been reading Tolstoy or Zola, you don't feel like reading Trigorin afterward.

SORIN

I must admit I am fond of writers, my boy. You know, years ago there were just two things I wanted passionately. One was to get married and the other was to be a novelist. I haven't managed to pull it off either way. Yes, even to be a minor writer must be rather nice, when all is said and done.

TREPLEV

Listening I can hear footsteps. *throws his arms around his uncle* I can't live without her. The very sound of her footsteps is beautiful. I feel insanely happy. *quickly walking to meet Nina Zarechnaya, who comes in* You . . . enchanting being . . . My dream.

NINA

Agitated I'm not late. Surely I'm not late.

TREPLEV

Kissing her hands
No, no, no.

NINA

I've been worrying the whole day. I've been feeling so afraid! I was afraid father wouldn't let me come . . . but he's just gone out with my stepmother. The sky was red, the moon was coming up, and I kept hurrying the horse, urging it on and on. *laughs* I'm glad, all the same! *shakes Sorin warmly by the hand*

SORIN

Laughing Your dear little eyes look as if they'd been crying. He-he! That isn't as it should be, you know.

NINA

It's nothing. . . . Look how out of breath I am! I'll have to leave in half an hour. We must hurry. I can't, I

can't! Don't try to keep me, for heaven's sake! My
father doesn't know I've come.

TREPLEV

It's time to begin, as a matter of fact. We must go and
call everybody.

SORIN

I'll go and call them, and all that sort of thing. I'll go
at once. *walks left, singing "The Two Grenadiers,"
then glances back* I remember I once burst into song
like this and the assistant public prosecutor said to
me, "My, Your Excellency, that's a powerful voice
you've got." Then he thought a bit and added, "But a
revolting one too." *laughs and goes out*

NINA

My father and stepmother won't let me come here.
They say this place is bohemian. They're afraid of my
going on the stage. And I am drawn to this place, to
this lake, as if I were a sea gull.

TREPLEV

We are alone.

NINA

I believe there's someone there.

TREPLEV

There isn't anybody. *they kiss*

NINA

What sort of a tree is this?

TREPLEV

An elm.

NINA

Why is it so dark?

TREPLEV

It's late; everything's turning dark now. Don't go
early, I implore you.

NINA   THE
I can't stay.   SEAGULL

TREPLEV

And what if I followed you home, Nina? I would stay in the garden all night, watching your window.

NINA

You can't do that; the watchman would notice you. And Tresor isn't used to you yet. He'd bark.

TREPLEV

I love you.

NINA

Sh-sh!

TREPLEV

Hearing footsteps Who's there? Is it you, Yakov?

YAKOV

Behind the stage

Yes, sir.

TREPLEV

Take up your positions. It's time to begin. Is the moon coming up?

YAKOV

Yes, sir.

TREPLEV

Have you got the wood alcohol? Have you got the sulfur? There must be a smell of sulfur as soon as the red eyes are seen.   *to Nina*   You can go now; everything is ready for you there. Are you nervous?

NINA

Yes, very. Your mother—she's all right; I'm not afraid of her. But there's Trigorin. I'm so afraid and ashamed of acting in front of him . . . a famous writer. Is he young?

TREPLEV

Yes.

ANTON
CHEKHOV

NINA

What marvelous stories he's written!

TREPLEV

Coldly I don't know about that. I haven't read them.

NINA

It's difficult to act in your play. There are no real living characters in it.

TREPLEV

Living characters! We don't have to depict life as it is or as it ought to be, but as we see it in our dreams.

NINA

But there's hardly any action in your play; there are only speeches. And then I do think there ought to be love in a play. *both go behind the stage*

Polina Andreyevna and Dorn come in

POLINA

It's getting damp out here. Please do go back and put on your galoshes.

DORN

I feel hot.

POLINA

You don't take care of yourself. It's just sheer obstinacy. You're a doctor, and you know perfectly well that the damp air is bad for you, but you just want to cause me pain and anxiety. Yesterday you stayed outside on the terrace the whole evening on purpose.

DORN

Hums "Say not your youth was ruined . . ."

POLINA

You were so absorbed in your conversation with Irina Nikolaevna that you simply weren't aware of the cold. Now own up, you do find her attractive.

DORN

I'm fifty-five.

THE
SEAGULL

POLINA

That's nothing. A man's not old at that age. You've kept your good looks and you're still attractive to women.

DORN

Well, what am I to do about it?

POLINA

You're so anxious to prostrate yourselves before an actress. Every single one of you!

DORN

Hums "Again I stand before you . . ." It's in the nature of things for people to admire artists and treat them differently from . . . well, let us say, tradesmen. It's a sort of idealism.

POLINA

Women always used to be falling in love with you and throwing themselves at you. Was that idealism too?

DORN

Shrugging his shoulders

Well, what of it? There was a lot that was good in the feelings these women had for me. What they mostly loved in me was my skill as a doctor. Ten or fifteen years ago, you remember, I was the only good obstetrician in the whole district. Besides I've always been honorable.

POLINA

Seizing him by the hand

You dear man!

DORN

Sh-sh! They're coming.

Enter Arkadina on Sorin's arm, accompanied by Trigorin, Shamrayev, Medvedenko, and Masha

ANTON
CHEKHOV

SHAMRAYEV

I remember I saw her play marvelously at the Poltava

Fair in '73! A sheer delight! Marvelous acting! *to Arkadina* I wonder if you happen to know where Chadin—Pavel Semënych Chadin, the comedian—is at present? He was quite inimitable in the part of Raspliuyev, better than Sadovski himself. I'm willing to swear he was, my dear lady! But where is he now?

ARKADINA
You're always inquiring about some old fossil or other. How should I know? *sits down*

SHAMRAYEV
With a sigh
Pashka Chadin! We don't have men like him nowadays! The theater is in a decline, Irina Nikolaevna. We used to have massive oak trees; now we see nothing but stumps.

DORN
It's true enough, there aren't so many outstandingly gifted people nowadays. On the other hand, the average actor is much more competent.

SHAMRAYEV
I can't agree at all with you there. However, it's a matter of taste. *De gustibus aut bene, aut nihil.*

Treplev enters from behind the stage

ARKADINA
To her son
When is it going to start, my dear?

TREPLEV
In a minute. Please have patience.

ARKADINA
Reciting from Hamlet
    "Oh, Hamlet, speak no more!
        Thou turn'st mine eyes into my very soul;
        And there I see such black and grained spots
        As will not leave their tinct."

TREPLEV

From Hamlet

  "And let me wring thy heart, for so I shall,
  If it be made of penetrable stuff."

A horn is sounded behind the stage

Ladies and gentlemen, we are about to begin! Attention please! *pause* I'll start now. *taps with a stick and recites in a loud voice* O venerable shades of ancient days, you who float over this lake at night, lull us to sleep and bring us dreams of things as they will be two hundred thousand years from now.

SORIN

Two hundred thousand years from now there will be just nothing.

TREPLEV

Well then, let them show us that nothing!

ARKADINA

Yes, let them. We are asleep already.

The curtain rises, revealing the view of the lake, with the moon above the horizon and its reflection in the water. Nina Zarechnaya, in white, is sitting on a rock

NINA

The men, the lions, the eagles, the partridges, the antlered deer, the geese, the spiders, the silent fishes of the deep, starfishes, and creatures unseen to the eye— in short—all living things, all living things, having completed their mournful cycle, have been snuffed out. For thousands of years the earth has borne no living thing, and this poor moon now lights its lamp in vain. The cranes no longer wake in the meadows with a cry; no longer are May beetles heard humming in the groves of lime trees. It is cold, cold, cold. . . . It is deserted, deserted, deserted. . . . It is terrifying, terri-

ANTON
CHEKHOV

fying, terrifying. *pause*   All living bodies have

turned to dust and the Eternal Matter has transformed
them into stones, into water, into clouds, while their
souls have all been merged into one. This common soul
of the world is I—I. . . . The souls of Alexander the
Great, of Caesar, of Shakespeare, of Napoleon, and of
the basest leech are contained in me! In me the
consciousness of men is merged with the instincts of
the animals. I remember all, all, all, and live every
single life anew in my own being!

Will-o'-the-wisps appear

ARKADINA
In a low voice
This sounds like the Decadent school.

TREPLEV
Imploringly and reproachfully
Mamma!

NINA
I am lonely. Once in a hundred years I open my lips to
speak, and then my voice rings dismally through this
void unheard by anybody. . . . And you too, pale
spirits, hear me not. The stagnant marsh gives birth
to you before dawn, and you wander until day breaks—
without thought, without will, without a quiver of
life. The Devil, father of the Eternal Matter, fearing
lest life reappear in you, has created in you, as also in
the rocks and water, a perpetual flux of atoms, so
that you are constantly changing. The spirit alone
remains constant and unchangeable in the whole
universe. *pause*   Like a prisoner cast into a deep
and empty well, I know not where I am or what awaits
me here. All I know is that I am destined to struggle
with the Devil, and in cruel and stubborn battle to
conquer the principle of material force, after which

THE
SEAGULL

matter and spirit will merge in beautiful harmony and the Kingdom of Cosmic Will will come into being. But this will only happen after a long succession of millennia during which time the moon, bright Sirius, and this earth will all have been gradually turned to dust. Until then horror, horror . . .

Pause. Two red spots appear over the lake

And now my powerful enemy, the Devil, is approaching. I see his terrifying, blood-red eyes.

ARKADINA

There's a smell of sulfur. Is that right?

TREPLEV

Yes.

ARKADINA

Laughing Ah! It's quite a good effect!

TREPLEV

Mamma!

NINA

He is bored without Man. . . .

POLINA

To Dorn You've taken off your hat. Put it on before you catch cold.

ARKADINA

The doctor's taken his hat off to the Devil, the father of Eternal Matter.

TREPLEV

Flaring up, loudly

The play's over! Enough of it! Curtain!

ARKADINA

But why get angry about it?

TREPLEV

That's enough! Curtain! Let down the curtain!

ANTON CHEKHOV

stamping his foot Curtain!

The curtain drops

I apologize! I overlooked the fact that only a select few
are permitted to write plays and act on the stage. I've
encroached on the preserves of a monopoly! To me . . .
I mean, I . . . *tries to continue, then makes a resigned*
gesture and goes out to the left

ARKADINA
What is the matter with him?

SORIN
Irina, my dear, you shouldn't hurt a young man's
self-esteem like this!

ARKADINA
But what have I said to him?

SORIN
You've offended him.

ARKADINA
He told us himself that it was going to be a joke, and I
treated it as a joke.

SORIN
All the same . . .

ARKADINA
And now it turns out he's written a great work of art!
Just think of that! So it wasn't for a joke that he got
up this show and perfumed the air with sulfur, but in
order to teach us something. He wanted to show us how
we ought to write plays and what plays we should act
in. Really this is becoming tedious! These perpetual
jibes at my expense, these pinpricks—anyone would
get tired of them, surely you'll grant me that! He's a
conceited, difficult boy!

SORIN
He wanted to give you pleasure.

ARKADINA
Did he? Even so, he didn't choose an ordinary play but
had to make us listen to these decadent ravings. I'm   THE
even prepared to listen to mad ravings for the sake of   SEAGULL

a joke, but here we have pretensions to new creative forms, to a new era in art. To my way of thinking, there are no new forms in this stuff at all, just a display of bad temper.

TRIGORIN

Everyone writes what he wants to and as he is able to.

ARKADINA

Let him write what he wants to and as he is able to, if only he leaves me out of it.

DORN

Jupiter! You are angry then.

ARKADINA

I'm not Jupiter; I'm a woman. *lights a cigarette* And I'm not angry. I'm merely irritated that a young man should spend his time in such a tiresome way. I had no wish to offend him.

MEDVEDENKO

There's no ground for making a distinction between spirit and matter, because spirit might consist of a combination of material atoms. *with animation to Trigorin* But you know, someone ought to write a play describing how our sort of people live—I mean we teachers—and get it produced somewhere. It's a hard life, a very hard life!

ARKADINA

That's not a bad idea. But let's not talk about plays now or atoms either. It's such a nice evening. Can you hear? There's someone singing.

All listen

How nice it is!

POLINA

It's on the other side of the lake. . . .

ARKADINA

After a pause, to Trigorin

Sit down here beside me. Ten or fifteen years ago you
could always hear music and singing on this lake—
almost every night. There are six country houses
around the lake. I remember such laughter and noise
and shooting—and love affairs, love affairs all the
time. . . . And the *jeune premier* and idol of all those
houses was—allow me to introduce him— *nods*
toward Dorn Doctor Yevgeni Sergeevich. He's
fascinating still, but in those days he was irresistible. . . .
Oh dear! My conscience is beginning to torment me.
Why did I hurt my poor boy's feelings? I'm so worried.
loudly Kostya! Kostya, dear!

MASHA
I'll go and look for him.

ARKADINA
Please do, my dear!

MASHA
Walks to the left
Yoo-hoo! Konstantin Gavriilovich! Yoo-hoo! *goes*
off

NINA
Coming out from behind the stage
Apparently we aren't going to continue, so I may as
well come out. Good evening! *kisses Arkadina and*
Polina

SORIN
Bravo! Bravo!

ARKADINA
Bravo! Bravo! We did admire you. You know, with
your looks and your lovely voice, you really shouldn't
stay in the country! It's a sin. I'm sure you have a gift
for acting. Listen to me! You must go on the stage!

NINA
Oh, it's my one dream! *sighs* But it'll never come
true.

ARKADINA

Who knows? Here now, let me introduce you—
Mr. Trigorin, Boris Alekseevich Trigorin.

NINA

Oh, I'm so glad. *overcome with embarrassment* I
always read everything you . . .

ARKADINA

Making her sit down beside them
Don't be shy, my dear. He's a famous man, but he
has a simple soul. You see, he's shy himself.

DORN

I think the curtain might be raised now. This place
gives me a sort of eerie feeling.

SHAMRAYEV

Loudly Yakov, pull the curtain up, will you!

The curtain goes up

NINA

To Trigorin It was a strange play, wasn't it?

TRIGORIN

I didn't understand it at all. But I watched it with
pleasure all the same. You acted with such sincerity.
And the scenery was beautiful. *pause* There must
be a lot of fish in this lake.

NINA

Yes.

TRIGORIN

I'm very fond of fishing. As far as I'm concerned,
there's no greater pleasure than to sit on the bank of a
river in the late afternoon and watch the float.

NINA

I would have thought that for anyone who'd experienced the joy of doing creative work no other pleasure
could exist.

ANTON
CHEKHOV

ARKADINA

Laughing You mustn't talk like that. When anyone talks high-flown language to him, he hasn't the least idea what to say.

SHAMRAYEV

I remember hearing the great Silva sing lower C one night at the Moscow Opera. As it happened, a bass from our parish church choir was sitting in the gallery. Suddenly—imagine our utter amazement—we heard, "Bravo, Silva!" from the gallery . . . but a whole octave lower. Like this. *in a deep bass* Bravo, Silva! And after that—dead silence. You could hear a pin drop. . . .

DORN

After a pause
The angel of silence has flown over us!

NINA

It's time for me to be going. Good-bye.

ARKADINA

Where are you off to? Why so early? We won't let you go.

NINA

My father is expecting me.

ARKADINA

What a man, really! *they embrace* Well, if it can't be helped . . . We're sorry, very sorry to let you go.

NINA

I wish you knew how hard it is for me to go.

ARKADINA

Someone ought to see you home, my little one.

NINA

Frightened Oh no, no!

SORIN

To Nina, imploringly
Do stay!

THE
SEAGULL

NINA

I can't, Pëtr Nikolaevich.

SORIN

Stay just for an hour, that's all. Why must you, really?

NINA

After a moment's thought, tearfully
It's impossible. *shakes hands with him and goes off
quickly*

ARKADINA

She's an unfortunate girl, really. They say her mother
left all her enormous fortune to her husband, every
kopeck of it; and now this girl has nothing, since her
father has already made a will in favor of his second
wife. It's really scandalous.

DORN

Yes, her charming father is a regular swine, to give
him his due.

SORIN

Rubbing his hands to warm them
Let us go too, friends. The air is getting damp. My
legs are hurting.

ARKADINA

Your legs! They might as well be made of wood; you
can hardly walk on them. Come along, you poor old
man! *takes his arm*

SHAMRAYEV

Offering his arm to his wife
Madame?

SORIN

I can hear that dog howling again. *to Shamrayev* Ilya
Afanasievich, I wish you'd be good enough to tell
them to let it off the chain.

SHAMRAYEV

It isn't possible, Pëtr Nikolaevich. I'm afraid of
thieves breaking into the barn. I've got millet there.

ANTON
CHEKHOV

to Medvedenko, who is walking beside him Yes,
lower by a whole octave, "Bravo, Silva!" And he
wasn't a professional singer either—just a fellow in
the church choir.

MEDVEDENKO
And what sort of pay does a fellow in the choir get?

All go out except Dorn

DORN
Alone I don't know, maybe I don't understand anything, maybe I've gone off my head, but I did like that
play. There is something in it. When that child was
holding forth about loneliness, and later when the
Devil's red eyes appeared, I was so moved that my
hands were shaking. It was fresh, unaffected. . . . Ah! I
think he's coming along now. I feel like telling him
a lot of nice things about it.

TREPLEV
Enters They've all gone already!

DORN
I'm here.

TREPLEV
Mashenka has been looking for me all over the park.
Insufferable creature!

DORN
Konstantin Gavriilovich, I liked your play exceedingly.
It's a bit strange and, of course, I didn't hear the end,
and yet it made a deep impression on me. You've got
talent and you must carry on.

*Treplev shakes his hand warmly and embraces him
impulsively*

Tut-tut! How strung up you are! Tears in your eyes!
What I mean to say is this. You took your subject from
the realm of abstract ideas. That was as it should be,

because a work of art must without fail convey some great idea. Only things conceived in high seriousness can be beautiful. How pale you are!

TREPLEV

So you're telling me to carry on?

DORN

Yes. But you must depict only what is significant and permanent. You know, I've lived a varied life; I've chosen my pleasures with discrimination. I'm satisfied. But if it had ever been my lot to experience the exaltation an artist feels at the moment of creative achievement, I believe I would have come to despise this material body of mine and all that goes with it, and my soul would have taken wings and soared into the heights.

TREPLEV

Forgive me, where's Zarechnaya?

DORN

There's one more thing. A work of art must express a clear, definite idea. You must know what you are aiming at when you write; for if you follow the enchanted path of literature without a definite goal in mind, you'll lose your way and your talent will ruin you.

TREPLEV

Impatiently Where is Zarechnaya?

DORN

She's gone home.

TREPLEV

In despair What shall I do? I want to see her. . . . I've got to see her. . . . I'm going.

Enter Masha

DORN

To Treplev Do be a little calmer, my friend.

But I'm going all the same. I must go.

MASHA

Please, Konstantin Gavriilovich, come indoors. Your
mamma is waiting for you. She's worried.

TREPLEV

Tell her I've gone away. And I beg you—all of you—
leave me alone! Leave me alone! Don't follow me
around.

DORN

But . . . but, my dear boy . . . You shouldn't. That's
not right.

TREPLEV

Tearfully Good-bye, Doctor. Thank you. *goes out*

DORN

With a sigh
Youth will have its own way! Youth!

MASHA

When people can't think of anything else to say, they
say, "Youth! Youth!" *takes snuff*

DORN

*Takes the snuff box from her and flings it into the
bushes*
Disgusting! *pause* I think I can hear music in the
house. We ought to go in.

MASHA

Wait a moment.

DORN

What is it?

MASHA

There's something I want to tell you again. I feel like
talking. *agitated* I'm not really fond of my father,
but I've a soft spot in my heart for you. For some
reason I feel a sort of deep affinity with you. . . . You
must help me. Help me or I'll do something stupid,

THE
SEAGULL

something that'll make a mockery of my life and mess it up. I can't go on like this.

DORN

But what is it? How am I to help you?

MASHA

I'm so unhappy. Nobody, nobody knows how unhappy I am! *leaning her head against his breast, softly* I love Konstantin.

DORN

How distraught they all are! How distraught! And what a quantity of love around! It's the magic lake! *tenderly* But what can I do, my child? Tell me, what can I do? What?

CURTAIN

ACT TWO

A croquet lawn and flower beds. In the background on the right, a house with a large terrace. On the left, a view of the lake with bright sunlight reflected in the water. It is midday and hot. On one side of the croquet lawn Arkadina, Dorn, and Masha are sitting on a garden seat in the shade of an old lime tree. Dorn has an open book on his lap

ARKADINA

To Masha Come, let us get up.   *both get up*   Stand by my side. You are twenty-two, and I'm nearly twice that. Yevgeni Sergeevich, which of us looks the younger?

DORN

You, of course.

ARKADINA

There you are! And why is it? Because I work, I care about things, I'm always on the go, while you stay in the same place all the time. You don't really live. And I have a rule: never to wonder about the future! I never think of old age or of death. What is to be, will be.

MASHA

And I feel as though I'd been born long, long ago, and
I'm trailing my life behind me like a dress with an
endless train. And often I don't feel like going on with
life at all. Of course, that's all nonsense. One ought
to shake oneself and throw it all off.

DORN

Hums quietly "Tell her, my flowers . . ."

ARKADINA

And one more thing—I am as particular about myself
as an Englishman. Yes, my dear, I keep myself in hand,
as they say. I'm always properly dressed and have my
hair done just *comme il faut*. Do you think I'd permit
myself to come out of the house, even into the garden,
like this, in a dressing gown or with my hair untidy?
Never. That's why it is I've kept so young looking—
because I've never been sloppy or let myself go, as
some women do. *walks up and down the lawn, her
hands on her hips* There! You see? I'm as brisk as a
bird. Fit to take the part of a fifteen-year-old girl!

DORN

Well, I may as well go on. *picks up the book* We'd
just come to the corn merchant and the rats.

ARKADINA

Yes, the rats. Go on reading. *sits down* No, give it
to me; I'll read. It's my turn. *takes the book and looks
for the place* The rats . . . Here it is. *reads* "And
it goes without saying that it is as dangerous for society
people to pamper and encourage writers of novels, as
it is for corn merchants to breed rats in their granaries.
And yet novelists are very much sought after. Thus,
when a woman has chosen a writer whom she wishes
to capture, she lays siege to him with the aid of
compliments, flattery, and favors." Well, that may
be true of the French, but there's nothing like that

ANTON
CHEKHOV

with us. We don't plan ahead. Over here, a woman is
usually head over heels in love with a writer long
before she decides to capture him, don't you see? To
go no further afield, take Trigorin and myself . . .

*Sorin enters leaning on his stick with Nina walking
beside him. They are followed by Medvedenko, who
pushes an empty wheel chair*

SORIN
Fondly, as to a child
Indeed? So we're quite delighted, are we? We're feeling
cheerful today after all?   *to his sister*   We're delighted!
Our father and stepmother have gone off to Tver,
and we are free now for three whole days.

NINA
Sits down beside Arkadina and embraces her
I'm so happy! Now I belong to you.

SORIN
Sits down in his wheel chair
She's looking very pretty today.

ARKADINA
Prettily dressed and interesting looking. That's a good
girl.   *kisses her*   But we mustn't praise her too much
or it may bring bad luck. Where's Boris Alekseevich?

NINA
He's down by the bathing shed—fishing.

ARKADINA
Surprising he doesn't get bored with it! *prepares to go
on reading*

NINA
What is that?

ARKADINA
Maupassant's *Sur l'eau*, my dear.   *reads a few lines
to herself*   Oh, well, the next bit isn't interesting or

true either.   *closes the book*   I'm worried. Tell me, what is the matter with my son? Why is he so sullen and depressed? He spends day after day on the lake and I hardly ever see him.

MASHA

His heart is troubled.   *to Nina, timidly*   Please, will you read us something from his play?

NINA

Shrugging her shoulders

Would you like me to? It's so uninteresting!

MASHA

Restraining her enthusiasm

When he reads himself, his eyes blaze and his face turns pale. He has a beautiful, sad voice and the bearing of a poet.

Sorin is heard snoring

DORN

Good night!

ARKADINA

Petrusha!

SORIN

Eh?

ARKADINA

Are you asleep?

SORIN

Not in the least. . . .

ARKADINA

After a pause

You're not taking any medical treatment, my friend. It's not wise, you know.

SORIN

I'd be glad to have some treatment, but the doctor here doesn't want me to.

DORN

Treatment! At sixty!

SORIN

Even at sixty one wants to go on living.

DORN

Tartly Oh, all right then, take some valerian drops.

ARKADINA

I believe it would do him good to go and stay at a spa.

DORN

Well, he might go. Or he might not.

ARKADINA

What is one to make of that?

DORN

There's nothing to make of it. It's perfectly clear. . . .

MEDVEDENKO

After a pause

Pëtr Nikolaevich ought to give up smoking.

SORIN

Nonsense.

DORN

No, it isn't nonsense. Wine and tobacco deprive you
of your individuality. After a cigar or a glass of vodka
you're no longer just Pëtr Nikolaevich, but Pëtr
Nikolaevich plus somebody else. Your "I" becomes
blurred, and you begin to think of yourself as if you
were someone quite different—as "he."

SORIN

Laughing It's all very well for you to talk. You've
had a good life, but what about me? I've served in the
Department of Justice for twenty-eight years, but I
haven't really lived. I haven't really experienced
anything yet, so obviously I feel very much like going
on living. You're satisfied and you don't care anymore,
so you're inclined to be philosophical. But I want to

THE
SEAGULL

live. That's why I drink sherry at dinner and smoke cigars, and all that. And there it is.

DORN

Life has to be taken seriously, but when it comes to taking cures at sixty and regretting that you didn't get enough enjoyment out of life when you were young—all that, forgive me, is just futile.

MASHA

Getting up It must be about lunch time. *walking languidly and with an effort* My leg's gone to sleep. *goes out*

DORN

She'll go and have a couple of drinks before lunch.

SORIN

She's not happy in her personal affairs, poor girl.

DORN

Rubbish, Your Excellency!

SORIN

You talk like a man who's had his fill of experience.

ARKADINA

Oh, what could be more boring than this cloying country boredom! So hot, so still, nobody doing anything, everybody talking like a philosopher. It's nice to be here with you, my friends. It's pleasant to listen to you, but . . . how much better to be sitting alone in a hotel room learning a part!

NINA

Enthusiastically How true! I do understand you!

SORIN

It's better in town, of course. You sit in your study, your footman doesn't let anyone in unannounced, you have a telephone. There are cabs in the streets, and all that sort of thing.

ANTON
CHEKHOV

DORN

Hums "Tell her, my flowers . . ."

SHAMRAYEV

Here they are! Good morning to you!   *kisses
Arkadina's hand, then Nina's*   So glad to see you
looking so well.   *to Arkadina*   My wife tells me that
you're thinking of going to town with her today. Is
that right?

ARKADINA

Yes, we are thinking of going.

SHAMRAYEV

Hm! That's splendid. But, my dear lady, how do you
propose to travel? We're carting the rye today, and
all the men are busy. What horses are you going to
have, may I ask?

ARKADINA

What horses? How am I to know what horses?

SORIN

But we have carriage horses.

SHAMRAYEV

Agitated   Carriage horses? Where am I to get collars
for carriage horses? Where am I to get collars? It
amazes me! It is really beyond my understanding! My
dear lady! Forgive me, I have the greatest admiration
for your talent; I'm prepared to give ten years of my
life for you—but I can't let you have the horses.

ARKADINA

But if I *have* to go? How very odd!

SHAMRAYEV

My dear lady! You don't realize what farming means.

ARKADINA

Flaring up   The old, old story! All right, then, I'm
leaving for Moscow this very day. Please have the
horses hired for me in the village, or I'll walk to the
station.

THE
SEAGULL

SHAMRAYEV

Flaring up   In that case, I'm giving up my post. You can look for another steward.   *goes out*

ARKADINA

Every summer it's like this. Every summer they insult me here. I won't set my foot in this place again!   *goes out to the left, in the direction of the bathing shed, which is offstage. A moment later she is seen entering the house, followed by Trigorin, who is carrying fishing rods and a pail*

SORIN

Flaring up   . This is pure insolence! It's the limit! I'm sick and tired of it, once and for all! Bring all the horses here this minute!

NINA

To Polina Andreyevna

To refuse Irina Nikolaevna, the famous actress! Surely, any wish of hers, even a mere whim, is more important than your farming? It's simply incredible.

POLINA

In despair   But what can I do? Put yourself in my position. What can I do?

SORIN

To Nina   Let us go along to my sister. We'll all try to persuade her not to go away, eh?   *looking in the direction in which Shamrayev has gone*   Insufferable fellow! Tyrant!

NINA

Preventing him from rising

Sit still, sit still. We'll take you along.   *she and Medvedenko push the wheel chair*   Oh, how dreadful all this is!

SORIN

ANTON
CHEKHOV   Yes, yes, it is dreadful. But he won't leave. I'll speak to him presently.   *they go out*

DORN

People *are* tiresome. Speaking candidly, your husband ought to be simply chucked out of here. But the end of it all will be that this old woman, Pëtr Nikolaevich, and his sister will go and apologize to him. You'll see.

POLINA

He's even sent the carriage horses to work in the fields. And misunderstandings like this happen every day. If you only knew how it upsets me! It makes me ill; you see I'm shaking. . . . I can't bear his rude manners. *entreating him* Yevgeni, my dear, dear man, won't you take me to live with you? Our time's passing; we're no longer young . . . and I wish we could stop concealing things and lying, now that we're so near the end of our lives.

DORN

I'm fifty-five; it's too late for me to change my way of life.

POLINA

I know you refuse me because there are other women you're intimate with. You can't take them all to live with you. I understand. Forgive me. You're tired of me.

Nina appears near the house. She is picking flowers

DORN

No, not really.

POLINA

I'm so tormented by jealousy. Of course, you're a doctor; you can't avoid women. I understand.

DORN

To Nina, who comes up
Well, how are things now?

THE
SEAGULL

NINA

Irina Nikolaevna's crying and Pëtr Nikolaevich has gotten an attack of asthma.

DORN

Getting up   I'd better go and give them some valerian drops.

NINA

Giving him the flowers
For you!

DORN

Merci bien!   *goes toward the house*

POLINA

Going with him
What pretty flowers!   *near the house, in a low voice*
Give me those flowers!

Dorn gives them to her and she tears them to pieces and throws them aside. Both go into the house

NINA

Alone   How strange it is to see a famous actress crying . . . and for such a trifling reason! And isn't it strange too? Here we have a famous author, a favorite with the public—they write about him in all the papers, they sell pictures of him everywhere, his works are translated into foreign languages—and he spends the whole day fishing and is quite delighted if he catches a couple of gudgeon. I used to think that famous people were proud and inaccessible and that they despised the crowd. I thought that the glory and luster of their names enabled them, as it were, to revenge themselves on people who put high birth and wealth above every-thing else. But here they are, crying, fishing, playing cards, laughing, and getting angry like anyone else.

ANTON
CHEKHOV

TREPLEV

Enters, hatless, carrying a gun and a dead sea gull
Are you alone here?

NINA
Yes, alone.

Treplev lays the sea gull at her feet

What does this mean?

TREPLEV
I was despicable enough to kill this sea gull today. I'm
laying it at your feet.

NINA
What is the matter with you?   *picks up the sea gull
and looks at it*

TREPLEV
After a pause
Soon I will kill myself in the same way.

NINA
This is not like you at all!

TREPLEV
True—but it's only since you've not been like yourself.
You've changed toward me, you look at me coldly,
my presence seems to embarrass you.

NINA
You've grown so irritable lately, and most of the time
you've been talking unintelligibly, in a sort of symbolic
way. And now this sea gull here is apparently another
symbol, but—you must forgive me—I don't understand it.   *puts the sea gull on the seat*   I'm too
simpleminded to understand you.

TREPLEV
It started that evening when my play was such a stupid
fiasco. Women don't forgive failure. I burned it all,

down to the last scrap. If you only knew how unhappy I am! Your growing coldness toward me is frightening; it's incredible! It is as if I woke up one day and saw this lake suddenly drying up or draining away into the ground. You said just now that you're too simple-minded to understand me. Oh, tell me—what is there to understand? My play wasn't liked, you despise my kind of inspiration, and now you think I'm commonplace and insignificant, just like all the rest. *stamping his foot* How well I understand it! I do indeed! It feels as though a nail has been knocked into my brain. Damn it—and my pride too, which is sucking my life blood, sucking it like a snake. *seeing Trigorin, who comes in reading a book* But here comes the real genius, stepping out like Hamlet himself, and with a book too. *mimics* "Words, words, words." The sun hasn't come near you yet, but you're smiling already and your eyes are melting in its rays. I won't inconvenience you further. *goes out quickly*

TRIGORIN
Making notes in his book
Takes snuff and drinks vodka. Always dresses in black. A schoolmaster in love with her . . .

NINA
Good morning, Boris Alekseevich!

TRIGORIN
Good morning. It turns out that we may have to leave here today, rather unexpectedly. It doesn't seem very likely that we will meet again. Girls don't often come my way, I mean girls who are young and interesting to meet. I've forgotten what it feels like to be eighteen or nineteen; indeed I can't imagine it at all clearly. That's why the girls in my novels and stories are usually so artificial. I wish I could exchange places with you, even if only for an hour, just to find out what your

thoughts are, and what kind of a pretty little thing
you are in a general sort of way.

NINA

And I would like to be in your place for a while.

TRIGORIN

Whatever for?

NINA

So that I could know what it feels like to be a famous,
gifted writer. How does one experience fame? What
sort of feeling does it give you to be famous?

TRIGORIN

What sort of feeling? Perhaps none. I've never thought
about it.   *after a moment's thought*   It's one thing
or the other: either you exaggerate the extent of my
fame, or I'm quite insensitive to it.

NINA

But what if you read about yourself in the papers?

TRIGORIN

When they praise me I am pleased, and when they
attack me I feel in a bad mood for a couple of days.

NINA

What a wonderful world you live in! How I envy
you—if only you knew! How different people's
destinies are! Some just drag out their obscure, tedious
existences, all very much like one another, and all
unhappy. And there are others—like you for instance,
one in a million—who are given an interesting life, a
life that is radiant and full of significance. You are
fortunate!

TRIGORIN

I?   *shrugs his shoulders*   Hm! You talk about fame
and happiness, and this radiant and interesting life,
but to me all these fine words of yours—you must
forgive me—are just like so many delicious sweets
which I never eat. You are very young and very kind.

NINA

Your life is beautiful.

TRIGORIN

But what is there beautiful about it? *looking at his watch* I must go and do some writing presently. Forgive me, I haven't much time to spare. *laughs* You've stepped on my favorite corn, as the saying goes, and here I am getting excited and a little bit angry too. All the same, let's talk. Let's talk about my radiant and beautiful life. Well, where shall we begin? *after a moment's thought* You know what it is to have a *fixed idea*, for instance when a man keeps on thinking about the same thing day and night, about . . . let us say, the moon. Well, I too have a kind of moon of my own. I'm obsessed day and night by one thought : I must write, I must write, I just must. For some reason, as soon as I've finished one novel, I feel I must start writing another, then another, then another. I write in a rush, without stopping, and can't do anything else. What is there radiant or beautiful in that, I ask you? Oh, it's a fatuous life! Here I am with you, I'm quite worked up, and yet not for a single moment do I forget that there's an unfinished novel waiting for me. I look over there and I see a cloud shaped like a grand piano. At once I think I must put it into some story or other—the fact that a cloud looking like a grand piano has floated by. There's the scent of heliotrope in the air. I make a mental note : "sickly scent . . . flower—the color of a widow's dress . . . mention when describing a summer evening." I snatch at every word and sentence I utter, and every word you utter too and hurriedly lock them up in my literary pantry—in case they might come in useful ! When I finish a piece of work, I dash off to the theater or go off on a fishing trip, and that's the time when I ought to relax and

ANTON
CHEKHOV

forget myself—but no! Something that feels like a heavy cast-iron ball begins to revolve in my brain— a new subject for a novel! So immediately I drag myself back to my desk again, and I have to push on with my writing once more, to keep on writing and writing. . . . And it's like that always, always . . . and I can't get any rest away from myself. I feel as though I'm devouring my own life, that for the sake of the honey I give to all and sundry I'm despoiling my best flowers of their pollen, that I'm plucking the flowers themselves and trampling on their roots. Am I out of my mind? Do you think my relatives and friends treat me like a sane person? "What are you jotting down now? What surprises have you in store for us?" It's the same thing over and over again, until I begin to imagine that this attentiveness on the part of my friends, all this praise and admiration, is just a sham, that they are trying to deceive me just as if I were insane. Sometimes I feel afraid of them stealing up on me from behind, seizing me and carrying me off, like Poprishchin,[1] to a lunatic asylum. As for the years when I was starting—my younger, better years—in those days my writing used to be one continuous torment. A minor writer, especially if he hasn't had much luck, sees himself as clumsy, awkward, and unwanted. He gets nervous and overwrought and feels irresistibly drawn toward people connected with literature or art; but then he just wanders among them unrecognized and unnoticed, unable to look them straight and courageously in the eye, like a passionate gambler who hasn't any money. I could not see my readers, but for some reason I always imagined them as unfriendly and skeptical. I was afraid of the public—it terrified

1. The principal character in the story *The Diary of a Madman*, by N. V. Gogol.

me—and whenever a new play of mine was produced, I always felt that the dark-haired people in the audience were hostile to it, and the fair-haired ones coldly indifferent. Oh, how dreadful it all was! What a torment!

NINA

But even so, don't you have moments of happiness and exaltation—moments when you feel inspired, when your creative work is actually in progress?

TRIGORIN

Yes, while I'm writing I enjoy it. I enjoy reading proofs too, but . . . as soon as the thing comes out in print I can no longer bear it. I immediately see that it's not what I intended, that it's a mistake, that it shouldn't have been written at all; and I feel angry and depressed. *laughing* And then the public reads it and says, "Yes, it's charming. So cleverly done. Charming, but a far cry from Tolstoy." Or "A very fine piece of work, but Turgenev's *Fathers and Children* is a better book." And so it will go on till my dying day—everything will be charming and clever—and nothing more. And when I die, my friends as they pass by my grave will say, "Here lies Trigorin. He was a good writer, but not as good as Turgenev."

NINA

You must forgive me, but I refuse to try to understand you. You've simply been spoiled by success.

TRIGORIN

What success? I've never liked myself. I dislike myself as a writer. But the worst of it is that I live in a sort of haze, and I often don't understand what I'm writing. I love this water here, the trees, the sky. I have a feeling for nature; it arouses a sort of passion in me, an irresistible desire to write. But you see, I'm not a mere landscape painter; I'm also a citizen of my country. I

ANTON
CHEKHOV

love it; I love its people. As an author, I feel I'm in
duty bound to write about the people, their sufferings,
their future—and about science, the rights of man, and
so on, and so forth. And I write about everything in a
great hurry while I'm being prodded and urged on from
all sides and people keep getting angry with me; so that
I dash around from one side to the other like a fox
badgered by the hounds. I see science and society
forging ahead, while I drop further and further behind,
like a peasant who's just missed his train. And in the
end I feel that all I can do is to paint landscapes, and
that everything else I write is a sham—false to the
very core.

NINA

You've been working too hard. You haven't the time
or the inclination to recognize your own importance.
You may be dissatisfied with yourself, but to others
you are a great and wonderful person! If I were a writer
like you, I would give my whole life to the ordinary
people, realizing at the same time that their happiness
lay in striving to rise to my level—and then they'd
have harnessed themselves to my chariot.

TRIGORIN

Chariot, indeed! Am I an Agamemnon or what? *both
smile*

NINA

For the sake of being happy like that—of being a writer
or an actress—I would put up with unfriendliness from
my family, with poverty and disappointment, with
living in a garret and having nothing to eat but rye
bread. I would gladly suffer dissatisfaction with myself
in the knowledge of my own imperfections, but in
return I would demand fame . . . real, resounding
fame. *covering her face with her hands* My head's
going around! Ugh!

ARKADINA'S VOICE

From the house

Boris Alekseevich!

TRIGORIN

They're calling me. To pack, I suppose. But I don't feel like leaving. *looks around at the lake* What a heavenly sight! How lovely it is!

NINA

Do you see a house with a garden on the other side?

TRIGORIN

Yes.

NINA

It belonged to my mother when she was alive. I was born there. I've spent all my life beside this lake and I know every tiny island on it.

TRIGORIN

It's a beautiful place! *noticing the sea gull* But what is this?

NINA

A sea gull. Konstantin Gavriilovich killed it.

TRIGORIN

What a beautiful bird! Really I don't feel like going away. Why don't you persuade Irina Nikolaevna to stay? *writes in his notebook*

NINA

What are you writing?

TRIGORIN

Just making a few notes. An idea suddenly came into my head. A subject for a short story: a young girl, like you, has lived beside a lake from childhood. She loves the lake as a sea gull does, and she's happy and free as a sea gull. But a man chances to come along, sees her, and, having nothing better to do, destroys her, just like this sea gull here.

ANTON
CHEKHOV

ARKADINA
Boris Alekseevich, where are you?

TRIGORIN
I'm coming! *goes, then looks back at Nina. To
Arkadina at the window* What is it?

ARKADINA
We're staying.

Trigorin goes into the house

NINA
*Advances to the footlights; after a few moments'
meditation*
It's a dream!

CURTAIN

ACT THREE

The dining room in Sorin's house. Doors right and left.
A sideboard and a medicine cupboard. In the middle
of the room a table. A trunk and some cardboard hat
boxes indicate preparations for departure. Trigorin is
having his breakfast while Masha stands beside the
table

MASHA

I'm telling you all this because you're a writer. You
can make use of it if you like. I tell you honestly—if he
had wounded himself badly, I wouldn't have lived
another minute. But I've got courage all the same. I
just decided I'd tear this love of mine out of my heart,
tear it out by the roots.

TRIGORIN

But how?

MASHA

I'm getting married. To Medvedenko.

TRIGORIN

You mean the schoolmaster?

MASHA

Yes.

ANTON
CHEKHOV

TRIGORIN

I don't see the point of it.

MASHA

What is the point of love without hope, of waiting whole years for something. . . . One doesn't know what. But when I'm married there'll be no time for love; new cares will drive out all the old ones. And anyway it'll be a change, you know. Shall we have another?

TRIGORIN

Do you think we ought to?

MASHA

Oh, come! *fills two glasses* Don't look at me like that. Women drink more often than you imagine. A few drink openly as I do, but most drink in secret. Yes. And it's always vodka or cognac. *clinks glasses with him* Here's good luck! You're a genuine, sincere man. I'm sorry to be parting from you. *they drink*

TRIGORIN

I don't feel like going away myself.

MASHA

Why don't you ask her to stay?

TRIGORIN

No, she won't stay now. Her son is behaving very tactlessly. First he shoots himself, and now they say he's going to challenge me to a duel. Whatever for? He sulks and snorts and preaches new forms of art. But there's room enough for all, for new and old alike. Why does he have to push and shove?

MASHA

There's jealousy too. However, it's not my affair.

A pause. Yakov passes from left to right carrying a suitcase. Nina comes in and stands by the window

My schoolmaster is not particularly clever, but he's kindhearted and poor, and he's very fond of me. I'm sorry for him. I'm sorry for his old mother too. Well,

THE
SEAGULL

let me wish you all the best. Don't think badly of me.
shakes his hand warmly I'm very grateful to you for
your friendly interest. Do send me your books and
be sure to autograph them. Only don't write, "To the
highly respected" and all that; but just put "To
Marya, who doesn't know where she belongs and has
no object in life." Good-bye! *goes out*

NINA

*Holding out her hand toward Trigorin, with her fist
clenched*
Odd or even?

TRIGORIN

Even.

NINA

With a sigh
That means "no." I've only got one pea in my hand.
I was trying to tell my fortune—whether to go on the
stage or not. If only someone would give me advice!

TRIGORIN

One can't give advice about that. . . .

NINA

After a pause
We are going to part now and . . . perhaps we will not
meet again. Will you take this little medallion to
remember me by? I had your initials engraved on it . . .
and on the other side, the title of a book of yours—
Days and Nights.

TRIGORIN

How exquisite! *kisses the medallion* A charming
gift!

NINA

Think of me sometimes.

TRIGORIN

I will indeed. I will think of you as you were on that
sunny day—do you remember?—a week ago, when

you were wearing that light-colored dress. We talked.
. . . There was a white sea gull lying on the seat.

NINA

Pensively Yes, a sea gull . . . *pause* We can't go
on talking; someone's coming. Let me have two
minutes with you before you go, I implore you. *goes
out on left*

*At the same time Arkadina and Sorin come in, the latter
wearing a frock coat with the star of an order on it.
They are followed by Yakov, who is looking after the
packing*

ARKADINA

Better stay at home, my friend. Are you really up to
running around visiting people, with your rheumatism?
to Trigorin Who was it just went out? Nina?

TRIGORIN

Yes.

ARKADINA

I'm sorry we've disturbed you. *sits down* I believe
I've packed everything. I'm worn out.

TRIGORIN

Reading the inscription on the medallion
Days and Nights, page 121, lines 11 and 12.

YAKOV

Clearing the table
Am I to pack your fishing rods too, sir?

TRIGORIN

Yes, I will be wanting them again. But you can give
the books away.

YAKOV

Yes, sir.

TRIGORIN

To himself Page 121, lines 11 and 12. What can they

be? *to Arkadina*   Are there any of my books in the house?

ARKADINA

Yes, in my brother's study, in the corner bookcase.

TRIGORIN

Page 121.   *goes out*

ARKADINA

Really, Petrusha, you'd better stay at home.

SORIN

You are going away. I'll find it hard to stay at home without you.

ARKADINA

But what is there to do in town?

SORIN

Nothing special, but all the same . . .   *laughs* There'll be the laying of the foundation stone of the County Hall, and all that sort of thing. I feel I'd like to shake myself out of this stagnant existence, if only for an hour or two. I've been lying around too long, like some old cigarette holder or something. I've ordered the horses for one o'clock, so that we'll be starting at the same time.

ARKADINA

After a pause

You must go on living here. Don't let yourself get bored and avoid catching cold. Watch over my son. Take care of him. Give him good advice.   *pause* Here I am going away, and I won't even know why Konstantin tried to shoot himself. I believe jealousy was the chief reason, and the sooner I take Trigorin away from here, the better.

SORIN

How shall I say it? There were other reasons too. It's not to be wondered at really—a young man, intelligent,

living in the country, in the wilds . . . with no money,
no position, no future. No occupation whatsoever.
Ashamed and afraid of his idleness. I am extremely
fond of him, and he's attached to me too. But all the
same, he does feel in a way that he doesn't belong here,
that he's a sponger, living on charity. It's not to be
wondered at—he's got pride.

ARKADINA

He's a great anxiety to me! *pondering* Should he
get some sort of job?

SORIN

Begins to whistle, then speaks irresolutely
I think quite the best thing would be if you were to . . .
give him a little money. In the first place, he ought
to have proper clothes, and all that sort of thing. Just
look at him; he's been wearing the same wretched
jacket for the last three years, and he's got no overcoat.
laughs And it wouldn't do the boy any harm to have
a little fun . . . to go abroad or something. It wouldn't
cost much.

ARKADINA

All the same. I might manage the suit, perhaps, but as
for going abroad . . . No, just at the moment I can't
even manage the suit. *resolutely* I haven't got the
money.

Sorin laughs

No!

SORIN

Begins to whistle
Quite so. Forgive me, my dear. Don't be annoyed. I
believe you. You're a generous, noblehearted woman.

ARKADINA   THE

Tearfully I have no money!   SEAGULL

SORIN

Naturally, if I had any money I would give it to him
myself, but I've got nothing, not a kopeck. *laughs*
My steward takes all my pension and spends it on
farming—on the cattle and the bees—and my money
is all wasted. The bees die, the cows die, and I'm never
allowed to use the horses.

ARKADINA

Well, I do have some money. But after all, I'm an
actress: my dress bill alone is enough to ruin me.

SORIN

You're a dear, kindhearted woman. I respect you.
Yes. . . . There's something the matter with me
again. . . . *sways* I feel dizzy. *holds on to the table*
I feel faint and all that sort of thing.

ARKADINA

Alarmed Petrusha! *trying to support him* Petrusha,
my dear! *calling* Help! Help!

*Treplev, with a bandage around his head, and
Medvedenko come in*

He's feeling faint!

SORIN

It's nothing, nothing. *smiles and drinks some water*
It's gone away already . . . and all that sort of . . .

TREPLEV

To his mother

Don't get alarmed, mamma; it's not serious. Uncle
often has these attacks nowadays. *to his uncle* You
ought to lie down for a while, uncle.

SORIN

Yes, for a while. . . . But I'll go to town all the same.
I'll lie down for a bit; then go. That's definite. *goes
out leaning on his stick*

Supporting him by the arm

Here's a riddle for you: in the morning on four legs, at
noon on two, in the evening on three.

SORIN

Laughing   Quite so. And at night on its back. I can
walk on my own, thank you.

MEDVEDENKO

Come, come, don't stand on ceremony.   *goes out with
Sorin*

ARKADINA

How he scared me!

TREPLEV

It doesn't do his health any good living in the country.
He gets depressed. Suppose you suddenly felt generous,
mamma, and lent him a couple of thousand? Then
he could spend a whole year in town.

ARKADINA

I have no money. I'm an actress, not a banker. . . .

TREPLEV

After a pause

Mamma, will you change my bandage for me? You do
it so well.

ARKADINA

*Takes some iodoform and a box of bandages out of the
medicine cupboard*

The doctor's late.

TREPLEV

He promised to be here by ten o'clock, and it's midday
already.

ARKADINA

Sit down.   *takes the bandage off his head*   You look
as if you're wearing a turban. Yesterday there was some
stranger in the kitchen asking what nationality you

were. But your wound is almost healed. There's only a tiny bit still open. *kisses him on the head* You won't play around with a gun again when I'm away, will you?

TREPLEV

No, mamma. That was a moment of mad despair, when I had no control over myself. It won't happen again. *kisses her hands* You've got magic hands. I remember ever so long ago, when you were still playing in the state-aided theaters—I was quite young then—there was a fight in our courtyard. One of the tenants, a washerwoman, was badly hurt. Do you remember? She was taken off unconscious . . . and you went to see her several times and took medicine to her and bathed her children in a tub. Don't you remember?

ARKADINA

No. *puts on a fresh bandage*

TREPLEV

Two ballet dancers lived in the same house as we did then. They used to come and have coffee with you.

ARKADINA

That I do remember.

TREPLEV

They were so religious. *pause* Just lately, these last few days, I've felt that I loved you as tenderly and uncritically as I did when I was a child. I have no one left but you now. Only why, why did you let yourself fall under the influence of that man?

ARKADINA

You don't understand him, Konstantin. He's such an honorable man.

TREPLEV

And yet, when he was told I was going to challenge him, his honor didn't prevent him from behaving like a coward. He's leaving. Ignominious flight!

ARKADINA

What nonsense! I asked him to go myself.

TREPLEV

A most honorable man, indeed! Here we are on the
point of quarreling about him, while at this very
moment he may be laughing at us in the garden or the
drawing room . . . bringing out Nina's potentialities,
trying to convince her finally that he's a genius.

ARKADINA

You take a delight in saying these unpleasant things.
I admire him, so please don't speak ill of him in my
presence.

TREPLEV

Well, I don't admire him. You want me to think he's a
genius too, but you must forgive me—I can't lie.
His books make me sick.

ARKADINA

That's envy. Mediocre people trying to make unjusti-
fiable claims about themselves have to run down
people with real talent. Poor comfort, I must say!

TREPLEV

Ironically Real talent! *wrathfully* I have more
talent than the lot of you if it comes to that! *tearing
the bandage off his head* It's conventional, hidebound
people like you who have grabbed the best places in the
arts today, who regard as genuine and legitimate only
what you do yourselves. Everything else you have to
smother and suppress! I refuse to accept you at your
own valuation! I refuse to accept you or him!

ARKADINA

You're decadent!

TREPLEV

Take yourself off to your lovely theater and go on
acting in your futile, miserable plays!

THE
SEAGULL

ARKADINA

I've never acted in futile, miserable plays! Leave me alone! You're incapable of writing even a couple of miserable scenes! You're just a little upstart from Kiev! A parasite!

TREPLEV

You miser!

ARKADINA

You beggar!

Treplev sits down and weeps quietly

Nonentity! *walks up and down in agitation, then stops* Don't cry. . . . You mustn't cry! *weeps* You mustn't. *kisses his forehead, then his cheeks and his head* My darling child, forgive me. Forgive your wicked mother. Forgive an unhappy woman.

TREPLEV

Embraces her If only you knew! I've lost everything. She doesn't love me, and I can't write anymore. . . . All my hopes are gone.

ARKADINA

Don't despair. Everything will turn out all right. He'll be leaving soon, and she'll love you again. *wipes away his tears* That's enough. We've made up now.

TREPLEV

Kissing her hands

Yes, mamma.

ARKADINA

Tenderly Make it up with him too. There's no need for a duel. Is there now?

TREPLEV

Very well. Only, mamma, don't make me see him. It's painful for me. It's too much for my strength.

ANTON
CHEKHOV

Trigorin comes in

There. I'm going. *quickly puts away the dressings in*
the cupboard The doctor will do the bandaging now.

TRIGORIN
Looking through the book
Page 121 . . . lines 11 and 12. Here it is. *reads* "If ever you need my life, come and take it."

Treplev picks up the bandage from the floor and goes out

ARKADINA
Glacing at her watch
The horses will soon be here.

TRIGORIN
To himself "If ever you need my life, come and take it."

ARKADINA
You've got all your things packed, I hope?

TRIGORIN
Impatiently Yes, yes. *musing* Why does it seem so sad to me, this cry from a pure soul? Why does it wring my heart so agonizingly? "If ever you need my life, come and take it." *to Arkadina* Let us stay one more day!

Arkadina shakes her head

Let us stay!

ARKADINA
Darling, I know what's holding you here. But do control yourself. You've become a little intoxicated. Try to sober down.

TRIGORIN
You must try to be sober too—and sensible and reasonable. Do try to see all this like a true friend, I implore you. *presses her hand* You are capable of sacrifice. Be a friend to me; release me.

ARKADINA

In great agitation

Has she fascinated you as much as that?

TRIGORIN

I'm drawn to her! Perhaps it is just what I need.

ARKADINA

The love of a provincial girl? Oh, how little you know yourself!

TRIGORIN

Sometimes people go to sleep on their feet, and that's just the state I'm in as I talk to you. All the time I feel as if I were asleep and dreaming of her. I'm possessed by sweet and wonderful dreams. Let me go.

ARKADINA

Trembling   No, no. . . . I'm just an ordinary woman. You mustn't talk to me like that. Don't torment me, Boris. I'm frightened.

TRIGORIN

You could be extraordinary, if you chose. Young love, enchanting, poetical—love that carries you off into a world of dreams—it's the only thing that can bring happiness on this earth! I've never yet known a love like that. In my youth I never had time; I was always hanging around on editors' doorsteps, struggling with poverty. And now it is here, it has come, it is beckoning to me. What's the sense in running away from it?

ARKADINA

Angrily   You're out of your mind!

TRIGORIN

And why not?

ARKADINA

You've all been conspiring to torment me today!

weeps

ANTON
CHEKHOV

TRIGORIN

Clasping his head with his hands

She doesn't understand! She doesn't want to understand!

ARKADINA

Am I really so old and ugly that you can talk to me about other women without embarrassment? *embraces and kisses him* Oh, you must have gone mad! My beautiful, my wonderful . . . You—the last page of my life! *kneels before him* My joy, my pride, my happiness! *embraces his knees* If you leave me even for a single hour I'll never survive it. I'll go out of my mind—my wonderful, magnificent man; my master.

TRIGORIN

Someone might come in. *helps her to her feet*

ARKADINA

Let them. I'm not ashamed of my love for you. *kisses his hands* My darling, reckless boy, you may want to behave as if you were mad, but I won't let you, I won't let you. *laughs* You're mine . . . mine. This forehead is mine, and these eyes, and this beautiful silky hair is mine too. All of you is mine. You're so gifted, so clever. You're the best of all the modern writers, the only hope of Russia. You have such sincerity, simplicity, freshness, stimulating humor. With a stroke of your pen you can convey the whole essence of a character or a landscape; people in your books are so alive. It is impossible to read your work and not be delighted by it. Do you think this is just hero worship? You think I'm flattering you? Come, look into my eyes. . . . Look. Do I look like a liar? There! You see— I alone know how to appreciate you. I'm the one person who tells you the truth, my darling, my wonderful man. Will you come? Yes? You'll not leave me?

TRIGORIN

I have no will of my own. I've never had a will of my

THE
SEAGULL

own. Sluggish, flabby, always submissive—how can any woman like that sort of thing? Take me, carry me off, but don't let me ever move a step away from you.

ARKADINA

To herself Now he's mine! *affecting an easy manner as if nothing had happened* But, of course, you can stay if you want to. I'll go myself, and you can come on afterward, a week later. After all, why should you hurry?

TRIGORIN

No, we may as well go together.

ARKADINA

Just as you like. Let's go together then.

A pause. Trigorin writes in his notebook

What is it?

TRIGORIN

I heard a good phrase this morning: "The Maiden's Forest." . . . Might come in useful. *stretches* So we are going? More railway carriages, stations, refreshment bars, veal cutlets, conversations . . .

SHAMRAYEV

Coming in I have come to inform you that the horses are ready, I am sorry to say. It's time, my dear lady, we were off to the station; the train comes in at five minutes past two. You will do me that little favor, won't you, Irina Nikolaevna? You won't forget to inquire where the actor Suzdaltsev is now? Is he alive? Is he well? We used to stand each other drinks years ago. He used to be quite inimitable in *The Mail Robbery*. I remember at that time there was Izmailov, an actor who always played with him at Elizavetgrad. He was a remarkable personality too. . . . Don't be in a hurry, my dear lady. You needn't start for another

five minutes. Once they were playing as conspirators in
a melodrama, and when they were suddenly discovered
they had to say, "We're caught in a trap." But Izmailov
said, "We're taught in a cap." *laughs loudly*
"Taught in a cap!"

*While he is speaking, Yakov fusses with the suitcases;
a maid brings Arkadina's hat, coat, umbrella, and
gloves; and everyone helps her to put them on. The chef
looks in through the door at left, and after some hesita-
tion, enters. Then Polina Andreyevna, and finally Sorin
and Medvedenko, come in*

POLINA
With a small basket in her hand
Here are some plums for your journey . . . very sweet.
You might feel like having something refreshing.

ARKADINA
You are very kind, Polina Andreyevna.

POLINA
Good-bye, my dear! If there has been anything that
wasn't quite as you like it, please forgive us. *weeps*

ARKADINA
Embracing her Everything was all right, everything!
Only you shouldn't cry!

POLINA
Our days are passing!

ARKADINA
There's nothing we can do about it.

SORIN
*Wearing an overcoat with a shoulder cape and a hat,
and carrying a cane, comes in from the door at left. He
speaks as he walks across the room*
It's time to go, sister. Let's not be late for the train
after all. I'm going to get into the carriage. *goes out*

THE
SEAGULL

MEDVEDENKO

I'll walk to the station . . . to see you off. I'll be there in no time. *goes out*

ARKADINA

Good-bye, my dears. If all goes well, we'll meet again next summer.

The maid, the chef, and Yakov kiss her hand

Don't forget me. *gives the chef a ruble* Here's a ruble between you three.

THE CHEF

Thank you kindly, madam. Good journey to you! We're most grateful for your kindness.

YAKOV

Godspeed to you!

SHAMRAYEV

Perhaps you'll write to us. It would make us so happy! Good-bye, Boris Alekseevich.

ARKADINA

Where is Konstantin? Tell him that I'm leaving. We must say good-bye. Think kindly of me. *to Yakov* I gave a ruble to the chef. It's between the three of you.

All go out at right. The stage is empty. There is the noise offstage of people being seen off. The maid returns to fetch the basket of plums from the table and goes out again

TRIGORIN

Returning I've forgotten my cane. I believe it's out there, on the terrace. *walks toward the door at the left and meets Nina, who comes in* It's you! We're going.

NINA

I felt sure that we should see each other again. *excitedly* Boris Alekseevich, I've decided irrevocably, the die is cast—I'm going on the stage. I will be gone

from here tomorrow. I'm leaving my father, leaving
everything. I'm beginning a new life. I'm going to
Moscow . . . like you. We'll see each other there.

TRIGORIN
Glancing behind him
Stay at the Slavianski Bazaar. Let me know at once . . .
at Molchanovka, Grokholski House. I must hurry.

NINA
After a pause
One minute more. . . .

TRIGORIN
In an undertone
You are so beautiful. Oh, how happy I am to think
that we'll be seeing each other soon!

She leans her head on his breast

I will see these wonderful eyes again, this indescribably
beautiful, tender smile . . . these sweet features, the
expression of angelic purity! My darling. . . .   *a prolonged kiss*

CURTAIN

*Between the Third and the Fourth Acts there is an
interval of two years*

ACT FOUR

*A drawing room in Sorin's house, converted into a study
by Konstantin Treplev. Doors right and left leading to
other rooms. In the center, a French window opening
onto the terrace. There is a writing desk in the corner
on the right and an ottoman by the door on the left;
also a bookcase and the usual drawing room furniture.
Books are lying on the windowsills and on chairs. It is
evening. The room is dimly lit by a shaded table lamp.
There is the noise of wind in the trees and the chimneys.*
A watchman is heard tapping.[1] *Enter Medvedenko
and Masha.*

MASHA

Calling Konstantin Gavriilovich! Konstantin
Gavriilovich! *looking around* No, there's no one
here. The old man keeps on asking: where's Kostya,
where's Kostya. He just can't live without him.

MEDVEDENKO

He's afraid of being alone. *listening* What dreadful
weather! It's been like this for nearly two days.

ANTON
CHEKHOV

1. In former days it was usual for a man to go around an estate,
striking a wooden board with a stick to frighten away potential thieves.

MASHA

Turning up the lamp
There are waves on the lake, enormous ones.

MEDVEDENKO

It's very dark outside. By the way, we might as well
tell them to pull down that stage in the garden. It
stands there naked and ugly like a skeleton, with the
curtain flapping in the wind. You know, last night as I
was walking past it, I thought I heard someone inside—
crying.

MASHA

What next. . . .

MEDVEDENKO

After a pause
Let's go home, Masha.

MASHA

Shaking her head
No, I will stay here for the night.

MEDVEDENKO

Imploringly   Masha, let us go! The baby may be
hungry.

MASHA

What nonsense! Matrëna will feed him. . . .

MEDVEDENKO

After a pause
I feel sorry for him. This is the third night he's been
without his mother.

MASHA

How boring you've become! In the old days you did at
least philosophize a bit now and again. Now all you
talk about is baby and home, baby and home. I never
hear anything else from you.

MEDVEDENKO

Let's go, Masha!

MASHA

You go by yourself.

THE
SEAGULL

MEDVEDENKO

Your father won't let me have a horse.

MASHA

Yes, he will. You go and ask him.

MEDVEDENKO

I suppose I might ask him. And you'll be coming home tomorrow then?

MASHA

Takes snuff Well, yes . . . tomorrow. How you pester me!

Enter Treplev and Polina Andreyevna. Treplev carries pillows and a blanket, and Polina Andreyevna, some sheets, which they put on the ottoman. Treplev then goes to his desk and sits down

What is this for, mamma?

POLINA

It's for Pëtr Nikolaevich. He wants his bed made in Kostya's room.

MASHA

Let me. *makes the bed*

POLINA

Sighing Old people are like children. *walks over to the writing desk and, leaning on her elbow, looks at an open manuscript*

MEDVEDENKO

After a pause

Well, I'd better go. Good-bye, Masha. *kisses his wife's hand* Good-bye, mother. *tries to kiss his mother-in-law's hand*

POLINA

With irritation Go on with you! It's time you went if you are going.

ANTON
CHEKHOV

MEDVEDENKO

Good-bye, Konstantin Gavriilovich.

Treplev gives him his hand without speaking.
Medvedenko goes out

POLINA
Looking at the manuscript
Who would have thought that you would turn out to
be a real writer, Kostya? But, thank God, here you
are getting money from magazines for your work.
strokes his hair   You've grown so good-looking too.
Kostya, my dear, you're so kind; couldn't you be a little
kinder to my Mashenka?

MASHA
Making the bed
Leave him alone, mamma.

POLINA
To Treplev   She's a nice girl, you know.   *pause*
Give a woman a kind glance sometimes, Kostya, and
she won't ask for more. I know that.

*Treplev gets up from his desk and goes out without
speaking*

MASHA
There! Now you've made him angry. What's the point
of pestering him?

POLINA
I feel so sorry for you, Mashenka!

MASHA
A lot of use that is to me!

POLINA
My heart's been aching for you. I see it all, you know.
I understand it all.

MASHA
All this is just nonsense. Love without hope—it only
happens in novels. It's really nothing. You've only
got to keep a firm hold on yourself, to stop yourself

hoping for . . . hoping for the tide to turn. If love sneaks into your heart the best thing to do is to chuck it out. My husband's been promised a transfer to another district. Once we get there, I'll forget it all. . . . Tear it out of my heart, roots and all.

A waltz with a melancholy tune is being played two rooms away

POLINA
That's Kostya playing. He must be feeling sad.

MASHA
Noiselessly takes two or three waltz turns
The most important thing, mamma, is not to have him constantly in front of me. Just let them give my Semën his transfer, and, you'll see, I'll forget it all in a month. The whole thing is just nonsense.

Door at left opens. Dorn and Medvedenko wheel in Sorin

MEDVEDENKO
I've got six people at home now, and flour is two kopecks a pound.

DORN
Yes, you've got to scrape and save!

MEDVEDENKO
It's all very well for you to laugh. You've got more money than you know what to do with.

DORN
Money? My dear fellow, in thirty years of practice—and very worrying practice at that, for I was day and night at everyone's beck and call—in all those years I've only managed to save two thousand rubles, and I've just spent that on a holiday abroad. I've got positively nothing.

To her husband
So you haven't gone after all?

MEDVEDENKO
Apologetically Well, how could I if they wouldn't
let me have a horse?

MASHA
Bitterly, in an undertone
I just can't bear the sight of you!

*Sorin is wheeled to the left side of the room. Polina,
Masha, and Dorn sit down beside him. Medvedenko,
looking depressed, stands a little apart from them*

DORN
What a lot of changes you've made though! You've
turned this drawing room into a study.

MASHA
Konstantin Gavriilovich is more comfortable working
here. He can walk out into the garden whenever he
likes, and he can think there.

The watchman can be heard tapping

SORIN
Where's my sister?

DORN
She's gone to the station to meet Trigorin. She'll be
back soon.

SORIN
I must be dangerously ill if you thought it necessary to
send for my sister. *after a short silence* Isn't it odd?
I'm dangerously ill; yet no one gives me any medicine.

DORN
Well, what would you like to have? Valerian drops?
Soda? Quinine?

THE
SEAGULL

SORIN

There he goes again, the philosopher! Oh, how trying it all is! *jerks his head in the direction of the ottoman* Has that been gotten ready for me?

POLINA

Yes, Pëtr Nikolaevich, it's for you.

SORIN

Thank you.

DORN

Hums "The moon floats through the night sky . . ."

SORIN

You know, I'd like to give Kostya a subject for a novel. I'd call it *The Man Who Wished.* "*L'homme qui a voulu.*" Long ago in my young days I wanted to become a writer—and I didn't. I wanted to be a fine speaker, and I spoke abominably *mimicking himself* —"and all that sort of thing, and all the rest of it, and so on, and so forth . . ." When I tried to sum up my argument, I'd go plodding on and on until I broke into perspiration. I wanted to get married—and I didn't. I always wanted to live in town—and here I am finishing my life in the country, and all that sort of thing.

DORN

You wanted to become a civil councillor—and you did.

SORIN

Laughs That was something I didn't strive for. It just happened.

DORN

Fancy expressing dissatisfaction with life at the age of sixty-two! It's a little indecent, you must admit.

SORIN

What a persistent fellow he is! Can't you understand anyone wanting to live?

DORN

That's just foolish. Every life must have an end—it's the law of nature.

SORIN

You talk like a man who's had his fill of experience. You've satisfied your hunger, and so life means nothing to you; you don't care about it. But when it comes to dying, you'll be afraid too.

DORN

The fear of death is an animal fear. You've got to suppress it. It's only religious people who consciously fear death, because they believe in a future life and are afraid they'll be punished for their sins. Your case is different: in the first place, you're not religious; and in the second, what sins have you committed? You've served in the Ministry of Justice for twenty-five years, that's all.

SORIN

Laughs Twenty-eight.

Enter Treplev, who sits down on a low stool at Sorin's feet. Masha gazes at him continuously

DORN

We're preventing Konstantin Gavriilovich from getting on with his work.

TREPLEV

Oh no, it doesn't matter. . . .

MEDVEDENKO

After a pause

If I might ask you, Doctor, which city do you like best of all those you've seen abroad?

DORN

Genoa.

TREPLEV

Why Genoa?

THE
SEAGULL

DORN

Because there's something very fine about the street crowds there. You go out of your hotel at night, and the whole street is packed with people. You just wander among them aimlessly, anywhere you like, up and down. You live with them, become part of the crowd spiritually, and you end by almost believing that a world-soul can really exist—something like the world-soul in your play, the one Nina Zarechnaya acted in some time back. By the way, where is Zarechnaya now? Do you know how she is?

TREPLEV

I suppose she's all right.

DORN

Someone told me she's been leading a rather peculiar kind of life. What's been happening?

TREPLEV

Well, Doctor, it's a long story.

DORN

Never mind, you can make it short. . . .

TREPLEV

After a pause

She ran away from home and had an affair with Trigorin. You knew that, didn't you?

DORN

Yes, I did know.

TREPLEV

She had a child. It died. Trigorin fell out of love with her and went back to his former attachments, as might have been expected. In fact he never gave them up, but in his spineless way he somehow managed to keep them all going. As far as I can make it out from what I've heard, Nina's personal life turned out a complete failure.

ANTON
CHEKHOV

DORN

And what about the stage?

TREPLEV

That was worse still, I believe. She started acting in a small theater at some holiday place near Moscow; then went to the provinces. I never lost sight of her at that time, and wherever she went, I followed. She would always take on big parts, but she acted them crudely, without distinction—with false intonations and violent gestures. There were moments when she showed talent—as when she uttered a cry, or died on the stage—but they were only moments.

DORN

Then she has some talent, after all?

TREPLEV

It's very hard to tell. I believe she has. I saw her, of course, but she refused to see me, and the servants wouldn't let me go up to her room at the hotel. I understood her state of mind and did not insist on seeing her. *pause* What more can I tell you? Afterward, when I got back home, I had letters from her— intelligent, warm, interesting letters. She did not complain, but I could feel that she was profoundly unhappy; every line was like an exposed, aching nerve. Her imagination seemed to be confused too. She signed herself "Sea gull." You remember, in Pushkin's play *The River Nymph* the miller says he's a raven. So in the same way she kept calling herself "the sea gull" in her letters. By the way, she is here now.

DORN

What do you mean—here?

TREPLEV

I mean she's staying in the town, at a hotel. She's been there for four or five days. I did go to call on her, and

THE
SEAGULL

Marya Ilyinichna here went too, but she won't see anyone. Semën Semënych insists that he saw her yesterday afternoon in the fields, a mile or so from here.

MEDVEDENKO

Yes, I did see her. She was walking away from here, toward the town. I bowed to her and asked why she didn't come to see us. She said she would.

TREPLEV

She won't come. *pause* Her father and stepmother won't have anything to do with her. They put men all around to make sure that she doesn't come near the house. *goes with the doctor toward the writing desk* How easy it is to be philosophical on paper, Doctor, and how difficult when it comes to real life.

SORIN

She was a most charming girl.

DORN

What?

SORIN

She was a most charming girl, I said. Councillor Sorin was actually in love with her for a time.

DORN

The old philanderer!

Offstage Shamrayev can be heard laughing

POLINA

I think they've arrived from the station.

TREPLEV

Yes, I can hear mamma.

Enter Arkadina and Trigorin, followed by Shamrayev

SHAMRAYEV

ANTON   *As he comes in*
CHEKHOV   We all of us get older; we wither away like trees

battered by the elements, but you, my dear lady, you're
still as young as ever. A light-colored blouse, vivacious
manner . . . grace in all your movements . . .

ARKADINA
You want to bring me ill luck again, you tiresome
man?

TRIGORIN
To Sorin How do you do, Pëtr Nikolaevich? So
you're still doing poorly? That's not so good! *seeing
Masha, happily* Ah, Marya Ilyinichna!

MASHA
So you remember me? *shakes hands with him*

TRIGORIN
Married?

MASHA
A long time now.

TRIGORIN
Happy? *bows to Dorn and Medvedenko, who bow in
return, then hesitatingly approaches Treplev* Irina
Nikolaevna has told me that you've forgotten the
past and aren't angry with me any longer.

Treplev holds out his hand

ARKADINA
To her son
Look, Boris Alekseevich has brought the magazine
with your new story in it.

TREPLEV
Taking the magazine, to Trigorin
Thank you, you're very kind.

TRIGORIN
Your admirers send their greetings to you. People in
Petersburg and Moscow are very intrigued by you—
always asking me what you are like, how old, and
whether you're fair or dark. For some reason they all

think that you're getting on in years. And no one knows
your real name; you always publish your work under
a pseudonym, don't you? You're as mysterious as the
Man in the Iron Mask.

TREPLEV

Will you be stopping with us for a while?

TRIGORIN

No, I think I'll go back to Moscow tomorrow. I've
got to, really. I'm in a hurry to finish a novel, and
besides, I've promised to give them something for an
anthology. In short it's just the same as ever.

*While they talk Arkadina and Polina move a card table
into the middle of the room and open it. Shamrayev
lights the candles and puts the chairs in place. A game
of lotto is brought out of the cupboard*

The weather isn't greeting me very kindly. There's a
cruel wind. Tomorrow morning, if it drops, I'll go
fishing on the lake. Besides, I want to have a look
around the garden and see the place where your play
was acted—you remember? I've a subject for a story.
I only want to revive my memories of the scene where
the action is supposed to take place.

MASHA

To her father

Papa, do let Semën have a horse! He must get home
somehow.

SHAMRAYEV

Mimics her   A horse. . . .   Must get home.   *sternly*
You saw the horses have just been to the station! How
can I send them out again?

MASHA

But there are other horses.   *on seeing that her father
says nothing, makes a gesture of discouragement*   Oh,
you're hopeless.

ANTON
CHEKHOV

MEDVEDENKO
I can walk, Masha. Really . . .

POLINA
With a sigh
Walk in this weather! *sits down at the card table*
Please come along, ladies and gentlemen.

MEDVEDENKO
It's only four miles after all. Good-bye. *kisses his wife's hand* Good-bye, mother.

Polina reluctantly holds out her hand for him to kiss

I wouldn't have made any bother if it weren't for the baby. *bows to the company* Good-bye. *goes out guiltily*

SHAMRAYEV
He can walk all right! He's not a general, after all!

POLINA
Tapping on the table
Come along, please! Let's not waste time; they'll be calling us to supper soon.

Shamrayev, Masha, and Dorn sit down at the table

ARKADINA
To Trigorin They always play lotto here when the long autumn evenings come on. Look, this is the same old set of lotto my mother used when she played with us children. Won't you have a game with us before supper? *sits down at the table with Trigorin* It's a dull game, but it's not so bad when you get used to it. *deals three cards to everyone*

TREPLEV
Turning over the pages of the magazine
He's read his own story, but he hasn't even cut the pages of mine. *puts the magazine down on his desk*

THE
SEAGULL

and walks toward the door at the left; as he passes his mother, he kisses her on the head

ARKADINA

What about you, Kostya?

TREPLEV

Please·forgive me; I don't feel like it somehow. I'll go for a stroll.   *goes out*

ARKADINA

The stake is ten kopecks. Put it down for me, Doctor, will you?

DORN

I will.

MASHA

Have you all put down your money? I'm starting. Twenty-two!

ARKADINA

Yes.

MASHA

Three.

DORN

Right!

MASHA

Did you play three? Eight! Eighty-one! Ten!

SHAMRAYEV

Don't be in such a hurry!

ARKADINA

What a reception I had in Kharkov! My goodness! It makes my head go around even now!

MASHA

Thirty-four!

A waltz with a melancholy tune is being played offstage

ARKADINA

The students gave me a regular ovation. Three baskets

of flowers, two garlands, and this as well. *unfastens*
a brooch on her throat and tosses it onto the table

SHAMRAYEV

Yes, that's really worth having.

MASHA

Fifty!

DORN

Just fifty?

ARKADINA

I had a wonderful dress on. I know how to dress, if I
know anything at all.

POLINA

Kostya's playing the piano. He's depressed, poor boy.

SHAMRAYEV

They've been attacking him a lot in the papers.

MASHA

Seventy-seven!

ARKADINA

He needn't take any notice of that!

TRIGORIN

He's unlucky. He still can't manage to strike the right
note somehow. There's something strange and vague
about his writing; at times it even suggests the ravings
of a sick man. And not a single living character!

MASHA

Eleven!

ARKADINA

Looking around at Sorin
Petrusha, are you bored? *pause* He's asleep.

DORN

The councillor is asleep.

MASHA

Seven! Ninety!

TRIGORIN

If I lived in a place like this, beside a lake, do you

THE
SEAGULL

suppose I would ever write anything? I would overcome this passion of mine and do nothing but fish.

MASHA

Twenty-eight!

TRIGORIN

Just to catch a perch or a ruff—how delightful it is!

DORN

Well, I believe in Konstantin Gavriilovich. He's got something! He certainly has! He thinks in images; his stories are vivid, full of color, and personally I'm deeply moved by them. But it's a pity he doesn't set himself any definite goal. He makes an impression, that's all, but an impression alone doesn't take you very far. Irina Nikolaevna, are you glad that you've got a writer for a son?

ARKADINA

Can you imagine it? I haven't read anything of his yet. There's never any time.

MASHA

Twenty-six!

Treplev comes in quietly and walks over to his desk

SHAMRAYEV

To Trigorin By the way, Boris Alekseevich, we've still got something of yours down here.

TRIGORIN

What is it?

SHAMRAYEV

Konstantin Gavriilovich shot a gull once, and you asked me to get it stuffed for you.

TRIGORIN

I don't remember. *pondering* No, I don't remember.

MASHA

Sixty-one! One!

TREPLEV

Throws open the window and listens
How dark it is! I can't understand why I'm feeling so
restless.

ARKADINA
Kostya, will you shut the window? There's a draft.

Treplev shuts the window

MASHA
Eighty-eight!

TRIGORIN
The game is mine, my friends.

ARKADINA
Gaily Bravo, Bravo!

SHAMRAYEV
Well done!

ARKADINA
This man's a lucky fellow, always and everywhere!
gets up But now let us go and have something to eat.
Our famous man hasn't had a decent meal today.
We'll go on with the game after supper. *to her son*
Kostya, do leave your writing and come to supper.

TREPLEV
I don't want any, mamma. I'm not hungry.

ARKADINA
Just as you like. *wakes Sorin* Petrusha, supper is
ready! *takes Shamrayev's arm* Let me tell you about
the reception I had at Kharkov.

*Polina Andreyevna blows out the candles on the table,
then she and Dorn wheel out Sorin's chair. Everyone
goes out by the door on the left except for Treplev, who
remains alone in the room sitting at his desk*

THE
SEAGULL

TREPLEV

Preparing to write, reads through what he has already written

I used to talk such a lot about new forms in art, and now I feel I'm slipping into a rut myself, little by little. *reads* "The placard on the wall proclaimed. A pale face in its frame of dark hair." Proclaimed . . . a frame of dark hair. . . . This won't do at all! *crosses out* I'll start with the passage where the hero is awakened by the noise of the rain. The rest will have to come out. The description of the moonlit evening is too long and rather precious. Trigorin has worked out his own methods—it comes easily to him. He would just mention the neck of a broken bottle glistening on the dam and the black shadow of a mill wheel—and there you'd have a moonlit night. But I have to put in the tremulous light, the soft twinkling of the stars, and the distant sounds of a piano, dying away in the still, fragrant air. It's excruciating! *pause* Yes, I'm becoming more and more convinced that it isn't a matter of old or new forms. One must write without thinking about forms, and just because it pours freely from one's soul.

There is a tap on the window nearest to his desk

What's that? *looks through the window* I can't see anything. *opens the French window and looks out into the garden* Someone ran down the steps. *calls* Who's there? *goes out and is heard walking rapidly along the terrace; then returns half a minute later with Nina Zarechnaya* Nina! Nina!

Nina leans her head against his breast and sobs quietly

ANTON CHEKHOV

deeply moved Nina! Nina! It's you . . . you. . . . I seem to have had a presentiment; my heart's been

aching terribly all day. *takes off her cape and hat*
Oh, my sweet, my precious girl, she's come at last!
Don't cry, don't!

NINA

There's someone here.

TREPLEV

There isn't anyone.

NINA

Please lock the doors or someone will come in.

TREPLEV

No one will come in.

NINA

I know Irina Nikolaevna is here. Lock the doors.

TREPLEV

Locks the door on the right, then crosses to the left
There's no lock on this one. I'll put a chair against it.
puts an armchair against the door Don't be afraid;
no one will come in.

NINA

Looks intently at his face
Let me look at you for a little while. *looking around*
How warm, how nice it is here! This used to be a
drawing room. Have I changed a lot?

TREPLEV

Yes. You are thinner and your eyes have grown bigger.
Nina, it's so strange to be seeing you! Why wouldn't
you let me see you? Why haven't you come here before
now? I know you've been in the town almost a week.
I've been to your place every day, several times a day.
I stood under your window like a beggar.

NINA

I was afraid that you might hate me. Every night I
dream that you look at me and don't recognize me. If
only you knew! Ever since I came I've been walking
around here . . . beside the lake. I've been near this

house many times, but I dared not come in. Let us
sit down. *they sit down* Let us sit and talk, talk. . . .
It's nice here, warm and comfortable. Do you hear
the wind? There's a passage in Turgenev: "Fortunate
is he who on such a night has a roof over him, who has
a warm corner of his own." I am a sea gull. No, that's
not it. *rubs her forehead* What was I saying?
Yes. . . . Turgenev. . . . "And heaven help the homeless wayfarers." . . . Never mind. *sobs*

TREPLEV

Nina, you're crying again! Nina!

NINA

Never mind, it does me good. I haven't cried for two
years. Yesterday, late in the evening I came into the
garden to see whether our stage was still there. And it
is still standing! I began to cry for the first time in two
years, and it lifted the weight from my heart, and I felt
more at ease. You see, I'm not crying now. *takes his
hand* And so you've become a writer. You are a
writer and I'm an actress. We've been drawn into the
whirlpool too. I used to live here joyously, like a child.
I used to wake up in the morning and burst into song.
I loved you and dreamed of fame. . . . And now?
Tomorrow morning early I have to go to Yelets in a
third-class carriage . . . with the peasants; and at Yelets
upstart businessmen will pester me with their atten-
tions. Life is coarse!

TREPLEV

Why do you have to go to Yelets?

NINA

I've accepted an engagement for the whole winter. It's
time to go.

ANTON
CHEKHOV

TREPLEV

Nina, I used to curse you: I hated you, I tore up your

letters and photographs. But all the time I knew that
I was bound to you heart and soul, and forever! It's
not in my power to stop loving you, Nina. Ever since
I lost you, ever since I began to get my work published,
my life's been intolerable. I'm miserable. I feel as if my
youth has been suddenly torn away from me, as if I've
been inhabiting this world for ninety years. I call out
your name; I kiss the ground where you've walked.
Wherever I look I seem to see your face, that sweet
smile that used to shine on me in the best years of my
life.

NINA

Bewildered Why does he talk like this? Why does he
talk like this?

TREPLEV

I am lonely. I've no one's love to warm me. I feel as
cold as if I were in a cellar—and everything I write
turns out lifeless and bitter and gloomy. Stay here,
Nina, I entreat you, or let me come with you!

Nina quickly puts on her hat and cape

Nina, why—for heaven's sake—Nina . . .   *looks at
her as she puts on her clothes*

NINA

After a pause
The horses are waiting for me at the gate. Don't see
me off. I'll go by myself.   *tearfully* Give me some
water.

TREPLEV

Gives her water
Where are you going now?

NINA

To the town.   *pause* Irina Nikolaevna's here, isn't
she?

TREPLEV

Yes. My uncle had an attack on Thursday, so we telegraphed for her.

NINA

Why did you say you kissed the ground where I walked? Someone ought to kill me. *droops over the table* I am so tired. Oh, I wish I could rest . . . just rest! *raising her head* I'm a sea gull. . . . No, that's not it. I'm an actress. Oh, well! *she hears Arkadina and Trigorin laughing offstage, listens, then runs to the door at the left and looks through the keyhole* So he is here too! *returning to Treplev* Oh, well! Never mind. . . . Yes. . . . He didn't believe in the theater. He was always laughing at my dreams, and so gradually I ceased to believe too and lost heart. . . . And then I was so preoccupied with love and jealousy and a constant fear for my baby. I became petty and common. When I acted I did it stupidly. I didn't know what to do with my hands or how to stand on the stage. I couldn't control my voice. But you can't imagine what it feels like—when you know that you are acting abominably. I'm a sea gull. No, that's not it again. . . . Do you remember you shot a sea gull? A man came along by chance, saw it, and destroyed it, just to pass the time. . . . A subject for a short story. . . . That's not it. *rubs her forehead* What was I talking about? . . . Yes, about the stage. I'm not like that now. Now I am a real actress. I act with intense enjoyment, with enthusiasm; on the stage I am intoxicated and I feel that I am beautiful. But now, while I'm living here, I go for walks a lot. I keep walking and thinking . . . thinking and feeling that I am growing stronger in spirit with every day that passes. I think I now know, Kostya, that what matters in our work—whether you act on the stage or write stories—what really matters is

ANTON
CHEKHOV

not fame or glamor, not the things I used to dream
about—but knowing how to endure things. How to
bear one's cross and have faith. I have faith now and
I'm not suffering quite so much, and when I think of
my vocation I'm not afraid of life.

TREPLEV

Sadly You have found your right path; you know
which way you're going. But I'm still floating around
in a chaotic world of dreams and images, without
knowing what use it all is. I have no faith, and I don't
know what my vocation is.

NINA

Listening Sh-sh! I'm going now. Good-bye. When I
become a great actress, come and see me act. Promise?
And now . . . *presses his hand* It's late. I can
hardly stand up. I'm so tired and hungry.

TREPLEV

Do stay; I'll give you some supper.

NINA

No, no. Don't see me off; I'll go by myself. My horses
are not far off. . . . So she brought him with her? Oh,
well, it doesn't matter. When you see Trigorin don't
tell him anything. I love him. I love him even more
than before. A subject for a short story. . . . Yes, I love
him, I love him passionately, I love him desperately!
How nice it all used to be, Kostya! Do you remember?
How tranquil, warm, and joyous, and pure our life
was. What feelings we had—like tender, exquisite
flowers. Do you remember? *recites* "The men, the
lions, the eagles, the partridges, the antlered deer, the
geese, the spiders, the silent fishes of the deep, starfishes,
and creatures unseen to the eye—in short all living
things, all living things, all living things, having completed their mournful cycle, have been snuffed out.   THE
For thousands of years the earth has borne no living   SEAGULL

creature, and this poor moon now lights its lamp in vain. The cranes no longer wake up in the meadows with a cry; the May bugs are no longer heard humming in the groves of lime trees." *impulsively embraces Treplev and runs out through the French window*

TREPLEV

After a pause

It won't be very nice if someone meets her in the garden and tells mamma. It might upset mamma. *he spends the next two minutes silently tearing up all his manu-scripts and throwing them under the table, then unlocks the door at the right and goes out*

DORN

Trying to open the door at the left

That's strange. The door seems to be locked. *comes in and puts the armchair in its place* Quite an obstacle race.

Enter Arkadina and Polina, followed by Yakov carrying drinks, then Masha, Shamrayev, and Trigorin

ARKADINA

Put the red wine and the beer on the table here for Boris Alekseevich. We'll drink as we play. Let us sit down, friends.

POLINA

To Yakov Bring the tea in as well. *lights the candles and sits down at the card table*

SHAMRAYEV

Leads Trigorin to the cupboard

Here is the thing I was telling you about just now. *takes the stuffed sea gull out of the cupboard* This is what you ordered.

TRIGORIN

Looking at the sea gull

I don't remember. *musing* No, I don't remember!

ANTON
CHEKHOV

DORN

That's nothing. It must be something in my medicine
chest that's gone off. Don't worry.   *goes out through
the door at the right and returns in half a minute*   Just
as I thought. A bottle of ether has burst.   *hums*
"Again I stand before you, enchanted."

ARKADINA

Sitting down to the table
Ough, how it frightened me! It reminded me of
how . . .   *covers her face with her hands*   Everything
went dark for a moment.

DORN

Turning over the pages of a magazine, to Trigorin
There was an article here about two months ago . . . a
letter from America, and I wanted to ask you . . .   *puts
his arm around Trigorin's waist and leads him to the
footlights*   Because I'm very much interested in this
question. . . .   *dropping his voice, in a lower tone*
Take Irina Nikolaevna away from here somehow. The
fact is, Konstantin Gavriilovich has shot himself.

CURTAIN

UNCLE VANYA

SCENES FROM COUNTRY LIFE
IN FOUR ACTS

THE
CHARACTERS

SEREBRYAKOV, *Aleksandr Vladimirovich, a retired professor*
YELENA ANDREYEVNA (Hélène Lenochka), *his wife, aged twenty-seven*
SONYA (Sofya Aleksandrovna, Sonechka, Sonyushka), *his daughter by his first wife*
VOYNITSKAYA, *Marya Vasilievna, widow of a privy councillor and mother of the professor's first wife*
VOYNITSKI, *Ivan Petrovich* (Vanya), *her son*
ASTROV, *Mikhail Lvovich, a doctor*
TELEGIN, *Ilya Ilyich* (nicknamed "Waffles"), *a landowner reduced to poverty*
MARINA TIMOFEEVNA, *an old children's nurse*
A WORKMAN
   The action takes place on Serebryakov's estate

ACT ONE

A garden. Part of a house with a terrace can be seen.
There is a table set for tea under an old poplar in the
avenue. Garden seats and chairs; on one of them lies a
guitar. Not far from the table there is a swing. It is
between two and three o'clock in the afternoon. The sky
is overcast.
   Marina, a small, plump, slow-moving, elderly
woman, is sitting beside the samovar, knitting a stocking.
Astrov is pacing up and down the avenue near her.

MARINA
Pours out a glass of tea
Here, drink it, dearie.

ASTROV
Reluctantly accepting the glass
I don't feel like it somehow.

MARINA
Perhaps you'd like a drop of vodka?

ASTROV
No. I don't drink vodka every day. It's too close anyway.   *pause*   By the way, Nanny, how many years
have we known each other?

MARINA
Pondering   How many? The Lord help my memory.

You came to live around here . . . Well, when was it? Sonechka's mother, Vera Petrovna, was still living then. You came to see us for two winters when she was alive. . . . That means at least eleven years have gone by. *after a moment's thought* Maybe more.

ASTROV

Have I changed a lot since then?

MARINA

Yes, a lot. You were young and handsome then, but you've aged now. And you're not as good-looking as you were. There's another thing too—you take a drop of vodka now and again.

ASTROV

Yes. In ten years I've become a different man. And what's the cause of it? I've been working too hard, Nanny. I'm on my feet from morning till night; I never have any peace. At night as I lie under the blankets I feel afraid all the time that I may be dragged out to see a patient. During the whole time you and I have known each other I haven't had a single day free. How could I help ageing? Besides, the life itself is tedious, stupid, squalid. This sort of life drags you down. You're surrounded by queer people—they're a queer lot, all of them—and after you've lived with them for a year or two, you gradually become queer yourself, without noticing it. That's inevitable. *twisting his long moustache* Ugh, what a huge moustache I've grown. Silly moustache! I've become an eccentric, Nanny. I haven't grown stupid yet, thank God! My brains are still functioning all right, but my feelings are somewhat duller. I don't wish for anything, I don't feel I need anything, I don't love anybody. Except you perhaps; I believe I'm fond of you. *kisses her on the head* I had a nanny like you when I was a child.

ANTON
CHEKHOV

MARINA

Wouldn't you like something to eat?

ASTROV

No. You know, in the first week of Lent I went to
Malitskoye, because of the epidemic—spotted typhus.
In the houses you could hardly move for sick people.
Dirt, stench, and smoke everywhere . . . and calves
mixed up with the sick on the floor. Young pigs there
as well. I struggled with it all day—hadn't a moment
to sit down or to swallow a bit of food. But would
they let me rest when I got home? No, they brought me
a signalman from the railway. I laid him on the table
to operate, and he went and died on me under the
chloroform. And just when I least wanted it my feelings
seemed to wake up again, and my conscience began to
worry me as if I had killed him deliberately. I sat
down, closed my eyes—just like this—and I started to
think. I wondered whether the people who come after
us in a hundred years' time, the people for whom we
are now blasting a trail—would they remember us and
speak kindly of us? No, Nanny, I'll wager they won't!

MARINA

If people won't remember, God will.

ASTROV

Thank you. You've put it well.

VOYNITSKI

*Comes out of the house. He has had a sleep after lunch
and looks disheveled. He sits down on the garden seat
and adjusts his smart tie*

Yes. *pause* Yes.

ASTROV

Had a good sleep?

VOYNITSKI

Yes . . . very good. *yawns* Since the professor and
his consort came to live here, our usual routine has

UNCLE
VANYA

been completely upset. Now I sleep at the wrong time, I eat the wrong kinds of food at dinner and lunch, I drink wine; it's all bad for my health! In the past I never had a free moment—Sonya and I used to work like Trojans. But now only Sonya works while I just sleep, eat, and drink. It's a bad business!

MARINA

Nods her head disapprovingly

Such goings-on! The professor gets up at midday, but the samovar is kept boiling the whole morning waiting for him. Before they came we always had dinner soon after twelve, like everybody else, but now they are here we have it after six in the evening. The professor spends the night reading and writing, and then suddenly, past one o'clock, the bell rings. My goodness, what is it? He wants some tea! So you've got to wake people up to heat the samovar. Such goings-on!

ASTROV

Are they going to stay here much longer?

VOYNITSKI

Whistles A hundred years maybe! The professor's decided to settle here.

MARINA

You see, it's just the same now. The samovar's been on the table for two hours, and they've gone for a walk.

VOYNITSKI

They're coming, they're coming! Don't fuss!

Voices are heard. Serebryakov, Yelena Andreyevna, Sonya, and Telegin approach from the farther part of the garden, returning from their walk

SEREBRYAKOV

It was beautiful, beautiful! Wonderful scenery!

ANTON
CHEKHOV

TELEGIN

Yes, Your Excellency, the views are remarkable.

SONYA

Tomorrow we'll go to the plantation, papa. Would
you like to?

VOYNITSKI

Tea's ready, my friends!

SEREBRYAKOV

My friends, will you be good enough to send my tea to
my study? I've something more I must do today.

SONYA

I'm sure you will like it at the plantation.

*Yelena Andreyevna, Serebryakov, and Sonya go into
the house. Telegin goes to the table and sits down beside
Marina*

VOYNITSKI

It's hot and close, but our great man of learning has
got his overcoat and galoshes on, and he's carrying his
umbrella and gloves.

ASTROV

He's obviously taking care of himself.

VOYNITSKI

But how lovely *she* is! How lovely! I've never seen a
more beautiful woman in all my life.

TELEGIN

You know, Marina Timofeevna, whether I'm driving
through the fields or taking a walk in a shady garden
or even just looking at this table—I feel inexpressibly
happy! The weather is marvelous, the birds are singing,
and we all live here in peace and harmony. What more
do we need? *taking the glass she hands him* Thank
you kindly.

VOYNITSKI

Dreamily Her eyes . . . a wonderful woman!

ASTROV

Tell us something, Ivan Petrovich.

UNCLE
VANYA

VOYNITSKI

Listlessly   What do you want me to tell you?

ASTROV

Isn't there anything new?

VOYNITSKI

Nothing at all. Everything's old. I'm just the same as I was—perhaps worse, because I've grown lazy. I don't do anything; I just grumble like some old fogey. As for my *maman*, the old magpie still goes on chattering about the emancipation of women. With one eye she looks into her grave and with the other she studies her learned books looking for the dawn of a new life.

ASTROV

And the professor?

VOYNITSKI

And the professor, as usual, sits in his study writing from morning till dead of night. "With furrowed brows and thought intense, we write and write our odes immense, but no praise ever comes our way for what we are, or what we say." I feel sorry for the paper he writes on! It would be better if he wrote his auto-biography! What a superb subject! A retired professor—don't you see?—a dull old stick, a sort of scholarly dried fish. Afflicted with gout, rheumatism, migraine; his liver swollen with jealousy and envy. This dried fish is living on his first wife's country estate, living there against his will, because he can't afford to live in town. He's forever complaining about his misfortunes, though as a matter of fact he's been extraordinarily lucky.   *becoming excited*   Just think how lucky! The son of a common sexton, trained as a priest, he somehow managed to get university qualifications and a professorship. Later he became "Your Excellency" and the son-in-law of a senator, and so on and so forth. However, all that's not the main thing.

ANTON
CHEKHOV

Just consider this. The man has been lecturing and writing about art for exactly twenty-five years, and yet he understands nothing whatever about art. For twenty-five years he has been chewing over other people's ideas about realism, naturalism, and all that sort of nonsense. For twenty-five years he has been lecturing and writing about things that intelligent people have known all the time and stupid people aren't interested in anyway. In fact, for twenty-five years he's been just wasting time and energy. And yet what an opinion of himself! What pretensions! Now he's retired and not a living soul is aware of him. Today he is completely unknown, and that simply means that for twenty-five years he's been occupying a place to which he wasn't in the least entitled. But just look at him—he struts around like a little tin god!

ASTROV

Come now, I believe you envy him.

VOYNITSKI

Yes, I do envy him! And what a success with women! No Don Juan ever experienced success as complete as his. My sister, his first wife—a beautiful, gentle creature, as pure as that blue sky, generous and noble-hearted, who had more admirers than he has ever had pupils—loved him as only innocent-hearted angels can love beings as pure and beautiful as themselves. My mother still adores him; he still inspires her with a feeling of reverent awe. His second wife—you've just seen her; she's intelligent and a beauty—married him when he was already an old man. She gave him her youth, beauty, freedom—her whole brilliant personality. Whatever for? Why?

ASTROV

Is she faithful to the professor?

VOYNITSKI
I am sorry to say she is.

ASTROV
But why should you be sorry?

VOYNITSKI
Because that sort of loyalty is false from beginning to end. There's plenty of rhetoric in it, but no logic. To be unfaithful to an old husband whom she couldn't bear would be immoral; but to do her utmost to stifle within her all her youth, her vitality, her capacity to feel—that is not immoral!

TELEGIN
Tearfully Vanya, I don't like it when you say these things. Come, really! Anyone who can betray a wife or a husband is an unreliable person who might betray his own country too!

VOYNITSKI
With annoyance You dry up, Waffles!

TELEGIN
Forgive me, Vanya. My wife ran away from me the day after our wedding with a man she loved, because of my unprepossessing appearance. But even after that I never failed in my duty toward her. I still love her, I'm faithful to her, I help her as much as I can, and I've spent all I possessed on educating the children she had by the man she loved. I've lost my happiness, but I've still got my pride. And what about her? Her youth is gone, her beauty has faded, as nature ordains that it must, the man she loved has died. What has she got left?

Enter Sonya and Yelena Andreyevna. Shortly after Marya Vasilievna enters with a book. She sits down and reads. Tea is put before her; she drinks it without looking up

ANTON
CHEKHOV

SONYA

Hurriedly to the nurse
Nanny, some peasants have come to the door. Please
go and talk to them, and I'll see to the tea myself.
pours out tea

*The nurse goes out. Yelena Andreyevna takes her tea
and drinks it sitting on the swing*

ASTROV

To Yelena Andreyevna
You know I've come to see your husband. You wrote
and told me that he was very ill—rheumatism and
something else—but I find that he's perfectly well.

YELENA

Last night he was depressed and complained of pains
in his legs, but today he seems all right.

ASTROV

And I've galloped twenty miles at breakneck speed to
get here. Well, never mind, it's not the first time. At
least I can stay with you till tomorrow and get as
much sleep as I need—*quantum satis.*

SONYA

That's splendid. It's so rare for you to stay the night
with us. I don't suppose you've had dinner?

ASTROV

No, I haven't.

SONYA

Then you'll dine with us. We have dinner soon after
six nowadays.   *drinks her tea*   The tea's cold!

TELEGIN

There's been a big fall in the temperature of the
samovar.

YELENA

Never mind, Ivan Ivanovich, we will drink it cold.

UNCLE
VANYA

TELEGIN

Excuse me. My name's not Ivan Ivanovich; it's Ilya
Ilyich . . . Ilya Ilyich Telegin, or as some people call
me on account of my spotty face, Waffles. I'm
Sonechka's godfather and His Excellency, your
husband, knows me very well. I'm now living here
on your estate. You may have been so kind as to
notice that I have dinner with you every day.

SONYA

Ilya Ilyich is our helper, our right-hand man.   *tenderly*
Let me pour you out some tea, godfather dear.

MARYA

Oh!

SONYA

What's the matter, grandmamma?

MARYA

I forgot to tell Aleksandr. I'm losing my memory.
I had a letter today from Pavel Alekseevich, from
Kharkov. He sent us his new pamphlet.

ASTROV

Is it interesting?

MARYA

It's interesting, but somehow strange. He disproves
the very thing he was maintaining seven years ago.
That's dreadful!

VOYNITSKI

There's nothing dreadful in that. Drink your tea,
maman.

MARYA

But I want to talk!

VOYNITSKI

But we've been talking and talking and reading
pamphlets for the last fifty years! It's about time to
stop.

ANTON
CHEKHOV

For some reason you don't like listening when I talk.
Forgive my saying so, Jean, but you've changed so much
in the last year or so that I positively don't recognize
you. You used to be a man with definite convictions,
an inspiring personality.

VOYNITSKI

Oh, yes! I used to be an inspiring personality who
never inspired anybody! *pause* I used to be an
inspiring personality! You could hardly have made a
more wounding joke! I'm forty-seven now. Up to a
year ago I tried deliberately to pull the wool over my
eyes—just as you do yourself with the aid of all your
pedantic rubbish—so that I wouldn't see the realities
of life. And I thought I was doing the right thing. But
now—if you only knew! I lie awake, night after night,
in sheer vexation and anger that I let time slip by so
stupidly during the years when I could have had all
the things from which my age now cuts me off.

SONYA

Uncle Vanya, this is boring!

MARYA

To Voynitski You seem to be blaming those former
principles of yours for something or other. It isn't they
but you who are to blame. You're forgetting that
principles are nothing in themselves—just empty
phrases. You ought to have done something that
mattered.

VOYNITSKI

Something that mattered? It isn't everyone who's
capable of being a nonstop writer like your *Herr*
Professor.

MARYA

What do you mean by that?

UNCLE
VANYA

SONYA

Imploringly Grandmamma! Uncle Vanya! I entreat you!

VOYNITSKI

I'll be quiet. I'll hold my tongue . . . and apologize. . . .

YELENA

After a pause

What a lovely day! Not too hot either.

VOYNITSKI

It would even be pleasant to hang oneself on a day like this.

Telegin tunes the guitar. Marina walks back and forth near the house, calling the chickens

MARINA

Here, chick, chick, chick!

SONYA

Nanny, what did the peasants come for?

MARINA

The same as before—they are still going on about the wasteland. Chick, chick, chick. . .

SONYA

Which is it you're calling?

MARINA

The speckled one. She's gone off somewhere with her chicks. The crows might get them. *walks away*

Telegin plays a polka. All listen in silence. Enter a workman

THE WORKMAN

Is the doctor here? *to Astrov* Mikhail Lvovich, they've come for you, please.

ASTROV

Where from?

THE WORKMAN

From the factory.

ASTROV

With annoyance   Many thanks! Well, I'll have to go. *looks around for his cap*   Hang it! What a nuisance!

SONYA

It really is annoying. Come back to dinner from the factory.

ASTROV

No, it'll be too late. How could I anyway? How could I?   *to the workman*   My good fellow, you might get me a glass of vodka or something.

The workman goes out

How could I anyway? How could I?   *finds his cap* In a play by Ostrovski there's a man with a big moustache but very little brain. That's me. Well, I'll bid you all good-bye.   *to Yelena*   If you ever cared to look me up—with Sofya Aleksandrovna here—I'd be so pleased. I've a small estate, about ninety acres altogether, but if you're interested, there's a model orchard and nursery such as you won't find for hundreds of miles around. And next to my place there's a plantation belonging to the government. The forester there is old and he often gets ill, so that in fact I'm in charge of everything.

YELENA

Yes, I've been told that you're very fond of forestry. Of course, you can do a lot of good that way, but doesn't it interfere with your real vocation? You are a doctor, after all.

ASTROV

Only God knows what our real vocation is.

YELENA

Is it interesting?

UNCLE VANYA

ASTROV

Yes, it's interesting work.

VOYNITSKI

Ironically It must be.

YELENA

To Astrov You're still a young man. You don't look more than . . . well, thirty-six or thirty-seven. I doubt whether you find it as interesting as you say. Nothing but trees and trees. I would think it must be monotonous.

SONYA

No, it's extremely interesting. Mikhail Lvovich puts down new plantations every year, and he's already been awarded a bronze medal and a diploma. He does his best to stop the old forests from being laid waste. If you'd only listen to him, you'd understand what he means and agree with him. He says that forests add beauty to the country, that they teach men to appreciate beauty and induce lofty emotions. Forests make a harsh climate milder. In countries with a mild climate people spend less energy in the struggle with nature, and so man is gentler and more capable of tender feeling. In such countries people are beautiful, sensitive, and flexible in spirit. Their speech is elegant; their movements, graceful. Science and the fine arts flourish among them; their philosophy is cheerful and there is great refinement and courtesy in their attitude toward women.

VOYNITSKI

Laughing Bravo, bravo! This is all very charming, but it isn't convincing. *to Astrov* And so, my friend, you must allow me to go on burning logs in my stoves and building my barns of wood!

ANTON
CHEKHOV

ASTROV

You can burn turf in your stoves and build your barns

out of stone. Well, I would consent to cutting wood when people really need it, but why destroy the forests? The Russian forests are literally groaning under the ax, millions of trees are being destroyed, the homes of animals and birds are being laid waste, the rivers are getting shallow and drying up, wonderful scenery is disappearing forever—and all this is happening just because people are too lazy and stupid to stoop down and pick up the fuel from the ground. *to Yelena* Isn't it so, madam? Anyone who can burn up all that beauty in a stove, who can destroy something that we cannot create, must be a barbarian incapable of reason. Man is endowed with reason and creative power so that he can increase what has been given him, but up to the present he's been destroying and not creating. There are fewer and fewer forests, the rivers are drying up, the wild creatures are almost exterminated, the climate is being ruined, and the land is getting poorer and more hideous every day. *to Voynitski* I can see your ironic expression, and I believe that what I say doesn't seem at all serious to you, and . . . and maybe it is just crankiness. All the same when I go walking by the woods that belong to the peasants, the woods I saved from being cut down, or when I hear the rustling of the young trees I planted with my own hands, I'm conscious of the fact that the climate is to some extent in my power too, and that if mankind is happy in a thousand years' time, I'll be responsible for it even though only to a very minute extent. When I plant a little birch tree and then see it growing green and swaying in the wind, my heart fills with pride, and I . . . *sees the workman who has brought a glass of vodka on a tray* However . . . *drinks* It's time for me to go. After all that's probably just my

UNCLE
VANYA

crankiness. Permit me to take my leave! *goes toward the house*

SONYA
Takes his arm and walks with him
When are you coming to see us then?

ASTROV
I don't know.

SONYA
Not for another month again?

Astrov and Sonya go into the house. Marya Vasilievna and Telegin remain beside the table. Yelena Andreyevna and Voynitski walk toward the terrace

YELENA
And you have been behaving abominably again, Ivan Petrovich. Did you have to irritate Marya Vasilievna with your talk about "nonstop writers"? And at lunch today you argued with Aleksandr again. How petty it all is!

VOYNITSKI
But if I detest him?

YELENA
There is nothing you can detest Aleksandr for—he's just like anyone else. He's no worse than you are.

VOYNITSKI
If only you could see your face, your movements! You give the impression that life is too much of an effort for you. Oh, such an effort!

YELENA
Oh, yes, such an effort and such a bore! Everyone blames my husband. Everyone looks at me with compassion: an unfortunate woman—she's got an old husband! This sympathy for me—oh, how well I understand it! As Astrov said just now: you go on

destroying the forests senselessly, and soon there won't be anything left on the earth. Just in the same way you senselessly ruin human beings, and soon, thanks to you, there will be no loyalty, no integrity, no capacity for self-sacrifice left. Why can't you look at a woman with indifference unless she's yours? Because—that doctor is right—there's a devil of destruction in every one of you. You spare neither woods nor birds nor women nor one another.

VOYNITSKI

I don't like this sort of philosophy!

YELENA

After a pause

The doctor has a tired, sensitive face. An interesting face. Sonya is obviously attracted by him; she's in love with him, and I understand her feelings. He's visited the house three times since I've been here, but I'm shy and I haven't once had a proper talk with him or been nice to him. He must have thought me bad-tempered. Perhaps, Ivan Petrovich, you and I are such good friends just because we both are such tiresome and boring people. Tiresome! Don't look at me like that; I don't like it!

VOYNITSKI

How else can I look at you if I love you? You are my happiness, my life, my youth! I know the chances of your returning my feelings are negligible, just zero. But I don't want anything—only let me look at you and hear your voice.

YELENA

Hush, they might hear you!   *they go into the house*

VOYNITSKI

Following her   Let me talk of my love. Don't drive me away; that in itself will be such great happiness to me.

This is torture.   *both enter the house*

Telegin strikes the strings of his guitar and plays a polka. Marya Vasilievna makes notes in the margin of her pamphlet

CURTAIN

ACT TWO

Dining room in Serebryakov's house. Nighttime; a
watchman can be heard tapping in the garden.
Serebryakov is sitting in an armchair in front of an open
window, dozing. Yelena Andreyevna is sitting beside
him, also dozing.

SEREBRYAKOV
Waking up   Who's that? Sonya, is it you?

YELENA
It's me.

SEREBRYAKOV
You, Lenochka. This pain's unbearable!

YELENA
Your blanket's fallen onto the floor.   *wraps it around*
his legs   I'll shut the window, Aleksandr.

SEREBRYAKOV
No, I feel suffocated. I dozed off just now and I
dreamed that my left leg didn't belong to me. I was
woken up by an agonizing pain. No, it's not gout; it's
more like rheumatism. What time is it now?

YELENA
Twenty minutes past twelve. . . .

SEREBRYAKOV
After a pause
You might look up Batyushkov in the library in the
morning. I believe we have his works.

UNCLE
VANYA

YELENA

What?

SEREBRYAKOV

Look up Batyushkov in the morning. I seem to
remember we had him. But why is it so difficult for
me to breathe?

YELENA

You're tired. This is the second night you haven't slept.

SEREBRYAKOV

They say Turgenev got angina pectoris from gout.
I'm afraid I might get it. This damnable, disgusting
old age! The devil take it! Since I've aged so much I've
become revolting even to myself. And you must find
it revolting to look at me—all of you!

YELENA

You talk of your old age in a tone of voice which
suggests we're all to blame for it.

SEREBRYAKOV

You are the first to find me repulsive.

Yelena gets up and sits down farther away

You are right, of course. I'm not a fool and I understand. You're young, healthy, good-looking; you
want to live . . . whereas I am an old man, almost a
corpse. Well. . . . Do you suppose I don't understand?
Of course it's stupid of me to go on living. But wait
a little while; I'll soon set you all free. I won't have to
linger on much longer.

YELENA

I'm worn out. For God's sake be quiet.

SEREBRYAKOV

It looks as if everyone's worn out, bored, wasting their

ANTON
CHEKHOV

youth thanks to me—and I am the only one who's
content and enjoying life. Yes, yes, of course!

YELENA

Oh, do be quiet! You've worn me out!

SEREBRYAKOV

I've worn everyone out. Of course!

YELENA

Tearfully It's intolerable! Tell me: what is it you want from me?

SEREBRYAKOV

Nothing at all.

YELENA

Well, be quiet then. I implore you.

SEREBRYAKOV

It's a strange business: when Ivan Petrovich starts talking, or that old idiot Marya Vasilievna, it's all right, and everyone listens. But I only have to say a single word, and everyone begins to feel miserable. Even my voice disgusts them. Well, I suppose I am disgusting—an egoist, a despot. But haven't I a right to be selfish in my old age? Haven't I deserved it? I ask you, haven't I a right to a quiet old age, to a little personal attention?

YELENA

No one is disputing your rights.

The window bangs in the wind

The wind's blowing up; I'll shut the window.   *shuts it* It's going to rain presently. No one disputes your rights.

A pause. In the garden the watchman taps and starts singing

SEREBRYAKOV

After devoting all my life to learning; after growing used to my study, to my lecture room, to esteemed colleagues—to find myself suddenly, for no reason at all, in this crypt; to have to meet stupid people every

UNCLE
VANYA

day, to have to listen to their trivial conversation! I want to live, I love success, I like being a well-known figure, I like creating a stir—but here I feel an exile. To spend every minute regretting the past, watching others succeed, fearing death. I can't! It's more than I can bear! And they won't even forgive me for getting old!

YELENA

Wait a little; have patience! In five or six years I will be old too.

Enter Sonya

SONYA

Papa, you told us to send for Doctor Astrov, and now that he's come you refuse to see him. It's discourteous. We've troubled him for nothing.

SEREBRYAKOV

What do I need your Astrov for? He knows as much about medicine as astronomy.

SONYA

We can't send for the whole medical faculty to attend to your gout.

SEREBRYAKOV

I won't even speak to that crank.

SONYA

Just as you please.   *sits down*   It's all the same to me.

SEREBRYAKOV

What time is it now?

YELENA

It's after midnight.

SEREBRYAKOV

I'm suffocating. Sonya, hand me my drops from the table.

SONYA 227

SONYA
Just a moment.   *hands him the drops*

SEREBRYAKOV
Irritably   Oh, not those! It's no use asking for
anything!

SONYA
Please don't be peevish. Some people may like it, but
do spare me, for goodness' sake! I don't like it. And
I haven't the time. I must get up early tomorrow;
I've got to see to the haymaking.

*Enter Voynitski in a dressing gown with a candle
in his hand*

VOYNITSKI
There's a storm coming up.

A flash of lightning

There, did you see? Hélène and Sonya, do go to bed;
I've come to take your place.

SEREBRYAKOV
Alarmed   No, no! Don't leave me with him! Don't!
He'll kill me with his talking!

VOYNITSKI
But they must have some rest! It's the second night
they've had no sleep.

SEREBRYAKOV
Let them go to bed, but you go too. I'd be so grateful.
I do implore you. For the sake of our past friendship,
don't argue. We'll talk later on.

VOYNITSKI
With a sneer
Our past friendship. Past . . .

SONYA
Be quiet, Uncle Vanya.

UNCLE
VANYA

SEREBRYAKOV

To his wife

My dear, don't leave me alone with him. He'll kill me with his talking!

VOYNITSKI

This is becoming ridiculous.

Enter Marina with a candle

SONYA

You ought to go to bed, Nanny. It's late.

MARINA

The samovar hasn't been cleared away. I can't very well go to bed.

SEREBRYAKOV

Everyone's awake; everyone's worn out. Only I am thoroughly enjoying myself.

MARINA

Going up to Serebryakov, tenderly

What is it, my dear? Your pain again? I've got a grumbling pain in my legs too—such a pain! *tucks the blanket in* It's that old trouble of yours. Vera Petrovna, Sonechka's mother, used to get so upset about it—she couldn't sleep nights. Ever so fond of you she was. *pause* The old are just the same as the little ones; they like someone to pity them—but nobody pities the old. *kisses Serebryakov on the shoulder* Come to bed, my dear. . . . Come, darling. I'll give you some lime-flower tea and warm your feet . . . and say a prayer for you.

SEREBRYAKOV

Moved Let us go, Marina.

MARINA

ANTON
CHEKHOV

I've got such a grumbling pain in my legs myself, such a grumbler! *she and Sonya lead him off* Vera

Petrovna used to get so upset, she used to cry over you.
You were little then, Sonyushka; you didn't understand. . . . Come along, come along, sir.

Serebryakov, Sonya, and Marina go out

YELENA

I'm quite worn out with him. I can hardly keep on
my feet.

VOYNITSKI

You with him, and I with myself. It's the third night
I've had no sleep.

YELENA

Things have gone to pieces in this household. Your
mother hates everything except her pamphlets and the
professor. The professor is irritable; he doesn't trust
me and is afraid of you. Sonya is bad-tempered with
her father and angry with me : she hasn't spoken to me
for two weeks. You detest my husband and openly
despise your mother. I am on edge; I have been on the
point of crying twenty times today. Things have gone
wrong in this house.

VOYNITSKI

Let's leave philosophy out of it!

YELENA

You are cultured and intelligent, Ivan Petrovich. Surely
you ought to realize that the world is being destroyed
not by fire and pillage, but by hatred, enmity, and all
this petty quarreling. Your job should be to reconcile
people to one another and not to grumble.

VOYNITSKI

Reconcile me to myself first! Dearest.   *bends down*
impulsively and kisses her hand

YELENA

Don't!   *draws away her hand*   Go away!

VOYNITSKI

In a minute or two the rain will be over, and everything in nature will be refreshed and sigh with relief. Only I shall not be refreshed by the storm. Day and night I feel suffocated by the thought that my life has been irretrievably lost. I have no past—it has all been stupidly wasted on trifles—while the present is awful because it's so meaningless. My life, my love—look at them—where do they belong? What am I to do with them? My feeling for you is just wasted like a ray of sunlight falling into a well—and I am wasted too.

YELENA

When you talk to me of your love I feel quite stupid and I don't know what to say. Forgive me, there's nothing I can say to you. *starting to go out* Good night.

VOYNITSKI

Barring her way

And if you only knew how I suffer when I think that near to me, in the very same house, another life is being wasted—your life! What are you waiting for? What confounded philosophy is holding you back? Understand, do understand.

YELENA

Looks at him intently

Ivan Petrovich, you are drunk!

VOYNITSKI

Maybe, maybe . . .

YELENA

Where's the doctor?

VOYNITSKI

He's in there. He's staying the night with me. It may be, it may be. Anything may be!

ANTON
CHEKHOV

YELENA

So you have been drinking again today! Whatever for?

VOYNITSKI

At least it gives the illusion of life. Don't prevent
me, Hélène.

YELENA

You never used to drink and you never used to talk so
much. Do go to bed! You bore me.

VOYNITSKI

Impulsively kissing her hand
Dearest. You wonderful woman!

YELENA

With annoyance   Leave me alone. This is really
hateful!   *goes out*

VOYNITSKI

Alone She's gone.   *pause*   Ten years ago I used
to meet her at my sister's house. She was seventeen
then and I was thirty-seven. Why didn't I fall in love
with her then and ask her to marry me? It could have
been done so easily! She would have been my wife now.
Yes . . . and we two might have been awakened by
this storm; she would have been frightened by the
thunder and I would have held her in my arms and
whispered, "Don't be afraid; I'm here." Oh, what a
wonderful thought! How enchanting! It actually makes
me laugh with happiness. . . . But, oh, God! My
thoughts are in a tangle. . . . Why am I so old? Why
won't she understand me? Her fine phrases; her easy
moralizing; her silly, facile ideas about the ruin of the
world—how utterly hateful it all is to me!   *pause*
And how I've been cheated! I adored the professor, the
gouty old invalid, and I worked like an ox for him!
Sonya and I squeezed all we could out of this estate.
Like tightfisted peasants we traded in linseed oil, dried
peas, and curds; we saved on our food so that we
could scrape together kopecks and send him thousands
of rubles. I was proud of him and his learning; he was

the breath of my life! Everything he wrote or uttered seemed to me the work of a genius. . . . And now what, good God? He's retired down here, and now you can see what his life really amounts to. Not a page of his writing will survive him. He's completely unknown, a nonentity! A soap bubble! And I've been cheated. I see it now. . . . Stupidly cheated.

Enter Astrov, wearing a coat but without waistcoat or tie. He is slightly drunk. He is followed by Telegin with a guitar

ASTROV
Play us something!

TELEGIN
Everyone's gone to bed!

ASTROV
Come on! Play!

Telegin plays softly

to Voynitski Are you alone here? No ladies? *putting his arms akimbo, sings quietly* "Dance my hut and dance my fire; the master's nowhere to retire." The thunderstorm woke me up. A nice little rain! What time is it now?

VOYNITSKI
The devil knows!

ASTROV
I thought I heard Yelena Andreyevna's voice.

VOYNITSKI
She was in here a moment ago.

ASTROV
An exceptionally attractive woman! *examines the medicine bottles on the table* What a variety of medicines! From Kharkov, from Moscow, from Tula!

He must have plagued every town in Russia with his
gout. Is he really ill or faking it?

VOYNITSKI

He is ill. . . .

ASTROV

After a pause

Why are you so depressed today? Are you feeling sorry
for the professor or what?

VOYNITSKI

Leave me alone.

ASTROV

Or maybe you're in love with the professor's wife?

VOYNITSKI

She's my friend.

ASTROV

Already?

VOYNITSKI

What do you mean by "already"?

ASTROV

A woman can only become a man's friend in three
stages: first she's an agreeable acquaintance, then a
mistress, and only after that a friend.

VOYNITSKI

That's a crude sort of philosophy.

ASTROV

What? Well, yes. I must confess, I am becoming pretty
crude. You see, I'm drunk too. As a rule I get drunk
like this once a month. When I'm in this state I get
extremely provocative and audacious. Then there's
nothing I don't feel equal to! I undertake the most
difficult operations and do them beautifully. I draw
up the most far-reaching plans for the future! At such
times I no longer think of myself as a crank; I believe
that I'm doing a tremendous job for the good of man- UNCLE
kind—tremendous! On these occasions too I have VANYA

my own special system of philosophy according to which all of you, my good friends, appear as insignificant as insects or microbes. *to Telegin* Waffles, go on playing!

TELEGIN

My dear friend, I'd do anything for you, but do remember—everyone in the house has gone to bed!

ASTROV

Play, I tell you!

Telegin plays quietly

A drink would be nice. Come on, I believe there's still some brandy left. When it's daylight, shall we go to my place? All right with you? I've got an unqualified assistant who never says "all right" but always "aw-right." He's an awful rogue. Aw-right then? *sees Sonya entering* Excuse me, I haven't got my tie on. *goes out quickly; Telegin follows him*

SONYA

Uncle Vanya, so you got drunk again with the doctor? You're a fine pair! It's not becoming at your age!

VOYNITSKI

Age has nothing to do with it. When people have no real life, they live on their illusions. Anyway it's better than nothing.

SONYA

All the hay has been cut, it rains every day, everything is rotting, and you are living on illusions! You've been utterly neglecting the estate. I've had to work alone; I'm quite worn out. *alarmed* Uncle, there are tears in your eyes!

VOYNITSKI

Tears? It's nothing. . . . Nonsense! You looked at me
then as your dear mother used to. My dearest girl! *eagerly kisses her hands and face* My sister . . . my

dear sister. . . . Where is she now? If only she knew!
Ah, if she only knew!

SONYA

What, uncle? Knew what?

VOYNITSKI

It's painful, wrong somehow. Never mind. . . . Later
on . . . It's nothing. . . . I'll go. *goes out*

SONYA

Knocks at the door
Mikhail Lvovich! You're not asleep, are you? One
minute!

ASTROV

Through the door
Coming! *a moment later he comes out with his tie and
waistcoat on* What can I do for you?

SONYA

You can drink yourself if you don't find it disgusting,
but don't let my uncle drink, I implore you! It's bad
for him.

ASTROV

Very well. We won't drink any more. *pause* I will
go home at once. That's settled and signed. It'll be
daylight by the time they've got the horses ready.

SONYA

It's still raining. Wait till the morning.

ASTROV

The storm is passing us by; we'll only get a few drops.
I'll go. And please don't ask me to see your father
again. I tell him he has gout, and he tells me it's
rheumatism; I ask him to stay in bed, and he sits up
in a chair. And today he wouldn't even speak to me.

SONYA

Looks into the sideboard
Would you like something to eat?

UNCLE
VANYA

ASTROV

Well, perhaps.

SONYA

I like having little snacks at night. I believe there's something in the sideboard. They say he's had great success with the women, and he's been spoiled by them. Here, have some cheese. *both stand at the sideboard and eat*

ASTROV

I've had nothing to eat today, only drink. Your father is difficult. *takes a bottle from the sideboard* May I? *drinks a glass* There's no one here, and I can speak frankly. You know I don't believe I could stick it in your house for a month; I would be suffocated in this atmosphere. Your father, completely absorbed in his gout and his books; Uncle Vanya with his depression; your grandmother; and your stepmother too . . .

SONYA

What about my stepmother?

ASTROV

Everything ought to be beautiful about a human being: face, clothes, soul, and thoughts. She's beautiful, there's no denying that, but . . . she does nothing but eat, sleep, go for walks, charm us all by her beauty . . . nothing else. She has no responsibilities; other people work for her. Isn't that so? And an idle life can't be virtuous. *pause* However, perhaps I'm being too severe. I'm dissatisfied with life, like your Uncle Vanya, and so we're both turning into old grumblers.

SONYA

You're dissatisfied with life then?

ANTON
CHEKHOV

ASTROV

I love life as such—but our life, our everyday provincial

life in Russia, I just can't endure. I despise it with all my soul. As for my own life, God knows I can find nothing good in it at all. You know when you walk through a forest on a dark night and you see a small light gleaming in the distance, you don't notice your tiredness nor the darkness nor the prickly branches lashing you in the face. I work harder than anyone in the district—you know that. Fate batters me continuously; at times I suffer unbearably—but there's no small light in the distance. I'm not expecting anything for myself any longer. I don't love human beings. I haven't cared for anyone for years.

SONYA

Not for anyone?

ASTROV

No one. I feel a sort of fondness for your old nurse—for old times' sake. The peasants are all too much alike—undeveloped, living in squalor. As for the educated people—it's hard to get on with them. They tire me so. All of them, all our good friends here are shallow in thought, shallow in feeling, unable to see farther than their noses—or to put it quite bluntly—stupid. And the ones who are a bit more intelligent, of a higher mental caliber, are hysterical, positively rotten with introspection and futile cerebration. They whine; they are full of hatreds and are morbidly malicious; they sidle up to a man, look at him out of the corner of their eyes, and pronounce their judgment: "Oh, he's a psychopath!" or "Just a phrase-monger." And when they don't know how to label me, they say, "He's a queer fellow, very queer!" I love forests—that's queer; I don't eat meat—that's queer too. There isn't any direct, objective, unprejudiced attitude to people or nature left. No, there isn't! *about to drink*

Prevents him No, I beg you, I implore you, don't drink any more.

ASTROV

Why not?

SONYA

It's so unlike you! You have such poise; your voice is so soft. More than that, you are beautiful as no one else I know is beautiful. So why do you want to be like ordinary men, the kind who drink and play cards? Don't do it, I implore you! You always say that people don't create anything but merely destroy what has been given them from above. Then why, why are you destroying yourself? You mustn't, you mustn't, I beseech you, I implore you!

ASTROV

Holds out his hand to her
I won't drink any more!

SONYA

Give me your word.

ASTROV

My word of honor.

SONYA

Presses his hand warmly
Thank you!

ASTROV

Enough! My head's clear now. You see I'm quite sober—and I'll stay sober to the end of my days.   *looks at his watch*   Well, to continue. As I said, my time's over; it's too late for me now. I've aged too much, I've worked myself to a standstill, I've grown coarse and insensitive. I believe I could never really become fond of another human being. I don't love anybody and . . . never will now. What still does affect me is beauty.

ANTON
CHEKHOV

I can't remain indifferent to that. I believe that if
Yelena Andreyevna wanted to, for instance, she could
turn my head in a day. But that's not love, of course;
that's not affection.   *covers his eyes with his hand
and shudders*

SONYA

What is it?

ASTROV

Nothing. In Lent one of my patients died under
chloroform.

SONYA

It's time to forget about that.   *pause*   Tell me,
Mikhail Lvovich. If I had a girl friend or a young
sister and if you got to know that she . . . Well,
suppose that she loved you, what would you do?

ASTROV

Shrugging his shoulders

I don't know. Probably nothing. I would let her know
that I couldn't love her. Besides I've got too many
other things on my mind. However, if I'm going, I'd
better start now. I'll say good-bye, my dear girl, or we'll
not finish till morning.   *shakes hands with her*   I'll
go through the drawing room if I may, otherwise I'm
afraid your uncle may keep me.   *goes out*

SONYA

Alone   He didn't say anything to me. His soul and
his heart are still hidden from me, so why do I feel so
happy?   *laughs with happiness*   I told him: you have
poise and nobility of mind and such a soft voice. Did
it sound out of place? His voice vibrates and caresses.
I can almost feel it in the air now. But when I said that
to him about a younger sister, he didn't understand.
wringing her hands   Oh, how dreadful it is that I'm
not good-looking! How dreadful! I know I'm plain,
I know, I know! Last Sunday as people were coming

out of church I heard them talking about me and a woman said, "She's kind and generous, but what a pity she is so plain." So plain.

Enter Yelena Andreyevna

YELENA
Opens the windows
The storm's over. What lovely fresh air! *pause*
Where's the doctor?

SONYA
He's gone. . . .

YELENA
After a pause
Sofya!

SONYA
What?

YELENA
How long are you going to go on being sulky with me? We haven't done each other any harm, so why should we behave like enemies? Come, let us stop it.

SONYA
I wanted to myself. *embraces her* Yes, let's not be angry anymore.

YELENA
That's fine! *both are moved*

SONYA
Has papa gone to bed?

YELENA
No, he's sitting in the drawing room. We don't speak to each other for weeks on end, but heaven alone knows why. *seeing that the sideboard is open*
What's this?

ANTON
CHEKHOV

SONYA
Mikhail Lvovich has been having supper.

YELENA

There's wine too. Let's drink to our friendship.

SONYA

Yes, let's.

YELENA

Out of the same glass. *fills it* It's better like that.
Now we are real friends?

SONYA

Friends. *they drink and kiss each other* I've been
wanting to make up for ever so long, but I felt so
ashamed somehow. *cries*

YELENA

But why are you crying?

SONYA

Never mind. . . . There's no reason.

YELENA

Come, there, there. *cries* I'm a queer creature—I've
started crying too. *pause* You're angry with me
because you think I married your father for ulterior
motives. If you are impressed by oaths, I'll vow to you
that I married him for love. I was attracted by him as
a learned man, a celebrity. It wasn't real love; it was
all artificial—but you see at that time it seemed real
to me. I'm not to blame. But from the day of our
marriage you've been punishing me with those
shrewd, suspicious eyes of yours.

SONYA

Come, peace, peace! Let's forget about it!

YELENA

You mustn't look at people like that—it doesn't suit
you. You should believe everyone—or else you just
can't live. . . .

SONYA

After a pause
Tell me honestly, as a friend. Are you happy?

UNCLE
VANYA

YELENA

No.

SONYA

I knew that. One more question. Tell me frankly:
wouldn't you have liked your husband to be young?

YELENA

What a little girl you are still! Of course I would.
laughs Well, ask me something else, go ahead.

SONYA

Do you like the doctor?

YELENA

Yes, very much.

SONYA

Laughs Have I got a stupid face? Yes? He's gone,
but I can still hear his voice and his footsteps, and
when I glance at that dark window I can see his face
in it. Let me tell you about it. But I mustn't speak so
loudly; I feel ashamed. Come to my room; we'll talk
there. Do I seem stupid to you? Own up. Tell me
something about him.

YELENA

Well, what shall I tell you?

SONYA

He's so clever. He knows how to do things; he can do
anything. He treats the sick, and he plants forests too.

YELENA

It isn't a question of forests or medicine. My dear,
don't you understand? He's got talent! And do you
know what that means? Courage, freedom of mind,
breadth of outlook. He plants a tree and wonders what
will come of it in a thousand years' time and speculates
on the future happiness of mankind. Such people are
rare, and we must love them. He drinks; sometimes he
seems a little coarse—but what does it matter? A
talented man can't stay free from blemishes in Russia.

ANTON
CHEKHOV

Just think what sort of life this doctor leads! Impassable mud on the roads; frost; snow storms; vast distances; crude, primitive people; poverty and disease all around him—it's hard for a man who works and struggles day after day in such surroundings to keep pure and sober till he's forty. *kisses her* I wish you happiness with all my heart; you deserve it. *gets up* As for me, I'm just a tiresome person of no importance. In my music studies, in my home life, in my husband's house, in all my romantic affairs—in fact in everything I've just been a person of no importance. Really, Sonya, when you come to think of it, I'm a very, very unfortunate woman. *walks about in agitation* There's no happiness for me on this earth. None! Why do you laugh?

SONYA
Laughs, hiding her face
I am so happy. . . . So happy!

YELENA
I would like to play something. I would like to play something now.

SONYA
Do play! *embraces her* I can't sleep. Do play!

YELENA
In a minute. Your father isn't asleep. When he's unwell, music irritates him. Go and ask him. If he doesn't mind, I'll play. Go.

SONYA
I'm going. *goes out*

Watchman taps in the garden

YELENA
It's a long time since I played the piano. I will play and cry. . . . Cry like a foolish girl. *calling through the window* Is it you tapping, Yefim?

UNCLE
VANYA

WATCHMAN'S VOICE
Yes, me.

YELENA
Don't tap; the master's not well.

WATCHMAN'S VOICE
I'm just going.   *whistles*   Hey there! Good dog!
Come, boy! Good dog!

SONYA
After a pause, returning
We mustn't!

CURTAIN

ACT THREE

A drawing room in Serebryakov's house. Three doors, right, left, and center. Daytime.

Voynitski and Sonya are seated, and Yelena Andreyevna is walking about the stage, preoccupied.

VOYNITSKI

The *Herr* Professor has graciously expressed a wish that we should assemble in this drawing room at one o'clock. *looks at his watch* It is a quarter to. He wishes to make some communication to the world.

YELENA

Probably some business matter.

VOYNITSKI

He does no business of any kind. He just writes nonsense, grumbles, and feels jealous. He does nothing else.

SONYA

Reproachfully Uncle!

VOYNITSKI

Well, well, I apologize. *pointing to Yelena* Just look at her! She walks about staggering with sheer laziness. Wonderful! Wonderful!

YELENA

And you keep on droning away all the time, all day

long! Aren't you tired of it? *miserably* I'm dying of boredom. I don't know what to do.

SONYA

Shrugging her shoulders

Isn't there plenty to do? If only you wanted to . . .

YELENA

For instance?

SONYA

You could help in running the estate, teach children, help to look after the sick. Isn't there plenty to do? For instance, before you and papa came to live here, Uncle Vanya and I used to go to the market ourselves and sell the flour.

YELENA

I don't know how to. And I'm not interested. It's only in idealistic novels that people teach and doctor the peasants. How am I suddenly to start teaching and doctoring them for no earthly reason?

SONYA

Well, I just don't understand how you can help wanting to go and teach them. Wait a little; you'll get accustomed to the idea. *embraces her* Don't get bored, dear! *laughs* You're bored and you don't know what to do with yourself, but boredom and idleness are infectious. Look : Uncle Vanya isn't doing anything either, just following you like a shadow, and I've left my work and come running to you to have a chat. I've grown quite lazy; I can't help it! The doctor, Mikhail Lvovich, only used to come to see us very rarely, once a month—it was hard to persuade him to come. But now he comes here every day; he's neglecting his forestry and his practice. You must be a witch.

VOYNITSKI

Why be miserable? *with enthusiasm* Come, my

dear, wonderful woman, be sensible! A mermaid's
blood flows in your veins; so be a mermaid! Let
yourself go for once in your life! Fall head over heels
in love with some water sprite—and plunge headfirst
into deep water, so that the *Herr* Professor and all of
us just throw up our hands in amazement!

YELENA

Angrily   Leave me alone! How cruel all this is!   *is
about to go out*

VOYNITSKI

Prevents her   Come, come, my treasure, forgive me!
I apologize.   *kisses her hand*   Peace!

YELENA

Even an angel couldn't hold her patience with you,
you know.

VOYNITSKI

As a token of peace and harmony I'll bring you a
bunch of roses; I've had them ready for you since this
morning. Autumn roses; exquisite, mournful roses . . .
goes out

SONYA

Autumn roses; exquisite, mournful roses. . . .   *both
look through the window*

YELENA

It's September already. How are we going to live
through the winter here!   *pause*   Where's the doctor?

SONYA

In Uncle Vanya's room. Writing something. I'm glad
Uncle Vanya's gone. I must have a talk with you.

YELENA

What about?

SONYA

What about!   *lays her head on Yelena's bosom*

YELENA

Come, there, there.   *strokes her hair*   Don't . . .

UNCLE
VANYA

SONYA

I'm not good-looking.

YELENA

You have beautiful hair.

SONYA

No! *turns around to look at herself in a mirror* No! When a woman is plain, they always say, "You have beautiful eyes, you have beautiful hair. . . ." I've loved him now for six years; I love him more than I did my mother. Every moment I seem to hear him, to feel his hand in mine; and I look at the door, waiting, expecting him to come in at any moment. And you can see how I keep coming to you just to talk about him. Now he comes here every day, but he doesn't look at me—doesn't see me. . . . It's such a torment! I have no hope at all—none, none! *in despair* O Lord, give me strength. I've been praying all night. . . . I often go up to him, start talking to him, look into his eyes. I have no more pride, no strength left to control myself. I couldn't help it—yesterday I confessed to Uncle Vanya that I'm in love. And all the servants know that I love him.

YELENA

And he?

SONYA

He doesn't notice me.

YELENA

Musing He's a strange man. I've an idea. Let me have a talk with him. I'll be careful; I'll do it in a roundabout way. *pause* Yes, really. After all how much longer are you to remain in ignorance? Let me!

Sonya nods her head in consent

ANTON
CHEKHOV

That's fine. It won't be difficult to find out whether

he loves you or not. You must not feel ashamed,
darling. You don't need to worry—I'll question him so
carefully that he won't notice. All we want is to find
out whether it's yes or no.   *pause*   If not, then he
mustn't come here anymore, must he?

Sonya nods in agreement

It's easier to bear when you don't see him. We won't
put it off; I'll speak to him straight away. He was
going to show me some charts. Go and tell him that
I want to see him.

SONYA

In great agitation
You will tell me the whole truth?

YELENA

Yes, of course. I think it's better to know the truth
whatever it may be. It's not so dreadful as being kept
in ignorance. Trust me, dear.

SONYA

Yes, yes. I'll tell him that you want to see his charts.
is about to go, then stops near the door   No, ignorance
is better. At least there's some hope.

YELENA

What do you say?

SONYA

Nothing.   *goes out*

YELENA

Alone   There's nothing worse than knowing someone's secret and not being able to help.   *musing*   He's
not in love with her, that's obvious. But why shouldn't
he marry her? She is not pretty, but she'd make an
excellent wife for a country doctor at his time of life.   UNCLE
She's intelligent and so kind and pure. No, that's not   VANYA

the point. *pause* I understand the poor girl so well. In the middle of all this desperate boredom, with just gray shadows wandering around instead of human beings, with nothing but commonplace gossip to listen to from people who do nothing but eat, drink, and sleep, he appears from time to time—so different from the rest of them, handsome, interesting, attractive, like a bright moon rising in the darkness. To fall under the fascination of a man like that, to forget oneself. I believe I'm a little attracted myself. Yes, I'm bored when he's not around, and here I am smiling when I think of him. Uncle Vanya says I have mermaid's blood in my veins. "Let yourself go for once in your life." Well, perhaps that's what I ought to do. To fly away, free as a bird, away from all of you, from your sleepy faces and talk, to forget that you exist at all— every one of you!... But I'm too timid and shy. My conscience would torment me to distraction. He comes here every day. I can guess why he comes and already I feel guilty. I want to fall on my knees before Sonya, to ask her forgiveness and cry.

ASTROV

Comes in with a chart

Good morning to you! *shakes hands* You wanted to see my artistic handiwork?

YELENA

Yesterday you promised to show me some of your work. Are you free now?

ASTROV

But of course! *spreads the chart on a card table and fixes it down with thumbtacks* Tell me, where were you born?

ANTON
CHEKHOV

YELENA

Helping him In Petersburg.

ASTROV

And where did you study?

YELENA

At the School of Music.

ASTROV

I don't suppose this will interest you.

YELENA

Why not? It's true I don't know the country, but I've read a great deal.

ASTROV

I have a table of my own here. . . . In Ivan Petrovich's room. When I'm completely tired out—to the point of utter stupefaction—I leave everything and escape here to amuse myself for an hour or two with this thing. Ivan Petrovich and Sofya Aleksandrovna click away at their counting beads, and I sit beside them at my table and mess around with my paints—and I'm warm and quiet, and the cricket chirps. But I don't allow myself this pleasure very often, just once a month.   *pointing to the chart*   Now look at this. It's a map of our district as it was fifty years ago. The dark and light green stand for forest; half of the whole area was covered with forest. Where there's a sort of network of red over the green, elk and wild goats were common. I show both the flora and the fauna here. This lake was the home of swans, geese, and ducks. There was "a power" of birds, as the old people say, of all kinds, no end to them: they used to fly around in clouds. Besides the villages and hamlets you can see all sorts of small settlements scattered here and there— little farms, monasteries, water mills. Cattle and horses were numerous—that's shown by the blue color. For instance there's a lot of blue in this part of the region. There was any number of horses here, and every

UNCLE
VANYA

252 homestead had three on the average. *pause* Now let us look lower down. This is how it was twenty-five years ago. Already only a third of the area is under forest. The goats have disappeared, but there are still some elk. The green and the blue colors are paler, and so on. Now look at the third section—the map showing the district as it is now. There's still some green here and there, but it's not continuous—it's in patches. The elk, swans, and woodgrouse have all disappeared. There's not a trace of the small farms and monasteries and mills that were there before. In general it's an unmistakable picture of gradual decay which will obviously be completed in another ten or fifteen years. You may say that it is the influence of civilization, that the old way of life naturally had to give place to the new. Yes and I would agree—if on the site of these ruined forests there were now roads and railways, if there were workshops and factories and schools. Then the people would have been healthier, better off, and better educated. But there's nothing of the sort here! There are still the same swamps and mosquitoes, the same absence of roads and the dire poverty and typhus and diphtheria and fires. Here we have a picture of decay due to an insupportable struggle for existence. It is decay caused by inertia, by ignorance, by utter irresponsibility—as when a sick, hungry, shivering man, simply to save what is left of his life and to protect his children, instinctively, unconsciously clutches at anything that will satisfy his hunger and keep him warm and in doing so destroys everything, without a thought for tomorrow. Already practically everything has been destroyed, but nothing has been created to take its place. *coldly* I see from your expression that it doesn't interest you.

ANTON
CHEKHOV

YELENA

But I understand so little about all this.

ASTROV

There's nothing to understand. You're just not
interested.

YELENA

To be quite frank, my mind was on something else.
Forgive me. I want to put you through a little
interrogation, and I feel rather embarrassed. I don't
know how to begin.

ASTROV

An interrogation?

YELENA

Yes, an interrogation, but . . . a fairly innocent one.
Let's sit down! *they sit down* It concerns a certain
young person. We'll talk frankly, like friends, without
beating around the bush. We'll talk it over and forget
everything we said. Agreed?

ASTROV

Agreed.

YELENA

The matter concerns my stepdaughter, Sonya. Tell
me, do you like her?

ASTROV

Yes, I respect her.

YELENA

Do you like her as a woman?

ASTROV

After a brief pause
No.

YELENA

One thing more—and that'll be the end. Have you
noticed anything?

ASTROV

Nothing.

UNCLE
VANYA

YELENA

Taking him by the hand
You don't love her, I see it from your eyes. She is
suffering. Understand that, and . . . stop coming here.

ASTROV

Rises My time's past. Besides I've got too much to
do. *shrugging his shoulders* When could I find
time? *he is embarrassed*

YELENA

Ough! What an unpleasant conversation! I feel as
though I've been carrying a ton weight around. Anyway we've finished now, thank heaven! Let's forget it,
as if we hadn't talked at all, and . . . and go away.
You're an intelligent man; you will understand. *pause*
I feel I'm quite flushed.

ASTROV

If you'd told me a month or two ago, I might perhaps
have considered it, but now . . . *shrugs his shoulders*
But if she is suffering, then of course . . . There's only
one thing I don't understand: why did you have to have
this interrogation? *looks into her eyes and shakes his
finger at her* You're a sly one!

YELENA

What does that mean?

ASTROV

Laughs Sly! Suppose Sonya is suffering—I'm
prepared to think it probable—but what was the
purpose of this cross-examination? *preventing her
from speaking, with animation* Please don't try to
look astonished. You know perfectly well why I come
here every day. Why and on whose account—you know
very well indeed. You charming bird of prey, don't
look at me like that; I'm a wise old sparrow.

ANTON
CHEKHOV

YELENA

Perplexed Bird of prey! I don't understand at all!

ASTROV

A beautiful, fluffy weasel . . . You must have a
victim! Here I've been doing nothing for a whole
month. I've dropped everything. I seek you out
hungrily—and you are awfully pleased about it,
awfully. Well, what am I to say? I'm conquered, but
you knew that without an interrogation! *crossing
his arms and bowing his head* I submit. Here I am;
devour me!

YELENA

Have you gone out of your mind?

ASTROV

Laughs sardonically You are coy.

YELENA

Oh, I'm not so bad or not so mean as you think! On
my word of honor! *tries to go out*

ASTROV

Barring her way

I'll go away today. I won't come here again, but . . .
takes her by the hand and glances around Where
shall I see you? Tell me quickly, where? Someone may
come in here; tell me quickly. *passionately* How
wonderful, how glorious you are! One kiss . . . If I
could only kiss your fragrant hair . . .

YELENA

I swear to you . . .

ASTROV

Prevents her from speaking

Why swear anything? There's no need to. No need for
unnecessary words. Oh, how beautiful you are! What
lovely hands! *kisses her hands*

YELENA

That's enough. . . . Go away. *withdraws her hands*
You are forgetting yourself.

UNCLE
VANYA

ASTROV

Speak, speak! Where shall we meet tomorrow? *puts his arm around her waist* You see, it's inevitable— we must see each other. *kisses her*

At that moment Voynitski comes in with a bunch of roses and stops just inside the door

YELENA

Not seeing Voynitski
Spare me. . . . Leave me alone. *lays her head on Astrov's chest* No! *tries to go out*

ASTROV

Holding her by the waist
Come to the plantation tomorrow about two o'clock. Yes? Yes? You will come?

YELENA

Seeing Voynitski Let me go! *in extreme confusion goes to the window* This is dreadful!

VOYNITSKI

Lays the roses on a chair; in agitation wipes his face and neck with a handkerchief
Never mind . . . no . . . never mind.

ASTROV

With bravado The weather is not too bad today, my dear Ivan Petrovich. It was overcast in the morning as though it were going to rain, but now it's sunny. It must be admitted that the autumn has turned out very fine . . . and the winter corn is quite promising. *rolls up his chart* The only thing is—the days are getting short. *goes out*

YELENA

Goes quickly up to Voynitski
You will try, you will do your utmost to see that my
husband and I leave here today for certain? Do you hear? Today for certain!

VOYNITSKI
Wiping his face
What? Oh, yes . . . very well. . . .

YELENA
Nervously   Do you hear? I must get away from here
this very day!

Enter Serebryakov, Sonya, Telegin, and Marina

TELEGIN
I'm not feeling too well myself, Your Excellency. I've
been doing poorly for the last two days. Something
the matter with my head . . .

SEREBRYAKOV
But where are the others? I don't like this house. It's
like a sort of labyrinth. Twenty-six enormous rooms,
people wander off in all directions, and there's no
finding anyone.   *rings*   Ask Marya Vasilievna and
Yelena Andreyevna to come here!

YELENA
I'm here.

SEREBRYAKOV
Please sit down, my friends.

SONYA
Going up to Yelena, impatiently
What did he say?

YELENA
I'll tell you later.

SONYA
You're trembling? You're upset?   *looks searchingly
into her face*   I understand. He said he wouldn't be
coming here any more . . . yes?   *pause*   Tell me: yes?

Yelena nods her head

SEREBRYAKOV   UNCLE
To Telegin   One can put up with ill health after all.   VANYA

But what I can't stomach is the whole pattern of life in the country. I feel as if I had been cast off the earth on to some strange planet. Do sit down, friends, please! Sonya!

Sonya does not hear him; she stands and hangs her head sadly

Sonya! *pause* She doesn't hear. *to Marina* You sit down too, Nanny.

The nurse sits down and starts knitting a stocking

I beg you, my friends, lend me your ears, as the saying goes. *laughs*

VOYNITSKI
Agitated Maybe I'm not needed here? Can I go?

SEREBRYAKOV
No, you're needed more than anyone.

VOYNITSKI
What do you require from me?

SEREBRYAKOV
Require from you . . . Why—are you annoyed at something? *pause* If I've offended you in any way, please excuse me.

VOYNITSKI
You don't have to adopt that tone. Let's come to business. What is it you want?

Enter Marya Vasilievna

SEREBRYAKOV
Here is *maman.* Let me begin, my friends. *pause* I have invited you here, ladies and gentlemen, to inform you that the inspector general is coming to visit us. But, joking apart, this is a serious matter. I have called you together, my friends, to ask your help and advice

ANTON
CHEKHOV

and, knowing how obliging you always are, I hope to receive it. I'm an academic, bookish man, and I've never had anything to do with practical life. I must have guidance from people better informed than I am, and so I want to ask you, Ivan Petrovich, and also you, Ilya Ilyich, and you, *maman*. The point is, *manet omnes una nox:* we are all mortal. I'm an old and ailing man, and I think it's high time to settle the matter of my property in so far as it concerns my family. My own life is over now; I'm not thinking of myself. But I have a young wife and an unmarried daughter. *pause* It is impossible for me to go on living in the country. We are not made for country life. But to live in town on the income we are receiving from this estate is also impossible. Suppose we sold the forest—that would be an exceptional measure which could not be repeated every year. We must find ways which will guarantee us a permanent, more or less definite income. One such measure has occurred to me, and I would like to submit it for your consideration. Omitting the details, I will describe it in rough outline. Our estate yields on the average not more than two percent on its capital value. I suggest we sell it. If we invest the money in suitable securities, we should get from four to five percent, and I think we might even have a few thousand rubles to spare, which would enable us to buy a small villa in Finland.

VOYNITSKI
Wait a moment. Surely I haven't been hearing correctly. Say that again.

SEREBRYAKOV
I suggest putting the money in suitable securities and with whatever is left buying a villa in Finland.

VOYNITSKI
Not Finland. You said something else.

SEREBRYAKOV

I suggested we sell the estate.

VOYNITSKI

That's it. You sell the estate—that's a fine idea—
magnificent. And where do you propose I should go—
with my old mother and Sonya here?

SEREBRYAKOV

We will discuss all that in due course. We can't do
everything at once.

VOYNITSKI

Wait a moment. It looks as though I must have been
incredibly stupid all this time. Until now I've been
foolish enough to believe that this estate belonged to
Sonya. My father bought it as a dowry for my sister.
I've been too simple; not interpreting the law like a
Turk, I thought that my sister's estate passed to Sonya.

SEREBRYAKOV

Yes, the estate belongs to Sonya. Who's disputing it?
Without Sonya's consent I will not venture to sell it.
Besides I am suggesting that this should be done for
Sonya's benefit.

VOYNITSKI

Its inconceivable, inconceivable! Either I've gone out
of my mind or . . . or . . .

MARYA VASILIEVNA

Jean, don't contradict Aleksandr. Believe me, he
knows better than we do what's good for us and
what isn't.

VOYNITSKI

No, give me some water. *drinks water* Say what
you like, anything!

SEREBRYAKOV

I don't understand why you're so upset. I'm not saying
that my plan is ideal. If everybody finds it unsuitable,
I won't insist on it.

ANTON
CHEKHOV

TELEGIN

Embarrassed   Toward learning, Your Excellency,
I have not merely a feeling of reverence, but a sort of
family relationship as well. The brother of my
brother's wife, Konstantin Trofimovich Lakedemonov
—perhaps you know him?—was an M.A.

VOYNITSKI

Stop, Waffles, we're talking business. Wait a little. . . .
Later on.   *to Serebryakov*   Here, ask him. This
estate was bought from his uncle.

SEREBRYAKOV

Indeed! But why should I ask him? Why ever . . .?

VOYNITSKI

The estate was originally bought for ninety-five
thousand rubles. My father only paid seventy thousand,
and twenty-five thousand remained on mortgage. Now
please do listen. This estate would never have been
bought if I hadn't given up my share of the inheritance
in favor of my sister, whom I loved dearly. What's
more, I worked like an ox for ten years and paid off
the whole mortgage.

SEREBRYAKOV

I regret that I started this discussion.

VOYNITSKI

The estate is free from debt and in good condition
simply because of my own efforts. And now that I've
grown old, I'm to be kicked out!

SEREBRYAKOV

I don't understand what you're driving at!

VOYNITSKI

For twenty-five years I've been managing this estate!
I've been working and sending you money like the
most conscientious steward you could have, but all this
time you've never once thanked me for it. All this

time—when I was young, and now just the same—I've been getting a salary of five hundred rubles a year from you—a pittance!—and never once have you thought of adding a single ruble to it!

SEREBRYAKOV

Ivan Petrovich, how was I to know? I'm not a practical man. I don't understand anything about these matters. You could have added as much as you liked.

VOYNITSKI

Yes indeed, why didn't I steal? Why don't you all laugh at me now because I didn't steal? It would have been fair enough, and I wouldn't have been a pauper now!

MARYA VASILIEVNA

Sternly Jean!

TELEGIN

In agitation Vanya, my dear, don't, don't. . . . I'm all trembling. Why spoil our good relations? *embraces him* You mustn't.

VOYNITSKI

For twenty-five years I sat with my mother here, buried like a mole in these four walls. All our thoughts and feelings belonged to you alone. By day we talked of you and your work. We were proud of you; we uttered your name with reverence. We wasted our nights reading books and magazines which now fill me with contempt.

TELEGIN

Don't, Vanya, don't. . . . I can't bear it.

SEREBRYAKOV

Angrily I don't understand what it is you want.

VOYNITSKI

To us you were a being of a higher order, and we knew your articles by heart. But now my eyes are opened! I can see it all! You write about art, but you don't understand anything about art! All your works,

those works which I used to love, are not worth a
kopeck! You've been deceiving us!

SEREBRYAKOV

Make him stop this! I'll go!

YELENA

Ivan Petrovich, I insist that you stop. Do you hear?

VOYNITSKI

I will not be silent! *barring Serebryakov's way*
Wait; I haven't finished yet! You've ruined my life!
I haven't lived. I have not lived! Thanks to you I've
destroyed, I've annihilated, the best years of my life!
You've been my worst enemy!

TELEGIN

I can't bear it.... I can't.... I'm going. *goes out
in great agitation*

SEREBRYAKOV

What do you want from me? And what right have
you to speak to me like this? You nonentity! If the
estate is yours, take it! I don't need it!

YELENA

I'm going to get away from this hell this very
minute! *screams* I can't stand it any longer!

VOYNITSKI

My life is ruined! I have talent, courage, intelligence.
If I had had a normal life, I might have been a
Schopenhauer, a Dostoevski.... Oh, I'm talking
rubbish! I'm going out of my mind. Mother, I'm in
despair! Mother!

MARYA VASILIEVNA

Sternly Do as Aleksandr tells you.

SONYA

Kneels before the nurse and huddles up against her
Nanny! Nanny!

VOYNITSKI

Mother! What am I to do? No, you don't have to

UNCLE
VANYA

tell me! I know what I must do.   *to Serebryakov*
You'll remember me!   *goes out through middle door*

Marya Vasilievna follows him

SEREBRYAKOV

What does he mean by this behavior? Take the madman away! I can't possibly live under the same roof with him. He lives there   *points at the middle door*   almost next door to me. Make him move into the village or into the lodge—or I'll move—but I can't remain in the same house with him.

YELENA

To her husband

We'll leave here today! We must make arrangements immediately.

SEREBRYAKOV

That nonentity!

SONYA

On her knees, turns to her father and speaks tearfully and with agitation

You must have pity, papa! Uncle Vanya and I are so unhappy!   *restraining her despair*   You must have pity! Remember—when you were younger Uncle Vanya and grandmamma used to spend whole nights translating books for you, copying your papers. . . . Whole nights on end! Whole nights! Uncle Vanya and I worked incessantly; we were afraid to spend a kopeck on ourselves and sent it all to you. We really did earn our daily bread! I'm saying it all wrong—all wrong—but you must understand us, papa! You must be charitable!

YELENA

In agitation, to her husband

ANTON
CHEKHOV
Aleksandr, for heaven's sake, go and talk it over with him. I implore you!

Very well, I will talk it over with him. I'm not
accusing him of anything; I'm not angry. But you
must agree with me that his behavior is very strange,
to say the least of it. Very well, I'll go and see him.
goes out through the middle door

YELENA

Be as gentle as you can with him. Try to reassure
him.   *follows him*

SONYA

Nestling up to the nurse
Nanny! Nanny!

MARINA

Never mind, child. The ganders will cackle a bit—and
then they'll leave off. They'll cackle and leave off.

SONYA

Nanny!

MARINA

Stroking her head
You're shivering as if you were out in a frost! There,
there, my little orphan, God is merciful. A drink of
lime-flower tea or hot raspberry, and it'll go away. . . .
Don't get so upset, my little orphan.   *looking at the
middle door, with annoyance*   What a row they're
making, the ganders! Damn them!

*A shot is heard offstage, then a shriek from Yelena;
Sonya starts*

Ough! Damn them!

SEREBRYAKOV

Runs in, staggering in terror
Stop him! Stop him! He's gone mad!

UNCLE
VANYA

Yelena and Voynitski struggle in the doorway

YELENA

Trying to take a revolver from him
Give it to me! Give it to me, I tell you!

VOYNITSKI

Let me go, Hélène! Let me go! *freeing himself from
her, runs in and looks around for Serebryakov* Where
is he? Ah, there he is! *fires at him* Bang! *pause*
Missed? Missed again! *furiously* Damn it!...
Devil... devil take it! *flings the revolver on the floor
and sinks onto a chair, exhausted*

*Serebryakov looks stunned. Yelena leans against the
wall, almost fainting*

YELENA

Take me away from here! Take me away! Kill me!...
But I can't stay here, I can't!

VOYNITSKI

In despair Oh, what have I done? What am I doing?

SONYA

Softly Nanny, dear! Nanny!

CURTAIN

ACT FOUR

Voynitski's room, which serves both as his bedroom and his office. By the window a large table with account books and various papers; also a bureau, bookcases, and scales. A smaller table is set apart for Astrov with paints, drawing materials, and a large portfolio. A cage with a starling in it. On the wall a map of Africa, obviously serving no useful purpose here. A large divan upholstered in American cloth. On the left, a door leading to other rooms; on the right, a door into the hall. In front of the right-hand door there is a mat to protect the floor from mud from the peasants' boots. It is an autumn evening and is very quiet.

Telegin and Marina, sitting opposite one another, are winding wool.

TELEGIN

Hurry up, Marina Timofeevna. They'll soon be calling us to say good-bye. They've ordered the horses to be brought around.

MARINA

Tries to wind faster
There isn't much left.

TELEGIN

They're going to Kharkov. Going to live there.

MARINA

That will be much better.

TELEGIN

They've had a fright. Yelena Andreyevna keeps saying, "I won't stay here another hour. Let's get away. Let's get away." "When we've lived in Kharkov for a bit and had a look around, we'll send for our things," she says. They're traveling light. It seems they're not ordained to live here, Marina Timofeevna. They're not ordained to. Such is the will of Providence.

MARINA

It's better so. The row they made this morning—and shooting too—a regular disgrace!

TELEGIN

Yes, a subject worthy of the brush of Ayvazovski, one might say.

MARINA

What a sight for my old eyes! *pause* We'll be living again as we used to—in the old way. Morning tea soon after seven, dinner at twelve, and in the evening we'll sit down to supper. Everything as it should be, just like other people. . . . Like Christians. *with a sigh* It's a long time since I tasted noodles, sinner that I am!

TELEGIN

Yes, it's a long time since they had noodles in this house. *pause* A very long time. Marina Timofeevna, as I was walking through the village this morning, the shopkeeper shouted after me, "Hey, you scrounger . . . Living on other people, you are!" I felt so hurt!

ANTON
CHEKHOV

MARINA

You shouldn't take any notice, dearie. We all live on

God. You and Sonya and Ivan Petrovich are just the
same. None of us sits with folded hands; we are all
working—all of us! Where's Sonya?

TELEGIN

In the garden. She keeps walking around with the
doctor looking for Ivan Petrovich. They're afraid he
may do himself harm.

MARINA

Where's his revolver?

TELEGIN

In a whisper
I've hidden it in the cellar.

MARINA

With a smile
What goings-on!

Enter Voynitski and Astrov from outside

VOYNITSKI

Leave me alone. *to Marina and Telegin* Please go
away from here. Leave me alone—if it's only for an
hour! I can't stand this supervision.

TELEGIN

Of course, Vanya. *goes out on tiptoe*

MARINA

You old gander! Ga-ga-ga! *gathers up her wool and
goes out*

VOYNITSKI

Leave me alone!

ASTROV

With the greatest pleasure! I should have left here
hours ago, but I must repeat I'm not going away until
you give me back what you took from me.

VOYNITSKI

I haven't taken anything from you.

ASTROV

I'm speaking seriously—don't keep me waiting. I
should have gone long ago.

VOYNITSKI

I didn't take anything from you.   *both sit down*

ASTROV

No? Well, I'll wait a little longer; and then, I'm sorry,
but I'll have to use force. We'll tie your hands together
and search you. I'm speaking absolutely in earnest.

VOYNITSKI

As you please.   *pause*   To have made such a fool of
myself—firing twice and missing both times! I will
never forgive myself for that!

ASTROV

If you really felt like shooting someone, you might as
well have taken a potshot at yourself.

VOYNITSKI

Shrugging his shoulders

It's queer! Here I've tried to commit a murder, and
yet no one arrests me, no one charges me with
anything. It must mean they think I'm a madman.
with an angry laugh   I'm mad—but people who
conceal their utter lack of talent, their dullness, their
complete heartlessness, under the guise of the professor,
the purveyor of learned magic—they aren't mad.
Women aren't mad who marry old men and then
deceive them for everyone to see. I saw you with your
arms around her! I saw it!

ASTROV

Yes, I did put my arms around her, and as for you—you
can take this.   *thumbs his nose at him*

VOYNITSKI

ANTON   *Looking at the door*
CHEKHOV   The earth must be mad because it still supports you.

ASTROV

Now you're being just silly!

VOYNITSKI

Well, I'm mad. I'm irresponsible. I have the right to say silly things.

ASTROV

That's an old trick. You're not mad; you're simply a crank. A silly old fool. I used to think that every crank was sick or abnormal. But now I believe it's normal for a man to be a crank. You are perfectly normal.

VOYNITSKI

Covers his face with his hands

I feel so ashamed. If you only knew how ashamed I feel! This acute sense of shame—it's worse than any pain! *miserably* It's unbearable. *leans over the table* What am I to do? What am I to do?

ASTROV

Nothing.

VOYNITSKI

Give me something! Oh, my God! I'm forty-seven. If I live to be sixty, I've got another thirteen years. What a time! How am I to get through those thirteen years? What shall I do? How shall I fill in the time? Ah, don't you see . . . *squeezing Astrov's hand convulsively* Don't you see, if only you could live the rest of your life in some new way! To wake up on a clear, calm morning and feel that you're starting your life over again, that all your past is forgotten, blown away like smoke. *weeps* To begin a new life . . . Tell me how to begin. . . . What with . . .

ASTROV

With annoyance Oh, get away with you! A new life indeed! Our situation's hopeless—yours and mine!

VOYNITSKI

Do you mean that?

ASTROV

I'm certain of it.

VOYNITSKI

Give me something. *pointing at his heart* I've a
burning sensation here.

ASTROV

Shouts angrily Shut up! *softening* The people who
come a hundred years or a couple of hundred years after
us and despise us for having lived in so stupid and
tasteless a fashion—perhaps they'll find a way to be
happy. As for us . . . There's only one hope for you
and me. The hope that when we're at rest in our
graves we may see visions—perhaps even pleasant
ones. *with a sigh* Yes, my friend! In the whole of
this province there have only been two decent,
cultured people—you and I. But ten years of this
contemptible routine, this trivial provincial life, has
swallowed us up, poisoned our blood with its putrid
vapors, until now we've become just as petty as all the
rest. *with a sudden animation* But don't you try to
talk me out of it : give me back what you took from
me.

VOYNITSKI

I didn't take anything from you.

ASTROV

You took a bottle of morphine out of my traveling
medicine chest. *pause* Look here now : if you really
feel you must put an end to yourself, why don't you
go to the woods and shoot yourself there? But do give
me back the morphine or else there will be talk and
suspicion. People might think I'd given it to you. It'll be
quite enough to have to do your postmortem. Do you
think I will find it interesting?

Enter Sonya

ANTON
CHEKHOV

VOYNITSKI

Leave me alone.

ASTROV

To Sonya Sofya Aleksandrovna, your uncle has stolen a bottle of morphine from my medicine chest and won't give it back. Tell him that it's . . . well . . . it's not a bit clever of him. Besides I haven't the time to waste. I ought to be going.

SONYA

Uncle Vanya, did you take the morphine?

ASTROV

After a pause

He did. I'm certain of it.

SONYA

Give it back. Why do you frighten us like this? *with tenderness* Give it back, Uncle Vanya! I must say I'm just as unhappy as you are, but I don't despair all the same. I bear it, and I will continue to bear it till my life comes to its natural end. You must bear it too. *pause* Give it back! *kisses his hand* My dear, kind uncle—give it up, dear! *weeps* You're so good; I know you'll feel sorry for us and give it back. You'll have to bear it, uncle! You must bear it!

VOYNITSKI

Takes a bottle out of his desk and hands it to Astrov

Here, take it! *to Sonya* But we must start work at once; we must start doing something or else I can't . . . I can't . . .

SONYA

Yes, yes, work. As soon as we've seen the others off, we'll settle down to work. *nervously turning over the papers on the table* We've been neglecting everything.

ASTROV

Puts the bottle into his case and tightens the straps

Now I can be on my way.

UNCLE
VANYA

YELENA

Ivan Petrovich, are you here? We're just going. Go and see Aleksandr; he wants to say something to you.

SONYA

Go along, Uncle Vanya.   *takes Voynitski's arm*
Let's go. You and papa must make it up. It's essential.

Sonya and Voynitski go out

YELENA

I'm going away.   *gives Astrov her hand*

ASTROV

Already?

YELENA

The horses are waiting.

ASTROV

Good-bye.

YELENA

Today you promised me you'd go away from here.

ASTROV

I haven't forgotten. I'm just going.   *pause*   Did you get frightened?   *takes her hand*   Is it really so frightening?

YELENA

Yes.

ASTROV

Why not stay all the same? Well? Tomorrow, at the plantation . . .

YELENA

No. It's settled. The reason I'm looking at you so fearlessly now is just that our departure has been settled. I only ask one thing of you: do think better of me. I would like you to respect me.

ANTON
CHEKHOV

Oh! *makes a gesture of impatience* Stay, I beg you.
You must admit you have nothing whatever to do,
you have absolutely no object in life, nothing to
occupy your mind with; so that sooner or later you'll
be bound to give way to your feelings—it's inevitable.
And it will be better if that happens not in Kharkov
or somewhere in Kursk, but down here in the lap of
nature. At least it's poetical here, quite beautiful in
fact. There are forestry plantations, half-ruined
country houses in the Turgenev style. . . .

YELENA

How funny you are. . . . I'm angry with you, and
yet . . . I'll remember you with pleasure. You're an
interesting, original man. We will never see each other
again, and so why should I conceal it? You did turn
my head a little. Come, let us shake hands and part
friends. Think well of me.

ASTROV

Shakes hands with her
Yes, you'd better go. *musing* You seem to be so
good and warm-hearted, and yet there's something
strange about your personality. You just happened to
come along with your husband, and all of us here,
who'd been working and running around and trying
to create something, we all had to drop everything
and occupy ourselves wholly with you and your
husband's gout. You two infected all of us with your
indolence. I was attracted by you and I've done nothing
for a whole month. And in the meantime people have
been ill and the peasants have been using my woods,
my plantations of young trees, as pasture for their
cattle. So you see, wherever you and your husband go,
you bring along destruction with you. I'm joking, of
course, but still . . . it *is* strange. I'm convinced that

UNCLE
VANYA

if you'd stayed on here the devastation would have been immense. I would have been ruined . . . and you wouldn't have fared too well either. Go away then. *La commedia è finita!*

YELENA

Takes a pencil from his table and quickly puts it in her pocket

I'm taking this pencil as a keepsake.

ASTROV

It is strange somehow. Here we've known one another, and all at once for some reason . . . we will never see each other again. That's the way with everything in this world. While there's no one here—before Uncle Vanya comes in with a bunch of flowers—allow me . . . to kiss you . . . good-bye. Yes? *kisses her on the cheek* There . . . That's fine.

YELENA

I wish you every happiness. *looks around* Well, here goes—for once in my life! *embraces him impulsively, and both at once quickly step back from each other* I must be off.

ASTROV

Go as soon as you can. If the horses are ready, you'd better be off!

YELENA

I think someone's coming. *both listen*

ASTROV

Finita!

Enter Serebryakov, Voynitski, Marya Vasilievna carrying a book, Telegin, and Sonya

SEREBRYAKOV

Let us let bygones be bygones. What with everything that's happened, I've thought and lived through so much in the last few hours that I believe I could write

a whole treatise on how one should conduct one's
life—for the benefit of posterity. I gladly accept your
apologies and I ask you to forgive me too. Good-bye!
he and Voynitski embrace and kiss each other three times
VOYNITSKI
You'll be receiving the same amount as before,
regularly. Everything will be as it was before.

Yelena embraces Sonya

SEREBRYAKOV
Kisses Marya Vasilievna's hand
Maman . . .
MARYA
Kissing him Aleksandr, do have your photograph
taken again and send it to me. You know how much
you mean to me.
TELEGIN
Good-bye, Your Excellency! Don't forget us!
SEREBRYAKOV
Kisses his daughter
Good-bye. Good-bye everyone! *shakes hands with
Astrov* Thank you for the pleasure of your company.
I respect your attitude of mind, your enthusiasms, your
spontaneity; but permit an old man to add one thing
to his farewell greetings: you must try to do real work,
my friends, yes, real work! *he bows to them all* I
wish you all happiness and good fortune! *goes out,
followed by Marya Vasilievna and Sonya*
VOYNITSKI
Warmly kisses Yelena's hand
Good-bye. Forgive me. We will never see one another
again.
YELENA
Moved Good-bye, dear Ivan Petrovich. *kisses him
on the head and goes out*

ASTROV

To Telegin   Waffles, you might tell them to bring
my horses around too.

TELEGIN

Certainly, my dear friend.   *goes out*

Astrov and Voynitski remain alone

ASTROV

*Clears the paints from the table and puts them away
in his case*
Well, why don't you go and see them off?

VOYNITSKI

Let them go. As for me—I . . . I can't. I'm depressed.
I must occupy myself with something as soon as I can.
Work, work!   *rummages among the papers*

A pause; the sound of harness bells is heard

ASTROV

They've gone. The professor's glad, that's certain.
Wild horses won't drag him back.

MARINA

Enters   They've gone.   *sits down in an easy chair
and knits a stocking*

SONYA

Enters   They've gone.   *wipes her eyes*   God grant
them a safe journey.   *to her uncle*   Well, Uncle
Vanya, let's start doing something.

VOYNITSKI

Work, work . . .

SONYA

It's a long, long time since we sat at this table, just
the two of us.   *lights the lamp on the table*   There
doesn't seem to be any ink.   *takes the inkstand, goes
to the cupboard, and fills it with ink*   But I feel sad
now they've gone.

MARYA VASILIEVNA
Comes in slowly
Gone! *sits down and becomes absorbed in reading*
SONYA
*Sits down at the table and turns over the pages of the
account book*
First of all, Uncle Vanya, let's write out the bills.
We've neglected it all dreadfully. Someone sent for
his account again today. You make it out. While you
do one, I'll do another.
VOYNITSKI
Writes Delivered . . . to . . . Mr. . . . *both write in
silence*
MARINA
Yawns I feel like going to sleep. . . .
ASTROV
How quiet it is! The pens scratch, the cricket sings.
It's warm and snug. I don't feel like leaving here.

The sound of harness bells is heard

My horses are coming. There's nothing left for me but
to say good-bye to you, my friends—to say good-bye
to my table and—be off! *packs up his maps in the
portfolio*
MARINA
Why are you in such a hurry? I'd stay on if I were you.
ASTROV
I can't.
VOYNITSKI
Writes Remaining to your debit: two rubles,
seventy-five kopecks.

A workman comes in

WORKMAN
Mikhail Lvovich, the horses are ready.

UNCLE
VANYA

ASTROV

I heard them. *hands him the medicine chest, the bag, and the portfolio* Here, take these. See that you don't bend the portfolio.

WORKMAN

Very good, sir. *goes out*

ASTROV

Well . . . *approaches them to say good-bye*

SONYA

When will we see you again?

ASTROV

Not before next summer, I expect. Hardly in the winter. Naturally if anything happens you'll let me know and I'll come. *shakes hands with them* Thank you for your hospitality, your kindness—for everything, in fact. *goes to the nurse and kisses her on the head* Good-bye, old woman!

MARINA

So you're going before you've had tea?

ASTROV

I don't want any, nurse.

MARINA

Perhaps you'll have a drop of vodka?

ASTROV

Irresolutely Perhaps . . .

Marina goes out

after a pause One of my horses has gone lame for some reason. I noticed it yesterday when Petrushka took it to water.

VOYNITSKI

You must change its shoes.

ASTROV

I'll have to call in at the blacksmith's in Rozhdestvennoye. It can't be helped. *walks up to the map of*

Africa and looks at it I suppose down there in Africa
the heat must be terrific now!

VOYNITSKI
Yes, very likely.

MARINA
Returns carrying a tray with a glass of vodka and a
piece of bread
Here you are.

Astrov drinks vodka

Good health, my dear. *makes a low bow* Why don't
you eat some bread with it?

ASTROV
No, that'll do for me. Well, good luck to you all! *to*
Marina Don't see me off, nurse. There's no need to.

Astrov goes out, Sonya following with a candle to see
him off. Marina sits down in her easy chair

VOYNITSKI
Writing February the second, linseed oil, twenty
pounds. . . . February the sixteenth, linseed oil again,
twenty pounds. Buckwheat . . .

A pause. The sound of harness bells

MARINA
He's gone. . . .

SONYA
After a pause, comes back and puts the candle on the
table
He's gone.

VOYNITSKI
Counts on the abacus and writes down
Total . . . fifteen . . . twenty-five . . .

UNCLE
VANYA

MARINA

Yawns Lord forgive us our sins.

Telegin enters on tiptoe, sits down by the door, and quietly tunes his guitar

VOYNITSKI

To Sonya, passing his hand over her hair
My child, there's such a weight on my heart! Oh, if only you knew how my heart aches!

SONYA

Well, what can we do? We must go on living! *pause*
We will go on living, Uncle Vanya. We will live through a long, long succession of days and tedious evenings. We will patiently suffer the trials which fate imposes on us. We will work for others, now and in our old age, and we will have no rest. When our time comes we will die submissively, and over there, beyond the grave, we will say that we've suffered, that we've wept, that we've had a bitter life, and God will take pity on us. And then, uncle dear, we will both begin to know a life that is bright and beautiful and lovely. We will rejoice and look back at these troubles of ours with tender feelings, with a smile. And we will have rest. I believe it, uncle, I believe it fervently, passionately. *kneels before him and lays her head on his hands; then, in a tired voice* We will have rest!

Telegin plays softly on the guitar

We will rest! We will hear the angels, we will see all the heavens covered with stars like diamonds, we will see all earthly evil, all our sufferings, swept away by the grace that will fill the whole world. And our life will become peaceful, gentle, and sweet as a caress. I believe it, I believe it. . . . *wipes his eyes with her*

ANTON
CHEKHOV

handkerchief   Poor, poor Uncle Vanya, you're
crying.   *tearfully*   You've had no joy in your life,
but wait, Uncle Vanya, wait. . . . We will rest. . . .
embraces him   We will rest!

*The watchman taps. Marya Vasilievna makes notes on
the margin of her pamphlet. Marina knits her stocking*

We will rest!

THE CURTAIN DROPS SLOWLY

°

THE
THREE
SISTERS

A DRAMA IN FOUR ACTS

THE
CHARACTERS

PROZOROV, *Andrei Sergeevich*
NATASHA (Natalya Ivanovna), *his fiancée, afterward his wife*
OLGA (Olga Sergeevna, Olya, Olyushka, Olechka) ⎫
MASHA (Marya Sergeevna) ⎬ *his sisters*
IRINA (Irina Sergeevna, Irenushka) ⎭
KULYGIN, *Fëdor Ilyich, a teacher at the high school for boys and the husband of Masha*
VERSHININ, *Aleksandr Ignatievich, a lieutenant colonel and battery commander*
TUTZENBACH, *Nikolai Lvovich, baron and a lieutenant in the army*
SOLENI, *Vasili Vasilievich, a captain*
CHEBUTYKIN, *Ivan Romanovich, an army doctor*
FEDOTIK, *Aleksei Petrovich, a second lieutenant*
RODÉ, *Vladimir Karlovich, a second lieutenant*
FERAPONT (Ferapont Spiridonich), *an old porter from the County Office*
ANFISA, *the Prozorov's former nurse, an old woman of eighty*

The action takes place in a country town

ACT ONE

*A drawing room in the Prozorovs' house; it is separated
from a large ballroom[1] at the back by a row of columns.
It is midday; there is cheerful sunshine outside. In the
ballroom the table is being set for lunch. Olga, wearing
the regulation dark blue dress of a secondary schoolteacher, is correcting her pupils' work, standing or
walking around as she does so. Masha, in a black
dress, is sitting reading a book, her hat on her lap.
Irina, in white, stands lost in thought.*

OLGA

It's exactly a year ago that father died, isn't it? This
very day, the fifth of May—your saint's day, Irina.
I remember it was very cold and it was snowing. I felt
then as if I would never survive his death; and you
had fainted and were lying quite still, as if you were
dead. And now—a year's gone by, and we talk about
it so easily. You're wearing white, and your face is
positively radiant.

A clock strikes twelve

The clock struck twelve then too.   *pause*   I remember when father was being taken to the cemetery there

1. A large room, sparsely furnished, used for receptions and dances
in Russian houses.

was a military band, and a salute with rifle fire. That was because he was a general, in command of a brigade. And yet there weren't many people at the funeral. Of course it was raining hard, raining and snowing.

IRINA
Need we bring up all these memories?

Baron Tutzenbach, Chebutykin, and Soleni appear behind the columns by the table in the ballroom

OLGA
It's so warm today that we can keep the windows wide open, and yet there aren't any leaves showing on the birch trees. Father was made a brigadier eleven years ago, and then he left Moscow and took us with him. I remember so well how everything in Moscow was in blossom by now; everything was soaked in sunlight and warmth. Eleven years have gone by, yet I remember everything about it as if we'd only left yesterday. Oh, heavens! When I woke up this morning and saw this flood of sunshine, all this spring sunshine, I felt so moved and so happy! I felt such a longing to get back home to Moscow!

CHEBUTYKIN
To Tutzenbach   The devil you have!

TUTZENBACH
It's nonsense, I agree.

Masha, absorbed in her book, whistles a tune under her breath

OLGA
Masha, stop whistling! How can you?   *pause*   I suppose I must get this continual headache because I have to go to school every day and go on teaching right into the evening. I seem to have the thoughts of

someone quite old. Honestly, I've been feeling as if
my strength and youth were running out of me drop
by drop, day after day. Day after day, all these four
years that I've been working at the school. I just have
one longing and it seems to grow stronger and
stronger.

IRINA
If only we could go back to Moscow! Sell the house,
finish with our life here, and go back to Moscow.

OLGA
Yes, Moscow! As soon as we possibly can.

Chebutykin and Tutzenbach laugh

IRINA
I suppose Andrei will soon get a professorship. He isn't
likely to go on living here. The only problem is our
poor Masha.

OLGA
Masha can come and stay the whole summer with us
every year in Moscow.

Masha whistles a tune under her breath

IRINA
Everything will settle itself, with God's help. *looks
through the window* What lovely weather it is today!
Really I don't know why there's such joy in my heart.
I remembered this morning that it was my saint's day,
and suddenly I felt so happy; and I thought of the time
when we were children and mother was still alive.
And then such wonderful thoughts came to me, such
wonderful stirring thoughts!

OLGA
You're so lovely today; you really do look most
attractive. Masha looks pretty today too. Andrei
could be good-looking, but he's grown so fat. It doesn't

THE
THREE
SISTERS

suit him. As for me, I've just aged and grown a lot
thinner. I suppose it's from getting so irritated with
the girls at school. But today I'm at home, I'm free,
and my headache's gone, and I feel much younger than
I did yesterday. I'm only twenty-eight after all. . . .
I suppose everything that God wills must be right
and good, but I can't help thinking sometimes that if
I'd gotten married and stayed at home, it would have
been a better thing for me.   *pause*   I would have
been very fond of my husband.

TUTZENBACH

To Soleni   Really you talk such a lot of nonsense
that I'm tired of listening to you.   *comes into the
drawing room*   I forgot to tell you: Vershinin, our
new battery commander, is going to call on you today.
sits down by the piano

OLGA

I'm very glad to hear it.

IRINA

Is he old?

TUTZENBACH

No, not particularly. Forty, forty-five at the most.
plays quietly   He seems a nice fellow. Certainly not
a fool. His only weakness is that he talks too much.

IRINA

Is he interesting?

TUTZENBACH

He's all right, only he's got a wife, a mother-in-law,
and two little girls. What's more, she's his second
wife. He calls on everybody and tells them that he's
got a wife and two little girls. He'll tell you about it
too; I'm sure of that. His wife seems to be a bit soft
in the head. She wears a long braid like a girl, she is
always philosophizing and talking in high-flown
language, and then she often tries to commit suicide,

ANTON
CHEKHOV

apparently just to annoy her husband. I would have run
away from a wife like that years ago, but he puts up
with it and just grumbles about it.

SOLENI

Enters the drawing room with Chebutykin
Now I can only lift sixty pounds with one hand, but
with two I can lift two hundred pounds or even two
hundred and forty. So I conclude from that that two
men are not just twice as strong as one, but three times
as strong, if not more.

CHEBUTYKIN

Reads the paper as he comes in
Here's a recipe for falling hair: two ounces of
naphthaline, half a bottle of wood alcohol. Dissolve
and apply once a day. *writes it down in a notebook*
Must make a note of it. *to Soleni* Well, as I was
trying to explain to you, you cork the bottle and pass
a glass tube through the cork. Then you take a pinch of
ordinary powdered alum and . . .

IRINA

Ivan Romanich, dear Ivan Romanich!

CHEBUTYKIN

What is it, my child, what is it?

IRINA

Tell me, why is it I'm so happy today? Just as if I were
sailing along in a boat with big white sails, and above
me the wide, blue sky, and in the sky great white birds
floating around?

CHEBUTYKIN

Kisses both her hands, tenderly
My little white bird!

IRINA

You know when I woke up this morning, and after
I'd gotten up and washed, I suddenly felt as if everything in the world had become clear to me, and I knew

the way I ought to live. I know it all now, my dear
Ivan Romanich. Man must work by the sweat of his
brow whatever his class, and that should make up the
whole meaning and purpose of his life and happiness
and contentment. Oh, how good it must be to be a
workman, getting up with the sun and breaking stones
by the roadside—or a shepherd—or a schoolteacher
teaching the children—or an engine driver on the
railway. Good heavens! It's better to be a mere ox or
horse and work, than the sort of young woman who
wakes up at twelve and drinks her coffee in bed and
then takes two hours dressing. How dreadful! You
know how you long for a cool drink in hot weather?
Well, that's the way I long for work. And if I don't
get up early from now on and really work, you can
refuse to be friends with me any more, Ivan Romanich.

CHEBUTYKIN

Tenderly So I will, so I will.

OLGA

Father taught us to get up at seven o'clock and so
Irina always wakes up at seven—but then she stays
in bed till at least nine, thinking about something or
other. And with such a serious expression on her face
too! *laughs*

IRINA

You think it's strange when I look serious because you
always think of me as a little girl. I'm twenty you
know!

TUTZENBACH

All this longing for work. Heavens, how well I can
understand it! I've never done a stroke of work in my
life. I was born in Petersburg, an unfriendly, idle city—
born into a family where work and worries were
simply unknown. I remember a valet pulling off my
boots for me when I came home from the cadet school.

ANTON
CHEKHOV

I grumbled at the way he did it, and my mother looked
on in admiration. She was quite surprised when other
people looked at me in any other way. I was so
carefully protected from work! But I doubt whether
they succeeded in protecting me for good and all—yes,
I doubt it very much! The time's come: there's a
terrific thundercloud advancing upon us; a mighty
storm is coming to freshen us up! Yes, it's coming all
right. It's quite near already, and it's going to blow
away all this idleness and indifference and prejudice
against work, this rot of boredom that our society is
suffering from. I'm going to work, and in twenty-five
or thirty years' time every man and woman will be
working. Every one of us!

CHEBUTYKIN

I'm not going to work.

TUTZENBACH

You don't count.

SOLENI

In twenty-five years' time you won't be alive, thank
goodness. In a couple of years you'll die from a stroke—
or I'll lose my temper with you and put a bullet in
your head, my good fellow. *takes a cologne bottle
from his pocket and sprinkles the scent over his chest
and hands*

CHEBUTYKIN

Laughs It's quite true that I never have done any
work. Not a stroke since I left the university. I haven't
even read a book, only newspapers. *takes another
newspaper out of his pocket* For instance here. I know
from the paper that there was a person called
Dobrolyubov, but what he wrote about I haven't
the faintest idea. God alone knows.

Someone knocks on the floor from downstairs

There! They're calling me to come down: there's someone come to see me. I'll be back in a moment. *goes out hurriedly, stroking his beard*

IRINA

He's up to one of his little games.

TUTZENBACH

Yes. He looked very solemn as he left. He's obviously going to give you a present.

IRINA

I do dislike that sort of thing.

OLGA

Yes, isn't it dreadful? He's always doing something silly.

MASHA

"A green oak grows by a curving shore, and round that oak hangs a golden chain . . ." *gets up as she sings under her breath*

OLGA

You're sad today, Masha.

Masha puts on her hat, singing

Where are you going?

MASHA

Home.

IRINA

What a strange thing to do.

TUTZENBACH

What! Going away from your sister's party?

MASHA

What does it matter? I'll be back this evening. Goodbye, my darling. *kisses Irina* And once again, I wish you all the happiness in the world. In the old days when father was alive we used to have thirty or forty officers at our parties. What gay parties we had!

And today—what have we got today? A man and a
half, and the place is as quiet as a tomb. I'm going
home. I'm depressed today, I'm sad; so don't listen
to me. *laughs through her tears* We'll have a talk
later, but good-bye for now, my dear. I'll go somewhere or other.

IRINA

Displeased Really you are a . . .

OLGA

Tearfully I understand you, Masha.

SOLENI

If a man starts philosophizing, you call that philosophy
or possibly just sophistry; but if a woman or a couple
of women start philosophizing you call that . . . What
would you call it now? Ask me another!

MASHA

What are you talking about? You are a disconcerting
person!

SOLENI

Nothing.

"He had no time to say 'Oh, oh!'
Before that bear had struck him low . . ."

MASHA

After a pause, to Olga, crossly
Do stop sniveling!

*Enter Anfisa and Ferapont, the latter carrying a large
cake*

ANFISA

Come along, my dear, this way. Come in, your boots
are quite clean. *to Irina* A cake from Protopopov
at the Council Office.

IRINA

Thank you. Tell him I'm very grateful to him. *takes
the cake*

FERAPONT

What's that?

IRINA

Louder   Tell him I sent my thanks.

OLGA

Nanny, will you give him a piece of cake? Go along, Ferapont; they'll give you some cake.

FERAPONT

What's that?

ANFISA

Come along with me, Ferapont Spiridonich, my dear. Come along.   *goes out with Ferapont*

MASHA

I don't like that Protopopov fellow, Mikhail Potapich or Ivanich or whatever it is. It's best not to invite him here.

IRINA

I haven't invited him.

MASHA

Thank goodness.

Enter Chebutykin, followed by a soldier carrying a silver samovar. Murmurs of astonishment and displeasure

OLGA

Covering her face with her hands
A samovar! But this is dreadful!   *goes through to the ballroom and stands by the table*

IRINA

My dear Ivan Romanich, what are you thinking about?

TUTZENBACH

Laughs   Didn't I tell you?

MASHA

Ivan Romanich, you really ought to be ashamed of yourself!

CHEBUTYKIN
My dear, sweet girls, I've no one in the world but you.
You're dearer to me than anything in the world! I'm
nearly sixty; I'm an old man—a lonely, utterly
unimportant old man. The only thing that's worth
anything in me is my love for you, and if it weren't
for you, really I would have been dead long ago.   *to*
Irina   My dear, my sweet little girl, haven't I known
you since the very day you were born? Didn't I carry
you around in my arms? Didn't I love your dear mother?

IRINA
But why do you get such expensive presents?

CHEBUTYKIN
Tearfully and angrily
Expensive presents! Get along with you!   *to the*
orderly   Put the samovar over there.   *mimics Irina*
Expensive presents!

The orderly takes the samovar to the ballroom

ANFISA
Crosses the drawing room
My dears, there's a strange colonel just arrived. He's
taken off his coat and he's coming up now. Irenushka,
do be nice and polite to him, won't you?   *in the*
doorway   And it's high time we had lunch too.
Oh, dear!   *goes out*

TUTZENBACH
It's Vershinin, I suppose.

Enter Vershinin

Lieutenant Colonel Vershinin!

VERSHININ   THE
To Masha and Irina   THREE
Allow me to introduce myself—Lieutenant Colonel   SISTERS

Vershinin. I'm so glad, so very glad to be here at last. How you've changed! Dear, dear, how you've changed!

IRINA

Please, do sit down. We're very pleased to see you, I'm sure.

VERSHININ

Gaily I'm so glad to see you, so glad! But there were three of you, weren't there? Three sisters. I remember there were three little girls. I don't remember their faces, but I knew your father, Colonel Prozorov, and I remember he had three little girls. Oh, yes, I saw them myself. I remember them quite well. How time flies! Dear, dear, how it flies!

TUTZENBACH

Aleksandr Ignatievich comes from Moscow.

IRINA

From Moscow? You come from Moscow?

VERSHININ

Yes, from Moscow. Your father was a battery commander there, and I was an officer in the same brigade. *to Masha* I seem to remember your face a little.

MASHA

I don't remember you at all.

IRINA

Olya, Olya! *calls toward the ballroom* Olya, do come!

Olga enters from the ballroom

It seems that Lieutenant Colonel Vershinin comes from Moscow.

VERSHININ

ANTON
CHEKHOV

You must be Olga Sergeevna, the eldest. And you are Marya. And you are Irina, the youngest.

OLGA

You come from Moscow?

VERSHININ

Yes. I studied in Moscow and entered the service there.
I stayed there quite a long time, but then I was put in
charge of a battery here—so I moved out here, you see.
I don't really remember you, you know; I only
remember that there were three sisters. I remember
your father, though; I remember him very well. All
I need to do is to close my eyes and I can see him
standing there as if he were alive. I used to visit you
in Moscow.

OLGA

I thought I remembered everybody, and yet . . .

VERSHININ

My Christian names are Aleksandr Ignatievich.

IRINA

Aleksandr Ignatievich, and you come from Moscow!
Well, what a surprise!

OLGA

We're going to live there you know.

IRINA

We hope to be there by the autumn. It's our home
town; we were born there. On Staraya Basmannaya
Street. *both laugh happily*

MASHA

Fancy meeting a fellow townsman so unexpectedly!
eagerly I remember now. Do you remember, Olga,
there was someone they used to call "the lovesick
major"? You were a lieutenant then, weren't you, and
you were in love with someone or other, and everyone
used to tease you about it. They called you "major"
for some reason or other.

THE
THREE
SISTERS

VERSHININ

Laughs That's it, that's it. "The lovesick major,"
that's what they called me.

MASHA

In those days you only had a mustache. Oh, dear,
how much older you look! *tearfully* How much
older!

VERSHININ

Yes, I was still a young man in the days when they
called me "the lovesick major." I was in love then.
It's different now.

OLGA

But you haven't got a single gray hair! You've aged,
yes, but you're certainly not an old man.

VERSHININ

Nevertheless, I've turned forty-two. Is it long since
you left Moscow?

IRINA

Eleven years. Now what are you crying for, Masha,
you funny girl? *tearfully* You'll make me cry too.

MASHA

I'm not crying. What was the street you lived on?

VERSHININ

On the Staraya Basmannaya.

OLGA

We did too.

VERSHININ

At one time I lived on Nemetskaya Street. I used to
walk from there to the Krasny Barracks, and I
remember there was such a gloomy bridge I had to
cross. I used to hear the noise of the water rushing
under it. I remember how lonely and sad I felt there.
pause But what a magnificently wide river you have
here! It's a marvelous river!

ANTON
CHEKHOV

OLGA

Yes, but this is a cold place. It's cold here, and there are too many mosquitoes.

VERSHININ

Really? I would have said you had a really good, healthy climate here, a real Russian climate. Forest, river. . . birch trees too. The dear, unpretentious birch trees—I love them more than any of the other trees. It's nice living here. But there's one rather strange thing: the station is fifteen miles from the town. And no one knows why.

SOLENI

I know why it is.

Everyone looks at him

Because if the station were nearer, it wouldn't be so far away; and since it is so far away, it can't be nearer.

An awkward silence

TUTZENBACH

You like your little joke, Vasili Vasilievich.

OLGA

I'm sure I remember you now. I know I do.

VERSHININ

I knew your mother.

CHEBUTYKIN

She was a good woman, God bless her memory!

IRINA

Mamma was buried in Moscow.

OLGA

At the convent of Novo-Devichye.

MASHA

You know, I'm even beginning to forget what she looked like. I suppose people will lose all memory of us in just the same way. We'll be forgotten.

THE
THREE
SISTERS

VERSHININ

Yes, we will all be forgotten. Such is our fate, and we can't do anything about it. And all the things that seem serious, important, and full of meaning to us now will be forgotten one day—or anyway they won't seem important anymore. *pause* It's strange to think that we're utterly unable to tell what will be regarded as great and important in the future and what will be thought of as just paltry and ridiculous. Didn't the great discoveries of Copernicus—or of Columbus, if you like—appear useless and unimportant to begin with? Whereas some rubbish, written up by an eccentric fool, was regarded as a revelation of great truth? It may well be that in time to come the life we live today will seem strange and uncomfortable and stupid and not too clean either and perhaps even wicked.

TUTZENBACH

Who can tell? It's just as possible that future generations will think that we lived our lives on a very high plane and remember us with respect. After all we no longer have tortures and public executions and invasions, though there's still a great deal of suffering!

SOLENI

In a high-pitched voice as if calling to chickens Cluck, cluck, cluck! There's nothing our good baron loves as much as a nice bit of philosophizing.

TUTZENBACH

Vasili Vasilievich, will you kindly leave me alone? *moves to another chair* It's becoming tiresome.

SOLENI

As before Cluck, cluck, cluck!

TUTZENBACH

To Vershinin The suffering that we see around us— and there's so much of it—itself proves that our society has at least achieved a level of morality which is higher.

ANTON
CHEKHOV

Yes, yes, of course.

CHEBUTYKIN

You said just now, Baron, that our age will be called
great; but people are small all the same.   *gets up*
Look how small I am.

A violin is played offstage

MASHA

That's Andrei playing the violin; he's our brother
you know.

IRINA

We've got quite a clever brother. We're expecting him
to be a professor. Papa was a military man, but
Andrei chose an academic career.

OLGA

We've been teasing him today. We think he's in love,
just a little.

IRINA

With a girl who lives down here. She'll be calling in
today most likely.

MASHA

The way she dresses herself is awful! It's not that her
clothes are just ugly and old-fashioned, they're simply
pathetic. She'll put on some weird-looking, bright
yellow skirt with a crude sort of fringe affair, and then
a red blouse to go with it. And her cheeks look as
though they've been scrubbed, they're so shiny!
Andrei's not in love with her—I can't believe it; after
all he has got some taste. I think he's just playing the
fool just to annoy us. I heard yesterday that she's going
to get married to Protopopov, the chairman of the
local council. I thought it was an excellent idea.   *calls*
through the side door   Andrei, come here, will you?
Just for a moment, dear.

OLGA

This is my brother, Andrei Sergeevich.

VERSHININ

Vershinin.

ANDREI

Prozorov.   *wipes the perspiration from his face*   I believe you've been appointed battery commander here?

OLGA

What do you think, dear? Aleksandr Ignatievich comes from Moscow.

ANDREI

Do you really? Congratulations! You'll get no peace from my sisters now.

VERSHININ

I'm afraid your sisters must be getting tired of me already.

IRINA

Just look, Andrei gave me this little picture frame today.   *shows him the frame*   He made it himself.

VERSHININ

Looks at the frame, not knowing what to say
Yes, it's . . . it's very nice indeed.

IRINA

Do you see that little frame over the piano? He made that one too.

Andrei waves his hand impatiently and walks off

OLGA

He's awfully clever and he plays the violin and he makes all sorts of things too. In fact he's very gifted all around. Andrei, please don't go. He's got such a bad habit—always going off like this. Come here!

ANTON
CHEKHOV

MASHA

Now just you come here!

ANDREI

Leave me alone, please!

MASHA

You are a silly! They used to call Aleksandr Ignatievich
"the lovesick major," and he didn't get annoyed.

VERSHININ

Not in the least.

MASHA

I feel like calling you a "lovesick fiddler."

IRINA

Or a "lovesick professor."

OLGA

He's fallen in love! Our Andryusha's in love!

IRINA

Clapping her hands

Three cheers for Andryusha! Andryusha's in love!

CHEBUTYKIN

*Comes up behind Andrei and puts his arms around his
waist*

"Nature created us for love alone."   *laughs loudly,
still holding his paper in his hand*

ANDREI

That's enough of it, that's enough.   *wipes his face*   I
couldn't get to sleep all night, and I'm not feeling too
grand just now. I read till four o'clock and then I went
to bed, but nothing happened. I kept thinking about
one thing and another. And it gets light so early; the
sun just pours into my room. I'd like to translate a
book from the English while I'm here during the
summer.

VERSHININ

You read English then?

ANDREI

Yes. My father—God bless his memory—used to simply wear us out with learning. It sounds silly, I know, but I must confess that since he died I've begun to grow fat, as if I'd been physically relieved of the strain. I've grown quite stout in a year. Yes, thanks to father, my sisters and I know French and German and English, and Irina here knows Italian too. But what an effort it all cost us!

MASHA

Knowing three languages in a town like this is an unnecessary luxury. In fact, not even a luxury, but just a sort of useless encumbrance. It's rather like having a sixth finger on your hand. We know a lot of stuff that's just useless.

VERSHININ

Really! *laughs* You know a lot of stuff that's useless! It seems to me that there's no place on earth, however dull and depressing it may be, where intelligence and education can be useless. Let us suppose that among the hundred thousand people in this town— all of them, no doubt, very backward and uncultured— there are just three people like yourselves. Obviously you can't hope to triumph over all the mass of ignorance around you. As your life goes by, you'll have to keep giving in little by little until you get lost in the crowd, in the hundred thousand. Life will swallow you up, but you'll not quite disappear; you'll make some impression on it. After you've gone perhaps six more people like you will turn up, then twelve, and so on, until in the end most people will have become like you. So in two or three hundred years life on this old earth of ours will have become marvelously beautiful.

ANTON
CHEKHOV

Man longs for a life like that, and if it isn't here yet,
he must imagine it, wait for it, dream about it, prepare
for it. He must know and see more than his father
and his grandfather did. *laughs* And you're complaining because you know a lot of stuff that's useless.

MASHA
Takes off her hat
I'll be staying to lunch.

IRINA
With a sigh
Really someone should have written all that down.

Andrei has left the room, unnoticed

TUTZENBACH
You say that in time to come life will be marvelously
beautiful. That's probably true. But in order to share
in it now, at a distance so to speak, we must prepare
for it and work for it.

VERSHININ
Gets up Yes. . . . What a lot of flowers you've got
here! *looks around* And what a marvelous house! I
do envy you! All my life I seem to have been huddling
in small flats, with two chairs and a sofa and a stove
that always smokes. It's the flowers that I've missed
in my life, flowers like these! *rubs his hands* Oh,
well, never mind!

TUTZENBACH
Yes, we must work. I suppose you're thinking I'm a
sentimental German. But I assure you I'm not—I'm
Russian. I don't speak a word of German. My father
was brought up in the Greek Orthodox faith.

VERSHININ
Walks up and down the room
You know, I often wonder what it would be like if you

could start your life over again—deliberately, I mean, consciously. Suppose you could put aside the life you'd lived already, as though it were just a sort of rough draft, and then start another one like a clean copy. If that happened I think the thing you'd want most of all would be not to repeat yourself. You'd try at least to create a new environment for yourself, a flat like this one, for instance, with some flowers and plenty of light. I have a wife, you know, and two little girls; and my wife's not very well, and all that. Well, if I had to start my life all over again, I wouldn't marry. No, no!

Enter Kulygin, in the uniform of a teacher

KULYGIN

Approaches Irina Congratulations, dear sister—from the bottom of my heart—congratulations on your saint's day. I wish you good health and everything a girl of your age ought to have! And allow me to present you with this little book. *hands her a book* It's the history of our school covering the whole fifty years of its existence. I wrote it myself. Quite a trifle, of course—I wrote it in my spare time when I had nothing better to do—but I hope you'll read it nevertheless. Good morning to you all! *to Vershinin* Allow me to introduce myself. Kulygin's the name; I'm a teacher at the secondary school here. And a town councillor. *to Irina* You'll find a list in the book of all the pupils who have completed their studies at our school during the last fifty years. *Feci quod potui, faciant meliora potentes.* *kisses Masha*

IRINA

But you gave me this book last Easter!

KULYGIN

Laughs Did I really? In that case give it back to me—

or no, better give it to the colonel. Please do take it,
Colonel. Maybe you'll read it sometime when you've
nothing better to do.

VERSHININ

Thank you very much. *prepares to leave* I'm so
very glad to have made your acquaintance.

OLGA

You aren't going, are you? Really, you mustn't.

IRINA

But you'll stay and have lunch with us! Please.

OLGA

Please do.

VERSHININ

Bows I see I've intruded on your saint's day party.
I didn't know. Forgive me for not offering you my
congratulations. *goes into the ballroom with Olga*

KULYGIN

Today is Sunday, my friends, a day of rest; let us rest
and enjoy it, each according to his age and position
in life! We will have to roll up the carpets and put them
away till the winter. We must remember to put some
naphthaline on them or Persian powder. . . . The
Romans enjoyed good health because they knew how
to work *and* how to rest. They had *mens sana in
corpore sano.* Their life had a definite shape, a form.
The director of the school says that the most important
thing about life is form. A thing that loses its form is
finished—that's just as true of our ordinary, everyday
lives. *takes Masha by the waist and laughs* Masha
loves me. My wife loves me. Yes, and the curtains will
have to be put away with the carpets too. . . . I'm
cheerful today; I'm in quite excellent spirits. Masha,
we're invited to the director's at four o'clock today.
A country walk has been arranged for the teachers and
their families.

MASHA

I'm not going.

KULYGIN

Distressed Masha, darling, why not?

MASHA

I'll tell you later. *peevishly* All right, I'll come, only leave me alone now. *walks off*

KULYGIN

And after the walk we will all spend the evening at the director's house. In spite of weak health that man is certainly sparing no pains to be sociable. A first-rate, thoroughly enlightened man! A most excellent person! After the conference yesterday he said to me, "I'm tired, Fëdor Ilyich. I'm tired!" *looks at the clock, then at his watch* Your clock is seven minutes fast. Yes, "I'm tired," he said.

The sound of the violin is heard offstage

OLGA

Will you all come and sit down, please! Lunch is ready. There's a pie.

KULYGIN

Ah, Olga, my dear girl! Last night I worked up to eleven o'clock and I felt tired, but today I'm quite happy. *goes to the table in the ballroom* My dear Olga!

CHEBUTYKIN

Puts the newspaper in his pocket and combs his beard A pie? Excellent!

MASHA

Sternly to Chebutykin

Remember, you mustn't take anything to drink today. Do you hear? It's bad for you.

CHEBUTYKIN

Never mind. I've gotten over that weakness long ago!

ANTON
CHEKHOV

I haven't done any heavy drinking for two years.
impatiently Anyway, my dear, what does it matter?

MASHA

All the same, don't you dare drink anything. See that
you don't now! *petulantly, but taking care that her
husband does not hear* So now I've got to spend
another of these damnably boring evenings at the
director's!

TUTZENBACH

I wouldn't go if I were you, and that's that.

CHEBUTYKIN

Don't you go, my dear.

MASHA

Don't go, indeed! Oh, what a damnable life! It's
intolerable. *goes into the ballroom*

CHEBUTYKIN

Follows her Well, well!

SOLENI

As he passes Tutzenbach on the way to the ballroom
Cluck, cluck, cluck!

TUTZENBACH

Do stop it, Vasili Vasilievich. I've really had enough
of it.

SOLENI

Cluck, cluck, cluck!

KULYGIN

Gaily Your health, Colonel! I'm a schoolteacher and
I'm quite one of the family here, as it were. I'm
Masha's husband. She's got a sweet nature, such a very
sweet nature!

VERSHININ

I think I'll have a little of this dark vodka. *drinks*
Your health! *to Olga* I do feel so happy with you
people!

IRINA

Masha's in a bit of a bad mood today. You know, she got married when she was eighteen, and then her husband seemed the cleverest man in the world to her. It's different now. He's the kindest of men, but not the cleverest.

OLGA

Impatiently   Andrei, will you please come?

ANDREI

Offstage   Just coming.   *enters and goes to the table*

TUTZENBACH

What are you thinking about?

IRINA

Oh, nothing special. You know, I don't like this man Soleni; I'm quite afraid of him. Whenever he opens his mouth he says something silly.

TUTZENBACH

He's a strange fellow. I'm sorry for him, even though he irritates me. In fact I feel more sorry for him than irritated. I think he's shy. When he's alone with me, he can be quite sensible and friendly, but in company he's offensive and bullying. Don't go over there just yet; let them get settled down at the table. Let me stay with you for a bit. Tell me what you're thinking about. *pause*   You're twenty and I'm not thirty yet myself. What years and years we still have ahead of us—a whole long succession of years, all full of my love for you!

IRINA

Don't talk to me about love, Nikolai Lvovich.

ANTON
CHEKHOV

TUTZENBACH

Not listening   Oh, I long so passionately for life; I

long to work and strive so much. And all this longing
is somehow mingled with my love for you, Irina. And
just because you happen to be beautiful, life appears
beautiful to me! What are you thinking about?

IRINA

You say that life is beautiful. Maybe it is—but what if
it only seems to be beautiful? Our lives, I mean the
lives of us three sisters, haven't been beautiful up to
now. The truth is that life has been stifling us, like
weeds in a garden. I'm afraid I'm crying. . . . So
unnecessary. *quickly dries her eyes and smiles* We
must work, work! The reason we feel depressed and
take such a gloomy view of life is that we've never
known what it is to make a real effort. We're the
children of parents who despised work.

*Enter Natalya Ivanovna. She is wearing a pink dress
with a green belt*

NATASHA

They've gone in to lunch already. I'm late. *glances at
herself in a mirror and adjusts her dress* My hair
seems to be all right. *catches sight of Irina* My dear
Irina Sergeevna, congratulations! *gives her a vigorous
and prolonged kiss* You've got such a lot of visitors.
I feel quite shy. How do you do, Baron?

OLGA

Enters the drawing room
Oh, there you are, Natalya Ivanovna! How are you,
my dear? *they kiss each other*

NATASHA

Congratulations! You've such a lot of people here that
I feel dreadfully shy.

OLGA

It's all right; they're all old friends. *alarmed, dropping her voice* You've got a green belt on! My dear, that's surely a mistake!

NATASHA

Why, is it a bad omen or what?

OLGA

No, but it just doesn't go with your dress. It looks so strange.

NATASHA

Tearfully Really? But it isn't really green you know; it's a sort of dull color. *follows Olga to the ballroom*

All are now seated at the table; the drawing room is empty

KULYGIN

Irina, you know, I do wish you'd find yourself a good husband. In my view it's high time you got married.

CHEBUTYKIN

You ought to get yourself a nice little husband too, Natalya Ivanovna.

KULYGIN

Natalya Ivanovna already has a husband in view.

MASHA

Strikes her plate with her fork

A glass of wine for me, please! Three cheers for our jolly old life! We keep our end up, we do!

KULYGIN

Masha, you won't get more than five out of ten for good conduct!

VERSHININ

Say there, this liqueur's very nice. What is it made of?

SOLENI

Cockroaches!

ANTON
CHEKHOV

IRINA

Ugh! Ugh! How disgusting!

OLGA
We're having roast turkey for dinner tonight, and then apple tart. Thank goodness I'll be here all day today. . . . This evening too. You must all come this evening.

VERSHININ
May I come in the evening too?

IRINA
Yes, please do.

NATASHA
They don't stand on ceremony here.

CHEBUTYKIN
"Nature created us for love alone."   *laughs*

ANDREI
Irritably   Will you stop it please? Aren't you tired of it yet?

Fedotik and Rodé come in with a large basket of flowers

FEDOTIK
Just look here, they're having lunch already!

RODÉ
In a loud voice
Having their lunch? So they are; they're having lunch already.

FEDOTIK
Wait half a minute.   *takes a snapshot*   One! Just a minute more!   *takes another snapshot*   Two! All over now.

They pick up the basket and go into the ballroom, where they are greeted uproariously

RODÉ
Loudly   Congratulations, Irina Sergeevna! I wish you all the best—everything you'd wish for yourself! Gorgeous weather today, absolutely marvelous. I've been out walking the whole morning with the boys.

You do know that I teach gym at the high school, don't you?

FEDOTIK

You may move now, Irina Sergeevna, that is, if you want to.   *takes a snapshot*   You do look attractive today.   *takes a top out of his pocket*   By the way, look at this top. It's got a wonderful hum.

IRINA

What a sweet little thing!

MASHA

"A green oak grows by a curving shore, and round that oak hangs a golden chain . . ." A golden chain around that oak.   *peevishly*   Why do I keep on saying that? Those lines have been worrying me all day long!

KULYGIN

Do you know, we're thirteen at table?

RODÉ

Loudly   You don't really believe in these old super-stitions, do you?   *laughs*

KULYGIN

When thirteen people sit down at the table, it means that some of them are in love. Is it you, by any chance, Ivan Romanich?

CHEBUTYKIN

Oh, I'm just an old sinner. But what I can't make out is why Natalya Ivanovna looks so embarrassed.

Loud laughter. Natasha runs out into the drawing room. Andrei follows her

ANDREI

Please, Natasha, don't pay any attention to them! Stop. . . . Wait a moment. Please!

NATASHA

I feel so ashamed. I don't know what's the matter with me, and they're all laughing at me. It's awful of me to

leave the table like that, but I couldn't help it. I just
couldn't.   *covers her face with her hands*

ANDREI

My dear girl, please, please don't get upset. Honestly
they don't mean any harm; they're just teasing. My
dear, sweet girl, they're really good-natured folks, they
all are, and they're fond of us both. Come over to the
window; they can't see us there.   *looks around*

NATASHA

You see, I'm not used to being with a lot of people.

ANDREI

Oh, how young you are, Natasha—how wonderfully,
beautifully young! My dear, sweet girl, don't get so
upset! Do believe me, believe me. I'm so happy, so full
of love, of joy. . . . No, they can't see us here! They
can't see us! How did I come to love you? When was it?
I don't understand anything. My precious, my sweet,
my innocent girl, please—I want you to marry me!
I love you; I love you as I've never loved anybody.
kisses her

*Enter two officers and, seeing Natasha and Andrei
kissing, stand and stare in amazement*

CURTAIN

ACT TWO

*The scene is the same as in Act One. It is eight o'clock
in the evening. The faint sound of an accordion is heard
coming from the street.*

*The stage is unlighted. Enter Natalya Ivanovna in a
dressing gown, carrying a candle. She crosses the stage
and stops by the door leading to Andrei's room.*

NATASHA

What are you doing, Andryusha? Reading? It's all
right; I only wanted to know.   *goes to another door,
opens it, looks inside, and shuts it again*   No one's
left a light anywhere.

ANDREI

Enters with a book in his hand
What is it, Natasha?

NATASHA

I was just going around to see if anyone had left a light
anywhere. It's carnival week, and the servants are so
excited about it . . . anything might happen! You've
got to watch them. Last night about twelve o'clock
I happened to go into the dining room, and—would
you believe it?—there was a lighted candle on the table.
I haven't found out who lit it.   *puts the candle down*
What time is it?

ANTON
CHEKHOV

Glances at his watch
Quarter past eight.

NATASHA

And Olga and Irina still out. They aren't back from
work yet, poor things! Olga's still at some teachers'
conference, and Irina's at the post office. *sighs* This
morning I said to Irina, "Do take care of yourself, my
dear." But she won't listen. Did you say it was a
quarter past eight? I'm afraid Bobik is not at all well.
Why does he get so cold? Yesterday he had a temperature, but today he feels quite cold when you touch him.
I'm so afraid!

ANDREI

It's all right, Natasha. The boy's well enough.

NATASHA

Still, I think he ought to have a special diet. I'm so
anxious about him. By the way they tell me that some
carnival party's supposed to be coming here soon after
nine. I'd rather they didn't come, Andryusha.

ANDREI

Well, I really don't know what I can do. They've been
asked to come.

NATASHA

This morning the dear little fellow woke up and
looked at me, and then suddenly he smiled. He recognized me, you see. "Good morning, Bobik," I said,
"good morning, darling precious!" And then he
laughed. Babies understand everything you know; they
understand us perfectly well. Anyway, Andryusha, I'll
tell the servants not to let that carnival party in.

ANDREI

Irresolutely Well . . . it's really for my sisters to
decide, isn't it? It's their house after all.

THE
THREE
SISTERS

NATASHA

Yes, it's their house as well. I'll tell them too. They're so kind. *walks off* I've ordered sour milk for supper. The doctor says you ought to eat nothing but sour milk or you'll never get any thinner. *stops* Bobik feels so cold. I'm afraid his room is too cold for him. He ought to move into a warmer room, at least until the warm weather comes. Irina's room for instance. That's just a perfect room for a baby: it's dry and it gets the sun all day long. We must tell her. Perhaps she'd share Olga's room for a bit. In any case she's never at home during the day; she only sleeps there. *pause* Andryusha, why don't you say anything?

ANDREI

I was just daydreaming. There's nothing to say anyway.

NATASHA

Well. What was it I was going to tell you? Oh, yes! Ferapont from the Council Office wants to see you about something.

ANDREI

Yawns Tell him to come up.

Natasha goes out. Andrei, bending over the candle which she has left behind, begins to read his book. Enter Ferapont in an old shabby overcoat, his collar turned up, his ears muffled in a scarf

Hello, my friend! What did you want to see me about?

FERAPONT

The chairman's sent you the register and a letter or something. Here they are. *hands him the book and the letter*

ANDREI

Thanks. That's all right. Incidentally, why have you come so late? It's past eight already.

ANTON
CHEKHOV

FERAPONT

What's that?

ANDREI

Raising his voice

I said, why have you come so late? It's past eight already.

FERAPONT

That's right. It was still daylight when I came first, but they wouldn't let me see you. "The master's busy," they said. Well, if you're busy, you're busy. I'm not in a hurry. *thinking that Andrei has said something* What's that?

ANDREI

Nothing. *turns over the pages of the register* Tomorrow's Friday. There's no meeting, but I'll go to the office just the same. Do some work. I'm so bored at home! *pause* Yes, my dear old fellow, how things do change. What a fraud life is! So strange! Today I picked up this book, just out of boredom, because I hadn't anything to do. It's a copy of some lectures I attended at the university. Good heavens! Just think—I'm secretary of the local council now, and Protopopov's chairman. And the most I can ever hope for is to become a member of the council myself! Me—a member of the local council! I, who dream every night that I'm a professor in Moscow University, a famous academician, the pride of all Russia!

FERAPONT

I'm sorry, I can't tell you. I don't hear very well.

ANDREI

If you could hear properly I don't think I'd be talking to you like this. I must talk to someone, but my wife doesn't seem to understand me. And as for my sisters . . . I'm afraid of them for some reason or other; I'm afraid of them laughing at me and pulling my leg.

THE
THREE
SISTERS

I don't drink and I don't like going to bars, but oh, man! how I'd enjoy an hour or so at Testov's or the Great Moscow Restaurant! Yes, my dear fellow, I would indeed!

FERAPONT

The other day at the office a contractor was telling me about some businessmen who were eating pancakes in Moscow. One of them ate forty pancakes and died. It was either forty or fifty; I can't remember exactly.

ANDREI

You can sit in some huge restaurant in Moscow without knowing anyone, and no one knowing you; yet somehow you don't feel that you don't belong there. Whereas here you know everybody, and everybody knows you, and yet you don't feel you belong here; you feel you don't belong at all. You're lonely and you feel like a stranger.

FERAPONT

What's that? *pause* It was the same man that told me—of course he may have been lying—he said that there's an enormous rope stretched right across Moscow.

ANDREI

Whatever for?

FERAPONT

I'm sorry, I can't tell you. That's what he said.

ANDREI

What nonsense! *reads the book* Have you ever been to Moscow?

FERAPONT

After a pause

No. It wasn't God's wish. *pause* Shall I go now?

ANTON
CHEKHOV

ANDREI

Yes, you may go. Good-bye.

Good-bye.   *reading*   Come in the morning to take
some letters. You can go now.   *pause*   He's gone.

A bell rings

Yes, that's how it is.   *stretches and slowly goes to his
room*

*Singing is heard offstage; a nurse is putting a baby to
sleep. Enter Masha and Vershinin. While they talk
together, a maid lights a lamp and candles in the
ballroom*

MASHA
I don't know.   *pause*   I don't know. Habit's very
important of course. For instance, after father died, for
a long time we couldn't get accustomed to the idea
that we hadn't any orderlies to wait on us. But, habit
aside, I think it's quite right what I was saying. Perhaps
it's different in other places, but in this town the
military certainly do seem to be the nicest and most
generous and best-mannered people.

VERSHININ
I'm thirsty. I could do with a nice glass of tea.

MASHA
Glances at her watch
They'll bring it in presently. You see, they married me
off when I was eighteen. I was afraid of my husband
because he was a schoolteacher, and I had only just
left school myself. He seemed terribly learned then,
very clever and important. Now it's quite different,
unfortunately.

VERSHININ
Yes. I see.

THE
THREE
SISTERS

MASHA

I don't say anything against my husband—I'm used to him now—but there are such a lot of vulgar and unpleasant and offensive people among the other civilians. Vulgarity upsets me; it makes me feel insulted. I actually suffer when I meet someone who lacks refinement and gentle manners and courtesy. When I'm with the other teachers, my husband's friends, I just suffer.

VERSHININ

Yes, of course. But I would have thought that in a town like this the civilians and the army people were equally uninteresting. There's no difference between them. If you talk to any educated person here, civilian or military, he'll generally tell you that he's just worn out. It's either his wife or his house or his estate or his horse or something. We Russians are capable of such elevated thoughts, but why do we have such low ideals in practical life? Why is it, why?

MASHA

Why?

VERSHININ

Yes, why does his wife wear him out? Why do his children wear him out? And what about *him* wearing out his wife and children?

MASHA

You're a bit low-spirited today, aren't you?

VERSHININ

Perhaps. I haven't had any dinner today. I've had nothing to eat since morning. One of my daughters is a bit under the weather, and when the children are ill, I get so worried. I feel utterly conscience-stricken at having given them a mother like theirs. Oh, if only you could have seen her this morning! What a despicable woman! We started quarreling at seven o'clock,

ANTON
CHEKHOV

and at nine I just walked out and slammed the door.
pause I never talk about these things in the ordinary
way. It's a strange thing, but you're the only person
I feel I dare complain to. *kisses her hand* Don't be
angry with me. I've nobody, nobody but you.

MASHA
After a pause
What a noise the wind's making in the stove! Just
before father died the wind howled in the chimney just
like that.

VERSHININ
Are you superstitious?

MASHA
Yes.

VERSHININ
How strange. *kisses her hand* You really are a
wonderful creature, a marvelous creature! Wonderful,
marvelous! It's quite dark here, but I can see your eyes
shining.

MASHA
Moves to another chair
There's more light over here.

VERSHININ
I love you, I love you, I love you. I love your eyes. I
love your movements. I dream about them. A
wonderful, marvelous being!

MASHA
Laughing softly When you talk to me like that,
somehow I can't help laughing, although I'm afraid at
the same time. Don't say it again, please. *half audibly*
Well, no. . . . Go on. I don't mind. *covers her face
with her hands* I don't mind. . . . Someone's coming.
Let's talk about something else.

Enter Irina and Tutzenbach through the ballroom

TUTZENBACH

I have a triple-barreled name—Baron Tutzenbach-Krone-Altschauer—but actually I'm a Russian. I was baptized in the Greek Orthodox faith just like yourself. I haven't really got any German characteristics, except maybe the obstinate, patient way I keep on pestering you. Look how I bring you home every evening.

IRINA

How tired I am!

TUTZENBACH

And I'll go on meeting you at the post office and bringing you home every evening for the next twenty years—unless you send me away. *noticing Masha and Vershinin, with pleasure* Oh, it's you! How are you?

IRINA

Well, here I am, home at last! *to Masha* A woman came into the post office just before I left. She wanted to send a wire to her brother in Saratov to tell him her son had just died, but she couldn't remember the address. So we had to send the wire without an address, just to Saratov. She was crying and I was rude to her for no reason at all. "I've no time to waste," I told her. So stupid of me. We're having the carnival crowd today, aren't we?

MASHA

Yes.

IRINA

Sits down How nice it is to rest! I am tired!

TUTZENBACH

Smiling When you come back from work, you look so young, so pathetic, somehow.

IRINA

I'm tired. No, I don't like working at the post office. I don't like it at all.

You've gotten thinner. *whistles* You look younger
too, and your face looks quite boyish.

TUTZENBACH
It's the way she does her hair.

IRINA
I must look for another job. This one doesn't suit me.
It hasn't got what I always longed for and dreamed
about. It's the sort of work you do without inspiration,
without even thinking.

Someone knocks at the floor from below

That's the doctor knocking. *to Tutzenbach* Will
you answer him, dear? I can't. I'm so tired.

Tutzenbach knocks on the floor

He'll be up in a moment. We must do something about
all this. Andrei and the doctor went to the club last
night and lost at cards again. They say Andrei lost two
hundred rubles.

MASHA
With indifference Well, what are we to do about it?

IRINA
He lost two weeks ago, and he lost in December too.
I wish to goodness he'd lose everything we've got, and
soon too, and then perhaps we'd move out of this place.
Good heavens, I dream of Moscow every night. Sometimes I feel as if I were going mad. *laughs* We're
going to Moscow in June. How many months are
there till June? February, March, April, May . . .
Nearly half a year!

MASHA   THE
We must take care that Natasha doesn't get to know   THREE
about his losing at cards.   SISTERS

IRINA

I don't think she cares.

Enter Chebutykin. He has been resting on his bed since dinner and has just gotten up. He combs his beard, then sits down at the table and takes out a newspaper

MASHA

There he is. Has he paid his rent yet?

IRINA

Laughs No. Not a kopeck for the last eight months. I suppose he's forgotten.

MASHA

Laughs How solemn he looks sitting there!

They all laugh. A pause

IRINA

Why don't you say something, Aleksandr Ignatievich?

VERSHININ

I don't know. I'm just longing for some tea. I'd give my life for a glass of tea! I've had nothing to eat since morning.

CHEBUTYKIN

Irina Sergeevna!

IRINA

What is it?

CHEBUTYKIN

Please come here. *Venez ici!*

Irina goes over to him and sits down at the table

I can't do without you.

Irina lays out the cards for a game of solitaire

VERSHININ

Well, if we can't have any tea, let's do a bit of philosophizing anyway.

ANTON
CHEKHOV

TUTZENBACH

Yes, let's. What about?

VERSHININ

What about? Well . . . let's try to imagine what life will be like after we're dead, say in two or three hundred years.

TUTZENBACH

All right then. After we're dead, people will fly around in balloons, the cut of their coats will be different, the sixth sense will be discovered and possibly even developed and used for all I know. But I believe life itself will remain the same; it will still be difficult and full of mystery and full of happiness. And in a thousand years' time people will still be sighing and complaining, "How hard this business of living is!" And yet they'll still be scared of death and unwilling to die just as they are now.

VERSHININ

After a moment's thought

Well, you know . . . How shall I put it? I think everything in the world is bound to change gradually—in fact it's changing before our very eyes. In two or three hundred years or maybe in a thousand years—it doesn't matter how long exactly—life will be different. It will be happy. Of course we won't be able to enjoy that future life, but all the same what we're living for now is to create it; we work and . . . yes, we suffer in order to create it. That's the goal of our life, and you might say that's the only happiness we will ever achieve.

Masha laughs quietly

TUTZENBACH

Why are you laughing?

MASHA

I don't know. I've been laughing all day today.

VERSHININ

To Tutzenbach   I went to the same cadet school as

THE
THREE
SISTERS

you did but I never went on to the military academy. I read a great deal, of course, but I never know what books I ought to choose, and probably I read a lot of stuff that's not worth anything. But the longer I live the more I seem to long for knowledge. My hair's turning gray and I'm getting on in years, and yet how little I know, how little! All the same I think I do know one thing which is not only true but also most important. I'm sure of it. Oh, if only I could convince you that there's not going to be any happiness for our own generation, that there mustn't be and won't be. We've just got to work and work. All the happiness is reserved for our descendants, our remote descendants. *pause* Anyway if I'm not to be happy, then at least my children's children will be.

Fedotik and Rodé enter the ballroom. They sit down and sing quietly, one of them playing a guitar

TUTZENBACH
So you won't even allow us to dream of happiness! But what if I *am* happy?

VERSHININ
You're not.

TUTZENBACH
Flinging up his hands and laughing
We don't understand one another, that's obvious. How can I convince you?

Masha laughs quietly

holds up a finger to her
Show a finger to her and she'll laugh! *to Vershinin* And life will be just the same as ever not merely in a couple of hundred years' time, but in a million years. Life doesn't change. It always goes on the same; it follows its own laws, which don't concern us, which

we can't discover anyway. Think of the birds that migrate in the autumn—the cranes, for instance: they just fly on and on. It doesn't matter what sort of thoughts they've got in their heads—great thoughts or little thoughts—they just fly on and on, not knowing where or why. And they'll go on flying no matter how many philosophers they happen to have flying with them. Let them philosophize as much as they like, as long as they go on flying.

MASHA

Isn't there some meaning?

TUTZENBACH

Meaning? Look out there. It's snowing. What's the meaning of that?

MASHA

I think a human being has got to have some faith, or at least he's got to seek faith. Otherwise his life will be empty, empty. How can you live and not know why the cranes fly, why children are born, why the stars shine in the sky! You must either know why you live or else . . . nothing matters. . . . Everything's just wild grass.

VERSHININ

All the same I'm sorry my youth's over.

MASHA

"It's a bore to be alive in this world, friends." That's what Gogol says.

TUTZENBACH

And I feel like saying: it's hopeless arguing with you, friends! I give you up.

CHEBUTYKIN

Reads out of the paper

Balsac's marriage took place at Berdichev.[1]

1. A town in western Russia well known for its almost exclusively Jewish population.

Must write this down in my notebook.   *writes*
Balsac's marriage took place at Berdichev.   *reads on*

IRINA
Playing solitaire, pensively
Balsac's marriage took place at Berdichev.

TUTZENBACH
Well, I've thrown in my hand. Did you know that
I sent in my resignation, Marya Sergeevna?

MASHA
Yes, I heard about it. I don't see anything good in it
either. I don't like civilians.

TUTZENBACH
Never mind.   *gets up*   What sort of a soldier do I
make anyway? I'm not even good-looking. Well, what
does it matter? I'll work. I'd like to do such a hard
day's work that when I came home in the evening I'd
fall on my bed exhausted and go to sleep at once.   *goes
to the ballroom*   I would think working men sleep
well at nights!

FEDOTIK
To Irina   I've gotten you some colored crayons at
Pyzhikov's, on Moscow Street. And this little penknife
too.

IRINA
You still treat me as if I were a little girl. I wish you'd
remember I'm grown up now.   *takes the crayons and
the penknife joyfully*   They're awfully nice!

FEDOTIK
Look, I bought a knife for myself too. You see, it's got
another blade here, and then another. This thing's for
cleaning your ears, and these are nail scissors, and
this is for cleaning your nails.

ANTON
CHEKHOV

In a loud voice
Doctor, how old are you?

CHEBUTYKIN
Me? Thirty-two.

Laughter

FEDOTIK
I'll show you another kind of solitaire.   *sets out the cards*

The samovar is brought in, and Anfisa attends to it. Shortly afterward Natasha comes in and begins to fuss around the table. Soleni enters, bows to the company, and sits down at the table

VERSHININ
What a wind though!

MASHA
Yes. I'm tired of winter. I've almost forgotten what summer is like.

IRINA
Playing solitaire   It's coming out. We'll get to Moscow!

FEDOTIK
No, it's not coming out. You see, the eight has to go on the two of spades.   *laughs*   That means you won't go to Moscow.

CHEBUTYKIN
Reads the paper
Tsitsihar. Smallpox is raging.

ANFISA
Goes up to Masha
Masha, the tea's ready, dear.   *to Vershinin*   Will you please come to the table, Your Excellency? Forgive me, your name's slipped my memory.

MASHA

Bring it here, Nanny. I'm not coming over there.

IRINA

Nanny!

ANFISA

Comi-ing!

NATASHA

To Soleni   You know, even tiny babies understand what we say perfectly well! "Good morning, Bobik," I said to him only today, "good morning, my precious!" And then he looked at me in such a special sort of way. You may say it's only a mother's imagination, but it isn't, I do assure you. No, no! He really is an extraordinary child!

SOLENI

If that child were mine, I'd cook him up in a frying pan and eat him.   *picks up his glass, goes into the drawing room, and sits down in a corner*

NATASHA

Covers her face with her hands
What a rude, ill-mannered person!

MASHA

People who don't even notice whether it's summer or winter are lucky! I think I'd be indifferent to the weather if I were living in Moscow.

VERSHININ

I've just been reading the diary of some French cabinet minister—he wrote it in prison. He got sent to prison in connection with the Panama affair. He writes with such a passionate delight about the birds he can see through the prison window—the birds he never even noticed when he was a cabinet minister. Of course now that he's released he won't notice them anymore. And in the same way you won't notice Moscow once

you live there again. We're not happy and we can't
be happy: we only want happiness.

TUTZENBACH
Picks up a box from the table
Say there, where are all the chocolates?

IRINA
Soleni's eaten them.

TUTZENBACH
All of them?

ANFISA
Serving Vershinin tea
Here's a letter for you, sir.

VERSHININ
For me?   *takes the letter*   From my daughter.   *reads
it*   Yes, of course. Forgive me, Marya Sergeevna, I'll
just leave quietly. I won't have any tea.   *gets up,
agitated*   Always the same thing.

MASHA
What is it? Secret?

VERSHININ
In a low voice
My wife's taken poison again. I must go. I'll get away
without them seeing me. All this is so dreadfully
unpleasant.   *kisses Masha's hand*   My dear, good,
sweet girl. I'll go out this way quietly.   *goes out*

ANFISA
Where's he off to? And I've just brought him some tea!
What a queer fellow!

MASHA
Flaring up   Leave me alone! Why do you keep
worrying me? Why don't you leave me in peace?   *goes
to the table, cup in hand*   I'm sick and tired of you,
silly old woman!   THE
ANFISA   THREE
Why . . . I didn't mean to offend you, dear.   SISTERS

ANDREI'S VOICE

Offstage Anfisa!

ANFISA

Mimics him Anfisa! Sitting there in his den! *goes out*

MASHA

By the table in the ballroom, crossly

Do let me sit down somewhere! *jumbles up the cards laid out on the table* You take up the whole table with your cards! Why don't you get on with your tea?

IRINA

How bad-tempered you are, Mashka!

MASHA

Well, if I'm bad-tempered. don't talk to me then. Don't touch me!

CHEBUTYKIN

Laughs Don't touch her! Take care you don't touch her!

MASHA

You may be sixty, but you're always babbling some damn nonsense or other just like a child.

NATASHA

Sighs My dear Masha, need you use such expressions? You know, with your good looks you'd be thought so charming, even by the best people—yes, I honestly mean it—if only you wouldn't use these expressions of yours! *Je vous prie, pardonnez-moi, Marie, mais vous avez des manières un peu grossières.*

TUTZENBACH

With suppressed laughter

Pass me . . . Say there, will you please pass me . . . Is that cognac over there or what?

ANTON
CHEKHOV

NATASHA

Il paraît que mon Bobik déjà ne dort pas. I think he's

awake. He's not been too well today. I must go and
see him. Excuse me. *goes out*

IRINA

And where has Aleksandr Ignatievich gone to?

MASHA

He's gone home. His wife's done something queer
again.

TUTZENBACH

Goes over to Soleni with a decanter of cognac
You always sit alone brooding over something or
other—though what it's all about nobody knows. Well,
let's make up. Let's have a cognac together. *they
drink* I suppose I'll have to play the piano all night
tonight—a lot of rubbishy tunes of course. Never mind!

SOLENI

Why did you say, "Let's make up"? We haven't
quarreled.

TUTZENBACH

You always give me the feeling that there's something
wrong between us. You're a strange character, no
doubt about it.

SOLENI

Recites "I am strange, but who's not so? Don't be
angry, Aleko!"

TUTZENBACH

What's Aleko got to do with it?

SOLENI

After a pause
When I'm alone with somebody I'm all right; I'm just
like other people. But in company I get depressed and
shy, and . . . I talk all sorts of nonsense. All the same
I'm a good deal more honest and well intentioned
than plenty of others. I can prove I am.

TUTZENBACH

You often make me angry because you keep on pestering

me when we're in company. But all the same I do like you for some reason. I'm going to get drunk tonight, whatever happens! Let's have another drink!

SOLENI

Yes, let's. *pause* I've never had anything against you personally, Baron. But my temperament's rather like Lermontov's. *in a low voice* I even look a little like Lermontov, I've been told. *takes a cologne bottle from his pocket and sprinkles some cologne on his hands*

TUTZENBACH

I have sent in my resignation! Finished! I've been considering it for five years, and now I've made up my mind at last. I'm going to work.

SOLENI

Recites "Don't be angry, Aleko!... Away, away with all your dreams!"

During the conversation Andrei enters quietly with a book in his hand and sits down by the candle

TUTZENBACH

I'm going to work!

CHEBUTYKIN

Comes into the drawing room with Irina
And the food they treated me to was the genuine Caucasian stuff: onion soup, followed by chehartma— that's a meat dish, you know.

SOLENI

Cheremsha isn't meat at all; it's a plant, something like an onion.

CHEBUTYKIN

No-o, my dear friend. Chehartma isn't an onion; it's roast mutton.

ANTON
CHEKHOV

SOLENI

I tell you cheremsha is a kind of onion.

Well, why should I argue about it with you? You've never been to the Caucasus and you've never tasted chehartma.

SOLENI

I haven't tasted it because I can't stand the smell of it. Cheremsha stinks just like garlic.

ANDREI

Imploringly   Do stop it, friends! Please stop it!

TUTZENBACH

When's the carnival crowd coming?

IRINA

They promised to be here by nine—that means any moment now.

TUTZENBACH

Embraces Andrei and sings
"Ah, my beautiful porch, my lovely new porch, my . . ."[1]

ANDREI

Dances and sings
"My new porch all made of maple wood."

CHEBUTYKIN

Dances   "With fancy carving over the door."

Laughter

TUTZENBACH

Kisses Andrei   Let's have a drink, the hell with it! Andryusha, let's drink to eternal friendship. I'll come with you when you go back to Moscow University.

SOLENI

Which university? There are two universities in Moscow.

---

1. A traditional Russian dance song.

ANDREI

There's only one.

SOLENI

I tell you there are two.

ANDREI

Never mind, make it three. The more the merrier.

SOLENI

There are two universities in Moscow.

Murmurs of protest and cries of "hush!"

There are two universities in Moscow, an old one and a new one. But if you don't want to listen to what I'm saying, if my conversation irritates you, I can keep silent. In fact I can go to another room. *goes out through one of the doors*

TUTZENBACH

Bravo, bravo! *laughs* Let's get started, my friends. I'll play for you. What a funny creature that Soleni is! *sits down at the piano and plays a waltz*

MASHA

Dances alone The baron is drunk, the baron is drunk, the baron is drunk.

Enter Natasha

NATASHA

To Chebutykin Ivan Romanovich! *speaks to him, then goes out quietly*

Chebutykin touches Tutzenbach on the shoulder and whispers to him

IRINA

What is it?

ANTON
CHEKHOV

CHEBUTYKIN

It's time we were going. Good night.

IRINA
But really . . . What about the carnival party?

ANDREI
Embarrassed The carnival party's not coming. You
see, my dear, Natasha says that Bobik isn't very well,
and so . . . Anyway, I don't know . . . and I certainly
don't care.

IRINA
Shrugs her shoulders
Bobik's not very well!

MASHA
Never mind, we'll keep our end up! If they turn us out,
out we must go! *to Irina* It isn't Bobik who's not
well; it's her. There! *taps her forehead with her
finger* Petty little bourgeois housewife!

*Andrei goes to his room on the right. Chebutykin follows
him. The guests say good-bye in the ballroom*

FEDOTIK
What a pity! I'd been hoping to spend the evening
here, but of course, if the baby's ill . . . I'll bring him
some toys tomorrow.

RODÉ
In a loud voice
I had a good long sleep after lunch today on purpose.
I thought I'd be dancing all night. I mean to say, it's
only just nine o'clock.

MASHA
Let's go outside and talk it over. We can decide what
to do then.

*Voices are heard saying, "Good-bye! God bless you!"
and Tutzenbach is heard laughing gaily. Everyone goes
out. Anfisa and a maid clear the table and put out*

THE
THREE
SISTERS

the lights. The nurse sings to the baby offstage. Enter Andrei, wearing an overcoat and hat, followed by Chebutykin. They move quietly

CHEBUTYKIN

I've never found time to get married, somehow . . . partly because my life's just flashed past me like lightning, and partly because I was always madly in love with your mother and she was married.

ANDREI

One shouldn't marry. One shouldn't marry because it's so boring.

CHEBUTYKIN

That may be so, but what about loneliness? You can philosophize as much as you like, dear boy, but loneliness is a dreadful thing. Although really . . . Well, it doesn't make a damn bit of difference of course!

ANDREI

Let's go quickly.

CHEBUTYKIN

What's the hurry? There's plenty of time.

ANDREI

I'm afraid my wife may try to stop me.

CHEBUTYKIN

Ah!

ANDREI

I won't play cards tonight; I'll just sit and watch. I'm not feeling too well. What should I do for this breathlessness, Ivan Romanovich?

CHEBUTYKIN

Why ask me, dear boy? I can't remember. I simply don't know.

ANDREI

Let's go through the kitchen.

They go out. A bell rings. The ring is repeated; then
voices and laughter are heard

IRINA

Coming in   What's that?

ANFISA

In a whisper
The carnival party.

The bell rings again

IRINA

Tell them there's no one at home, Nanny. Apologize
to them.

*Anfisa goes out. Irina walks up and down the room,
lost in thought. She seems agitated. Enter Soleni*

SOLENI

Puzzled   There's no one here. Where is everybody?

IRINA

They've gone home.

SOLENI

How strange! Then you're alone here?

IRINA

Yes, alone.   *pause*   Well, good night.

SOLENI

I know I behaved tactlessly just now. I lost control of
myself. But you're different from the others; you stand
out high above them. You're pure; you can see where
the truth lies. You're the only person in the world who
can possibly understand me. I love you. I love you
with a deep, infinite . . .

IRINA

Do please go away. Good night!

SOLENI

I can't live without you.   *follows her*   Oh, it's such a

delight just to look at you! *with tears* Oh, my
happiness! Your glorious, marvelous, entrancing eyes—
eyes like no other woman's I've ever seen.

IRINA

Coldly Please stop it, Vasili Vasilievich!

SOLENI

I've never spoken to you of my love before. It makes
me feel as if I were living on a different planet. *rubs
his forehead* Never mind! I can't force you to love
me, obviously. But I don't intend to have any rivals—
successful rivals, I mean. No, no! I swear to you by
everything I hold sacred that if there's anyone else, I'll
kill him. Oh, how wonderful you are!

Enter Natasha carrying a candle

NATASHA

*Pokes her head into one room, then into another, but
passes the door leading to her husband's room*
Andrei's reading in there. Better let him read. Forgive
me, Vasili Vasilievich, I didn't know you were here.
I'm afraid I'm not properly dressed.

SOLENI

I don't care. Good-bye. *goes out*

NATASHA

You must be tired, my poor dear girl. *kisses Irina*
You ought to go to bed earlier.

IRINA

Is Bobik asleep?

NATASHA

Yes, he's asleep. But he's not sleeping peacefully. By the
way, my dear, I've been meaning to speak to you for
some time but there's always been something. Either
you're not here, or I'm too busy. You see, I think that
Bobik's nursery is so cold and damp. And your room

ANTON
CHEKHOV

is just ideal for a baby. Darling, do you think you
could move into Olga's room?

IRINA
Not understanding her
Where to?

*The sound of bells is heard outside, as a troika is driven
up to the house*

NATASHA
You can share a room with Olya for the time being,
and Bobik can have your room. He is such a darling!
This morning I said to him, "Bobik, you're my very
own! My very own!" And he just gazed at me with
his dear little eyes.

The doorbell rings

That must be Olga. How late she is!

A maid comes up to Natasha and whispers in her ear

Protopopov! What a funny fellow! Protopopov's come
to ask me to go for a drive with him. In a troika!
laughs Aren't these men strange creatures!

The doorbell rings again

Someone's ringing. Shall I go for a short drive? Just for
a quarter of an hour? *to the maid* Tell him I'll be
down in a minute.

The doorbell rings

That's the bell again. I suppose it's Olga. *goes out*

*The maid runs out. Irina sits lost in thought. Enter
Kulygin and Olga, followed by Vershinin*

KULYGIN
Well! What's the meaning of this? You said you were
going to have a party.

VERSHININ

It's a strange thing. I left here about half an hour ago, and they were expecting a carnival party then.

IRINA

They've all gone.

KULYGIN

Masha's gone too? Where has she gone to? And why is Protopopov waiting outside in a troika? Who's he waiting for?

IRINA

Please don't ask me questions. I'm tired.

KULYGIN

You spoiled child!

OLGA

The conference has only just ended. I'm quite worn out. The headmistress is ill and I'm substituting for her. My head's aching, oh, my head, my head.   *sits down* Andrei lost two hundred rubles at cards last night. The whole town's talking about it.

KULYGIN

Yes, the conference exhausted me too.   *sits down*

VERSHININ

So now my wife's taken it into her head to try to frighten me. She tried to poison herself. However, everything's all right now, so I can relax, thank goodness. So we've got to go away? Well, good night to you, all the best. Fëdor Ilyich, would you care to come along with me somewhere or other? I can't stay at home tonight, I really can't. Do come!

KULYGIN

I'm tired. I don't think I'll come.   *gets up*   I'm tired. Has my wife gone home?

IRINA

I think so.

KULYGIN

Kisses Irina's hand

Good night. We can rest tomorrow and the day after tomorrow, two whole days! Well, I wish you all the best. *going out* How I long for some tea! I planned on spending the evening in congenial company, but— *o fallacem hominum spem!* Always use the accusative case in exclamations.

VERSHININ

Well, it looks as if I'll have to go somewhere by myself. *goes out with Kulygin, whistling*

OLGA

My head aches, oh, my head. Andrei lost at cards. The whole town's talking. I'll go and lie down. *going out* Tomorrow I'm free. Heavens what a joy! Tomorrow I'm free, and the day after tomorrow I'm free. My head's aching, oh, my poor head.

IRINA

Alone They've all gone. No one's left.

Someone is playing an accordion in the street. The nurse sings in the next room

NATASHA

Crosses the ballroom, wearing a fur coat and cap. She is followed by the maid

I'll be back in half an hour. I'm just going for a little drive. *goes out*

IRINA

Alone, with intense longing

Moscow! Moscow! Moscow!

CURTAIN

ACT THREE

A bedroom now shared by Olga and Irina. There are two beds, one on the right, the other on the left, each screened off from the center of the room. It is past two o'clock in the morning. Offstage the alarm is being sounded on account of a fire which has been raging for some time. No one in the house has been to bed yet. Masha is lying on a couch, dressed as usual in black. Olga and Anfisa come in.

ANFISA

Now they're sitting down there, under the stairs. I keep telling them to come upstairs, that they shouldn't sit down there, but they just cry. "We don't know where our papa is," they say, "perhaps he got burned in the fire." What an idea! And there are people in the yard too . . . half-dressed.

OLGA

Takes a dress out of a wardrobe

Take this gray dress, Nanny. . . . And this one . . . This blouse too . . . And this skirt. Oh, heavens! What is happening! Apparently the whole of the Kirsanovski Street's been burned down. Take this . . . And this too . . . *throws the clothes into Anfisa's arms* The poor Vershinins had a fright. Their house only just escaped being burned down. They'll have to spend the

night here. We mustn't let them go home. Poor
Fedotik's lost everything; he's got nothing left.

ANFISA

I'd better call Ferapont, Olyushka; I can't carry all this.

OLGA

Rings No one pays any attention when I ring. *calls through the door* Is anyone there? Will someone come up, please!

A window, red with the glow of the fire, can be seen through the open door. The sound of a passing fire engine is heard

How dreadful it all is! And how tired of it I am!

Enter Ferapont

Take this downstairs please. The Kolotilin girls are sitting under the stairs. Give it to them. And this too.

FERAPONT

Very good, madam. Moscow was burned down in 1812 just the same. Mercy on us! Yes, the French were surprised all right.

OLGA

Go ahead now, take this down.

FERAPONT

Very good. *goes out*

OLGA

Give it all away, Nanny dear. We won't keep anything. Give it all away. I'm so tired, I can hardly keep on my feet. We mustn't let the Vershinins go home. The little girls can sleep in the drawing room, and Aleksandr Ignatievich can share the downstairs room with the baron. Fedotik can go in with the baron too, or maybe he'd better sleep in the ballroom. The doctor's gone and gotten drunk—you'd think he'd done it on purpose; he's so hopelessly drunk that we can't let anyone go into his room. Vershinin's wife will have to go into the drawing room too.

ANFISA

Wearily Don't send me away, Olyushka, darling! Don't send me away!

OLGA

What nonsense you're talking, Nanny! No one's sending you away.

ANFISA

Leans her head against Olga's breast
My dearest girl! I do work, you know; I work as hard as I can. I suppose now that I'm getting weaker, I'll be told to go. But where can I go? Where? I'm eighty years old. I'm over eighty-one!

OLGA

You sit down for a while, Nanny. You're tired, you poor dear. *makes her sit down* Just rest a bit. You've turned quite pale.

Enter Natasha

NATASHA

They're saying we ought to start a drive in aid of the victims of the fire. You know—form a society or something for the purpose. Well, why not? It's an excellent idea! In any case it's up to us to help the poor as best we can. Bobik and Sofochka are fast alseep as if nothing had happened. We've got such a crowd of people in the house; the place seems full of people whichever way you turn. There's flu around in the town. I'm so afraid the children might catch it.

OLGA

Without listening to her
You can't see the fire from this room; it's quiet in here.

NATASHA

Yes. I suppose my hair is all over the place. *stands in*

front of the mirror They say I've gotten fatter, but
it's not true! I'm not a bit fatter. Masha's alseep. She's
tired, poor girl. *to Anfisa, coldly* How dare you
sit down in my presence! Get up! Get out of here!

Anfisa goes out. There is a pause

I can't understand why you keep that old woman in
the house.

OLGA
Taken aback Forgive me for saying it, but I can't
understand how you . . .

NATASHA
She's quite useless here. She's just a peasant woman; her
right place is in the country. You're spoiling her. I do
like order in the home. I don't like having useless
people around. *strokes Olga's cheek* You're tired,
my poor dear! Our headmistress is tired! You know,
when my Sofochka grows up and goes to school, I'll
be frightened of you.

OLGA
I'm not going to be a headmistress.

NATASHA
You'll be asked to, Olechka. It's settled.

OLGA
I'll refuse. I couldn't do it. I wouldn't be strong enough.
drinks water You spoke so harshly to nanny just
now. You must forgive me for saying so, but I just
can't stand that sort of thing. It made me feel quite
faint.

NATASHA
Agitated Forgive me, Olya, forgive me. I didn't
mean to upset you.

*Masha gets up, picks up a pillow, and starts to go
out in a huff*

OLGA

Please try to understand me, dear. It may be that we've been brought up in a peculiar way, but anyway I just can't bear it. When people are treated like that, it gets me down, I feel quite ill. . . . I simply get unnerved.

NATASHA

Forgive me, dear, forgive me! *kisses her*

OLGA

Any cruel or tactless remark, even the slightest dis-courtesy, upsets me.

NATASHA

It's quite true, I know I often say things which would be better left unsaid—but you must agree with me, dear, that she'd be better in the country somewhere.

OLGA

She's been with us for thirty years.

NATASHA

But she can't do any work now, can she? Either I don't understand you, or you don't want to understand me. She can't work; she just sleeps or sits around.

OLGA

Well, let her sit around.

NATASHA

In surprise What do you mean, let her sit around? Surely she is a servant! *tearfully* No, I don't under-stand you, Olya! I have a nurse for the children and a wet nurse and we share a maid and a cook. Whatever do we want this old woman for? What for?

The alarm is sounded again

OLGA

I've aged ten years tonight.

ANTON
CHEKHOV

NATASHA

We must sort things out, Olya. You're working at your

school, and I'm working at home. You're teaching
and I'm running the house. And when I say anything
about the servants, I know what I'm talking about.
That old thief, that old witch, must get out of this
house tomorrow! *stamps her feet* How dare you
annoy me like this? How dare you? *recovering her
self-control* Really if you don't move downstairs,
we'll always be quarreling. This is quite dreadful!

Enter Kulygin

KULYGIN

Where's Masha? It's time we went home. They say the
fire's getting less fierce. *stretches* Only one block
got burned down, but to begin with it looked as if the
whole town was going to be set on fire by that wind.
sits down I'm so tired, Olechka, my dear. You know,
I've often thought that if I hadn't marrried Masha, I'd
have married you, Olechka. You're so kind. I'm worn
out. *listens*

OLGA

What is it?

KULYGIN

The doctor's gotten drunk just as if he'd done it on
purpose. Hopelessly drunk. As if he'd done it on
purpose. *gets up* I think he's coming up here. Can
you hear him? Yes, he's coming up. *laughs* What a
fellow really! I'm going to hide myself. *goes to the
wardrobe and stands between it and the wall* What a
scoundrel!

OLGA

He's been off drinking for two years, and now suddenly
he goes and gets drunk. *walks with Natasha toward
the back of the room*

Chebutykin enters; walking firmly and soberly he crosses

*the room, stops, looks around, then goes to the wash-
stand, and begins to wash his hands*

CHEBUTYKIN
Glumly The devil take them all . . . all the lot of
them! They think I can treat anything just because I'm
a doctor, but I know positively nothing at all. I've
forgotten everything I used to know. I remember
nothing, positively nothing.

Olga and Natasha leave the room without his noticing

The devil take them! Last Wednesday I attended a
woman at Zasyp. She died, and it's all my fault that
she did die. Yes. I used to know a thing or two twenty-
five years ago, but now I don't remember anything.
Not a thing! Perhaps I'm not a man at all, but I just
imagine that I've got hands and feet and a head.
Perhaps I don't exist at all, and I only imagine that I'm
walking around and eating and sleeping. *weeps* Oh,
if only I could simply stop existing! *stops crying,
glumly* God knows. . . . The other day they were
talking about Shakespeare and Voltaire at the club.
I haven't read either—never read a single line of
either—but I tried to make out by my expression that
I had. The others did the same. How petty it all is!
How despicable! And then suddenly I thought of the
woman I killed on Wednesday. It all came back to me,
and I felt like such a swine, so sick of myself that I went
and got drunk.

*Enter Irina, Vershinin, and Tutzenbach. Tutzenbach
is wearing a fashionable, new civilian suit*

IRINA
Let's sit down here for a while. No one will come in
here.

VERSHININ

The whole town would have been burned down if it weren't for the soldiers. They're a fine lot of fellows! *rubs his hands with pleasure* Excellent fellows! Yes, they're a fine lot!

KULYGIN

Approaches them What's the time?

TUTZENBACH

It's past three. It's beginning to get light.

IRINA

Everyone's sitting in the ballroom and nobody thinks of leaving. That man Soleni's there too. *to Chebutykin* You ought to go to bed, Doctor.

CHEBUTYKIN

I'm all right. Thanks. *combs his beard*

KULYGIN

Laughs A bit tipsy, Ivan Romanovich! *slaps him on the shoulder* You're a fine one! *In vino veritas,* as they used to say in Rome.

TUTZENBACH

Everyone keeps asking me to arrange a concert in aid of the victims of the fire.

IRINA

Well, who'd you get to perform in it?

TUTZENBACH

It could be done if we wanted to. Marya Sergeevna plays the piano wonderfully well, in my opinion.

KULYGIN

Yes, wonderfully well!

IRINA

She's forgotten how to. She hasn't played for three years . . . or maybe it's four.

TUTZENBACH

Nobody understands music in this town, not a single person. But I do—I really do—and I assure you quite

THE
THREE
SISTERS

definitely that Marya Sergeevna plays magnificently. She's almost a genius for it.

KULYGIN

You're right, Baron. I'm very fond of Masha. She's such a nice girl.

TUTZENBACH

Fancy being able to play so exquisitely, and yet having nobody, nobody at all, to appreciate it!

KULYGIN

Sighs Yes. But would it be quite proper for her to play in a concert? *pause* I don't know anything about these matters, my friends. Perhaps it'll be perfectly all right. But you know, although our director is a good man, a very good man indeed and most intelligent, I know that he does hold certain views. . . . Of course this doesn't really concern him, but I'll have a word with him about it all the same, if you like.

Chebutykin picks up a china clock and examines it

VERSHININ

I've gotten my clothes in such a mess helping to put out the fire, I must look like nothing on earth. *pause* I believe they were saying yesterday that our brigade might be transferred to somewhere a long way away. Some said it was to be Poland, and some said it was Chita, in Siberia.

TUTZENBACH

I heard that too. Well, the town will seem quite deserted.

IRINA

We'll go away too!

CHEBUTYKIN

Drops the clock and breaks it
Smashed to smithereens!

KULYGIN
Picks up the pieces
Fancy breaking such a valuable thing! Ah, Ivan
Romanich, Ivan Romanich! You'll get a bad mark for
that!

IRINA
It was my mother's clock.

CHEBUTYKIN
Well, supposing it was. If it was your mother's, then it
was your mother's. Perhaps I didn't smash it. Perhaps
it only appears that I did. Perhaps it only appears to
us that we exist, whereas in reality we don't exist at all.
I don't know anything; no one knows anything.
stops at the door   Why are you staring at me?
Natasha's having a nice little affair with Protopopov,
and you don't see it. You sit here seeing nothing, and
meanwhile Natasha's having a nice little affair with
Protopopov.   *sings*   Would you like a date?   *goes
out*

VERSHININ
So.   *laughs*   How odd it all is really!   *pause*   When
the fire started, I ran home as fast as I could. When I
got near, I could see that our house was all right and
out of danger, but the two little girls were standing
there, in the doorway, in their night clothes. Their
mother wasn't there. People were rushing around,
horses, dogs . . . And in the kids' faces I saw a
frightened, anxious, appealing look, I don't know
what! My heart sank when I saw their faces. My God,
I thought, what will these children have to go through   THE
in the course of their poor lives? And they may live a   THREE
long time too! I picked them up and ran back here with   SISTERS

them, and all the time I was running, I was thinking the same thing: what will they have to go through?

The alarm is sounded. A pause

When I got here, my wife was here already . . . angry, shouting!

Enter Masha carrying a pillow. She sits down on the couch

And when my little girls were standing in the doorway with nothing on but their night clothes, and the street was red with the glow of the fire and full of terrifying noises, it struck me that the same sort of thing used to happen years ago, when armies used to make sudden raids on towns and plunder them and set them on fire. Anyway is there any essential difference between things as they were and as they are now? And before very long, say, in another two or three hundred years, people may be looking at our present life just as we look at the past now, with horror and scorn. Our own times may seem uncouth to them, boring and frightfully uncomfortable and strange. Oh, what a great life it'll be then, what a life! *laughs* Forgive me, I'm philosophizing my head off again . . . but may I go on, please? I'm bursting to philosophize just at the moment. I'm in the mood for it. *pause* You seem as if you've all gone to sleep. As I was saying: what a great life it will be in the future! Just try to imagine it. . . . At the present time there are only three people of your intellectual caliber in the whole of this town, but future generations will be more productive of people like you. They'll go on producing more and more of the same sort until at last the time will come when everything will be just as you'd wish it yourselves.

ANTON
CHEKHOV

People will live their lives in your way, and then even 361
you may be outmoded, and a new lot will come along
who will be even better than you are. *laughs* I'm in
quite a special mood today. I feel full of a tremendous
urge to live. *sings*
    "To Love all ages are in fee,
        The passion's good for you and me." *laughs*

MASHA
Sings Tara-tara-tara . . .

VERSHININ
Tum-tum . . .

MASHA
Tara-tara . . .

VERSHININ
Tum-tum, tum-tum . . . *laughs*

Enter Fedotik

FEDOTIK
Dancing about Burned, burned! Everything I've got
burned!

All laugh

IRINA
It's hardly a joking matter. Has everything really been
burned?

FEDOTIK
Laughs Everything, completely. I've got nothing
left. My guitar's burned, my photographs are burned,
all my letters are burned. Even the little notebook I was
going to give you has been burned.

Enter Soleni

IRINA
No, please go away, Vasili Vasilievich. You can't
come in here.

SOLENI

Can't I? Why can the baron come in here if I can't?

VERSHININ

We really must go, all of us. What's the fire doing?

SOLENI

It's dying down, they say. Well, I must say it's a peculiar thing that the baron can come in here and I can't.   *takes a cologne bottle from his pocket and sprinkles himself with cologne*

VERSHININ

Tara-tara.

MASHA

Tum-tum, tum-tum.

VERSHININ

Laughs, to Soleni

Let's go to the ballroom.

SOLENI

Very well, we'll make a note of this. "I hardly need to make my moral yet more clear: that might be teasing geese, I fear!"[1]   *looks at Tutzenbach*   Cluck, cluck, cluck!   *goes out with Vershinin and Fedotik*

IRINA

That Soleni has smoked the room out.   *puzzled*   The baron's asleep. Baron! Baron!

TUTZENBACH

Waking out of his dose

I must be tired. The brickworks . . . No, I'm not talking in my sleep. I really do intend to go to the brickworks and start working there quite soon. I've had a talk with the manager.   *to Irina, tenderly*   You are so pale, so beautiful, so fascinating. Your pallor seems to light up the darkness around you, as if it were luminous, somehow. You're sad; you're dissatisfied

ANTON
CHEKHOV

1. From Krylov's fable *Geese*.

with the life you have to live. Oh, come away with me;
let's go away and work together!

MASHA

Nikolai Lvovich, I wish you'd go away.

TUTZENBACH

Laughs Oh, you're here, are you? I didn't see you.
kisses Irina's hand Good-bye, I'm going. You know,
as I look at you now, I keep thinking of the day—it
was a long time ago, your saint's day—when you
talked to us about the joy of work. You were so gay
and high-spirited then. And what a happy life I saw
ahead of me! Where is it all now? *kisses her hand*
There are tears in your eyes. You should go to bed; it's
beginning to get light. It's almost morning. Oh, if
only I could give my life for you!

MASHA

Nikolai Lvovich, please go away! Really now.

TUTZENBACH

I'm going. *goes out*

MASHA

Lies down Are you asleep, Fëdor?

KULYGIN

Eh?

MASHA

Why don't you go home?

KULYGIN

My darling Masha, my sweet, my precious Masha . . .

IRINA

She's tired. Let her rest a while, Fedya.

KULYGIN

I'll go in a moment. My wife, my dear, good wife!
How I love you! Only you!

MASHA

Crossly Amo, amas, amat, amamus, amatis, amant!

THE
THREE
SISTERS

KULYGIN

Laughs Really, she's an amazing woman! I've been married to you for seven years, but I feel as if we were only married yesterday. Yes, on my word of honor, I do! You really are amazing! Oh, I'm so happy, happy, happy!

MASHA

And I'm so bored, bored, bored! *sits up* I can't get it out of my head. It's simply disgusting. It's like having a nail driven into my head. No, I can't keep silent about it anymore. It's about Andrei. He's actually mortgaged this house to a bank, and his wife's got hold of all the money. And yet the house doesn't belong to him; it belongs to all four of us! Surely, he must realize that, if he's got any honesty.

KULYGIN

Why bring all this up, Masha? Why bother about it now? Andryusha owes money everywhere. Leave him alone.

MASHA

Anyway it's disgusting. *lies down*

KULYGIN

Well, we aren't poor, Masha. I've got work, I teach at the county school, I give private lessons in my spare time. I'm just a plain, honest man. *Omnia mea mecum porto*, as they say.

MASHA

I don't ask for anything, but I'm just disgusted by injustice. *pause* Why don't you go home, Fëdor?

KULYGIN

Kisses her You're tired. Just rest here for a while. I'll go home and wait for you. Go to sleep. *goes to the door* I'm happy, happy, happy! *goes out*

IRINA

The truth is that Andrei is getting to be shallow-

minded. He's aging and since he's been living with
that woman he's lost all the inspiration he used to have!
Not long ago he was working for a professorship, and
yet yesterday he boasted of having at last been elected
a member of the County Council. Fancy him a member,
with Protopopov as chairman! They say the whole
town's laughing at him; he's the only one who doesn't
know anything or see anything. And now, you see,
everyone's at the fire, while he's just sitting in his room,
not taking the slightest notice of it. Just playing his
violin. *agitated* Oh, how dreadful it is, how dreadful, how dreadful! I can't bear it any longer, I can't,
I really can't!

*Enter Olga. She starts arranging things on her bedside
table*

sobs loudly You must turn me out of here! Turn me
out; I can't stand it anymore!

OLGA
Alarmed What is it? What is it, darling?

IRINA
Sobbing Where? Where has it all gone to? Where is
it? Oh, God! I've forgotten. I've forgotten everything. . . . There's nothing but a muddle in my head.
I don't remember what the Italian for "window" is or
for "ceiling." . . . Every day I'm forgetting more and
more, and life's slipping by, and it will never, never
come back. We will never go to Moscow. I can see
that we will never go.

OLGA
Don't, my dear, don't.

IRINA
Trying to control herself
Oh, I'm so miserable! I can't work! I won't work! I've

THE
THREE
SISTERS

had enough of it, enough! First I worked on the tele-graph, now I'm in the County Council office, and I hate and despise everything they give me to do there. I'm twenty-three years old, I've been working all this time, and I feel as if my brain's dried up. I know I've gotten thinner and uglier and older, and I find no kind of satisfaction in anything, none at all. And the time's passing . . . and I feel as if I'm moving away from any hope of a genuine, fine life. I'm moving further and further away and sinking into a kind of abyss. I feel in despair, and I don't know why I'm still alive, why I haven't killed myself.

OLGA

Don't cry, my dear child, don't cry. It hurts me.

IRINA

I'm not crying anymore. That's enough of it. Look, I'm not crying now. Enough of it, enough!

OLGA

Darling, let me tell you something. I just want to speak as your sister, as your friend. That is, if you want my advice. Why don't you marry the baron?

Irina weeps quietly

After all you do respect him; you think a lot of him. It's true, he's not good-looking, but he's such a decent, clean-minded sort of man. After all one doesn't marry for love, but to fulfill a duty. At least I think so, and I'd marry even if I weren't in love. I'd marry anyone that proposed to me, as long as he was a decent man. I'd even marry an old man.

IRINA

I've been waiting all this time, imagining that we'd be moving to Moscow, and I'd meet the man I'm meant for there. I've dreamed about him and I've loved him

ANTON
CHEKHOV

in my dreams. But it's all turned out to be nonsense. . . .
Nonsense.

OLGA

Embracing her My darling sweetheart, I understand
everything perfectly. When the baron resigned his
commission and came to see us in his civilian clothes,
I thought he looked so plain that I actually started to
cry. He asked me why I was crying. How could I tell
him? But, of course, if it were God's will that he should
marry you, I'd feel perfectly happy about it. That's
quite a different matter, quite different!

*Natasha, carrying a candle, comes out of the door on
the right, crosses the stage, and goes out through the
door on the left without saying anything*

MASHA

Sits up She goes around looking as if she'd started
the fire.

OLGA

You're silly, Masha. You're the stupidest person in our
family. Forgive me for saying so. . . .

MASHA

After a pause
My dear sisters, I've got something to confess to you.
I must get some relief; I feel the need of it in my heart.
I'll confess it to you two alone, and then never again,
never to anybody! I'll tell you in a minute.   *in a low
voice*   It's a secret, but you'll have to know everything.
I can't keep silent anymore.   *pause*   I'm in love,
in love. I love that man. You saw him there just now.
Well, what's the use? I love Vershinin.

OLGA

Goes behind her screen
Don't say it. I don't want to hear it.

MASHA

Well, what's to be done? *holding her head* I thought
he was queer at first; then I started to pity him. Then
I began to love him . . . love everything about him—
his voice, his talk, his misfortunes, his two little girls.

OLGA

Nevertheless, I don't want to hear it. You can say any
nonsense you like, I'm not listening.

MASHA

Oh, you're stupid, Olya! If I love him, well—that's
my fate! That's my destiny. He loves me too. It's all
rather frightening, isn't it? Not a good thing, is it?
takes Irina by the hand and draws her to her Oh, my
dear! How are we going to live through the rest of our
lives? What's going to become of us? When you read
a novel, everything in it seems so old and obvious. But
when you fall in love yourself, you suddenly discover
that you don't really know anything, and you've got
to make your own decisions. . . . My dear sisters, my
dear sisters! I've confessed it all to you, and now I'll
keep quiet. I'll be like that madman in the story by
Gogol—silence . . . silence!

Enter Andrei followed by Ferapont

ANDREI

Irritably What do you want? I don't understand you.

FERAPONT

Stopping in the doorway, impatiently
I've asked you about ten times already, Andrei
Sergeevich.

ANDREI

In the first place you're not to call me Andrei
Sergeevich; call me "Your Honor."

ANTON
CHEKHOV

FERAPONT

The firemen are asking Your Honor if they may drive

through your garden to get to the river. They've been going a long way around all this time—it's a terrible business!

ANDREI

All right. Tell them it's all right.

Ferapont goes out

They keep on plaguing me. Where's Olga?

Olga comes from behind the screen

I wanted to see you. Will you give me the key to the cupboard? I've lost mine. You know the key I mean, the small one you've got.

Olga silently hands him the key. Irina goes behind the screen on her side of the room

What a terrific fire! It's going down though. That Ferapont annoyed me, the devil take him! Silly thing he made me say. Telling him to call me "Your Honor"! *pause* Why don't you say anything, Olya? *pause* It's about time you stopped this nonsense. Sulking like this for no reason whatever.... You here, Masha? And Irina's here too. That's excellent! We can talk it over then, frankly once and for all. What have you got against me? What is it?

OLGA

Drop it now, Andryusha. Let's talk it over tomorrow. *agitated* What a dreadful night!

ANDREI
In great embarrassment
Don't get upset. I'm asking you quite calmly: what have you got against me? Tell me frankly.

VERSHININ'S VOICE

Offstage Tum-tum-tum!

MASHA

In a loud voice, getting up
Tara-tara-tara! *to Olga* Good-bye, Olya, God bless
you! *goes behind the screen and kisses Irina* Sleep
well. Good-bye, Andrei. I would leave them now;
they're tired. Talk it over tomorrow. *goes out*

OLGA

Really, Andryusha, let's leave it till tomorrow. *goes
behind the screen on her side of the room* It's time to
go to bed.

ANDREI

I only want to say one thing; then I'll go. In a moment.
First of all, you've got something against my wife,
against Natasha. I've always been conscious of it from
the day we got married. Natasha is a fine woman; she's
honest and straightforward and high-principled. That's
my opinion. I love and respect my wife. You understand that I respect her, and I expect others to respect
her too. I repeat: she's an honest, high-principled
woman, and all your grievances against her—if you
don't mind my saying so—are just imagination and
nothing more. *pause* Secondly, you seem to be
annoyed with me for not making myself a professor
and not doing any academic work. But I'm working
in the Council Office, I'm a member of the County
Council, and I feel my service there is just as fine and
valuable as any academic work I might do. I'm a
member of the County Council, and if you want to
know, I'm proud of it! *pause* Thirdly, there's
something else I must tell you. . . . I know I mortgaged
the house without asking your permission. That was
wrong, I admit it, and I ask you to forgive me. I was
driven to it by my debts. I'm in debt for about thirty-
five thousand rubles. I don't play cards anymore; I've
given it up long ago. The only thing I can say to justify

ANTON
CHEKHOV

myself is that you girls get an annuity, while I don't get anything. No income, I mean.

KULYGIN

Calling through the door

Is Masha there? She's not there? *alarmed* Where can she be then? It's very strange. *goes away*

ANDREI

So you won't listen? Natasha is a good, honest woman, I tell you. *walks up and down the stage, then stops* When I married her, I thought we were going to be happy; I thought we would all be happy. But . . . oh, my God! *weeps* My dear sisters, my dear, good sisters, don't believe what I've been saying, don't believe it. *goes out*

KULYGIN

Through the door, agitated

Where's Masha? Isn't Masha here? Extraordinary! *goes away*

The alarm is heard again. The stage is empty

IRINA

Speaking from behind the screen

Olya! Who's that knocking on the floor?

OLGA

It's the doctor, Ivan Romanovich. He's drunk.

IRINA

It's been one thing after another all night. *pause* Olya! *peeps out from behind the screen* Have you heard? The troops are being moved from the district. They're being sent somewhere a long way off.

OLGA

That's only a rumor.

IRINA

We'll be left quite alone then. Olya!

THE
THREE
SISTERS

OLGA

Well?

IRINA

Olya, darling, I do respect the baron. I think a lot of
him; he's a very good man. I'll marry him, Olya. I'll
agree to marry him, if only we can go to Moscow!
Let's go! Please let's go! There's nowhere in all the
world like Moscow. Let's go, Olya! Let's go!

CURTAIN

ACT FOUR

The old garden belonging to the Prozorovs' house. A river is seen at the end of a long avenue of fir trees, and on the far bank of the river, a forest. On the right of the stage there is a veranda with a table on which champagne bottles and glasses have been left. It is midday. From time to time people from the street pass through the garden to get to the river. Five or six soldiers march through quickly.

Chebutykin, radiating a mood of benevolence which does not leave him throughout the act, is sitting in a chair in the garden. He is wearing his army cap and is holding a walking stick, as if ready to be called away at any moment. Kulygin, with a decoration around his neck and with his mustache shaved off, Tutzenbach, and Irina are standing on the veranda saying good-bye to Fedotik and Rodé, who are coming down the steps. Both officers are in marching uniform.

TUTZENBACH

Embracing Fedotik You're a good fellow, Fedotik; we've been good friends! *embraces Rodé* Once more then. . . . Good-bye, my dear friends!

IRINA

Au revoir!

FEDOTIK

It's not *au revoir*. It's good-bye. We will never meet
again!

KULYGIN

Who knows? *wipes his eyes, smiling* There!
You've made me cry.

IRINA

We'll meet some time.

FEDOTIK

Perhaps in ten or fifteen years' time. But then we'll
hardly know one another. We will just meet and say
"how are you?" coldly. *takes a snapshot* Wait a
moment. Just one more, for the last time.

RODÉ

Embraces Tutzenbach We're not likely to meet
again. *kisses Irina's hand* Thank you for everything . . . everything!

FEDOTIK

Annoyed Just wait a second!

TUTZENBACH

We'll meet again if we're fated to meet. Do write to
us. Be sure to write.

RODÉ

Glancing around the garden
Good-bye, trees! *shouts* Hey! *pauses* Good-
bye, echo!

KULYGIN

I wouldn't be surprised if you got married out there, in
Poland. You'll get a Polish wife, and she'll put her
arms around you and say, "*kochany*"![1] *laughs*

FEDOTIK

Glances at his watch
There's less than an hour to go. Soleni is the only one

ANTON
CHEKHOV

1. A Polish word meaning "beloved."

from our battery who's going down the river on the
barge. All the others are marching with the division.
Three batteries are leaving today by road and three
more tomorrow—then the town will be quite peaceful.

TUTZENBACH

Yes, and dreadfully dull too.

RODÉ

By the way, where's Marya Sergeevna?

KULYGIN

She's somewhere in the garden.

FEDOTIK

We must say good-bye to her.

RODÉ

Good-bye. I really must go or I'll burst into tears.
*quickly embraces Tutzenbach and Kulygin, then kisses
Irina's hand* Life's been very pleasant here.

FEDOTIK

To Kulygin Here's something for a souvenir for
you—a notebook with a pencil. We'll go down to the
river through here. *they go off, glancing back*

RODÉ

Shouts Heigh-ho!

KULYGIN

Shouts Good-bye!

*At the back of the stage Fedotik and Rodé meet Masha
and say good-bye to her. She goes off with them*

IRINA

They've gone. . . . *sits down on the bottom step of the
veranda*

CHEBUTYKIN

They forgot to say good-bye to me.

IRINA

Well, what about you?

THE
THREE
SISTERS

CHEBUTYKIN

That's true; I forgot too. Never mind, I'll be seeing them again quite soon. I'll be leaving tomorrow. Yes . . . only one more day. And then in a year's time I'll be retiring. I'll come back here and finish the rest of my life near you. There's just one more year to go and then I get my pension. *puts a newspaper in his pocket and takes out another* I'll come back here and lead a reformed life. I'll be a nice, quiet, well-behaved little man.

IRINA

Yes, it's really time you reformed, my dear friend. You ought to live a different sort of life somehow.

CHEBUTYKIN

Yes, I think so too. *sings quietly* Tarara-boom-di-ay. . . . I'm sitting on a tomb-di-ay.

KULYGIN

Ivan Romanovich is incorrigible! Incorrigible!

CHEBUTYKIN

Yes, you ought to have taken me in hand. You'd have reformed me!

IRINA

Fëdor's shaved his mustache off. I can't bear to look at him.

KULYGIN

Why not?

CHEBUTYKIN

If I could just tell you what your face looks like now— but I don't dare.

KULYGIN

Well! Such are the conventions of life! *Modus vivendi*, you know. The director shaved his mustache off, so I shaved mine off when they gave me an inspectorship. No one likes it, but personally I'm quite indifferent.

ANTON
CHEKHOV

I'm content. Whether I've got a mustache or not, it's
all the same to me. *sits down*

Andrei passes across the back of the stage pushing a
carriage with a child asleep in it

IRINA

Ivan Romanovich, my dear friend, I'm awfully
worried about something. You were out in the town
garden last night. Tell me what happened there.

CHEBUTYKIN

What happened? Nothing. Just a trifling thing. *reads*
his paper It doesn't matter anyway.

KULYGIN

They say that Soleni and the baron met in the town
garden outside the theater last night and . . .

TUTZENBACH

Don't, please! What's the good? *waves his hand at*
him deprecatingly and goes into the house

KULYGIN

It was outside the theater. Soleni started badgering the
baron, and he lost patience and said something that
offended him.

CHEBUTYKIN

I don't know anything about it. It's all nonsense.

KULYGIN

A schoolteacher once wrote "nonsense" in Russian
over a pupil's essay, and the pupil puzzled over it,
thinking it was a Latin word. *laughs* Frightfully
funny, you know! They say that Soleni's in love with
Irina and that he got to hate the baron more and more.
Well, that's understandable. Irina's a very nice girl.
She's a bit like Masha; she tends to get wrapped up in
her own thoughts. *to Irina* But your disposition is
more easygoing than Masha's. And yet Masha has a
very nice disposition too. I love her, I love my Masha.

IRINA

Starts Anything seems to startle me today. *pause* I've got everything ready too. I'm sending my luggage off after lunch. The baron and I are going to get married tomorrow, and directly afterward we're moving to the brickworks, and the day after tomorrow I'm starting work at the school. So our new life will begin, God willing! When I was sitting for my teacher's diploma, I suddenly started crying for sheer joy, with a sort of feeling of blessedness. *pause* The carrier will be coming for my luggage in a minute.

KULYGIN

That's all very well, but somehow I can't feel that it's meant to be serious. All ideas and theories, but nothing really serious. Anyway I wish you luck from the bottom of my heart.

CHEBUTYKIN

Moved My dearest girl, my precious child! You've gone on so far ahead of me, I'll never catch up now. I've gotten left behind like a bird that has grown too old and can't keep up with the rest of the flock. Fly away, my dears, fly away, and God be with you! *pause* It's a pity you've shaved your mustache off, Fëdor Ilyich.

KULYGIN

Don't keep on about it, please! *sighs* Well, the soldiers will be leaving today, and everything will go back to what it was before. Anyway whatever they say, Masha is a good, loyal wife. Yes, I love her dearly and I'm thankful for what God has given me. Fate treats people so differently. For instance there's an excise clerk here called Kozyrev. He was at school with me and he was expelled in his fifth year because he just

ANTON
CHEKHOV

couldn't grasp the *ut consecutivum*. He's dreadfully
hard up now and in bad health too, and whenever I
meet him, I just say to him, "Hello, *ut consecutivum!*"
"Yes," he replies, "that's just the trouble—*consecutivum*" and he starts coughing. Whereas I—I've been
lucky all my life. I'm happy; I've actually been awarded
the order of Saint Stanislav, second class—and now I'm
teaching the children the same old *ut consecutivum*.
Of course, I'm clever, cleverer than plenty of other
people, but happiness does not consist of merely being
clever.

In the house someone plays "The Maiden's Prayer"

IRINA
Tomorrow night I won't have to listen to "The
Maiden's Prayer." I won't have to meet Protopopov.
pause By the way, he's in the sitting room. He's
come again.

KULYGIN
Hasn't our headmistress arrived yet?

IRINA
No, we've sent for her. If you only knew how difficult
it is for me to live here by myself, without Olya! She
lives at the school now; she's the headmistress and she's
busy the whole day. And I'm here alone, bored, with
nothing to do, and I hate the very room I live in. So
I've just made up my mind—if I'm really not going
to be able to live in Moscow, that's that. It's my fate,
that's all. Nothing can be done about it. It's God's
will, everything that happens, and that's the truth.
Nikolai Lvovich proposed to me. Well, I thought it
over, and I made up my mind. He's such a nice man;
it's really extraordinary how nice he is. And then   THE
suddenly I felt as though my soul had grown wings; I   THREE
felt more cheerful and so relieved somehow that I   SISTERS

wanted to work again. Just to start work! Only something happened yesterday, and now I feel as though something mysterious is hanging over me.

CHEBUTYKIN

Nonsense!

NATASHA

Speaking through the window
Our headmistress!

KULYGIN

Our headmistress has arrived! Let's go indoors.   *goes indoors with Irina*

CHEBUTYKIN

Reads his paper and sings quietly to himself
Tarara-boom-di-ay. I'm sitting on a tomb-di-ay.

Masha walks up to him. Andrei passes across the back of the stage pushing the carriage

MASHA

You look very comfortable sitting here.

CHEBUTYKIN

Well, why not? Anything happening?

MASHA

Sits down No, nothing. *pause* Tell me something. Were you in love with my mother?

CHEBUTYKIN

Yes, very much in love.

MASHA

Did she love you?

CHEBUTYKIN

After a pause
I can't remember now.

MASHA

Is my man here? Our cook Marfa always used to call her policeman "my man." Is he here?

CHEBUTYKIN

Not yet.

MASHA

When you have to take your happiness in snatches, in little bits, as I do, and then lose it, as I've lost it, you gradually get hardened and bad-tempered. *points at her breast* Something's boiling over inside me, here. *looking at Andrei, who again crosses the stage with the carriage* There's Andrei, our dear brother. All our hopes are gone. It's the same as when thousands of people haul a huge bell up into a tower. Untold labor and money is spent on it, and then suddenly it falls and gets smashed. Suddenly, without rhyme or reason. It was the same with Andrei.

ANDREI

When are they going to settle down in the house? They're making such a row.

CHEBUTYKIN

They will soon. *looks at his watch* This is an old-fashioned watch: it strikes. *winds his watch, which then strikes* The first, second, and fifth batteries will be leaving punctually at one o'clock. *pause* And I will leave tomorrow.

ANDREI

For good?

CHEBUTYKIN

I don't know. I may return in about a year. Although God knows, it's all the same.

The sounds of a harp and a violin are heard

ANDREI

The town will seem quite empty. Life will be snuffed out like a candle. *pause* Something happened yesterday outside the theater; everybody's talking about it. I'm the only one that doesn't seem to know about it.

THE
THREE
SISTERS

CHEBUTYKIN

It was nothing. A lot of nonsense. Soleni started badgering the baron or something. The baron lost his temper and insulted him, and in the end Soleni had to challenge him to a duel. *looks at his watch* I think it's time to go. At half past twelve, in the forest over there, on the other side of the river . . . Bang-bang! *laughs* Soleni imagines he's like Lermontov. He actually writes poems. But, joking apart, this is his third duel.

MASHA

Whose third duel?

CHEBUTYKIN

Soleni's.

MASHA

What about the baron?

CHEBUTYKIN

Well, what about him?

MASHA

My thoughts are all in a muddle. But what I mean to say is that they shouldn't be allowed to fight. He might wound the baron or even kill him.

CHEBUTYKIN

The baron's a good enough fellow, but what does it really matter if there's one baron more or less in the world? Well, let it be! It's all the same.

The shouts of "ah-hoo!" and "yoo-hoo!" are heard from beyond the garden

That's Skvortsov, the second, shouting from the boat. He can wait.

ANDREI

I think it's simply immoral to fight a duel, or even to be present at one as a doctor.

CHEBUTYKIN

That's only how it seems. We don't exist; nothing exists. It only seems to us that we do. And what difference does it make?

MASHA

Talk, talk, nothing but talk all day long! *starts to go* Having to live in this awful climate with the snow threatening to fall at any moment, and then on top of it having to listen to all this sort of talk. *stops* I won't go into the house; I can't bear going in there. Will you let me know when Vershinin comes? *walks off along the avenue* Look, the birds are beginning to fly away already! *looks up* Swans or geese . . . Dear birds, happy birds . . . *goes off*

ANDREI

Our house will seem quite deserted. The officers will go, you'll go, my sister will get married, and I'll be left alone in the house.

CHEBUTYKIN

What about your wife?

Enter Ferapont with some papers

ANDREI

My wife is my wife. She's a good, decent sort of woman. She's really very kind too, but there's something about her which pulls her down to the level of an animal—a sort of mean, blind, thick-skinned animal—anyway not a human being. I'm telling you this as a friend, the only person I can talk openly to. I love Natasha, it's true. But at times she appears to me so utterly vulgar that I feel quite bewildered by it, and then I can't understand why, for what reasons I love her—or anyway did love her.

CHEBUTYKIN

Gets up Well, dear boy, I'm going away tomorrow

THE
THREE
SISTERS

and it may be we will never see each other again. So
I'll give you a bit of advice. Put on your hat, take a
walking stick, and go away. Go away and don't ever
look back. And the farther you go, the better.

*Soleni passes across the back of the stage accompanied
by two officers. Seeing Chebutykin, he turns toward him,
while the officers walk on*

SOLENI

It's time, Doctor. Half past twelve already.   *shakes
hands with Andrei*

CHEBUTYKIN

In a moment. Oh, I'm tired of you all.   *to Andrei*
Andryusha, if anyone asks for me, tell them I'll be back
presently.   *sighs*   Oh-ho-ho!

SOLENI

     "He had not time to say 'Oh, oh!'
     Before that bear had struck him low."
walks off with him   What are you groaning about, old
man?

CHEBUTYKIN

Oh, well!

SOLENI

How do you feel?

CHEBUTYKIN

Sourly   Like a last year's bird's nest.

SOLENI

You don't have to be so agitated about it, old boy. I
won't indulge in anything much; I'll just scorch his
wings a little, like a woodcock's.   *takes out a cologne
bottle and sprinkles cologne over his hands*   I've used
up a whole bottle today, but my hands still smell. They
smell like a corpse.   *pause*   Yes. Do you remember
that poem of Lermontov's?

ANTON
CHEKHOV

"And he, rebellious, seeks a storm,
As if in storms there were tranquillity."

CHEBUTYKIN

Yes.

"He had not time to say 'Oh, oh!'
Before that bear had struck him low."

goes out with Soleni

*Shouts of "yoo-hoo, ah-hoo!" are heard. Enter Andrei
and Ferapont*

FERAPONT

Will you sign these papers please?

ANDREI

With irritation   Leave me alone! Leave me alone, for
heaven's sake.   *goes off with the carriage*

FERAPONT

Well, what am I supposed to do with the papers then?
They are meant to be signed, aren't they?   *goes to back
of stage*

*Enter Irina and Tutzenbach, the latter wearing a straw
hat. Kulygin crosses the stage, calling, "Yoo-hoo,
Masha! Yoo-hoo!"*

TUTZENBACH

I think he's the only person in the whole town who's
glad that the army is leaving.

IRINA

That's quite understandable really.   *pause*   The town
will look quite empty.

TUTZENBACH

My dear, I'll be back in a moment.

IRINA

Where are you going?

THE
THREE
SISTERS

TUTZENBACH

I must slip back to the town, and then . . . I want to see some of my colleagues off.

IRINA

It's not true. Nikolai, why are you so absentminded today? *pause* What happened outside the theater last night?

TUTZENBACH

With a movement of impatience
I'll be back in an hour. I'll be back with you again. *kisses her hands* My treasure! *gazes into her eyes* It's five years since I first began to love you, and still I can't get used to it, and you seem more beautiful every day. What wonderful, lovely hair! What marvelous eyes! I'll take you away tomorrow. We'll work, we'll be rich, my dreams will come to life again. And you'll be happy! But—there's only one "but," only one—you don't love me!

IRINA

I can't help that! I'll be your wife. I'll be loyal and obedient to you, but I can't love you. What's to be done? *weeps* I've never loved anyone in my life. Oh, I've had such dreams about being in love! I've been dreaming about it for ever so long, day and night. But somehow my soul seems like an expensive piano that someone has locked up and the key's gotten lost. *pause* Your eyes are so restless.

TUTZENBACH

I was awake all night. Not that there's anything to be afraid of in my life, nothing threatening. Only the thought of that lost key torments me and keeps me awake. Say something to me. *pause* Say something!

ANTON
CHEKHOV

IRINA

What? What am I to say? What?

Anything.

IRINA

Don't, my dear, don't.

TUTZENBACH

Such trifles, such silly little things, sometimes become
so important suddenly for no apparent reason! You
laugh at them, just as you always have done, you still
regard them as trifles, and yet you suddenly find they're
in control, and you haven't the power to stop them.
But let's not talk about all that! Really I feel quite
elated. I feel as if I were seeing those fir trees and
maples and birches for the first time in my life. They
all seem to be looking at me with a sort of inquisitive
look and waiting for something. What beautiful trees—
and how beautiful, when you think of it, life ought to
be with trees like these!

Shouts of "ah-hoo, yoo-hoo!" are heard

I must go; it's time. Look at that dead tree; it's all
dried up, but it's still swaying in the wind along with
the others. And in the same way, it seems to me that,
if I die, I will still have a share in life somehow or
other. Good-bye, my dear.   *kisses her hands*   Your
papers, the ones you gave me, are on my desk, under
the calendar.

IRINA

I'm coming with you.

TUTZENBACH

Alarmed   No, no!   *goes off quickly, then stops in the
avenue*   Irina!

IRINA

What?

THE
THREE
SISTERS

TUTZENBACH

Not knowing what to say

I didn't have any coffee this morning. Will you tell them to get some ready for me?   *goes off quickly*

Irina stands lost in thought, then goes to the back of the stage and sits down on a swing. Enter Andrei with the carriage. Ferapont appears

FERAPONT

Andrei Sergeevich, the papers aren't mine, you know; they're the office papers. I didn't make them up.

ANDREI

Oh, where has all my past life gone to? The time when I was young and gay and clever, when I used to have fine dreams and great thoughts, and the present and the future were bright with hope? Why do we become so dull and commonplace and uninteresting almost before we've begun to live? Why do we get lazy, indifferent, useless, unhappy? This town's been in existence for two hundred years; a hundred thousand people live in it, but there's not one who's any different from all the others! There's never been a scholar or an artist or a saint in this place, never a single man sufficiently out-standing to make you feel passionately that you wanted to emulate him. People here do nothing but eat, drink, and sleep. Then they die and some more take their places, and they eat, drink, and sleep too. And just to introduce a bit of variety into their lives, so they'll avoid getting completely stupid with boredom, they indulge in their disgusting gossip and vodka and gambling and lawsuits. The wives deceive their hus-bands, and the husbands lie to their wives and pretend they don't see anything and don't hear anything. And all this overwhelming vulgarity and pettiness crushes

ANTON
CHEKHOV

the children and puts out any spark they might have in
them, so that they too become miserable, half-dead
creatures, just like one another and just like their
parents! *to Ferapont, curtly* What do you want?

FERAPONT

What? Here are the papers to sign.

ANDREI

What a nuisance you are!

FERAPONT

Hands him the papers
The porter at the finance department told me just now;
he said last winter they had two hundred degrees of
frost in Petersburg.

ANDREI

I hate the life I live at present, but oh, the sense of
elation when I think of the future! Then I feel so light-
hearted, such a sense of release! I seem to see light ahead,
light and freedom. I see myself free, and my children
too—free from idleness, free from kvass, free from
eternal meals of goose and cabbage, free from after-
dinner naps, free from all this degrading parasitism!

FERAPONT

They say two thousand people were frozen to death.
They say everyone was scared stiff. It was either in
Petersburg or in Moscow; I can't remember exactly.

ANDREI

With sudden emotion, tenderly
My dear sisters, my dear good sisters! *tearfully*
Masha, my dear sister!

NATASHA

Through the window
Who's that talking so loudly there? Is that you,
Andryusha? You'll wake Sofochka. *Il ne faut pas faire
du bruit; la Sophie est dormie déjà. Vous êtes un ours.*
getting angry If you want to talk, give the baby

buggy to someone else. Ferapont, take the carriage from the master.

FERAPONT

Yes, madam. *takes the carriage*

ANDREI

Embarrassed I was talking quietly.

NATASHA

In the window, caressing her small son
Bobik! Naughty Bobik! Aren't you a naughty boy!

ANDREI

Glancing through the papers
All right, I'll go through them and sign them if they need it. You can take them back to the office later.
goes into the house, reading the papers

Ferapont wheels the carriage into the garden

NATASHA

In the window
What's mommy's name, Bobik? You darling! And who's that lady? Auntie Olya. Say, "Hello, Auntie Olya."

Two street musicians, a man and a girl, enter and begin to play on a violin and a harp. Vershinin, Olga, and Anfisa come out of the house and listen in silence for a few moments. Then Irina approaches them

OLGA

Our garden's like a public road; everybody goes through it. Nanny, give something to the musicians.

ANFISA

Giving them money
Go along now. God bless you, good people!

The musicians bow and go away

ANTON
CHEKHOV

Poor, homeless folk! Whoever would go dragging

around the streets playing tunes if he had enough to eat?
to Irina How are you, Irenushka? *kisses her* Ah,
my child, what a life I'm having! Such comfort! In a
large flat at the school with Olyushka—and no rent
to pay either! The Lord's been kind to me in my old
age. I've never had such a comfortable time in my life,
old sinner that I am! A big flat, and no rent to pay, and
a whole room to myself, with my own bed. All free.
Sometimes when I wake up in the night I begin to
think, and then—Oh, Lord! Oh, Holy Mother of
God!—there's no one happier in the world than me!

VERSHININ
Glances at his watch
We will be starting in a moment, Olga Sergeevna. It's
time I went. *pause* I wish you all the happiness
in the world. . . . Everything. Where's Marya
Sergeevna?

IRINA
She's somewhere in the garden. I'll go and look for her.

VERSHININ
That's kind of you. I really must hurry.

ANFISA
I'll come and help to look for her. *calls out*
Mashenka, yoo-hoo! *goes with Irina toward the far
end of the garden* Yoo-hoo! Yoo-hoo!

VERSHININ
Everything comes to an end. Well, here we are—and
now it's going to be good-bye. *looks at his watch*
The city gave us a sort of farewell lunch. There was
champagne, and the mayor made a speech, and I ate
and listened, but in spirit I was with you here.
glances around the garden I've grown so . . . so
accustomed to you.

OLGA
Will we meet again some day I wonder?

THE
THREE
SISTERS

VERSHININ

Most likely not! *pause* My wife and the two little girls will be staying on here for a month or two. Please, if anything happens, if they need anything . . .

OLGA

Yes, yes, of course. You needn't worry about that. *pause* Tomorrow there won't be a single officer or soldier in the town. All that will be just a memory, and, of course, a new life will begin for us here. *pause* Nothing ever happens as we'd like it to. I didn't want to be a headmistress, and yet now I am one. It means we won't be going to live in Moscow.

VERSHININ

Well, thank you for everything. Forgive me if ever I've done anything. . . . I've talked a lot too much, far too much. Forgive me for that; don't think too unkindly of me.

OLGA

Wipes her eyes

Now . . . why is Masha so long in coming?

VERSHININ

What else can I tell you now that it's time to say good-bye? What shall I philosophize about now? *laughs* Yes, life is difficult. It seems quite hopeless for a lot of us, just a kind of impasse. And yet you must admit that it is gradually getting easier and brighter, and it's clear that the time isn't far off when the light will spread everywhere. *looks at his watch* Time, it's time for me to go. In the old days the human race was always making war; its entire existence was taken up with campaigns, advances, retreats, victories. But now all that's out of date, and in its place there's a huge vacuum, clamoring to be filled. Humanity is passionately seeking something to fill it with and, of course, it will find something some day. Oh, if only it

ANTON
CHEKHOV

would happen soon! *pause* If only we could educate
the industrious people and make the educated people
industrious. *looks at his watch* I really must go.

OLGA
Here she comes!

Enter Masha

VERSHININ
I've come to say good-bye.

*Olga walks off and stands a little to one side so as not
to interfere with their parting*

MASHA
Looking into his face
Good-bye! *a long kiss*
OLGA
That'll do, that'll do.

Masha sobs loudly

VERSHININ
Write to me. Don't forget me! Let me go. . . . It's
time. Olga Sergeevna, please take her away. . . . I
must go. . . . I'm late already. *deeply moved, kisses
Olga's hands, then embraces Masha once again, and
goes out quickly*
OLGA
That'll do, Masha! Don't, my dear, don't.

Enter Kulygin

KULYGIN
Embarrassed Never mind, let her cry, let her. My
dear Masha, my dear, sweet Masha. You're my wife,
and I'm happy in spite of everything. I'm not com- THE
plaining; I've no reproach to make—not a single one. THREE
Olga here is my witness. We'll start our life over again SISTERS

in the same old way, and you won't hear a word from me . . . not a hint.

MASHA
Suppressing her sobs
"A green oak grows by a curving shore, and round that oak hangs a golden chain . . ." A golden chain round that oak. . . . Oh, I'm going mad. By a curving shore . . . a green oak . . .

OLGA
Calm yourself, Masha, calm yourself. Give her some water.

MASHA
I'm not crying anymore.

KULYGIN
She's not crying anymore. She's a good girl.

The hollow sound of a gunshot is heard in the distance

MASHA
"A green oak grows by a curving shore, and round that oak hangs a golden chain . . ." A green cat . . . A green oak . . . I've got it all mixed up. *drinks water* My life's messed up. . . . I don't want anything now. . . . I'll calm down in a moment. . . . It doesn't matter. . . . What *is* "the curving shore"? Why does it keep coming into my head all the time? My thoughts are all mixed up.

Enter Irina

OLGA
Calm down, Masha. That's right. . . . Good girl! Let's go indoors.

MASHA
Irritably I'm not going in there! *sobs, but immediately checks herself* I don't go into that house now, and I'm not going to . . .

ANTON
CHEKHOV

IRINA

Let's sit down together for a moment and not talk about anything. I'm going away tomorrow you know. . . .

KULYGIN

After a pause

Yesterday I took away a false beard and a mustache from a boy in the third grade. I've got them here. *puts them on* Do I look like our German teacher? *laughs* I do, don't I? The boys are funny.

MASHA

It's true, you do look like that German of yours.

OLGA

Laughs Yes, he does.

Masha cries

IRINA

That's enough, Masha!

KULYGIN

Very much like him, I think!

Enter Natasha

NATASHA

To the maid

What? Oh, yes. Mr. Protopopov is going to keep an eye on Sofochka, and Andrei Sergeevich is going to take Bobik out in the baby buggy. What a lot of work these children make! *to Irina* Irina, you're really leaving tomorrow? What a pity! Stay just another week, won't you? *catching sight of Kulygin, shrieks; he laughs and takes off the false beard and mustache* Get away with you! How you scared me! *to Irina* I've grown so accustomed to you being here. You mustn't think it's going to be easy for me to be without

THE
THREE
SISTERS

you. I'll get Andrei and his old violin to move into your room: he can saw away at it as much as he likes there. And then we'll move Sofochka into his room. She's such a wonderful child, really! Such a lovely little girl! This morning she looked at me with such a sweet expression, and then she said, "Mamma!"

KULYGIN

It's quite true; she is a beautiful child.

NATASHA

So tomorrow I'll be alone here. *sighs* I'll have this fir tree avenue cut down first, then that maple tree over there. It looks so awful in the evenings. *to Irina* My dear, that belt you're wearing doesn't suit you at all. Not at all good taste. You want something brighter to go with that dress. I'll tell them to put flowers all around here, lots of flowers, so that we get plenty of scent from them. *sternly* Why is there a fork lying on this seat? *going into the house, to the maid* Why is that fork left on the seat there? *shouts* Don't answer me back!

KULYGIN

There she goes again!

A band plays a military march offstage. All listen

OLGA

They're going.

Enter Chebutykin

MASHA

The soldiers are going. Well, happy journey to them! *to her husband* We must go home. Where's my hat and cape?

ANTON CHEKHOV

KULYGIN

I took them indoors. I'll bring them at once.

OLGA

Yes, we can go home now. It's time.

CHEBUTYKIN

Olga Sergeevna!

OLGA

What is it? *pause* What?

CHEBUTYKIN

Nothing. I don't know quite how to tell you. *whispers into her ear*

OLGA

Frightened It can't be true!

CHEBUTYKIN

Yes. . . . A bad business. I'm so tired. . . . Quite worn out. I don't want to say another word. *with annoyance* Anyway nothing matters!

MASHA

What's happened?

OLGA

Puts her arms around Irina

What a dreadful day! I don't know how to tell you, dear.

IRINA

What is it? Tell me quickly, what is it? For heaven's sake! *cries*

CHEBUTYKIN

The baron's just been killed in a duel.

IRINA

Cries quietly I knew it, I knew it.

CHEBUTYKIN

Goes to the back of the stage and sits down

I'm tired. *takes a newspaper out of his pocket* Let them cry for a bit. *sings quietly to himself* Tarara-boom-di-ay, I'm sitting on a tomb-di-ay. What difference does it make?

THE
THREE
SISTERS

MASHA

Oh, listen to that band! They're leaving us. . . . One
of them's gone for good . . . forever! We're left
alone . . . to start our lives all over again. We must
go on living. . . . We must go on living.

IRINA

Puts her head on Olga's breast

Someday people will know why such things happen,
and what the purpose of all this suffering is. Then
there won't be any more riddles. Meanwhile we must
go on living . . . and working. Yes, we must just go on
working! Tomorrow I'll go away alone and teach in
a school somewhere; I'll give my life to people who
need it. It's autumn now, winter will soon be here, and
the snow will cover everything. . . . But I'll go on
working and working!

OLGA

Puts her arms around both her sisters

How cheerfully and jauntily that band's playing—
really I feel as if I wanted to live! Merciful God! The
years will pass, and we will all be gone for good and
quite forgotten. Our faces and our voices will be
forgotten and people won't even know that there were
once three of us here. But our sufferings may mean
happiness for the people who come after us. There'll be
a time when peace and happiness reign in the world,
and then we will be remembered kindly and blessed.
No, my dear sisters, life isn't finished for us yet! We're
going to live! The band is playing so cheerfully and
joyfully—maybe if we wait a little longer, we will
find out why we live, why we suffer. . . . Oh, if we
only knew, if only we knew!

ANTON
CHEKHOV

The music grows fainter and fainter. Kulygin, smiling
happily, brings out the hat and the cape. Andrei enters;
he is pushing the carriage with Bobik sitting in it

CHEBUTYKIN
Sings quietly to himself
Tarara-boom-di-ay . . . I'm sitting on a tomb-di-ay.
reads the paper   What does it matter? Nothing
matters!

OLGA
If only we knew, if only we knew!

CURTAIN

THE
CHERRY
ORCHARD

A DRAMA IN FOUR ACTS

THE
CHARACTERS

RANEVSKAYA, *Lyubov Andreyevna* (Lyuba), *a landowner*

ANYA (Anichka), *her daughter, aged seventeen*

VARYA (Varvara Mikhailovna), *her adopted daughter, aged twenty-four*

GAYEV, *Leonid Andreyevich* (Lenya), *brother of Madame Ranevskaya*

LOPAKHIN, *Yermolai Alekseevich, a businessman*

TROFIMOV, *Pëtr Sergeevich* (Petya), *a student*

SIMEONOV-PISHCHIK, *Boris Borisovich, a landowner*

CHARLOTTA IVANOVNA, *a German governess*

YEPIKHODOV, *Semën Panteleyevich, a clerk on Ranevskaya's estate*

DUNYASHA (Avdotya Fëdorovna), *a parlormaid*

FIRS (Firs Nikolaevich), *a manservant, aged eighty-seven*

YASHA, *a young manservant*

A TRAMP

STATIONMASTER

POST OFFICE CLERK
GUESTS, SERVANTS

*The action takes place on the estate
of Madame Ranevskaya*

ACT ONE

A room which used to be the children's bedroom and is
still referred to as the nursery. There are several doors:
one of them leads into Anya's room. It is early morning:
the sun is just coming up. The windows of the room are
shut, but through them the cherry trees can be seen in
blossom. It is May, but in the orchard there is morning
frost.
Enter Dunyasha, carrying a candle, and Lopakhin
with a book in his hand.

LOPAKHIN

The train's arrived, thank God. What time is it?

DUNYASHA

It's nearly two.   *blows out the candle*   It's light
already.

LOPAKHIN

How late was the train then? Two hours at least.
yawns and stretches   How stupid I am! What a fool
I've made of myself! Came here on purpose to go to the
station and meet them—and then overslept! Dropped
off to sleep in the chair. Annoying. . . . I wish you'd
woken me up.

DUNYASHA

I thought you'd gone. *listens* Sounds as if they're coming.

LOPAKHIN

Also listens No. They'll have to get their luggage out and all that. *pause* Lyubov Andreyevna has been abroad for five years; I don't know what she's like now. She used to be a good soul. An easygoing, simple kind of person. I remember when I was a boy of about fifteen, my father—he had a small shop in the village then—hit me in the face and made my nose bleed. We had come to the manor for something or other, and he'd been drinking. I remember it as if it happened yesterday: Lyubov Andreyevna—she was still young and slender then—brought me in and took me to the washstand in this very room, the nursery it was then. "Don't cry, little peasant," she said, "it'll be better before you're old enough to get married." *pause* "Little peasant." She was right enough; my father was a peasant. Yet here I am—all dressed up in a white waistcoat and brown shoes. But you can't make a silk purse out of a sow's ear. I am rich; I've got a lot of money. But anyone can see I'm just a peasant, anyone who takes the trouble to think about me and look under my skin. *turning over pages in the book* I've been reading this book, and I haven't understood a word of it. I fell asleep reading it.

DUNYASHA

The dogs didn't sleep all night; they know their masters are coming.

LOPAKHIN

What's the matter, Dunyasha?

ANTON
CHEKHOV

DUNYASHA

My hands are trembling. I feel as if I'm going to faint.

LOPAKHIN
You're too refined and sensitive, Dunyasha. You dress yourself up like a lady, and you do your hair like one too. That won't do you know. You must remember your place.

Enter Yepikhodov with a bunch of flowers. He wears a jacket and brightly polished high boots which squeak loudly. As he comes in, he drops the flowers

YEPIKHODOV
Picks up the flowers
The gardener sent these. He says they're to go in the dining room.   *hands the flowers to Dunyasha*

LOPAKHIN
And bring me some kvass.

DUNYASHA
Very well.

YEPIKHODOV
Outside it's about three degrees below freezing, and the cherry trees are covered with bloom. I can't approve of this climate of ours, you know.   *sighs*   No, I can't. It doesn't contribute to—to things, I mean. And do you know, Yermolai Alekseevich, I bought myself a pair of boots the day before yesterday, and they squeak so terribly. Well, I mean to say, it's utterly impossible you know. What can I put on them?

LOPAKHIN
Oh, leave me alone. You make me tired.

YEPIKHODOV
Every day something or other unpleasant happens to me. But I don't complain. I'm accustomed to it; I even laugh at it.

Enter Dunyasha; she serves Lopakhin kvass

THE
CHERRY
ORCHARD

I'll leave you now. *bumps into a chair, which falls over* You see! *triumphantly* You can see for yourself what it is, I mean to say. . . . So to speak. It's simply extraordinary! *goes out*

DUNYASHA

I want to tell you a secret, Yermolai Alekseevich. Yepikhodov proposed to me.

LOPAKHIN

Ah!

DUNYASHA

I don't know what to do. He's a quiet man, but sometimes he gets talking, and then you can't understand anything he says. It sounds nice; it sounds very moving, but you just can't understand it. I think I like him a little, and he's madly in love with me. He's an unlucky sort of person; something unpleasant seems to happen to him every day. That's why they tease him and call him "twenty-two misfortunes."

LOPAKHIN

Listens I think I can hear them coming.

DUNYASHA

Coming! Oh, dear! I don't know what's the matter with me. I feel cold all over.

LOPAKHIN

Yes, they really are coming! Let's go and meet them at the door. I wonder if she'll recognize me? We haven't met for five years.

DUNYASHA

Agitated I'm going to faint. . . . Oh, I'm fainting!

The sound of two coaches driving up to the house is heard. Lopakhin and Dunyasha go out quickly. The stage is empty. Then there are sounds of people arriving in the adjoining room. Firs, leaning on a stick, crosses the stage hurriedly: he has been to the station to meet

ANTON
CHEKHOV

Lyubov Andreyevna. He is dressed in an old-fashioned
livery coat and a top hat and is muttering to himself,
though it is impossible to make out what he is saying.
The noises offstage become louder. A voice says, "Let's
go through here." Enter Lyubov Andreyevna, Anya,
and Charlotta Ivanovna leading a small dog—all in
traveling clothes; Varya, wearing an overcoat and a
kerchief over her head; Gayev; Simeonov-Pishchik;
Lopakhin; Dunyasha, carrying a bundle and an
umbrella; and other servants with luggage

ANYA

Let's go through here. You remember what room this
is, mamma?

LYUBOV ANDREYEVNA

Joyfully, through her tears
The nursery!

VARYA

How cold it is! My hands are quite numb.   *to Lyubov*
Andreyevna   Your rooms are just as you left them,
mamma dear, the white one and the mauve one.

LYUBOV ANDREYEVNA

The nursery, my dear, my beautiful room! I used to
sleep here when I was little.   *cries*   And now I feel as
if I were little again.   *she kisses her brother, then*
Varya, then her brother again   And Varya is just the
same as ever, looking like a nun. I recognized Dunyasha
too.   *kisses Dunyasha*

GAYEV

The train was two hours late. Just think of it! What
efficiency!

CHARLOTTA

To Pishchik   My dog actually eats nuts.

PISHCHIK

Astonished   Fancy that!

THE
CHERRY
ORCHARD

They all go out except Anya and Dunyasha

DUNYASHA

We've waited and waited for you.   *helps Anya to take off her hat and coat*

ANYA

I haven't slept for four nights. I'm frozen.

DUNYASHA

You went away during Lent and it was snowing and freezing then, but now it's springtime. Darling!   *she laughs and kisses her*   I could hardly bear waiting for you, my pet, my precious. But I must tell you at once, I can't wait a minute longer.

ANYA

Without enthusiasm   What is it this time?

DUNYASHA

Yepikhodov, the clerk, proposed to me just after Easter.

ANYA

You never talk about anything else.   *tidies her hair* I've lost all my hairpins.   *she is very tired and can hardly keep on her feet*

DUNYASHA

I really don't know what to think. He loves me. He does love me so!

ANYA

Looking through the door into her room, tenderly My own room, my own windows, just as if I had never been away! I'm home again! Tomorrow I'm going to get up and run straight into the garden! Oh, if only I could go to bed and sleep now! I couldn't sleep all the way back, I was so worried.

DUNYASHA

Pëtr Sergeevich arrived the day before yesterday.

ANTON
CHEKHOV

ANYA

Joyfully   Petya!

DUNYASHA

He's sleeping in the bathhouse and living there too. "I wouldn't like to inconvenience them," he said.   *looks at her watch*   I ought to wake him up, but Varvara Mikhailovna told me not to. "Don't you wake him," she said.

Enter Varya with a bunch of keys at her waist

VARYA

Dunyasha, make some coffee, quick! Mamma is asking for coffee.

DUNYASHA

It'll be ready in a moment.   *goes out*

VARYA

Thank God you've arrived. You're home again. *embracing her*   My darling's come back! My precious!

ANYA

If you only knew the things I had to put up with!

VARYA

I can just imagine it.

ANYA

I left just before Easter: it was cold then. Charlotta never stopped talking, never quit doing her silly magic tricks all the way. Why did you make me take Charlotta?

VARYA

But how could you go alone, darling? At seventeen!

ANYA

When we arrived in Paris it was cold and snowing. My French was awful. Mamma was living on the fifth floor, and when I got there she had visitors. There were some French ladies there and an old priest with a little book; and the room was full of cigarette smoke, so untidy and uncomfortable. Suddenly I felt so sorry for mamma, so sorry, that I took her head between my

THE
CHERRY
ORCHARD

hands and just couldn't let it go. Afterward mamma cried and was very sweet to me.

VARYA

Tearfully   I can hardly bear listening to you.

ANYA

She had already sold her villa near Menton and she had nothing left, positively nothing. And I hadn't any money left either, not a kopeck; I had hardly enough to get to Paris. And mamma couldn't grasp that! In station restaurants she would order the most expensive dishes and tip the waiters a ruble each. Charlotta was just the same. And Yasha expected a full-course dinner for himself: it was simply dreadful. You know, Yasha is mamma's valet; we brought him with us.

VARYA

Yes, I've seen the wretch.

ANYA

Well, how are things going? Have we paid the interest?

VARYA

Far from it.

ANYA

Oh dear! Oh dear!

VARYA

The estate will be up for sale in August.

ANYA

Oh dear!

LOPAKHIN

Puts his head through the door and bleats
Me-e-e.   *disappears*

VARYA

Tearfully   I'd like to give him this.   *clenches her fist*

ANYA

Her arms around Varya, dropping her voice
Varya, has he proposed to you?

ANTON
CHEKHOV

But he loves you. Why don't you talk it over with him?
What are you waiting for?

VARYA

I don't believe anything will come of it. He's too busy;
he has no time to think of me. He pays no attention to
me at all. I'd rather he didn't come; it makes me miserable to see him. Everyone's talking of our wedding.
Everyone's congratulating me, but in fact there's
nothing in it—it's all a kind of dream. *in a changed
tone of voice* You've got a new brooch—a bee, isn't it?

ANYA

Sadly Mamma bought it for me. *she goes into her
room and now speaks gaily, like a child* You know,
I went up in a balloon in Paris!

VARYA

My darling's home again! My precious girl!

Dunyasha returns with a coffeepot and prepares coffee

standing by Anya's door You know, dearest, as I go
about the house doing my odd jobs, I'm always
dreaming and dreaming. If only we could marry you
to some rich man, I feel my mind would be at ease.
I'd go away then, first to a hermitage, then on to Kiev,
to Moscow . . . walking from one holy place to
another. I'd go on and on. Oh, what a beautiful life!

ANYA

The birds are singing in the garden. What time is it?

VARYA

It must be past two. Time you went to bed, darling.
goes into Anya's room A beautiful life!

*Enter Yasha, carrying a traveling blanket and a small
bag*

THE
CHERRY
ORCHARD

YASHA

Crossing the stage, in an affectedly genteel voice
May I go through here?

DUNYASHA

I can hardly recognize you, Yasha. You've changed so abroad.

YASHA

Hm! And who are you?

DUNYASHA

When you left here, I was no bigger than this.   *shows her height from the floor with her hand*   I'm Dunyasha, Fëdor Kozoyedov's daughter. You can't remember!

YASHA

Hm! Quite a little peach!   *looks around, puts his arms around her. She cries out and drops a saucer. Yasha goes out quickly*

VARYA

In the doorway, angrily
What's going on here?

DUNYASHA

Tearfully   I've broken a saucer.

VARYA

That's a good omen.

ANYA

Coming out of her room
We ought to warn mamma that Petya is here.

VARYA

I gave orders not to wake him.

ANYA

Pensively   It was six years ago that father died, and then, only a month after that, little brother Grisha was drowned in the river. He was only seven, such a pretty little boy! Mamma couldn't bear it and went away. She never looked back.   *shivers*   How well I understand her! If she only knew how I understand her!

pause And, of course, Petya Trofimov was Grisha's
tutor; he might remind her . . .

Enter Firs, wearing a jacket and a white waistcoat

FIRS
Goes to the coffeepot, preoccupied
Madam will have her coffee here.   *puts on white
gloves*   Is the coffee ready?   *to Dunyasha, severely*
What about the cream?

DUNYASHA
Oh, my goodness!   *goes out quickly*

FIRS
Fussing around the coffeepot
The girl's daft.   *mutters*   From Paris . . . The
master used to go to Paris years ago. . . . Used to go
by coach.   *laughs*

VARYA
Firs, what are you laughing at?

FIRS
What can I get you, madam?   *happily*   The mistress
is home again! Home at last! I don't mind if I die
now.   *weeps with joy*

*Enter Lyubov Andreyevna, Lopakhin, Gayev, and
Simeonov-Pishchik, the last wearing a long peasant
coat of finely woven cloth and wide trousers tucked
inside high boots. Gayev, as he comes in, moves his arms
and body as if he were playing billiards*

LYUBOV ANDREYEVNA
How does it go now? Let me think. . . . I sink the red.
I go in off into the middle pocket!

GAYEV
I put mine into the corner pocket! . . . Years ago you
and I slept in this room, little brother and sister together; and now I'm fifty-one, strange as it may seem.

LOPAKHIN

Yes, time flies.

GAYEV

What?

LOPAKHIN

Time flies, I say.

GAYEV

This place smells of patchouli.

ANYA

I think I'll go to bed. Good night, mamma.   *kisses her*

LYUBOV ANDREYEVNA

My precious child!   *kisses her hands*   You're glad to be home, aren't you? I still feel dazed.

ANYA

Good night, uncle.

GAYEV

Kisses her face and hands

God bless you. How like your mother you are!   *to his sister*   You looked exactly like her at her age, Lyuba.

Anya shakes hands with Lopakhin and Pishchik, goes out and shuts the door after her

LYUBOV ANDREYEVNA

She's very tired.

PISHCHIK

It's a long journey.

VARYA

To Lopakhin and Pishchik

Well, gentlemen? It's past two; time to break up the party.

LYUBOV ANDREYEVNA

Laughs   You're just the same, Varya.   *draws Varya to her and kisses her*   Let me have some coffee; then we'll all go.

Thank you, my dear. I've gotten into the habit of
drinking coffee. I drink it day and night. Thank you,
my dear old friend.   *kisses Firs*

VARYA
I'd better see if all the luggage is there.   *goes out*

LYUBOV ANDREYEVNA
Is it really me sitting here?   *laughs*   I feel like
dancing and flinging my arms around.   *hides her face
in her hands*   What if I'm just dreaming? God, how I
love my own country! I love it so much. I could hardly
see it from the train; I was crying all the time.   *through
tears*   However, I must drink my coffee. Thank you,
Firs, thank you, my dear old friend. I am so glad I
found you still alive.

FIRS
The day before yesterday.

GAYEV
He doesn't hear very well.

LOPAKHIN
I've got to leave for Kharkov soon after four. What
a nuisance! I'd like to have a good look at you, to have
a talk. You look as lovely as ever.

PISHCHIK
Breathing heavily   She looks prettier. In her Parisian
clothes . . . enough to turn anybody's head!

LOPAKHIN
Your brother here, Leonid Andreyevich, says that I'm
a country bumpkin, a tightfisted peasant, but I don't
pay any attention to that. Let him say what he likes.
The only thing I want is for you to have faith in me as
you did before. Merciful God! My father was your
father's serf and your grandfather's too, but you did so
much for me in the past that I forget everything and

THE
CHERRY
ORCHARD

love you as if you were my own sister . . . more than
my own sister.

LYUBOV ANDREYEVNA

I just can't sit still! I simply can't! *she jumps up and
walks around the room in great agitation* This happiness is too much for me. You can laugh at me; I'm
foolish. My dear bookcase! *kisses bookcase* My own
little table!

GAYEV

You know, old Nanny died while you were away.

LYUBOV ANDREYEVNA

Sits down and drinks coffee

Yes, I know. May the Kingdom of Heaven be hers.
They wrote to tell me.

GAYEV

Anastasi died too. Petrushka Kosoi has left me and is
working for the police in town. *takes a box of boiled
sweets from his pocket and puts one in his mouth*

PISHCHIK

My daughter, Dashenka, sends her greetings to you.

LOPAKHIN

I feel I'd like to tell you something nice, something
jolly. *glances at his watch* I'll have to go in a
moment; there's no time to talk. However, I could
tell you in a few words. You know, of course, that your
cherry orchard is going to be sold to pay your debts.
The auction is to take place on the twenty-second of
August, but there's no need for you to worry. You can
sleep in peace, my dear; there's a way out. This is my
plan. Please listen carefully. Your estate is only twenty
miles from town, and the railway line is not far away.
Now if your cherry orchard and the land along the
river are divided into plots and leased out for summer
residences, you'll have a yearly income of at least
twenty-five thousand rubles.

But what nonsense!

LYUBOV ANDREYEVNA

I don't quite understand you, Yermolai Alekseevich.

LOPAKHIN

You'll charge the tenants at least twenty-five rubles a year for a plot of one acre, and if you advertise now, I'm prepared to stake any amount you like that you won't have a spot of land unoccupied by the autumn; it will be snatched up. In fact I really feel I must congratulate you; you're saved after all! It's a marvelous location and the river's deep enough for bathing. But, of course, the place will have to be cleaned up, put in order. For instance all the old outbuildings will have to be pulled down, as well as this house, which is no good to anybody. The old cherry orchard would be cut down too.

LYUBOV ANDREYEVNA

Cut down? My dear man, forgive me, you don't seem to understand. If there's one thing interesting, one thing really outstanding, in the whole county, it's our cherry orchard.

LOPAKHIN

The only outstanding thing about this orchard is that it's very large. It only produces a crop every other year, and then there's nobody to buy it.

GAYEV

This orchard is actually mentioned in the encyclopedia.

LOPAKHIN

Glancing at his watch

If you can't think clearly about it or come to a decision, the cherry orchard and the whole estate as well will be sold by auction. You must decide! There's no other way out, I assure you. There's no other way.

FIRS
In the old days, forty or fifty years ago, the cherries were dried, preserved, marinated, made into jam, and sometimes . . .

GAYEV
Be quiet, Firs.

FIRS
And sometimes whole cartloads of dried cherries were sent to Moscow and Kharkov. The money they brought in! And the dried cherries in those days were soft, juicy, sweet, tasty. They knew how to do it then. They had a recipe.

LYUBOV ANDREYEVNA
And where is that recipe now?

FIRS
Forgotten. No one can remember it.

PISHCHIK
To Lyubov Andreyevna
What was it like in Paris? Did you eat frogs?

LYUBOV ANDREYEVNA
I ate crocodiles.

PISHCHIK
Fancy that!

LOPAKHIN
Up to just recently there were only gentry and peasants living in the country, but now there are all these summer residents. All the towns, even quite small ones, are surrounded with villas. And probably in the course of the next twenty years or so, these people will multiply tremendously. At present they merely drink tea on the veranda, but they might start cultivating their plots of land, and then your cherry orchard would be gay with life and wealth and luxury.

ANTON
CHEKHOV

GAYEV

Indignantly What nonsense!

Enter Varya and Yasha

VARYA

Here are two telegrams for you, mamma dear. *picks out a key and unlocks an old bookcase with a jingling noise* Here they are.

LYUBOV ANDREYEVNA

They are from Paris. *tears them up without reading them* I've finished with Paris.

GAYEV

Do you know, Lyuba, how old this bookcase is? A week ago I pulled out the bottom drawer, and I found some figures burned in the wood. It was made exactly a hundred years ago. What do you think of that, eh? We ought to celebrate its anniversary. An inanimate object, true, but still—a bookcase!

PISHCHIK

Astonished A hundred years! Fancy that!

GAYEV

Yes. This is a valuable piece of furniture. *feeling around the bookcase with his hands* My dear, venerable bookcase! I salute you! For more than a hundred years you have devoted yourself to the highest ideals of goodness and justice. For a hundred years you have never failed to fill us with an urge to useful work. Several generations of our family have had their courage sustained and their faith in a better future fortified by your silent call. You have fostered in us the ideal of public good and social consciousness. . . .

LOPAKHIN

After a pause

Yes.

THE
CHERRY
ORCHARD

LYUBOV ANDREYEVNA
You're just the same, Lenya.

GAYEV
Slightly embarrassed I put it into the corner pocket!
I drop it into the middle pocket!

LOPAKHIN
Glances at his watch
Well, it's time for me to be going.

YASHA
Brings medicine to Lyubov Andreyevna
Would you care to take your pills now?

PISHCHIK
Don't take medicines, my dear. They don't do you any
good . . . or harm either. Let me have them. *takes the
box from her, pours the pills into the palm of his hand,
blows on them, puts them all into his mouth, and takes
a drink of kvass* There!

LYUBOV ANDREYEVNA
Alarmed But you're mad!

PISHCHIK
I've taken all the pills.

LOPAKHIN
What a digestion!

All laugh

FIRS
His Honor came to see us in Holy Week and ate half
a bucketful of salt cucumbers. *mutters*

LYUBOV ANDREYEVNA
What is it he's saying?

VARYA
He's been muttering for the last three years. We're
accustomed to it.

ANTON
CHEKHOV

YASHA
It's his age.

Charlotta Ivanovna, very thin and tightly laced in a
white dress, with a lorgnette at her waist, passes across
the stage

LOPAKHIN

Forgive me, Charlotta Ivanovna, I haven't yet had
time to say how d'you do to you.   *tries to kiss her hand*

CHARLOTTA

Withdrawing her hand
If you were permitted to kiss a lady's hand, you'd want
to kiss her elbow next and then her shoulder.

LOPAKHIN

I'm unlucky today.

All laugh

Charlotta Ivanovna, do a trick for us.

CHARLOTTA

There's no need to now. I want to go to bed.   *goes out*

LOPAKHIN

I'll see you in three weeks' time.   *kisses Lyubov
Andreyevna's hand*   Meanwhile, good-bye. Time to
go.   *to Gayev*   Au revoir.   *embraces Pishchik*   Au
revoir.   *shakes hands with Varya, then with Firs and
Yasha*   I don't want to go really.   *to Lyubov
Andreyevna*   If you think over this question of
country villas and come to a decision, let me know, and
I'll get you a loan of fifty thousand or more. Think
it over seriously.

VARYA

Angrily   Will you ever go away?

LOPAKHIN

I'm going, I'm going.   *goes out*

GAYEV

What a boor! I beg your pardon. Varya's going to
marry him. He's Varya's precious fiancé.

THE
CHERRY
ORCHARD

VARYA

Please don't say anything uncalled for, uncle dear.

LYUBOV ANDREYEVNA

Well, Varya, I will be very glad. He's a good man.

PISHCHIK

He's a man—let's admit it—a most admirable fellow. . . . My Dashenka says so too. . . . She says all sorts of things. *he drops asleep and snores but wakes up again at once* Incidentally, my dear, will you lend me two hundred and forty rubles? I've got to pay the interest on the mortgage tomorrow.

VARYA

In alarm We haven't got it; we really haven't!

LYUBOV ANDREYEVNA

It's quite true. I have nothing.

PISHCHIK

It'll turn up. *laughs* I never lose hope. Sometimes I think everything's lost, I'm ruined, and then—lo and behold!—a railway line is built through my land, and they pay me for it! Something or other is sure to happen tomorrow if not today. Perhaps Dashenka will win two hundred thousand rubles. She's got a lottery ticket.

LYUBOV ANDREYEVNA

I've finished my coffee; now I can go and rest.

FIRS

Brushing Gayev's clothes, admonishing him
You've put on the wrong pair of trousers again! What am I to do with you?

VARYA

In a low voice
Anya's asleep. *quietly opens a window* The sun has risen; it's warmer already. Look, mamma dear, how wonderful the trees are! Heavens what lovely air! The starlings are singing!

ANTON
CHEKHOV

GAYEV

Opens another window

The orchard is all white. You haven't forgotten, Lyuba? How straight this long avenue is—quite straight, just like a ribbon that's been stretched taut. It glitters on moonlit nights. Do you remember? You haven't forgotten?

LYUBOV ANDREYEVNA

Looks through the window at the orchard

Oh, my childhood, my innocent childhood! I used to sleep in this nursery. I used to look at the orchard from here, and I woke up happy every morning. In those days the orchard was just as it is now; nothing has changed. *laughs happily* All, all white! Oh, my orchard! After the dark, stormy autumn and the cold winter, you are young and joyous again; the angels have not forsaken you! If only this burden could be taken from me. If only I could forget my past!

GAYEV

Yes, and now the orchard is going to be sold to pay our debts, strange as it seems.

LYUBOV ANDREYEVNA

Look, there's mother walking through the orchard . . . in a white dress! *laughs happily* It is her!

GAYEV

Where?

VARYA

Bless you, mamma dear!

LYUBOV ANDREYEVNA

It's no one; I only imagined it. Over there, you see, on the right, as you turn to the summer house there's a small white tree and it's bending over. It looks like a woman.

Enter Trofimov. He is dressed in a shabby student's uniform and wears glasses

THE
CHERRY
ORCHARD

What a wonderful orchard! Masses of white blossom, the blue sky . . .

TROFIMOV

Lyubov Andreyevna! *she turns to him* I'll just make my bow and go at once. *kisses her hand warmly* I was told to wait until the morning, but it was too much for my patience.

Lyubov Andreyevna looks at him, puzzled

VARYA

Through tears This is Petya Trofimov.

TROFIMOV

Petya Trofimov, I used to be tutor to your Grisha. Have I really changed so much?

Lyubov Andreyevna puts her arms around him and weeps quietly

GAYEV

Embarrassed Now, now, Lyuba . . .

VARYA

Weeps Didn't I tell you to wait until tomorrow, Petya?

LYUBOV ANDREYEVNA

My Grisha . . . my little boy . . . Grisha . . . my son . . .

VARYA

There's nothing we can do about it, mamma darling. It was God's will.

TROFIMOV

Gently, with emotion

Don't, don't . . .

LYUBOV ANDREYEVNA

Quietly weeping My little boy was lost . . . drowned. What for? What for, my friend? *more quietly* Anya's asleep there, and here I am, shouting and making a

scene. Well, Petya? How is it you've lost your good
looks? Why have you aged so?

TROFIMOV

A peasant woman in the train called me "that moth-
eaten gent."

LYUBOV ANDREYEVNA

In those days you were quite a boy, a nice young
student, and now your hair is thin, you wear glasses.
Are you still a student?   *walks to the door*

TROFIMOV

I expect I will be a student to the end of my days.

LYUBOV ANDREYEVNA

Kisses her brother, then Varya
Well, go to bed now. You have aged too, Leonid.

PISHCHIK

Following her   So you're going to bed now? Ouch,
my gout! I'd better stay the night here. And tomorrow
morning, Lyubov Andreyevna, my dear, I'd like to
borrow those two hundred and forty rubles.

GAYEV

How the fellow keeps at it!

PISHCHIK

Two hundred and forty rubles. You see, I've got to pay
the interest on the mortgage.

LYUBOV ANDREYEVNA

I have no money, my dear.

PISHCHIK

I'll pay you back, my dear lady. It's a trifling amount
after all.

LYUBOV ANDREYEVNA

Very well then. Leonid will give you the money. You
give him the money, Leonid.

GAYEV

I'll be delighted; anything he wants, of course!

THE
CHERRY
ORCHARD

LYUBOV ANDREYEVNA

What else can we do? He needs it. He'll pay it back.

*Lyubov Andreyevna, Trofimov, Pishchik, and Firs go
out. Gayev, Varya, and Yasha remain*

GAYEV

My sister hasn't lost her habit of throwing money
away.   *to Yasha*   Out of the way, my man, you
smell of the kitchen.

YASHA

With a sneer

I see you're just the same as you used to be, Leonid
Andreyevich.

GAYEV

What's that?   *to Varya*   What did he say?

VARYA

To Yasha   Your mother's come from the village.
She's been sitting in the servants' hall since yesterday,
wanting to see you.

YASHA

I wish she'd leave me alone!

VARYA

You . . . aren't you ashamed of yourself?

YASHA

It's quite unnecessary. She could have come tomorrow.
goes out

VARYA

Dear mamma is just the same as she used to be; she
hasn't changed a bit. If she had her own way, she'd
give away everything.

GAYEV

Yes. You know, if a lot of cures are suggested for a
disease, it means that the disease is incurable. I've been
thinking and puzzling my brains, and I've thought of
plenty of ways out, plenty—which means there aren't

any. It would be a good thing if somebody left us
some money, or if we married off our Anya to some
very rich man, or if one of us went to Yaroslavl and
tried our luck with the old aunt, the countess. You
know she's very rich.

VARYA

Weeping If only God would help us.

GAYEV

Do stop blubbering! The countess is very rich, but she
doesn't like us. First because my sister married a
lawyer and not a nobleman.

Anya appears in the doorway

She married a man who wasn't of noble birth; and then
you can't say her behavior's been exactly virtuous.
She's a good, kind, lovable person, and I'm very fond
of her, but whatever extenuating circumstances you
may think of, you must admit that she's a bit easygoing
morally. You can sense it in every movement.

VARYA

In a whisper
Anya's standing in the doorway.

GAYEV

What? *pause* Funny thing, something's gotten into
my right eye. I can't see properly. And on Thursday,
when I was at the District Court . . .

Anya comes in

VARYA

Well, why aren't you asleep, Anya?

ANYA

I can't get to sleep. I just can't.

GAYEV

My dear little girl! *kisses Anya's face and hands*
My dear child! *through tears* You're not just a

THE
CHERRY
ORCHARD

niece to me, you're an angel, you're everything to me. Please believe me, believe . . .

ANYA

I believe you, uncle. Everyone loves you, respects you. But, dear uncle, you shouldn't talk; you should try to keep quiet. What was that you were saying just now about my mother, about your own sister? Why were you saying it?

GAYEV

Yes, yes! *he takes her hand and puts it over his face* You're quite right; it's dreadful! My God! My God! And the speech I made today in front of the book-case . . . so foolish! And it was only after I'd finished that I realized it was foolish.

VARYA

It's true, uncle dear; you ought to try to keep quiet. Just keep quiet, that's all.

ANYA

If you keep quiet, you'll be happier inside.

GAYEV

I'll be quiet. *kisses Anya's and Varya's hands* I'll be quiet. But I must tell you something important. Last Thursday I went to the District Court, and I got talking with some friends, and from what they said it looks as if it might be possible to get a loan on promissory notes in order to pay the interest to the bank.

VARYA

If only God would help us!

GAYEV

I'll go there again on Tuesday and have another talk. *to Varya* Don't keep crying. *to Anya* Your mother's going to have a talk with Lopakhin; he won't refuse her of course. And after you've had a rest, you will go to Yaroslavl to see the countess, your grandmother. And so we'll approach the matter from three angles, and—the thing's done! We'll pay the interest, I'm sure of it. *he puts a sweet into his mouth* I swear on my honor, on anything you like, that the estate will not be sold! *excited* I'll stake my happiness! Here's my hand, you can call me a good-for-nothing liar if I allow the auction to take place. I swear on my soul!

ANYA

Calmer, with an air of happiness
How good you are, uncle, and how sensible! *puts her arms around him* I feel calmer now. I feel so calm and happy.

Enter Firs

FIRS

Reproachfully Leonid Andreyevich, aren't you ashamed of yourself? When are you going to bed?

GAYEV

Presently, presently. You go away, Firs. I don't need your help. Well, children dear, bye-bye now. All the news tomorrow; you must go to bed now. *kisses Anya and Varya* You know, I'm a man of the eighties. People don't think much of that period, but all the same, I can say that I've suffered quite a lot in the course of my life for my convictions. It's not for nothing that the peasants love me. You have to know the peasants! You have to know from which side . . .

ANYA

You're starting it again, uncle!

VARYA

You'd better keep quiet, uncle dear.

FIRS

Sternly Leonid Andreyevich!

Coming, coming! Go to bed! In off the cushion! I sink the white!   *goes out. Firs hobbles after him*

ANYA

My mind is at rest now. I don't really feel like going to Yaroslavl; I don't like grandmamma. But still, I'm not worrying. I'm grateful to uncle.   *she sits down*

VARYA

I must get some sleep. I'm going. Oh, by the way, while you were away something unpleasant happened here. You know, there are only a few old servants living in the servants' quarters: just Yefimyushka, Polya, Yevstignei, and Karp. Well, they let some tramps sleep there, and I didn't say anything about it. But some time afterward I heard some gossip; people said I had ordered them to be fed on nothing but dried peas. Because I was mean, you see. Yevstignei was at the bottom of it all. "Well," I said to myself, "if that's how the matter stands, just you wait!" So I sent for Yevstignei.   *yawns*   In he comes. "What's all this, Yevstignei," I said to him, "idiot that you are."   *she walks up to Anya*   Anichka!   *pause*   She's asleep!   *takes her arm*   Come to bed! Come!   *leads her away*   My darling's fallen asleep! Come.   *they go toward the door*

The sound of a shepherd's pipe is heard from far away, beyond the orchard. Trofimov crosses the stage, but, seeing Varya and Anya, stops

Sh-sh! She's asleep. . . . Asleep. Come, my dear.

ANYA

Softly, half-asleep   I'm so tired. I can hear bells tinkling all the time. Uncle . . . dear. . . . Mamma and uncle.

ANTON
CHEKHOV

VARYA

Come, darling, come.   *they go into Anya's room*

TROFIMOV

Deeply moved   Anya, my one bright star! My spring flower!

CURTAIN

ACT TWO

An old wayside shrine in the open country; it leans slightly to one side and has evidently been long abandoned. Beside it there are a well, an old seat, and a number of large stones which apparently served as gravestones in the past. A road leads to Gayev's estate. On one side and some distance away is a row of dark poplars, and it is there that the cherry orchard begins. Farther away is seen a line of telegraph poles, and beyond them, on the horizon, the vague outlines of a large town, visible only in very good, clear weather.

The sun is about to set. Charlotta, Yasha, and Dunyasha are sitting on the seat. Yepikhodov is standing nearby, playing a guitar. All look pensive. Charlotta is wearing a man's old peaked cap; she has taken a shotgun off her shoulder and is adjusting a buckle on the strap.

CHARLOTTA

Thoughtfully I don't know how old I am. I haven't got a proper identity card you see. And I keep on imagining I'm still quite young. When I was little father and mother used to tour the fairs and give performances—very good ones they were too. And I used to jump the *salto mortale* and do all sorts of other

ANTON
CHEKHOV

tricks. When papa and mamma died a German lady
took me into her house and began to give me lessons.
So then I grew up and became a governess. But where
I come from and who I am, I don't know. Who my
parents were—perhaps they weren't properly married—
I don't know. *she takes a cucumber from her pocket
and begins to eat it* I don't know anything. *pause*
I'm longing to talk to someone, but there isn't anyone.
I haven't anyone.

YEPIKHODOV

Plays the guitar and sings
"What care I for the noisy world? What are friends
and foes to me?" How pleasant it is to play the
mandolin!

DUNYASHA

That's a guitar, not a mandolin. *she looks at herself
in a hand mirror and powders her face*

YEPIKHODOV

To a man that's crazy with love this is a mandolin.
sings quietly "If only my heart might be warmed by
the ardor of love requited."

Yasha joins in

CHARLOTTA

How dreadful their singing is! Ach! It is like the
jackals.

DUNYASHA

To Yasha You are lucky to have been abroad!

YASHA

Of course I am. I'm bound to agree with you there.
yawns, then lights a cigar

YEPIKHODOV

Stands to reason. Abroad everything's been in full
swing. I mean to say, everything's been going on for
ever so long.

THE
CHERRY
ORCHARD

YASHA

Obviously.

YEPIKHODOV

Personally, I'm a cultured sort of fellow. I read all sorts
of extraordinary books, you know, but somehow I
can't seem to make out where I'm going, what it is I
really want, I mean to say—to live or to shoot myself,
so to speak. All the same I always carry a revolver on
me. Here it is. *shows the revolver*

CHARLOTTA

I have finished. Now I'm going. *slips the strap of the
gun over her shoulder* Yes, you are a very clever man,
Yepikhodov, and rather frightening too; the women
must fall madly in love with you! Brrr! *walks off*
All these clever people are so stupid. I have no one to
talk to. I am so lonely, always so lonely. No one
belongs to me, and . . . and who I am, what I exist for,
nobody knows. *goes out leisurely*

YEPIKHODOV

Candidly speaking—and I do want to keep strictly to
the point, by the way—I feel I simply must explain
that fate, so to speak, treats me absolutely without
mercy, just like a storm treats a small ship, as it were.
I mean to say, supposing I'm wrong, for instance, then
why should I wake up this morning and suddenly see a
simply colossal spider sitting on my chest like this?
makes a gesture with both hands Or supposing I pick
up a jug to have a drink of kvass, there's sure to be
something frightful inside it, like a cockroach. *pause*
Have you read Buckle? *pause* May I trouble you
for a word, Avdotya Fëdorovna?

DUNYASHA

All right, go on.

ANTON
CHEKHOV

YEPIKHODOV

I'd very much like to speak to you alone. *sighs*

DUNYASHA

Embarrassed Very well then. Only will you bring
me my little cape first? It's hanging beside the wardrobe. It's rather chilly here.

YEPIKHODOV

Very well, I'll bring it. Now I know what to do with
my revolver. *picks up his guitar and goes, twanging
it*

YASHA

Twenty-two misfortunes! He's a stupid fellow,
between you and me. *yawns*

DUNYASHA

I hope to God he won't shoot himself. *pause* I've
gotten sort of anxious, worrying all the time. I came to
live here with the master and mistress when I was still
a little girl you see. Now I've lost the habit of living a
simple life, and my hands are as white . . . as white
as a young lady's. I've grown sensitive and delicate,
just as if I were one of the nobility. I'm afraid of
everything. . . . Just afraid. If you deceive me, Yasha,
I don't know what will happen to my nerves.

YASHA

Kisses her Little peach! Mind you, a girl ought to
keep herself in hand you know. Personally I dislike it
more than anything if a girl doesn't behave herself.

DUNYASHA

I love you so much, so much! You're educated; you
can reason about everything. . . .

YASHA

After a pause, yawns
Y-yes. To my way of thinking, it's like this: if a girl
loves somebody, it means she's immoral. *pause* It's
nice to smoke a cigar in the open air. *listens* Someone's coming this way. Our ladies and gentlemen.

THE
CHERRY
ORCHARD

438 *Dunyasha impulsively puts her arms around him*

Go home now, as if you'd been down to the river
bathing. Go by this path or you'll meet them, and they
might think I've been keeping company with you.
I couldn't stand that.

DUNYASHA

Coughing softly My head's aching from that cigar.
goes out

*Yasha remains sitting by the shrine. Enter Lyubov
Andreyevna, Gayev, and Lopakhin*

LOPAKHIN

We must decide once and for all; time won't wait.
After all, my question's quite a simple one. Do you
consent to lease your land for villas or don't you? You
can answer in one word: yes or no? Just one word!

LYUBOV ANDREYEVNA

Who's been smoking such abominable cigars here?
sits down

GAYEV

How very convenient it is having a railway here. *sits
down* Here we are—we've been up to town for lunch
and we're back home already. I sink the red into the
middle pocket! I'd like to go indoors now and have
just one game.

LYUBOV ANDREYEVNA

You've plenty of time.

LOPAKHIN

Just one word! *beseechingly* Do give me an answer!

GAYEV

Yawns What do you say?

LYUBOV ANDREYEVNA

Looking into her purse

Yesterday I had a lot of money, but today there's

ANTON
CHEKHOV

hardly any left. My poor Varya is feeding everyone on
milk soups to economize, the old servants in the
kitchen get nothing but dried peas to eat, and here I am
spending money senselessly. I don't know why.   *she
drops the purse, scattering gold coins*   Now I've
scattered it all over the place.   *annoyed*

YASHA

Allow me, madam; I'll pick them up in a minute.
gathers up the money

LYUBOV ANDREYEVNA

Thank you, Yasha. Why did I go out to lunch? It was
quite vile, that restaurant of yours, with its beastly
music; and the tablecloths smelt of soap too. Do you
have to drink so much, Lenya? Do you have to eat so
much? And talk so much? Today at the restaurant you
talked too much again, and it was all so pointless.
About the seventies, about the decadents. And to
whom? Imagine talking about the decadents to the
restaurant waiters!

LOPAKHIN

Yes, imagine.

GAYEV

Waving his hand
I'm hopeless, I know.   *to Yasha, with irritation*   Why
are you always buzzing around in front of me?

YASHA

Laughs   I can never hear you talk without laughing.

GAYEV

To his sister
Either he goes or I do.

LYUBOV ANDREYEVNA

Go away, Yasha, go along.

YASHA

Hands the purse to Lyubov Andreyevna

I'll go now.   *he can hardly restrain his laughter*   This very minute.   *goes out*

LOPAKHIN

You know, that wealthy fellow Deriganov, he's intending to buy your estate. They say he's coming to the auction himself.

LYUBOV ANDREYEVNA

Where did you hear that?

LOPAKHIN

They were saying so in town.

GAYEV

Our aunt in Yaroslavl promised to send us money, but when and how much it will be we don't know.

LOPAKHIN

How much will she send you? A hundred thousand? Two hundred?

LYUBOV ANDREYEVNA

Well, hardly. Ten or twelve thousand perhaps. We'll be thankful for that much.

LOPAKHIN

You must forgive me for saying it, but really I've never met such irresponsible, unbusinesslike, queer people as you are. You are told in plain language that your estate is up for sale, and you simply don't seem to understand it.

LYUBOV ANDREYEVNA

But what are we to do? Tell us: what?

LOPAKHIN

I keep on telling you. Every day I tell you the same thing. You must lease the cherry orchard and the land for villas, and you must do it now, as soon as possible. The auction is going to be held almost at once. Please try to understand! Once you definitely decide to have the villas, you'll be able to borrow as much money as you like, and then you'll be out of the woods.

ANTON
CHEKHOV

LYUBOV ANDREYEVNA

Villas and summer visitors! Forgive me, but it's so
vulgar.

GAYEV

I absolutely agree with you.

LOPAKHIN

Honestly, I feel I'll burst into tears or shriek or fall
down and faint. I simply can't stand it. You've literally
worn me out. *to Gayev*   An old woman, that's what
you are!

GAYEV

What's that?

LOPAKHIN

An old woman!

LYUBOV ANDREYEVNA

Alarmed   No, don't go. Do stay, my dear. Please stay!
Perhaps we could think of something.

LOPAKHIN

It hardly seems worth trying.

LYUBOV ANDREYEVNA

Don't go, please! Somehow it's more cheerful with you
here.   *pause*   I keep expecting something dreadful to
happen, as if the house were going to fall down on us.

GAYEV

In deep thought

Carom off the cushions! I sink it into the middle
pocket.

LYUBOV ANDREYEVNA

We've sinned too much.

LOPAKHIN

Sinned, indeed! What were your sins?

GAYEV

Puts a sweet into his mouth

They say I've eaten up my whole fortune in sweets.
laughs

THE
CHERRY
ORCHARD

LYUBOV ANDREYEVNA

Oh, my sins! Look at the way I've always squandered
money continually. It was sheer madness. And then I
got married to a man who only knew how to get into
debt. Champagne killed him—he was a terrific
drinker—and then, worse luck, I fell in love with
someone else. We had an affair, and just at that very
time—it was my first punishment, a blow straight to
my heart—my little boy was drowned here, in this
river . . . and then I went abroad. I went away for good
and never meant to return; I never meant to see the
river again. I just shut my eyes and ran away in a frenzy
of grief, but *he* . . . he followed me. It was so cruel and
brutal of him! I bought a villa near Menton because
he became ill there, you see, and for three years I never
had any rest, day or night. He was a sick man; he quite
wore me out. My soul seemed to dry right up. Then
last year when the villa had to be sold to pay the debts,
I went to Paris, and there he robbed me and left me.
He went away and lived with another woman. . . .
I tried to poison myself. . . . It was all so foolish, so
shameful! And then suddenly I felt an urge to come
back to Russia, to my own country and my little girl.
wipes away her tears Oh, Lord, Lord, be merciful;
forgive me my sins! Don't punish me anymore!
takes a telegram out of her pocket I had this from
Paris today. He's asking my forgiveness, begging me
to return. *tears up the telegram* Sounds like music
somewhere. *listens*

GAYEV

That's our famous Jewish band. Do you remember:
four violins, a flute, and a contrabass?

LYUBOV ANDREYEVNA

Is that still in existence? It would be nice to get them

to come to the house one day, and we could have a little dance.

LOPAKHIN

Listens I can't hear anything. *sings quietly* "And the Germans, if you pay, will turn Russian into Frenchman, so they say." *laughs* I saw such a good play at the theater yesterday. Very amusing.

LYUBOV ANDREYEVNA

I'm sure it wasn't at all amusing. Instead of going to see plays, you should take a good look at yourself. Just think what a drab kind of life you lead, what a lot of nonsense you talk!

LOPAKHIN

It's perfectly true. Yes, I admit it—we lead an idiotic existence. *pause* My dad was a peasant, a blockhead. He didn't understand anything, and he didn't teach me anything but just beat me when he was drunk, and always with a stick at that. As a matter of fact, I'm just as much of a fool and a half-wit myself. No one taught me anything. My writing is awful; I'm ashamed even to show it to people: it's just like a pig's.

LYUBOV ANDREYEVNA

You ought to get married, my friend.

LOPAKHIN

Yes. That's true.

LYUBOV ANDREYEVNA

You ought to marry our Varya. She's a nice girl.

LOPAKHIN

Yes.

LYUBOV ANDREYEVNA

She comes from the common folk, and she's a hardworking girl: she can work the whole day without stopping. But the main thing is that she loves you, and you've been attracted to her for a long time yourself.

THE
CHERRY
ORCHARD

LOPAKHIN

Well, I'm quite willing. She's a nice girl. . . .

GAYEV

After a pause

I've been offered a job at the bank. Six thousand a year. Have you heard?

LYUBOV ANDREYEVNA

Indeed I have. You'd better stay where you are.

Enter Firs with an overcoat

FIRS

To Gayev   Will you please put it on, sir. It's so chilly.

GAYEV

Puts on the overcoat

You *are* a nuisance.

FIRS

Tut, tut! You went off this morning and never told me you were going.   *looks him over*

LYUBOV ANDREYEVNA

How you've aged, Firs!

FIRS

What can I get you, madam?

LOPAKHIN

They say that you've aged a lot.

FIRS

I've been alive a long time. They were going to marry me off before your dad was born.   *laughs*   And when freedom was granted to the people, I'd already been made a chief valet. I wouldn't take my freedom then; I stayed with the master and mistress.   *pause*   I remember everyone was glad at the time, but what they were glad about, no one knew.

LOPAKHIN

ANTON
CHEKHOV

Oh, yes, it was a good life all right! At least people got flogged!

FIRS

Not hearing him

Rather! The peasants belonged to the gentry, and the gentry belonged to the peasants; but now everything's separate, and you can't understand anything.

GAYEV

Be quiet, Firs. Tomorrow I must go to town. I was promised an introduction to some general or other who'll lend us some money on a promissory note.

LOPAKHIN

Nothing will come of that. And you won't be able to pay the interest anyway.

LYUBOV ANDREYEVNA

He's talking through his hat. There aren't any generals.

Enter Trofimov, Anya, and Varya

GAYEV

Here come the children.

ANYA

There's mamma.

LYUBOV ANDREYEVNA

Come here, my dears. My dear children.   *embraces Anya and Varya*   If you both only knew how much I love you! Sit down beside me here.

All sit down

LOPAKHIN

Our "eternal student" is always with the young ladies.

TROFIMOV

It's none of your business anyway.

LOPAKHIN

He'll soon be fifty, yet he's still a student.

TROFIMOV

I wish you'd drop your idiotic jokes.

THE
CHERRY
ORCHARD

LOPAKHIN

But why are you getting annoyed? You *are* a queer fellow!

TROFIMOV

Why do you keep pestering me?

LOPAKHIN

Laughs Just let me ask you one question: what do you make of me?

TROFIMOV

My opinion of you, Yermolai Alekseevich, is simply this: you're a wealthy man, and before long you'll be a millionaire. And in so far as a wild beast is necessary because it devours everything in its path and so converts one kind of matter into another, you are necessary also.

Everybody laughs

VARYA

You'd better tell us about the planets, Petya.

LYUBOV ANDREYEVNA

No, let's continue what we were talking about yesterday.

TROFIMOV

What were we talking about?

GAYEV

About pride.

TROFIMOV

We talked a lot yesterday, but we didn't agree on anything. The proud man, in the sense you understand him, has something mystical about him. Maybe you're right in a way, but if we try to think it out simply, without being too farfetched about it, the question arises: why should he be proud? Where's the sense in being proud when you consider that man, as a species, is not very well constructed physiologically, and in the vast majority of cases is coarse, stupid, and profoundly unhappy too? We ought to stop all this self-admiration. We ought to—just work.

GAYEV

You'll die just the same whatever you do.

TROFIMOV

Who knows? And anyway what does it mean—to die? It may be that man possesses a hundred senses, and only the five that are known to us perish in death, while the remaining ninety-five live on afterward.

LYUBOV ANDREYEVNA

How clever you are, Petya!

LOPAKHIN

Ironically Oh, awfully clever!

TROFIMOV

Humanity is perpetually advancing, always seeking to perfect its own powers. One day all the things that are beyond our grasp at present are going to fall within our reach, only to achieve this we've got to work with all our might, to help the people who are seeking after truth. Here in Russia very few people have started to work so far. Nearly all the members of the intelligentsia that I know care for nothing, do nothing, and are still incapable of work. They call themselves "intelligentsia," but they still talk contemptuously to their servants, they treat the peasants as if they were animals, they study without achieving anything, they don't read anything serious, they just do nothing. As for science they only talk about it, and they don't understand much about art either. They all look very grave and go around with grim expressions on their faces, and they only discuss important matters and philosophize. Yet all the time anyone can see that our working people are abominably fed and have to sleep without proper beds, thirty to forty to a room, with bedbugs, bad

THE
CHERRY
ORCHARD

smells, dampness, and immorality everywhere. It's perfectly obvious that all our nice-sounding talk is intended only to mislead ourselves and others. Tell me then, where are the day nurseries that we're always talking about, where are the reading rooms? We only write about them in novels, but actually there just aren't any. There's nothing but dirt, bestiality, Asiatic customs. I'm afraid of these deadly serious faces; I don't like them. I'm afraid of serious talk. It would be better for us just to keep quiet.

LOPAKHIN

Well, let me tell you that *I'm* up soon after four every morning, and I work from morning till night. I always have money in hand, my own and other people's, and I have plenty of opportunities to learn what the people around me are like. You only have to start on a project to realize how few honest, decent people there are around. Sometimes when I can't sleep, I start brooding over it. The Lord God has given us vast forests, immense fields, wide horizons; surely we ought to be giants, living in such a country as this.

LYUBOV ANDREYEVNA

Whatever do you want giants for? They're all right in fairy tales; otherwise they're just terrifying.

Yepikhodov crosses the stage in the background, playing his guitar

pensively   There goes Yepikhodov.

ANYA

Pensively   There goes Yepikhodov.

GAYEV

The sun's gone down, ladies and gentlemen.

ANTON
CHEKHOV

TROFIMOV

Yes.

GAYEV

In a subdued voice, as if reciting a poem
Oh, glorious nature, shining with eternal light, so
beautiful, yet so indifferent to our fate . . . You, whom
we call mother, uniting in yourself both life and death,
you live and you destroy.

VARYA

Imploringly Uncle, dear!

ANYA

You're starting again, uncle!

TROFIMOV

You'd better screw back off the red into the middle
pocket.

GAYEV

I'll keep quiet, I'll keep quiet.

*They all sit deep in thought. The silence is only broken
by the subdued muttering of Firs. Suddenly a distant
sound is heard, coming as if out of the sky, like the
sound of a string snapping, slowly and sadly dying
away*

LYUBOV ANDREYEVNA

What was that?

LOPAKHIN

I don't know. Somewhere a long way off a lift cable in
one of the mines must have broken. But it must be
somewhere very far away.

GAYEV

Or perhaps it was some bird. A heron perhaps.

TROFIMOV

Or an owl.

LYUBOV ANDREYEVNA

Shudders It sounded unpleasant, somehow. . . .

FIRS

After a pause

It was the same before the misfortune; the owl hooted and the samovar kept singing.

GAYEV

What misfortune?

FIRS

Before they gave us freedom. . . .

LYUBOV ANDREYEVNA

After a pause

Come along, my friends! Let us go home; it's getting dark. *to Anya* You've got tears in your eyes. What is it, my little one? *embraces her*

ANYA

Never mind, mamma. It's nothing.

TROFIMOV

Someone's coming.

Enter a tramp in a white, battered peaked cap and an overcoat; he is slightly tipsy

THE TRAMP

Excuse me, can I get straight to the station through here?

GAYEV

You can. Follow the road.

THE TRAMP

I'm greatly obliged to you, sir. *coughs* Lovely weather today. *recites* "Oh, my brother, my suffering brother! Come to mother Volga, whose groans . . ." *to Varya* Mademoiselle, may a starving Russian citizen trouble you for a few coppers?

Varya cries out, frightened

ANTON
CHEKHOV

LOPAKHIN

Angrily Really there's a limit to everything!

At a loss what to do
Take this. . . . Here you are.   *searches in her purse*
I have no silver. Never mind, here's a gold one.

THE TRAMP
I'm deeply grateful to you!   *goes off*

Laughter

VARYA
Frightened   I'm going. I'm going. Oh, mamma dear,
you know there's no food in the house, and you gave
him all that!

LYUBOV ANDREYEVNA
Well, what can you do with a fool like me? I'll give
you all I've got when we get home. Yermolai
Alekseevich, you'll lend me some more, won't you?

LOPAKHIN
Certainly I will.

LYUBOV ANDREYEVNA
Let's go on now; it's time. By the way, Varya, we
almost fixed up your marriage just now. I congratulate
you.

VARYA
Through her tears
It's no laughing matter, mamma!

LOPAKHIN
Get thee to a nunnery, Ophelia!

GAYEV
Look how my hands are trembling: I haven't played
billiards for a long time.

LOPAKHIN
Ophelia, nymph, in thy orisons be all my sins remembered!

LYUBOV ANDREYEVNA
Come along, everybody. It's almost supper time.

THE
CHERRY
ORCHARD

VARYA

That man scared me so. My heart keeps thumping.

LOPAKHIN

My friends, just one word, please just one word: on the twenty-second of August the cherry orchard is going to be sold. Just consider that! Just think . . .

All go out, except Trofimov and Anya

ANYA

Laughs   Thank the tramp for this! He frightened Varya; now we are alone.

TROFIMOV

Varya's afraid—afraid we might suddenly fall in love with each other—so she follows us around all day long. She's so narrow-minded, she can't grasp that we are above falling in love. To rid ourselves of all that's petty and unreal, all that prevents us from being happy and free—that's the whole aim and meaning of our life. Forward! Let's march on irresistibly toward that bright star over there, shining in the distance! Forward! Don't fall behind, friends!

ANYA

Raising her hands

How well you talk!   *pause*   It's wonderful here today.

TROFIMOV

Yes, the weather's marvelous.

ANYA

What have you done to me, Petya? Why is it that I don't love the cherry orchard as I used to? I used to love it so dearly. It seemed to me that there wasn't a better place in all the world than our orchard.

TROFIMOV

The whole of Russia is our orchard. The earth is great and beautiful and there are many, many wonderful

ANTON
CHEKHOV

places on it. *pause* Just think, Anya : your grandfather, your great-grandfather, and all your forefathers
were serf owners—they owned living souls. Don't you
see human beings gazing at you from every cherry tree
in your orchard; from every leaf and every tree trunk,
don't you hear voices? They owned living souls—and
it has perverted you all, those who came before you,
and you who are living now; so that your mother, your
uncle, and even you yourself no longer realize that
you're living in debt, at other people's expense, at the
expense of people you don't admit farther than the
kitchen. We are at least two hundred years behind the
times; we still have no real background, no clear
attitude to our past. We just philosophize and complain of depression or drink vodka. Yet it's perfectly
clear that to begin to live in the present, we must first
atone for our past and be finished with it, and we can
only atone for it by suffering, by extraordinary,
unceasing exertion. You must understand this, Anya.

ANYA

The house we live in hasn't really been ours for a long
time. I'll leave it; I give you my word.

TROFIMOV

Leave it, and if you have any keys to it, throw them
down a well. Be free like the wind.

ANYA

In rapture How well you put it!

TROFIMOV

You must believe me, Anya, you must. I'm not thirty
yet, I'm young, and I'm still a student, but I've suffered
so much already. As soon as the winter comes, I get
half-starved and ill and worried, poor as a beggar, and
there's hardly anywhere I haven't been where I
haven't been driven by fate. And yet, always, every
moment of the day and night my soul has been filled

THE
CHERRY
ORCHARD

with such marvelous hopes and visions. I can see happiness, Anya; I can see it coming.

ANYA

Pensively The moon's coming up.

Yepikhodov can be heard playing his guitar, the same melancholy tune as before. The moon rises. Somewhere in the vicinity of the poplars Varya is looking for Anya and calling, "Anya! Where are you?"

TROFIMOV

Yes, the moon is rising. *pause* There it is— happiness—it's coming nearer and nearer. I seem to hear its footsteps. And if we don't see it, if we don't know when it comes, what does it matter? Other people will see it!

VARYA'S VOICE

Anya! Where are you?

TROFIMOV

That Varya again! *angrily* It's disgusting!

ANYA

Well? Let us go to the river. It's nice there.

TROFIMOV

Let's go.

Trofimov and Anya go out

VARYA'S VOICE

Anya! Anya!

CURTAIN

ACT THREE

The drawing room of the Ranevskaya house. Adjoining the drawing room at the back, and connected to it by an archway, is the ballroom. A Jewish band, the same that was mentioned in Act Two, is heard playing in the hall. It is evening; the candles in a chandelier are lit. In the ballroom a party is dancing the grand rond. *Simeonov-Pishchik is heard calling out, "Promenade à une paire!"; then all come into the drawing room. Pishchik and Charlotta Ivanovna form the leading couple; then come Trofimov and Lyubov Andreyevna, Anya with a post office clerk, Varya with the station-master, and so on. Varya cries quietly and wipes away her tears as she dances. Dunyasha is in the last couple. They walk across the drawing room. Pishchik shouts,* "Grand rond balancez!" *and* "Les cavaliers à genoux et remerciez vos dames!"

Firs, wearing a tailcoat, crosses the room with soda water on a tray.

PISHCHIK

I've got this high blood pressure—I've had a stroke twice already, you know—and it makes dancing difficult; but if you're one of a pack, as the saying goes, you've got to wag your tail, whether you bark or not.

Actually I'm as strong as a horse. My dear father—he liked his little joke, God bless him—he used to say that the ancient family of Simeonov-Pishchik was descended from the very same horse that Caligula sat in the Senate. *sits down* But the trouble is, we've no money. A hungry dog can only think about food. . . . *falls asleep and snores but wakes up almost at once* Just like myself—I can't think of anything but money.

TROFIMOV

It's quite true; there *is* something horsy about your build.

PISHCHIK

Oh, well, the horse is a good animal. You can sell a horse.

From the adjoining room comes the sound of someone playing billiards. Varya appears in the ballroom, under the arch

TROFIMOV

Teasing her Madame Lopakhin! Madame Lopakhin!

VARYA

Angrily The "moth-eaten gent"!

TROFIMOV

Yes, I am a moth-eaten gent, and I'm proud of it.

VARYA

Brooding bitterly So now we've hired a band—but how are we going to pay for it? *goes out*

TROFIMOV

To Pishchik If all the energy you've wasted in the course of a lifetime looking for money to pay interest on your debts—if all that energy had been used for something else, you'd probably have turned the world upside down by now.

ANTON
CHEKHOV

PISHCHIK

The philosopher Nietzsche, the greatest, the most

famous—a man of the highest intellect in fact—says
it's justifiable to forge bank notes.

TROFIMOV

Have you read Nietzsche then?

PISHCHIK

Well, no. Dashenka told me. But just now I'm in such
a frightful position that I wouldn't mind forging a few
bank notes. The day after tomorrow I've got to pay
three hundred and ten rubles. I've borrowed one
hundred and thirty already. *feels in his pockets with
alarm* The money's gone! I've lost the money. *tearfully* Where's the money? *with an expression of joy*
Here it is, inside the lining! The shock's made me
sweat!

Enter Lyubov Andreyevna and Charlotta

LYUBOV ANDREYEVNA

*Singing "Lezginka," a popular dance tune, under her
breath*
Why is Leonid so late? What's he doing in town? *to
Dunyasha* Dunyasha, offer the musicians some tea.

TROFIMOV

I suppose the auction didn't take place.

LYUBOV ANDREYEVNA

The band came at the wrong time, and the party started
at the wrong time. Well, never mind. *sits down and
sings quietly*

CHARLOTTA

Hands a pack of cards to Pishchik
Here's a pack of cards—think of any card now.

PISHCHIK

I've thought of one.

CHARLOTTA

Now shuffle the pack. That's right. Now give it to me,

THE
CHERRY
ORCHARD

my good Monsieur Pishchik. *Eins, zwei, drei!* Now look for it. There it is, in your breast pocket.

PISHCHIK

Takes the card out of his breast pocket
The eight of spades, absolutely right! *in astonishment* Fancy that!

CHARLOTTA

Holding the pack of cards on the palm of her hand, to Trofimov
Tell me quickly, which card is on top?

TROFIMOV

Well. Let us say the queen of spades.

CHARLOTTA

Here it is! *she claps her hand over the pack of cards, which disappears* What fine weather we're having today!

A woman's voice, apparently coming from beneath the floor, answers her, "Oh yes, madam, the weather's perfectly marvelous!"

addressing the voice How charming you are, quite delightful!

VOICE

And I like you very much also, madam.

STATIONMASTER

Applauding Madame ventriloquist, well done!

PISHCHIK

Astonished Fancy that! Charlotta Ivanovna, how fascinating you are! I'm quite in love with you!

CHARLOTTA

Shrugging her shoulders
ANTON   In love? Do you know how to love? *Guter Mensch,*
CHEKHOV *aber schlechter Musikant.*

TROFIMOV
Slaps Pishchik on the shoulder
A regular old horse!

CHARLOTTA
Attention please! Here's just one more trick. *she takes a blanket from a chair* Now I'm offering this very nice blanket for sale. *shakes it out* Would anyone like to buy it?

PISHCHIK
Astonished Just imagine!

CHARLOTTA
Eins, zwei, drei! she lifts up the blanket and discloses Anya standing behind it.

Anya drops a curtsy, runs to her mother, gives her a hug, then runs back into the ballroom. Everyone is delighted

LYUBOV ANDREYEVNA
Clapping Bravo, bravo!

CHARLOTTA
Just once more. *Eins, zwei, drei! lifts the blanket; behind it stands Varya, who bows*

PISHCHIK
Astonished Fancy that!

CHARLOTTA
Finished! *she throws the blanket over Pishchik, curtsies, and runs off to the ballroom*

PISHCHIK
Hurries after her
The little rascal! Have you ever seen anything like it? Have you ever . . .? *goes out*

LYUBOV ANDREYEVNA
Still no Leonid. I can't understand what he's doing all this time in town. In any case everything must be over

by now; either the estate's been sold or the auction never took place. Why must he keep us in ignorance so long?

VARYA
Trying to comfort her
Uncle bought it; dear uncle, I'm sure he did.

TROFIMOV
Sarcastically Oh yes?

VARYA
Grandmamma sent him power of attorney to buy the estate in her name and transfer the mortgage to her. She's done it for Anya's sake. God will help us. I'm sure of it. Uncle will buy the estate.

LYUBOV ANDREYEVNA
Grandmamma sent us fifteen thousand rubles to buy the estate in her name—she doesn't trust us, you see— but the money wouldn't even pay the interest. *she covers her face with her hands* Today my fate is being decided, my fate.

TROFIMOV
To Varya, teasingly
Madame Lopakhin!

VARYA
Irritably The eternal student! Why, you've been thrown out of the university twice already!

LYUBOV ANDREYEVNA
Why get so cross, Varya? He does tease you about Lopakhin, but what's the harm? If you feel inclined to, why don't you marry Lopakhin; he's a nice, interesting fellow. Of course, if you don't feel like it, don't. No one's trying to force you, darling.

VARYA
I do take it very seriously, mamma dear . . . and I want to be frank with you about it. He's a nice man and I like him.

LYUBOV ANDREYEVNA

Then marry him. What are you waiting for? I can't understand you.

VARYA

Mamma darling, I can't propose to him myself, can I? It's two years now since everyone started talking to me about him, and everyone is still doing it, but he either says nothing or else he just talks in a sort of teasing way. I understand what's the matter. He's getting rich, he's occupied with his business, and he has no time for me. If only I had some money, just a little, even a hundred rubles, then I'd have left everything and gone away, the farther the better. I'd have gone into a convent.

TROFIMOV

A beautiful life!

VARYA

To Trofimov Of course a student like you has to be clever! *softly and tearfully* How plain you've become, Petya. How much older you look! *to Lyubov Andreyevna, her tearfulness gone* The only thing I can't bear, mamma dear, is to be without work. I must be doing something all the time.

Enter Yasha

YASHA

With difficulty restraining his laughter Yepikhodov's broken a billiard cue! *goes out*

VARYA

But why is Yepikhodov here? Who allowed him to play billiards? I can't understand these people. *goes out*

LYUBOV ANDREYEVNA

Don't tease her, Petya. Don't you see she's upset already?

TROFIMOV

She's too much of a busybody; she will poke her nose into other people's affairs. She wouldn't leave us alone the whole summer, neither Anya nor me. She was afraid we might fall in love with each other. Why should she mind? Besides, I didn't show any sign of it. I'm too far removed from such trivialities. We are above love!

LYUBOV ANDREYEVNA

And I suppose I'm below love.   *in great agitation* Why isn't Leonid back? I only want to know whether the estate's sold or not. Such a calamity seems so incredible that somehow I don't even know what to think. I feel quite lost. Honestly I feel I could shriek out loud this very moment. I will be doing something silly. Help me, Petya. Say something, speak!

TROFIMOV

Isn't it all the same whether the estate's sold today or not? It's finished and done with long ago, there's no turning back, the bridges are burned. You must keep calm, my dear. You mustn't deceive yourself; for once in your life you must look the truth straight in the face.

LYUBOV ANDREYEVNA

What truth? *You* can see where the truth is and where it isn't, but I seem to have lost my power of vision; I don't see anything. You're able to solve all your problems in a resolute way—but, tell me, my dear boy, isn't that because you're young, because you're not old enough yet to have suffered on account of your problems? You look ahead so boldly—but isn't that because life is still hidden from your young eyes, so that you're not able to foresee anything dreadful or expect it? You've a more courageous and honest and serious nature than we have, but do consider our position carefully; do be generous—even if only a little

ANTON
CHEKHOV

bit—and spare me. I was born here you know. My
father and mother lived here, and my grandfather too,
and I love this house. I can't conceive of life without
the cherry orchard, and if it really has to be sold, then
sell me with it. *embraces Trofimov and kisses him on
the forehead* You know, my son was drowned here.
weeps Have pity on me, my dear, dear friend.

TROFIMOV

You know that I sympathize with you with all my
heart.

LYUBOV ANDREYEVNA

But you must say it differently. . . . Differently. *takes
out a handkerchief; a telegram falls onto the floor*
There's such a weight on my mind today, you can't
imagine. This place is too noisy, my very soul seems
to shudder with every sound, and I'm trembling all
over—yet I can't go to my room for fear of being alone
and quiet. Don't blame me, Petya. I love you as if you
were my own child. I would willingly let Anya marry
you, honestly I would, but, my dear boy, you must
study, you must finish your course. You don't do
anything; fate seems to drive you from one place to
another—such a strange thing. Isn't it? Isn't it? And
you should do something about your beard; make it
grow somehow. *laughs* You are a funny boy!

TROFIMOV

Picks up the telegram
I don't want to be a dandy.

LYUBOV ANDREYEVNA

That telegram's from Paris. I get one every day.
Yesterday and today. That savage is ill again, and
things are going badly with him. He wants me to
forgive him, implores me to return; and really I do feel
I ought to go to Paris and stay near him for a bit.
You're looking very stern, Petya, but what's to be done,

my dear boy? What am I to do? He's ill and lonely and unhappy. And who's there to take care of him, to prevent him from making a fool of himself, and give him his medicine at the proper time? And anyway why should I hide it or keep quiet about it? I love him, of course I love him. I do, I do. It's a millstone around my neck, and I'm going to the bottom with it—but I love him and I can't live without him. *she presses Trofimov's hand* Don't think badly of me, Petya; don't speak, don't say anything.

TROFIMOV

With strong emotion

Please, please forgive my frankness, but that man's been robbing you!

LYUBOV ANDREYEVNA

No, no, no, you mustn't talk like that. *puts her hands over her ears*

TROFIMOV

He's a cad. You're the only one who doesn't know it! He's a petty cad, a worthless . . .

LYUBOV ANDREYEVNA

Angry, but in control of herself

You're twenty-six or twenty-seven years old but you're still like a schoolboy in a prep school!

TROFIMOV

Never mind me!

LYUBOV ANDREYEVNA

You ought to be a man. At your age you ought to understand people who are in love. And you ought to be able to love, to fall in love! *angrily* Yes, yes! And you're not "pure," but you just make a fad of purity. You're a ridiculous crank, a freak.

TROFIMOV

Horrified What is she saying?

LYUBOV ANDREYEVNA   465

"I'm above love!" You're not above love; you're daft,
as our Firs would say. Not to have a mistress at your
age!

TROFIMOV

Horrified This is dreadful! What's she saying?
*walks quickly toward the ballroom, his head between
his hands* This is dreadful. I can't; I'm going. *goes
out but returns at once* Everything's finished between
us! *goes out through the door into the hall*

LYUBOV ANDREYEVNA

Calls after him
Petya, wait! You funny fellow, I was joking! Petya!

*From the hall comes the sound of someone running
quickly upstairs, then falling down with a crash. There
are shrieks from Anya and Varya, followed by laughter*

What's happened?

Anya runs in

ANYA

Laughing Petya's fallen downstairs. *runs out*

LYUBOV ANDREYEVNA

What a queer fellow he is!

*The stationmaster stands in the middle of the ballroom
and begins to recite "The Sinner" by Aleksei Tolstoy.
The others listen, but he has hardly had time to recite
more than a few lines when the sound of a waltz
reaches them from the hall, and the recitation breaks off.
Everyone dances. Enter from the hall Trofimov, Anya,
and Varya*

LYUBOV ANDREYEVNA
Now, Petya. There, my dear boy. I ask your forgiveness. Let's dance. *she dances with Petya*

THE
CHERRY
ORCHARD

Anya and Varya dance. Enter Firs, then Yasha. Firs stands his walking stick by the side door. Yasha looks at the dancers from the drawing room

YASHA

How goes it, grandad?

FIRS

I'm not too well. We used to have generals, barons, and admirals dancing at our balls, but now we send for the post office clerk and the stationmaster, and even they don't come too willingly. I seem to have grown so weak somehow. . . . My old master, that's the mistress's grandfather, used to give everyone powdered sealing wax for medicine, whatever the illness was. I've been taking it every day for the last twenty years or perhaps even longer. Maybe that's why I'm still alive.

YASHA

How you weary me, grandad! *yawns* I wish you'd go away and die soon.

FIRS

Eh, you! You're daft. *mutters*

Trofimov and Lyubov Andreyevna dance in the ball-room, then in the drawing room

LYUBOV ANDREYEVNA

Thank you. I'd like to sit down for a bit. *sits down* I'm tired.

Enter Anya

ANYA

Agitated A man in the kitchen was saying just now that the cherry orchard was sold today.

ANTON CHEKHOV

LYUBOV ANDREYEVNA

Sold? Who to?

ANYA

He didn't say. He's gone.   *she dances with Trofimov.*
Both go to the ballroom

YASHA

There was some old man there gossiping away. A
stranger.

FIRS

And Leonid Andreyevich's not back yet; he's still not
back. He's only got his light overcoat on—his
"between seasons" coat—and he might easily catch
a cold. These youngsters!

LYUBOV ANDREYEVNA

I feel as though I'm going to die. Yasha, go and find
out who bought it.

YASHA

But the old man's been gone a long time.   *laughs*

LYUBOV ANDREYEVNA

With a touch of annoyance

Well, what are you laughing at? What are you so happy
about?

YASHA

Yepikhodov's such a comic guy—a stupid fellow.
Twenty-two misfortunes!

LYUBOV ANDREYEVNA

Firs, if the estate is sold, where will you go?

FIRS

I'll go wherever you order me to.

LYUBOV ANDREYEVNA

Why are you looking like that? Are you ill? I would go
to bed, you know.

FIRS

Yes.   *with a faint smile*   If I went to bed, who'd wait
on the guests? Who'd keep things going? There's no
one in the house but me.

YASHA

To Lyubov Andreyevna

Lyubov Andreyevna! I want to ask you for something, please! If you go to Paris again, do me a favor and take me with you. It's quite impossible for me to stay here. *looking around, in a subdued voice* There's no need for me to say it. You can see it for yourself: the people are uneducated, and they're immoral too. Besides it's so boring, and the food they give you in the kitchen is abominable. Then this Firs keeps on walking around and muttering all sorts of silly things. Take me with you, please!

Enter Pishchik

PISHCHIK

Allow me to ask you for a dance, beautiful lady.

Lyubov Andreyevna gets up to dance

I'll have that hundred and eighty rubles from you all the same, my charmer, Yes, I will. *dances* Just one hundred and eighty rubles, that's all. *they go into the ballroom*

YASHA

Sings quietly "Will you understand the agitation of my soul?"

In the ballroom a woman in checked trousers and a gray top hat starts jumping in the air and throwing her arms around. There are shouts of "bravo, Charlotta Ivanovna!"

DUNYASHA

Stops to powder her face

The young mistress ordered me to dance—there are so many gentlemen and only a few ladies—but I get so dizzy from dancing, and my heart beats too fast. Firs

ANTON
CHEKHOV

Nikolaevich, the post office clerk told me something 469
just now that quite took my breath away.

The music stops

FIRS
What did he tell you?

DUNYASHA
"You are like a flower," he said.

YASHA
Yawns What ignorance! *goes out*

DUNYASHA
Like a flower . . . I'm so sensitive. I love it when
people say nice things to me.

FIRS
You'll get your head turned all right.

Enter Yepikhodov

YEPIKHODOV
Avdotya Fëdorovna, you don't seem to want to look
at me, as if I were some sort of insect. *sighs* What
a life!

DUNYASHA
What is it you want?

YEPIKHODOV
Perhaps you may be right, no doubt. *sighs* But, of
course, if one looks at it from a certain point of view—
if I may so express myself, forgive my frankness—
you've driven me into such a state. I know what my
fate is; every day some misfortune's sure to happen to
me, but I've been so long accustomed to it, that I look
at life with a smile. You gave me your word, and
though I . . .

DUNYASHA
Please, please, let's have a talk later, but now leave me

THE
CHERRY
ORCHARD

alone. I feel in a kind of dream just now. *plays with her fan*

YEPIKHODOV
Some misfortune or other happens to me every day, and yet—if I may so express myself—I only smile; I even laugh.

Varya enters from the ballroom

VARYA
Haven't you gone yet, Semën? What an ill-mannered fellow you are really! *to Dunyasha* You'd better go, Dunyasha. *to Yepikhodov* First you go and play billiards and break a cue, and now you're walking around the drawing room like a visitor.

YEPIKHODOV
Permit me to inform you that you can't start imposing penalties on me.

VARYA
I'm not imposing penalties; I'm merely telling you. All you do is walk from one place to another, instead of getting on with your work. We keep a clerk, but what for no one knows.

YEPIKHODOV
Offended Whether I work, walk around, eat, or play billiards, the only people who are entitled to judge my actions are those who are older than me and know what they're talking about.

VARYA
You dare say that to me? *flying into a temper* You dare to say that? You're suggesting I don't know what I'm talking about? Get out of here! This very minute!

YEPIKHODOV
Cowed I wish you'd express yourself more delicately.

Beside herself   Get out this minute! Out!

He goes to the door. She follows him

Twenty-two misfortunes! I don't want any more of
you here! I don't want ever to set eyes on you again!

*Yepikhodov goes out. He is heard from outside the door
saying, "I'll complain about you."*

Ah, you're coming back, are you?   *she seizes the stick
which Firs left by the door*   Come on, come on . . . I'll
show you! Ah, you're coming back, are you? There,
I'll give it to you.   *swings the stick, and at that
moment Lopakhin enters*

LOPAKHIN
Whom the stick did not, in fact, touch
Thank you very much!

VARYA
Angry and sarcastic
I beg your pardon!

LOPAKHIN
Don't mention it. Thanks for a pleasant surprise.

VARYA
It's not worth thanking me for.   *goes to the side, then
looks around and says gently*   I haven't hurt you,
have I?

LOPAKHIN
No, not at all. There's a huge bump coming up though.

VOICES IN THE BALLROOM
Lopakhin's arrived! Yermolai Alekseevich!

PISHCHIK
Look here, you can see him, you can hear him!   *embraces Lopakhin*   You smell of cognac, my dear
fellow, my fine boy! We're making merry here too.

THE
CHERRY
ORCHARD

LYUBOV ANDREYEVNA

It's you, Yermolai Alekseevich? Why have you been so long? Where is Leonid?

LOPAKHIN

Leonid Andreyevich returned with me; he's coming along.

LYUBOV ANDREYEVNA

Agitated Well, what happened? Was there an auction? Speak, tell me!

LOPAKHIN

Embarrassed, fearing to betray his joy
The auction was over by four o'clock. We missed our train and had to wait until half past nine.   *with a deep sigh* Ugh! My head's going around.

Enter Gayev. He carries some parcels in his right hand and wipes away his tears with his left

LYUBOV ANDREYEVNA

Lenya, what happened? Well, Lenya?   *impatiently, with tears* Tell me quickly, for God's sake!...

GAYEV

Does not reply but waves his hand at her. To Firs, weeping
Here, take this. It's some anchovies and Kerch herrings. I've had nothing to eat all day. What I've been through!

Through the open door leading to the billiard room comes the sound of billiard balls in play and Yasha's voice saying, "Seven and eighteen." Gayev's expression changes and he stops crying

ANTON
CHEKHOV

I'm dreadfully tired. Come, Firs, I want to change. *goes out through the ballroom, Firs following*

PISHCHIK

What happened at the auction? Come, tell us!

LYUBOV ANDREYEVNA

Has the cherry orchard been sold?

LOPAKHIN

It has.

LYUBOV ANDREYEVNA

Who bought it?

LOPAKHIN

I did.

A pause. Lyubov Andreyevna is overcome; only the fact that she is standing beside a table and a chair prevents her from falling. Varya takes a bundle of keys off her belt, throws them on the floor in the middle of the drawing room, and walks out

Yes, I bought it. Wait a moment, ladies and gentlemen, please. I don't feel quite clear in my head. I hardly know how to talk.   *laughs*   When we got to the auction, Deriganov was there already. Of course Leonid Andreyevich only had fifteen thousand rubles, and Deriganov at once bid thirty over and above the mortgage. I could see how things were going, so I muscled in and offered forty. He bid forty-five, I bid fifty-five; he kept on adding five thousand each time and I added ten thousand each time. Well, it finished at last. I bid ninety thousand over and above the mortgage, and I got the property. Yes, the cherry orchard's mine now! Mine!   *laughs*   My God! The cherry orchard's mine! Come on, tell me I'm drunk, tell me I'm out of my mind, say I've imagined all this.   *stamps his foot* Don't laugh at me! If only my father and grandfather could rise from their graves and see everything that's happened—how their Yermolai, their much-beaten, half-literate Yermolai, the lad who used to run around

THE
CHERRY
ORCHARD

with bare feet in the winter—how he's bought this estate, the most beautiful place on God's earth! Yes, I've bought the very estate where my father and grandfather were serfs, where they weren't even admitted to the kitchen! I must be asleep, I must be dreaming, I only think it's true. It's all just my imagination; my imagination's been wandering. *picks up the keys, smiling tenderly* She threw these down because she wanted to show she's not mistress here anymore. *jingles the keys* Well, never mind. *the band is heard tuning up* Hey, you musicians, come on now, play something! I want some music! Now then, all of you, just you wait and see Yermolai Lopakhin take an ax to the cherry orchard, just you see the trees come crashing down! We're going to build a whole lot of new villas, and our children and great-grandchildren are going to see a new living world growing up here. Come on there, let's have some music!

The band plays. Lyubov Andreyevna has sunk into a chair and is crying bitterly

reproachfully Why didn't you listen to me before, why didn't you? My poor, dear lady, you can't undo it now. *with great emotion* Oh, if only we could be done with all this, if only we could alter this distorted, unhappy life somehow!

PISHCHIK
Taking his arm, in a subdued voice
She's crying. Come into the ballroom; leave her alone. Come on. *takes his arm and leads him away to the ballroom*

LOPAKHIN
Never mind! Come on, band, play, play! Everything must be just as *I* wish it now. *ironically* Here comes the new landowner! Here comes the owner of

the cherry orchard! *he pushes a small table acci-*
dentally and nearly knocks over some candlesticks
Never mind, I can pay for everything! *goes out with*
Pishchik

No one remains in the ballroom or drawing room except
Lyubov Andreyevna, who sits hunched up in a chair,
crying bitterly. The band continues playing quietly.
Anya and Trofimov enter quickly. Anya goes up to her
mother and kneels beside her. Trofimov remains standing
by the entrance to the ballroom

ANYA
Mamma! Mamma, you're crying? Dear, kind, sweet
mamma, my darling precious, how I love you! God
bless you, mamma! The cherry orchard's sold, it's
quite true; there isn't any cherry orchard anymore, it's
true. But don't cry, mamma—you still have your life
ahead of you, you still have your dear, innocent heart.
You must come away with me, darling; we must get
away from here! We'll plant a new orchard, even more
splendid than this one—and when you see it, you'll
understand everything, your heart will be filled with
happiness, like the sun in the evening. And then you'll
smile again, mamma! Come with me, darling, come!

CURTAIN

ACT FOUR

*The same setting as for Act One. There are no pictures
on the walls or curtains at the windows; only a few
remaining pieces of furniture are piled up in a corner
as if for sale. There is an oppressive sense of emptiness.
At the back of the stage, beside the door, suitcases
and other pieces of luggage have been piled together as
if ready for a journey. The voices of Varya and Anya
can be heard through the door on the left, which is open.
Lopakhin stands waiting. Yasha is holding a tray
laden with glasses of champagne. In the hall
Yepikhodov is tying up a large box. From somewhere
behind the scenes comes the low hum of voices: the
peasants have called to say good-bye. Gayev's voice is
heard saying, "Thank you, friends, thank you."*

YASHA

The villagers have come to say good-bye. In my view,
Yermolai Alekseevich, they're kindhearted folk, but
they haven't much understanding.

*The hum subsides. Lyubov Andreyevna and Gayev
enter from the hall. Lyubov Andreyevna is not crying
but her face is pale and tremulous. She seems unable
to speak*

ANTON
CHEKHOV

GAYEV

You gave them your purse, Lyuba. You shouldn't have done that. You really shouldn't.

LYUBOV ANDREYEVNA

I couldn't help myself, I couldn't help myself! *both go out*

LOPAKHIN

Calls after them through the door

Have some champagne, please do, please! Just one little glass before you go. I didn't think of bringing any from town, and I could only get one bottle at the station. Have some, please. *pause* Won't you have any, ladies and gentlemen? *walks away from the door* If I'd known, I wouldn't have brought any. Then I won't have any either.

Yasha carefully puts the tray on a chair

You have a drink, Yasha, if nobody else will.

YASHA

Here's to the travelers! And here's to you staying behind. *drinks* This champagne isn't the real thing, I can tell you.

LOPAKHIN

Eight rubles a bottle. *pause* It's devilishly cold here.

YASHA

The stoves weren't lighted today. It doesn't matter since we're going. *laughs*

LOPAKHIN

Why are you laughing?

YASHA

Because I'm feeling glad.

LOPAKHIN

October's here, but it's still sunny and calm, as if it were summer. Good building weather. *looks at his*

THE
CHERRY
ORCHARD

watch, then at the door Ladies and gentlemen, don't forget there are only forty-six minutes before the train's due to leave. That means we must start in twenty minutes. Hurry up.

Trofimov, wearing an overcoat, comes in from outdoors

TROFIMOV

I think it's time to start. The horses are at the door. God knows where my galoshes are; they've disappeared. *calls through the door* Anya, my galoshes aren't here; I can't find them.

LOPAKHIN

And I must be off to Kharkov. I'll travel with you on the same train. I will stay the whole winter in Kharkov. I've hung around here too long, and it's torture having no work to do. I can't be without work. I just don't know what to do with my hands; they feel limp and strange, as if they didn't belong to me.

TROFIMOV

We'll soon be gone; then you can start your useful labors again.

LOPAKHIN

Have a little drink.

TROFIMOV

No, thanks.

LOPAKHIN

You're going to Moscow then?

TROFIMOV

Yes, I'll see them off to town, and then tomorrow I'm off to Moscow.

LOPAKHIN

Well, well. I expect the professors are holding up their lectures, waiting for your arrival!

ANTON
CHEKHOV

TROFIMOV

That's none of your business.

LOPAKHIN

How many years have you been studying at the
university?

TROFIMOV

I wish you'd think up something new; that's old and
stale. *looks for his galoshes* Incidentally since we're
not likely to meet again, I'd like to give you a bit of
advice, by way of a farewell: stop throwing your arms
around! Try to get rid of that habit of making wide,
sweeping gestures. Yes, and all this talk too about
building villas, these calculations about summer residents that are going to turn into small property owners,
these forecasts—they're all sweeping gestures too.
When all's said and done, I like you, despite everything.
You've slender, delicate fingers, like an artist's; you've
a fine, sensitive soul.

LOPAKHIN

Embraces him Good-bye, my friend. Thank you for
everything. I can let you have some money for your
journey if you need it.

TROFIMOV

Whatever for? I don't want it.

LOPAKHIN

But you haven't any!

TROFIMOV

Yes, I have, thank you. I've just gotten some for a
translation. Here it is, in my pocket. *anxiously* But
I can't see my galoshes anywhere.

VARYA

From the other room
Take your beastly things! *she throws a pair of rubber
galoshes into the room*

TROFIMOV

But why are you angry, Varya? Hm . . . but these
aren't my galoshes!

THE
CHERRY
ORCHARD

LOPAKHIN

I had a thousand acres of poppies sown last spring, and now I've just made forty thousand net profit on it. And when they were in bloom, what a picture it was! What I want to say is that I've made the forty thousand, and now I'm offering to lend you money because I'm in a position to do it. Why are you so stuck up? I'm a peasant. I've no manners.

TROFIMOV

Your father was a peasant; mine had a chemist's shop. But there's nothing in that.

Lopakhin takes out his wallet

Leave it alone, leave it alone. Even if you offered me two hundred thousand, I wouldn't take it. I'm a free man. And all that you value so highly and hold so dear, you rich men—and beggars too for that matter—none of it has the slightest power over me. It's all just so much fluff blowing around in the air. I'm strong, I'm proud, I can do without you, I can pass you by. Humanity is advancing toward the highest truth, the greatest happiness that it is possible to achieve on earth, and I am in the vanguard!

LOPAKHIN

Will you get there?

TROFIMOV

Yes.   *pause*   I'll get there myself or show others the way to get there.

The sound of an ax striking a tree is heard in the distance

LOPAKHIN

Well, good-bye, my friend, it's time to go. We show off in front of one another, and in the meantime life is slipping by. When I work for long hours on end, without taking any time off, I feel happier in my mind and I even imagine I know why I exist. But how many people there are in Russia, my friend, who exist for no purpose whatever! Well, never mind, perhaps it doesn't matter. They say Leonid Andreyevich has taken a post at the bank, at six thousand a year. I don't expect he'll stick to it; he's too lazy.

ANYA

In the doorway

Mamma asks you not to cut the orchard down until she's left.

TROFIMOV

I should say not! Haven't you got any tact? *goes out through the hall*

LOPAKHIN

All right, all right. These people! *follows Trofimov*

ANYA

Has Firs been taken to the hospital?

YASHA

I told them to take him this morning. He's gone, I think.

ANYA

To Yepikhodov, who passes through the ballroom

Semën Panteleyevich, will you please find out whether Firs has been taken to the hospital?

YASHA

Offended I told Yegor this morning. Do you have to ask ten times?

YEPIKHODOV

This superannuated Firs—candidly speaking, I mean—he's beyond repair; he ought to go and join his ancestors. As for me, I can only envy him. *he places a suitcase on top of a cardboard hatbox and squashes it* There you are, you see! I might have known it! *goes out*

YASHA

Sardonically Twenty-two misfortunes!

VARYA

From behind the door

Has Firs been taken to the hospital?

ANYA

Yes.

VARYA

Why haven't they taken the letter to the doctor then?

ANYA

I'll send someone after them with it. *goes out*

VARYA

From the adjoining room

Where's Yasha? Tell him his mother is here and wants to say good-bye to him.

YASHA

Waves his hand

She makes me lose patience with her.

While the foregoing action has been taking place, Dunyasha has been fussing with the luggage. Now that Yasha is alone, she comes up to him

DUNYASHA

If only you'd look at me once, Yasha! You're going. You're leaving me behind! *she cries and throws her arms around his neck*

YASHA

What's the point of crying? *drinks champagne* In a week's time I'll be in Paris again. Tomorrow we'll get into an express train—and off we'll go. We will just disappear! I can hardly believe it. *Vive la France!* This place doesn't suit me; I can't live here—there's nothing going on. I've seen enough of all this ignorance. I've had enough of it. *drinks* What are you crying for?

ANTON
CHEKHOV

Behave like a respectable girl, then there won't be
any need to cry.

DUNYASHA

Looking into a hand mirror and powdering her nose
Write to me from Paris, won't you? You know that
I've loved you, Yasha. I've loved you so much! I've
got a soft heart, Yasha!

YASHA

Someone's coming.   *pretends to be busy with a suitcase, singing quietly to himself*

*Enter Lyubov Andreyevna, Gayev, Anya, and Charlotta
Ivanovna*

GAYEV

We ought to be going. There isn't much time left.
looks at Yasha   Who smells of herring here?

LYUBOV ANDREYEVNA

In ten minutes we ought to be getting into the carriage.
glances around the room   Good-bye, dear house, old
grandfather house. Winter will pass, spring will come
again, and then you won't be here anymore; you'll
be pulled down. How much these walls have seen!
kisses her daughter ardently   My little treasure, you
look simply radiant; your eyes are shining like
diamonds. Are you glad? Very glad?

ANYA

Yes, very. Our new life is just beginning, mamma!

GAYEV

Brightly   So it is indeed. Everything's all right now.
Before the cherry orchard was sold everybody was
worried and upset, but as soon as it was all settled
finally and once and for all, everybody calmed down
and felt quite cheerful in fact. I'm an employee of a
bank now, a financier. . . . I sink the red. . . . And you,

THE
CHERRY
ORCHARD

Lyuba, you're looking better too when all's said and done. There's no doubt about it.

LYUBOV ANDREYEVNA

Yes, my nerves are better, it's true.

Someone helps her on with her hat and coat

I'm sleeping better too. Take my things out, Yasha; it's time. *to Anya* My little girl, we'll soon be seeing each other again. I'm going to Paris—I will live there on the money which your grandmamma in Yaroslavl sent us to buy the estate—God bless grandmamma!—and that money won't last long either.

ANYA

You'll come back soon, mamma—quite soon, won't you? I will study and pass my exams at the high school and then I'll work and help you. We'll read all sorts of books together, mamma, won't we? *she kisses her mother's hands* We'll read during the long autumn evenings; we'll read lots of books, and a new, wonderful world will open up before us. *dreamily* Mamma, come back.

LYUBOV ANDREYEVNA

I'll come back, my precious. *embraces her*

Enter Lopakhin. Charlotta quietly sings to herself

GAYEV

Happy Charlotta! She's singing.

CHARLOTTA

Picks up a bundle that looks like a baby in swaddling clothes

Bye-bye, little baby. *a sound like a baby crying is heard* Be quiet, my sweet, be a good little boy. *the crying continues* My heart goes out to you, baby! *throws the bundle down* Are you going to find me another job, please? I can't do without one.

ANTON
CHEKHOV

LOPAKHIN

We'll find you one, Charlotta Ivanovna, don't worry.

GAYEV

Everybody's leaving us. Varya's going away. We've
suddenly become unwanted.

CHARLOTTA

I haven't got anywhere to live in town. I'll have to go.
hums Oh, well, never mind.

Enter Pishchik

LOPAKHIN

What a phenomenon!

PISHCHIK

Out of breath
Ouch, let me get my breath. . . . I'm worn out. My
good friends. Give me some water.

GAYEV

I suppose you've come to borrow money? I'd better go.
Excuse me. *goes out*

PISHCHIK

I've not been to see you for a long time, my beautiful
lady. *to Lopakhin* So you're here. I'm glad to see
you; you're a man of great intelligence. Here . . . take
this. *hands money to Lopakhin* Four hundred rubles.
I still owe you eight hundred and forty.

LOPAKHIN

Shrugs his shoulders, bewildered
It's like a dream. Where did you get it from?

PISHCHIK

Wait a moment. . . . I'm so hot. A most extraordinary
thing happened. Some English people came to see me
and discovered a sort of white clay on my land. *to
Lyubov Andreyevna* Here's four hundred for you
also, my dear enchantress. *hands her the money*
You'll get the rest later on. *takes a drink of water*

THE
CHERRY
ORCHARD

Just now a young fellow in the train was telling me that some great philosopher or other advises people to jump off roofs. You just jump off, he says, and that settles the whole problem. *as though astonished at what he has just said* Fancy that! More water, please.

LOPAKHIN

Who were these Englishmen?

PISHCHIK

I leased the land with the clay to them for twenty-four years. And now you must excuse me; I'm in a hurry. I've got to get along as quickly as I can. I'm going to Znoykov's, then to Kardamonov's. I owe money to all of them. *drinks* Good health to you all. I'll call again on Thursday.

LYUBOV ANDREYEVNA

We're just on the point of moving to town, and tomorrow I'm going abroad.

PISHCHIK

What's that? *in agitation* What are you going to town for? I see now. This furniture and the suitcases . . . Well, never mind. *tearfully* Never mind. These Englishmen, you know, they're men of the greatest intelligence. Never mind. I wish you every happiness. God be with you. Never mind, everything comes to an end eventually. *kisses Lyubov Andreyevna's hand* And when you hear that my end has come, just think of—a horse and say, "There used to be a fellow like that once. Simeonov-Pishchik his name was. God be with him!" Wonderful weather we're having. Yes. *goes out, overcome with embarrassment, but returns at once and stands in the doorway* Dashenka sent greetings to you. *goes out*

LYUBOV ANDREYEVNA

Well, we can go now. I'm leaving with two worries

on my mind. One is Firs—he's sick you know.
glances at her watch We have another five minutes
or so.

ANYA

Mamma, Firs has been taken to the hospital already.
Yasha sent him this morning.

LYUBOV ANDREYEVNA

The other is Varya. She's been accustomed to getting
up early and working, and now without work she's
like a fish out of water. She's gotten so thin and pale,
and she cries a lot, poor thing. *pause* You know
very well, Yermolai Alekseevich, that I'd been hoping
to get her married to you, and everything seemed to
show that you meant to marry her too. *whispers to
Anya, who nods to Charlotta, and they both go out* She
loves you, and you must be fond of her too. And I just
don't know, I just don't know why you seem to keep
away from each other. I don't understand it.

LOPAKHIN

Neither do I myself, I must confess. It's all so strange
somehow. If there's still time, I'm ready even now.
Let's settle it at once—and get it over! Without you
here, I don't feel I shall ever propose to her.

LYUBOV ANDREYEVNA

That's an excellent idea! You'll hardly need more than
a minute, that's all. I'll call her at once.

LOPAKHIN

There's champagne here too, quite suitable for the
occasion. *takes a look at the glasses* But they're
empty; someone's drunk it up.

Yasha coughs

I should have said lapped it up. THE
CHERRY
LYUBOV ANDREYEVNA ORCHARD
With animation I'm so glad. We'll go outside.

Yasha, *allez!* I'll call her. *through the door* Varya, come here a moment; leave what you're doing for a minute! Varya! *goes out with Yasha*

LOPAKHIN

Glancing at his watch

Yes.

Suppressed laughter and whispering is heard from behind the door, and finally Varya comes in and starts examining the luggage.

VARYA

After some time

It's strange, I just can't find . . .

LOPAKHIN

What are you looking for?

VARYA

I packed the things myself, yet I can't remember . . .

LOPAKHIN

After a pause

Where are you going to now, Varvara Mikhailovna?

VARYA

I? To the Ragulins. I've agreed to look after the house for them—to be their housekeeper or something.

LOPAKHIN

That's at Yashnevo, isn't it? About seventy miles from here. *pause* So this is the end of life in this house.

VARYA

Examining the luggage

But where could it be? Or perhaps I've packed it in the trunk? Yes, life in this house has come to an end; there won't be any more.

LOPAKHIN

And I'm going to Kharkov presently. On the next train. I've got a lot to do there. And I'm leaving Yepikhodov here. I've engaged him.

ANTON
CHEKHOV

VARYA

Well!

LOPAKHIN

Do you remember, last year about this time it was
snowing already, but now it's quite still and sunny. It's
rather cold though. About three degrees below freezing.

VARYA

I haven't looked.   *pause*   Besides our thermometer's
broken.

*A voice is heard from outside the door: "Yermolai
Alekseevich!"*

LOPAKHIN

As if he had long been expecting it
Coming this moment!   *goes out quickly*

*Varya, sitting on the floor, with her head on the bundle
of clothes, sobs softly. The door opens; Lyubov
Andreyevna enters quietly*

LYUBOV ANDREYEVNA

Well?   *pause*   We must go.

VARYA

Stops crying and wipes her eyes
Yes, it's time, mamma dear. I'll just be able to get to
the Ragulins today, if only we don't miss the train.

LYUBOV ANDREYEVNA

Calls through the door
Anya, put your coat on.

*Enter Anya, followed by Gayev and Charlotta Ivanovna.
Gayev wears a heavy overcoat with a hood. Servants
and coachmen come into the room. Yepikhodov fusses
with the luggage*

Now we can start on our journey!

THE
CHERRY
ORCHARD

ANYA

Joyfully   Yes, our journey!

GAYEV

My friends, my dear, kind friends! Now as I leave this house forever, how can I remain silent, how can I refrain from expressing to you, as a last farewell, the feelings which now overwhelm me?

ANYA

Imploringly   Uncle!

VARYA

Uncle, dear, please don't!

GAYEV

Downcast   I sink the red and follow through. . . . I'll keep quiet.

Enter Trofimov, then Lopakhin

TROFIMOV

Well, ladies and gentlemen, it's time to go.

LOPAKHIN

Yepikhodov, my coat!

LYUBOV ANDREYEVNA

I'll just sit down for one little minute more. I feel as if I'd never seen the walls and ceilings of this house before, and now I look at them with such longing and affection.

GAYEV

I remember when I was six years old—it was Holy Trinity day—I was sitting on this windowsill, looking at father. He was just going to church. . . .

LYUBOV ANDREYEVNA

Have they taken out all the luggage?

LOPAKHIN

It looks as if they have.   *to Yepikhodov, as he puts on his coat*   See that everything's all right, Yepikhodov.

YEPIKHODOV

In a husky voice
Don't worry, Yermolai Alekseevich!

LOPAKHIN
What are you talking like that for?

YEPIKHODOV
I've just had a drink of water. I must have swallowed something.

YASHA
With contempt   What ignorance!

LYUBOV ANDREYEVNA
When we leave here there won't be a soul in the place

LOPAKHIN
Until the spring.

Varya pulls an umbrella from a bundle of clothes.
Lopakhin pretends to be frightened that she is going to
strike him

Now, why . . . why are you doing that? I never thought of . . .

TROFIMOV
Ladies and gentlemen, come, let's get into the carriage. It's high time. The train will be in soon.

VARYA
Petya, here they are, your galoshes, beside the suitcase.
tearfully   And how dirty and worn-out they are!

TROFIMOV
Puts them on
Come along, ladies and gentlemen!

GAYEV
Greatly embarrassed, afraid of breaking into tears
The train, the station . . . In off into the middle pocket.

LYUBOV ANDREYEVNA
Let us go!

LOPAKHIN

Is everyone here? No one left behind? *locks the door on the left* There are some things put away there; it had better be locked up. Come along!

ANYA

Good-bye, old house! Good-bye, old life!

TROFIMOV

Greetings to the new life! *goes out with Anya*

Varya glances around the room and goes out slowly. Yasha and Charlotta, with her little dog, follow

LOPAKHIN

And so, until the spring. Come along, ladies and gentlemen. *Au revoir!* *goes out*

Lyubov Andreyevna and Gayev are left alone. They seem to have been waiting for this moment, and now they embrace each other and sob quietly, with restraint, so as not to be heard

GAYEV

With despair in his voice

Sister, my sister . . .

LYUBOV ANDREYEVNA

Oh, my darling, my precious, my beautiful orchard! My life, my youth, my happiness . . . good-bye! . . . Good-bye!

ANYA'S VOICE

Gaily Mamma!

TROFIMOV'S VOICE

Gaily and excitedly

Yoo-hoo!

LYUBOV ANDREYEVNA

For the last time—to look at these walls, these windows. . . . Mother used to love walking up and down this room.

ANTON
CHEKHOV

GAYEV

Sister, my sister!

ANYA'S VOICE

Mamma!

TROFIMOV'S VOICE

Yoo-hoo!

LYUBOV ANDREYEVNA

We're coming.   *both go out*

The stage is empty. The sound of doors being locked is heard, then of carriages driving off. It grows quiet. The stillness is broken by the dull thuds of an ax on a tree. They sound forlorn and sad.

   There is a sound of footsteps and from the door on the right Firs appears. He is dressed as usual in a coat and white waistcoat and is wearing slippers. He looks ill

FIRS

Walks up to the middle door and tries the handle Locked. They've gone.   *sits down on a sofa* They forgot about me. Never mind. . . . I'll sit here for a bit. I don't suppose Leonid Andreyevich put on his fur coat. I expect he's gone in his light one.   *sighs, preoccupied* I didn't see to it. These youngsters!   *mutters something unintelligible* My life's gone as if I'd never lived. *lies down*   I'll lie down a bit. You haven't got any strength left, nothing's left, nothing. . . . Oh, you . . . you're daft!   *lies motionless*

A distant sound is heard, coming as if out of the sky, like the sound of a string snapping, slowly and sadly dying away. Silence ensues, broken only by the sound of an ax striking a tree in the orchard far away

CURTAIN

THE
BEAR

A JEST IN ONE ACT

THE
CHARACTERS

POPOVA, *Yelena Ivanovna, the young widow of a landowner, pretty, with dimpled cheeks*
SMIRNOV, *Grigori Stepanovich, a middle-aged landowner*
LUKA, *Madame Popova's old manservant*

The action takes place in the drawing room of Madame Popova's house in the country

Popova in deep mourning with her eyes fixed on a photograph, and Luka.

LUKA

It's not right, madam. You're just killing yourself.
The cook and the chambermaid have gone to pick
strawberries in the woods. Every living thing's happy.
Even the cat knows how to enjoy herself—promenading
in the courtyard and chasing birds. And you sit indoors
all day, as if you were in a nunnery, taking no pleasure
in anything. Yes indeed! I believe it's nearly a year
since you went out of the house!

POPOVA

And I never will go out. Why should I? My life is over.
He lies in his grave; I have buried myself in these four
walls. We are both dead.

LUKA

There you go again! I wish I didn't have to listen to it!
Nikolai Mikhailovich is dead—that's as it had to be.
It was God's will, and the Kingdom of Heaven be his!
You've done your mourning, and now that'll do—it's
time to stop. Surely you can't go on weeping and
wearing mourning all your life. I lost my missus too.
Well, what of it? I grieved and cried for a month or so,

THE
BEAR

and that was enough for her. Suppose I kept on wailing like Lazarus all my life—it would be more than the old woman was worth. *sighs* You've forgotten all your neighbors. You don't visit them, and you won't receive them. We live like spiders, if you'll pardon my saying so. We don't see the light of day. The mice have eaten our liveries. It's not as though there weren't any nice people around—the district is full of them. There's a regiment stationed at Ryblov, and the officers are handsome devils—you simply can't take your eyes off them! In the camp not a Friday goes by without a ball, and the military band plays music every day, they say. Ah! Madam, my dear lady! You're young, pretty, blooming with health—all you need is to live and enjoy yourself to the full. You know, beauty isn't given you to keep forever! In another ten years you may be wanting to show off before the officers too—spreading your tail like a peacock—but it will be too late then!

POPOVA

Resolutely I must ask you never to speak to me like this again! You know quite well that ever since Nikolai Mikhailovich died, life has lost all its value to me. It may seem to you that I'm alive, but that's only what you think! I made a vow never to take off this mourning, never to look at the light of day till I go to my grave. Do you hear? May his departed spirit see how I love him. Yes, I know, it was no secret to you that he was often mean to me, harsh, and . . . and even unfaithful. But I will be faithful to the grave, and I will let him see how well I can love. There, from the other side of the grave, he will see me just as I was before he died.

ANTON
CHEKHOV

LUKA

Instead of talking like that, you'd do better to take a

walk in the garden or maybe have Toby or Giant put
into harness and go and drop in on your neighbors.

POPOVA

Oh! *weeps*

LUKA

Madam! My dear lady! What is the matter? God be
with you!

POPOVA

He was so fond of Toby! He always used to drive him
when he went to visit the Korchagins and the Vlasovs.
How wonderfully he used to drive! How graceful he
looked when he pulled at the reins with all his strength!
Do you remember? Toby, Toby! Tell them to give
him an extra bag of oats today.

LUKA

Yes, madam.

A loud ring at the door

POPOVA

Starts Who is that? Say that I'm not seeing anyone!

LUKA

Yes, madam. *goes out*

POPOVA

Alone, looking at the photograph
You will see, Nicolas, how well I can love and forgive.
My love will only fade away when I do, when my poor
heart stops beating. *laughs, half-weeping* Aren't
you ashamed of yourself? I'm such a good little woman,
such a loyal wife. I've shut myself up and I'll remain
faithful to you all my life, while you . . . aren't you
ashamed of yourself, you brute? How you deceived me
and made scenes and left me on my own for weeks on
end!

THE
BEAR

LUKA

Enters, flustered Madam, there's someone asking for you. He wants to see you.

POPOVA

But didn't you tell him that I'm not seeing anybody since my husband died?

LUKA

I did, but he won't listen. He says it's a very urgent matter.

POPOVA

I won't see *anybody!*

LUKA

I kept telling him, but he's a real devil. He swore and shoved past me. He's in the dining room now.

POPOVA

Irritably Very well, show him in. How rude these people are!

Luka goes out

How difficult they are! What do they want from me? Why will they keep upsetting my peace of mind? *sighs* No, it looks as if I really will have to enter a convent. *ponders* Yes, a convent.

Enter Luka with Smirnov

SMIRNOV

As he enters, to Luka

You blockhead—you're a lot too fond of talking. Fool! *seeing Popova, assumes a dignified manner* Madam, I have the honor of introducing myself: Grigori Stepanovich Smirnov, landowner and retired lieutenant of artillery. I'm obliged to trouble you on a very important matter.

ANTON
CHEKHOV

POPOVA

Not offering her hand
What is it you want?

SMIRNOV

At the time of his death, your late husband, with whom
I had the honor of being acquainted, owed me twelve
hundred rubles on two bills of exchange. As I have to
make a payment of interest to the Agricultural Bank
tomorrow, I would be obliged to you, madam, if you
would pay the sum owing to me today.

POPOVA

Twelve hundred. And what did my husband owe you
money for?

SMIRNOV

He used to buy oats from me.

POPOVA

With a sigh, to Luka
Don't forget, Luka, to tell them to give Toby that
extra bag of oats.

Luka goes out

to Smirnov If Nikolai Mikhailovich owed you something, then of course I'll pay, but I must ask you to
excuse me—I have no money in hand today. The day
after tomorrow my steward will be back from town,
and I'll tell him to pay you what's owing; till then
I can't settle with you. Besides it's exactly seven
months ago today since my husband died, and just now
I'm in such a state of mind that I don't feel at all
disposed to occupy myself with money matters.

SMIRNOV

And I'm in such a state of pocket that if I don't pay
the interest tomorrow, I'll be completely and utterly
bankrupt! My estate will be put up for auction!

THE
BEAR

POPOVA

The day after tomorrow you will receive the money.

SMIRNOV

I need the money today, not the day after tomorrow!

POPOVA

Forgive me, I can't pay you today.

SMIRNOV

And I can't wait till the day after tomorrow!

POPOVA

But how can I help it if I haven't any money?

SMIRNOV

You mean you can't pay?

POPOVA

No, I can't.

SMIRNOV

Hm. Is that your last word?

POPOVA

Yes, my last.

SMIRNOV

Your last? Positively?

POPOVA

Positively.

SMIRNOV

Thank you very much indeed! We'll make a note of that! *shrugs his shoulders* And yet they expect me to keep my temper! Just now on the way here I met the excise officer and he asked me, "Why are you always in such a bad mood, Grigori Stepanovich?" I wish people would be fair—how can I help being in a bad mood? I need money desperately. I left home at daybreak yesterday, and went the round of all my debtors, but— would you believe it?—not a single one of them paid me! I was dog-tired, and I spent the night in a low- down hole—a Jewish tavern—lying beside an empty

barrel of vodka. When at last I got here, forty miles
from home and hoping to be paid my money, I'm
treated to "a state of mind"! How can I help being in
a bad mood?

POPOVA

I think I've explained the position clearly; when my
steward comes back from town, you'll get your money.

SMIRNOV

I've come to see you, not your steward! What the
hell—excuse the language—do I want your steward for?

POPOVA

Forgive me, sir, I'm not used to such strange expressions or to such a tone. I won't listen to you any longer!
goes out quickly

SMIRNOV

Alone I like that! "A state of mind"! Her husband
died seven months ago! But have I got to pay the
interest or haven't I? I ask you: have I got to pay the
interest or haven't I? I grant you, your husband died,
you're in a state, and all that hogwash. Your steward's
gone off somewhere, the devil take him! But what am
I supposed to do? Fly away from my creditors on a
balloon or what? Or take a run and bash the wall in
with my head? I arrive at Gruzdev's—he's not at home.
Yaroshevich has gone into hiding, and as for Kuritsyn,
I had such an awful row with him that I nearly threw
him out of the window. Mazutov had a bellyache, and
this one is—in a state! Not one of the wretches has
paid me! And all because I've been too indulgent with
them—because I'm soft-hearted, a milksop, an old
woman! I'm too gentle with them! Well, you wait!
I'll soon show you what I'm made of! I won't let you
play your tricks on me, devil take you! I'll stay here
and stick around until she pays me! Brr! How mad I

THE
BEAR

feel today, how furious! I'm positively shaking with rage! I can hardly breathe. . . . Ugh! My God! I'm almost fainting! *shouts* You there!

Enter Luka

LUKA
What is it?

SMIRNOV
Bring me some kvass, or a glass of water!

Luka goes out

And just look at the logic of it! A man needs money so desperately that it's like a noose around his neck, but she won't pay because, if you please, she's not disposed to occupy herself with money matters! Proper petticoat logic! That's why I never like and never have liked talking to women. I'd rather sit on a barrel of gunpowder than talk to a woman. Brr! I've got the shivers all over. That little hussy has put me in such a rage! I've only got to set eyes on a poetical creature like that even from a distance, and it makes me so angry that I get a cramp in my legs! I almost want to shout for help.

LUKA
Enters and serves him water
Madam is indisposed and is seeing no one.

SMIRNOV
Get out!

Luka goes out

Indisposed and seeing no one! Very well, you don't have to see me. I'll just sit here till you pay me back. If you're ill for a week, I'll stay here a week. If you're ill for a year, I'll stay a year. I'll get my own back, my

good woman! I won't be appeased by your mourning
or your dimpled cheeks. We know all about those
dimples! *shouts through the window* Semën,
unharness the horses! We're not leaving for quite a
time! I'm stopping here! Tell them at the stables to
give the horses some oats! You lout, you've let the
left-hand horse get its legs all tangled up with the reins
again! *mimics him* It's no-othing! I'll give you
something for nothing! *goes away from the window*
Disgusting! The weather's unbearably hot, no one will
pay, I've had a bad night, and on top of it all there's
this mourning female with her "states." My head's
aching. Should I have some vodka, I wonder? *shouts*
You there!

LUKA
Enters What is it?

SMIRNOV
Bring me a glass of vodka!

Luka goes out

Ugh! *sits down and examines himself* I cut a fine
figure, I must say! All covered with dust, my boots
dirty, unwashed, uncombed, bits of straw on my
waistcoat. I think the little lady took me for a thug.
yawns It's hardly polite to present myself in a drawing
room looking like this. Well, who cares? I'm not a
visitor here; I'm a creditor, and there's no regulation
dress for creditors.

LUKA
Enters and serves him vodka
You're taking too much of a liberty, sir.

SMIRNOV
Angrily What's that?

LUKA
I . . . It's nothing. I only . . .

SMIRNOV

Whom are you talking to? Keep your mouth shut!

LUKA

Aside There's a brute for you! A real imposition! The devil himself must have brought him here.

goes out

SMIRNOV

Oh, what a rage I'm in! So angry, I could crush the whole world to powder! I feel almost faint. *shouts* You there!

POPOVA

Enters with downcast eyes

Sir, for some time I've not been accustomed to hearing human voices in my solitude, and I can't bear shouting. I beg you most earnestly not to disturb my peace.

SMIRNOV

Pay me back my money and I'll go.

POPOVA

I've told you in plain language: I have no money in hand just now. Wait till the day after tomorrow.

SMIRNOV

And with the greatest respect I told you in plain language that I need money today, not the day after tomorrow. If you don't pay me today, I will have to hang myself tomorrow.

POPOVA

But what am I to do if I haven't the money?

SMIRNOV

So you won't pay me right away? You won't?

POPOVA

I can't.

SMIRNOV

In that case I'll stay here; I'll sit here till I get my money. *sits down* So you'll pay me the day after tomorrow? Very good! Then I'll sit it out till the day

ANTON
CHEKHOV

after tomorrow. I'll keep on sitting just like this. . . .
jumps up   I ask you: do I have to pay the interest
tomorrow or don't I? Or do you think I'm joking?

POPOVA

Sir, I beg you not to shout! This isn't a stable!

SMIRNOV

I'm not asking you about a stable, I'm asking: do I
have to pay the interest tomorrow or not?

POPOVA

You don't seem to know how to behave in the company of a lady.

SMIRNOV

Yes, I do know how to behave in the company of a
lady.

POPOVA

No, you don't. You're a coarse, ill-mannered fellow!
Respectable people don't talk like this to a lady.

SMIRNOV

Well, this *is* a surprise! How would you like me to talk
to you then? In French or what?   *affectedly and with
exasperation*   Madame, *je vous prie.* I'm so happy
to know that you're not paying me my money. Ah,
pardon me for having troubled you! What delightful
weather it is today! This mourning dress you're wearing
is so becoming!   *bows and clicks his heels*

POPOVA

That's rude and not in the least clever!

SMIRNOV

Mimics her   Rude and not in the least clever! I don't
know how to behave in the company of ladies!
Madam, in my time I've seen more women than you
have sparrows! I've fought three duels over women,
I've jilted twelve, and nine have jilted me. Yes indeed!
There was a time when I used to play the fool; when I   THE
sentimentalized over women and flattered them; when   BEAR

I scattered compliments, bowed, and scraped. I loved,
I suffered, I sighed at the moon, I went limp, I melted,
I shivered in turn. I loved passionately, madly, in
every way you can think of—the devil take me! I
chattered away like a magpie about the emancipation
of women and I spent half my fortune pandering to my
tender emotions! But now—thank you very much!
You won't take me in now! I've had enough of it!
Black eyes, passionate eyes, red lips, dimpled cheeks,
moonlight, whisperings, bated breath—madam, I
won't give you two kopecks for all the lot of it! I'm not
referring to present company, but all women, young
and old alike, are affected and deceitful—spiteful
gossips and consummate liars. They are vain too,
petty, merciless, outrageously illogical, and as for
this   *slaps his forehead*   excuse my frankness—
any sparrow could give ten points to a philosopher in
petticoats. You gaze at one of these poetical beings—
all muslin and airs and graces—a demigoddess, and
you go into a million raptures! But peep inside her mind
and you see just the most ordinary crocodile!   *clutches
the back of a chair; the chair creaks and breaks*   But
what revolts me more than anything is that this
crocodile imagines for some reason that her monopoly
and privilege, in fact, her special gift is the capacity for
experiencing the tender passion! The devil take it!
You can hang me head downward on that nail there if
a woman is capable of loving any living thing apart
from a lap dog! All she can do when she's in love is to
moan and blubber. While the man suffers and makes
sacrifices, she expresses all the love she feels for him by
trailing her skirts about and trying to lead him more
ANTON   and more firmly by the nose. You have the misfortune
CHEKHOV   to be a woman, so you must know woman's nature

from your own. Very well then, tell me on your honor:
have you ever in your life met a woman who was
really sincere, loyal, and constant? You haven't! Only
the old and ugly women are faithful and constant!
You'd be more likely to meet a cat with horns or a
white snipe than a constant woman!

POPOVA

Excuse me—then who do you think is faithful and
constant in love? Surely not the man?

SMIRNOV

Yes, the man, of course.

POPOVA

The man! *laughs angrily* The man is faithful and
constant in love! That's news indeed! *with feeling*
But what right have you to say that? Men are faithful
and constant! If it comes to that, I may tell you that of
all the men I have ever known, my late husband was
the best. I loved him passionately, with all my being,
as only a young, thoughtful woman can love. I gave
him my life, my youth, my happiness, my fortune. He
was the breath of my life; I worshipped him as if I were
a pagan and he my god, and . . . and—what do you
think? That best of men deceived me at every turn in
the most unscrupulous way! After his death I found a
drawer full of love letters in his desk, and when he was
alive—it's dreadful to remember it!—he used to leave
me alone for weeks on end. He made love to other
women before my very eyes and was actually unfaithful
to me. He spent my money recklessly and laughed at
my feeling for him. Yet despite everything, I loved him
and was loyal to him. More than that: though he is
dead now, I am still faithful and loyal to him. I've
buried myself within these four walls forever, and I   THE
won't take off this mourning till my dying day.   BEAR

SMIRNOV

Laughs scornfully Mourning! I don't know what you take me for! As if I didn't know why you wear this black domino and bury yourself inside these four walls! Come now! It's so mysterious, so poetical! Suppose some youngster from a military school or some little fool of a poet happened to pass by your house, wouldn't he glance up at your windows and think, "There lives the mysterious Tamara who has buried herself within four walls out of love for her husband." We know all these tricks!

POPOVA

Flaring up What? How dare you say this to me?

SMIRNOV

You've buried yourself alive, yet you haven't forgotten to powder your face!

POPOVA

But . . . how dare you speak to me like this?

SMIRNOV

Please don't shout; I'm not your steward! Allow me to call a spade a spade. I'm not a woman and I'm used to expressing my views without beating around the bush. So please don't shout.

POPOVA

It isn't I who does the shouting, it's you. Be so good as to leave me alone!

SMIRNOV

Pay me back my money and I'll go.

POPOVA

I'm not going to give you the money.

SMIRNOV

Yes, you are!

POPOVA

ANTON
CHEKHOV
Just to spite you, I won't give you a kopeck! Leave me alone!

SMIRNOV

Since I haven't the pleasure of being either your spouse
or your betrothed, there's no need to make scenes for
my benefit.   *sits down*   I don't like it.

POPOVA

Breathless with anger
You dare to sit down?

SMIRNOV

Yes, I do.

POPOVA

I ask you to go away.

SMIRNOV

Give me back my money.   *aside*   Ah, how furious
I am! How furious!

POPOVA

I refuse to talk to insolent people! Be so good as to get
out of here!   *pause*   You're not going? Well?

SMIRNOV

No.

POPOVA

No?

SMIRNOV

No.

POPOVA

Very well then.   *rings*

Enter Luka

Luka, put this gentleman out!

LUKA

Approaches Smirnov   Sir, be so good as to leave when
you're told to. You mustn't . . .

SMIRNOV

Leaping up   Shut up! Whom are you talking to? I'll
make mincemeat out of you!

THE
BEAR

LUKA

Clutches at his heart

Holy Fathers! Saints! *sinks into an armchair*   Oh, I feel ill, I feel ill! I can't get my breath!

POPOVA

Where's Dasha? Dasha! *shouts*   Dasha, Pelageya, Dasha! *rings*

LUKA

Ough! They've all gone to pick strawberries. There's no one at home. I feel faint! Water!

POPOVA

To Smirnov   Will you please get out of here!

SMIRNOV

Will you please be more polite?

POPOVA

Clenching her fists and stamping her feet

You're a boor! An ill-mannered bear! A brute! A monster!

SMIRNOV

What did you say?

POPOVA

I said that you're a bear, a monster!

SMIRNOV

Advancing toward her

Excuse me, what right have you to insult me?

POPOVA

Yes, I am insulting you. What of it? Do you imagine I'm afraid of you?

SMIRNOV

And do you imagine that because you happen to be one of those poetical beings you have the right to insult others with impunity? You do? I challenge you!

LUKA

Holy Fathers. . . . Saints. . . . Water!

SMIRNOV

Pistols!

POPOVA

Do you imagine that because you have huge fists and
can bellow like a bull, I'm going to be afraid of you?
Do you? You bully!

SMIRNOV

I challenge you! I won't allow anyone to insult me,
and I don't care if you are a woman, a fragile creature!

POPOVA

Trying to shout him down

Bear, bear, bear!

SMIRNOV

It's high time we gave up the notion that only men
have to answer for their insults! If women are to have
equal rights, let them be equal, the devil take it! I
challenge you!

POPOVA

You want a duel? By all means!

SMIRNOV

Now, this minute!

POPOVA

This very minute! My husband had some pistols. I'll
go at once and get them.   *goes out hurriedly, then
returns* How I'll enjoy putting a bullet slap through
your brazen head! Damn you!   *goes out*

SMIRNOV

I'll pot her off like a chicken! I'm not a youngster, a
sentimental puppy! Delicate creatures don't exist for
me.

LUKA

Good, kind sir!   *kneels before him* Do me a favor;
take pity on an old man! Go away from here! You've
scared me to death, and now you're going to fight a
duel!

THE
BEAR

SMIRNOV

Ignoring him A duel! Yes, that's equality of rights, that's emancipation! There's equality of sexes for you! I'll pop her off just as a matter of principle! But what a woman! *mimics her* "Damn you! I'll put a bullet slap through your brazen head." What a woman! Her face flushed, her eyes sparkled! She accepted my challenge! My word! I've never seen one like her in my life!

LUKA

Kind sir, do go away! I'll say prayers for you for the rest of my life!

SMIRNOV

That's a woman for you! That's the kind I appreciate! A real woman! Not one of these soft, weak females, but a creature of fire, gunpowder, fireworks! I'm almost sorry to have to kill her!

LUKA

Weeps My good sir, go away!

SMIRNOV

I positively like her! Positively! Even if she does have dimples in her cheeks, I like her! I am even ready to let her off her debt . . . and my anger's vanished. A wonderful woman!

POPOVA

Enters carrying pistols

Here they are, the pistols. But before we begin, be good enough to show me how to fire. I've never had a pistol in my hands before.

LUKA

The Lord save us, the Lord have mercy on us! I'll go and look for the gardener and the coachman. What can have brought this trouble upon our heads? *goes out*

ANTON
CHEKHOV

SMIRNOV

Examining the pistols

You see, there are several sorts of pistols. There are
special dueling pistols; that's the Mortimer make with
capsules. But these pistols of yours are Smith-Wessons,
triple action with extractor. Beautiful pistols! They're
worth at least ninety rubles the brace. You must hold
the revolver like this.   *aside*   What eyes, what eyes!
A woman to set you on fire!

POPOVA

Like this?

SMIRNOV

Yes, that's right. Then you raise the cock . . . take aim
like this. Hold your head back a little! Stretch your
arm full length. . . . That's it. Then with this finger
press on that little thing—and that's all. But the most
important rule is not to get excited and to take your
aim without hurrying. You must try to keep your hand
from shaking.

POPOVA

Very well. It's not very convenient to shoot indoors.
Let's go into the garden.

SMIRNOV

All right. Only I warn you that I will fire into the air.

POPOVA

What next? Why?

SMIRNOV

Because . . . because. It's my business why.

POPOVA

You're trying to get out of it, aren't you? Is that it?
Ah-ah! No, sir! No wriggling! Be good enough to
follow me! I won't rest a wink till I've made a hole in
your forehead—that forehead I detest so much! So
you're getting cold feet?

SMIRNOV

Yes, I am.

THE
BEAR

POPOVA

That's a lie! Why won't you fight?

SMIRNOV

Because . . . because you . . . I like you.

POPOVA

Laughs angrily He likes me! He dares to say that he likes me! *points to the door* You can go.

SMIRNOV

Puts down the revolver in silence, picks up his cap, and goes to the door. He stops by the door and for about half a minute they look at each other without speaking. Then he approaches her hesitantly
Listen. Are you still angry? I'm devilishly angry too, but, don't you see? How can I explain? . . . The fact is that . . . you see . . . strictly speaking . . . it's something like this. *shouts* Anyway is it my fault that I've taken a liking to you? *clutches the back of a chair, which creaks and breaks* Damn it, what fragile furniture you've got! I like you! Do you understand? I . . . I'm almost in love with you.

POPOVA

Keep away from me! I hate you!

SMIRNOV

My God, what a woman! I've never seen anything like it in my life! I'm lost! I'm done for! I'm caught like a mouse in a trap!

POPOVA

Keep away or I'll shoot!

SMIRNOV

Shoot! You can't imagine how happy I'd be to die with those wonderful eyes looking at me, to be killed by a bullet from a weapon held by that little velvet-smooth hand! I've gone out of my mind! You must consider and decide now, because if I once leave here, we will never see each other again. You must decide!

ANTON
CHEKHOV

I come from a good family, I'm an honest man, I've an
income of ten thousand rubles a year. I can put a bullet
through a kopeck tossed in the air. I have excellent
horses. Will you be my wife?

POPOVA
Indignant, brandishes the revolver
A duel! I challenge you!

SMIRNOV
I've gone out of my mind. I don't understand anything.
shouts   You there! Water!

POPOVA
Shouts   Let us fight!

SMIRNOV
I've gone out of my head. I've fallen in love like a
youngster, like a fool!   *seizes her by the hand; she
shrieks with pain*   I love you!   *kneels before her*   I
love you as I've never loved before! I've jilted twelve
women, nine have jilted me, but I've never loved any
of them as I love you! I've gone all soft and soppy.
Here I am on my knees like a fool, offering you my
hand. It's a shame, a disgrace! I haven't fallen in love
for five years. I vowed I wouldn't; and all of a sudden
here I am—up to my neck in it! I'm offering my hand
in marriage! Yes or no? You don't want it? Very well,
you don't have to!   *gets up and walks quickly to the
door*

POPOVA
Wait a minute.

SMIRNOV
Stopping   Well?

POPOVA
No, it's nothing. You can go. . . . Wait though. . . .
No, go away, go! I hate you! However . . . No, don't
go. Oh, if you only knew how furious I am, how
furious!   *flings the revolver onto the table*   My

fingers are quite numb from holding the horrid thing! *tears her handkerchief in a fury*   Well, why are you standing there? Get out!

SMIRNOV

Good-bye!

POPOVA

Yes, yes, go!   *shouts*   Where are you going? Wait.... You'd better go, though. Oh, how angry I feel! Don't come near me, don't come near me!

SMIRNOV

Going up to her

How angry I am with myself! I've fallen in love like a schoolboy. I've been on my knees. It positively makes my flesh creep.   *gruffly*   I love you! It's the last thing I wanted to do! I've got to pay the interest tomorrow, the haymaking's just started, and now you.   *takes her by the waist*   I'll never forgive myself for it!

POPOVA

Keep away from me! Take your hands off! I . . . I hate you. I . . . challenge you!

A prolonged kiss. Luka enters, carrying an ax. He is followed by a gardener with a rake, a coachman with a pitchfork, and several workmen with clubs

LUKA

Seeing the embracing couple

Holy Fathers!

POPOVA

After a pause, with downcast eyes

Luka, tell them not to give Toby any oats at all today.

CURTAIN

THE
PROPOSAL

A JEST IN ONE ACT

THE
CHARACTERS

CHUBUKOV, *Stepan Stepanovich, a landowner*
NATALYA STEPANOVNA (Natasha), *his
daughter, aged twenty-six*
LOMOV, Ivan Vasilievich, *a landowner and
neighbor of Chubukov's, a healthy, well-nourished but
hypochondriacal person*

*The action takes place on the
estate of Chubukov*

*The drawing room in Chubukov's house. Chubukov and
Lomov; the latter enters wearing evening dress and
white gloves.*

CHUBUKOV
Going to meet him
My dearest friend, fancy seeing you! Ivan Vasilievich!
I'm so glad! *shakes hands* Well, this is a real
surprise, dear old boy! How are you?
LOMOV
Thank you. And how are you?
CHUBUKOV
We're getting on reasonably well, my cherub—thanks
to your prayers and all that. Please do sit down. You
know it's too bad of you to forget your neighbors, old
fellow. But, my dear friend, why all this formality?
Tails, gloves, and all the rest of it! Are you going
visiting or what, dear boy?
LOMOV
No, I've only come to see you, my dear Stepan
Stepanovich.
CHUBUKOV
Then why wear tails, dear boy? As though you were
making a formal call on New Year's day!

THE
PROPOSAL

LOMOV

The fact is, you see . . . *takes his arm* I've come to
ask a favor of you, my dear Stepan Stepanovich—if I'm
not causing too much trouble. I've taken the liberty of
seeking your help more than once in the past, and
you've always, so to speak . . . But forgive me, I'm in
such a state. I'll take a drink of water, my dear Stepan
Stepanovich. *drinks water*

CHUBUKOV

Aside He's come to ask for money! I won't give him
any! *to Lomov* What's the matter, my dear young
fellow?

LOMOV

You see, my dear Stepanich . . . Forgive me, Stepan,
my dear . . . I mean I'm in such a state of nerves, as
you can see. In short you're the only man who can
possibly help me, though, of course, I haven't done
anything to deserve it, and . . . and I have no right to
count on your assistance.

CHUBUKOV

Oh, don't spin it out, dear boy! Out with it! Well?

LOMOV

Yes, yes. I'll tell you right away. The fact is that I've
come to ask for the hand of your daughter, Natalya
Stepanovna.

CHUBUKOV

Joyfully Ivan Vasilievich! My dearest friend! Say it
again—I didn't quite hear you!

LOMOV

I have the honor to ask . . .

CHUBUKOV

Interrupting him My dear man! I am so very glad,
and so forth. Yes, indeed—and all that sort of thing.
embraces and kisses him I've wished it for a long

ANTON
CHEKHOV

time. It always has been my wish. *sheds a tear* I've
always loved you as if you were my own son, my
dearest fellow! May God grant you love and sweet
harmony, and all the rest of it. As for myself, I've
always wished . . . But why am I standing here like an
idiot? I'm stunned with joy, simply stunned! Oh, with
all my heart. I'll go and call Natasha, and so on.

LOMOV

Moved My dear Stepan Stepanich, what do you
think she'll say? May I count on her consenting?

CHUBUKOV

She not consent to it? And you such a handsome one
too! I bet she's up to her ears in love with you, and so
forth. I'll tell her right away! *goes out*

LOMOV

Alone I'm cold. I'm trembling all over as if I were
going in for an examination. The main thing is to
make up your mind. If you think too long, keep talking
and hesitating and waiting for the ideal woman or for
real true love, you'll never get married. Brr! I'm cold!
Natalya Stepanovna is an excellent housekeeper, educated, not bad-looking. What more do I want? But
I'm in such a state that I'm beginning to have noises in
my head. *drinks water* Yet I mustn't stay single.
In the first place, I'm thirty-five already—a critical age,
so to speak. Secondly, I must have an ordered, regular
life. I've got a heart condition, with continual palpitations. I flare up so easily, and I'm always getting
terribly agitated. Even now my lips are trembling and
my right eyelid's twitching. But the worst thing is my
sleep. No sooner do I get into bed and start dropping
off to sleep than something stabs me in my left side.
Stab! And it goes right through my shoulder to my
head. I jump up like a madman, walk around for a bit,

and lie down again. But as soon as I start dozing off, there it goes again in my side—stab! And the same thing happens twenty times over.

Enter Natalya

NATALYA

Oh, so it's you! And papa said, "Go along, there's a customer come for the goods." How do you do, Ivan Vasilievich?

LOMOV

How do you do, my dear Natalya Stepanovna?

NATALYA

Excuse my wearing this apron and not being properly dressed. We're shelling peas for drying. Why haven't you been to see us for so long? Do sit down.

They sit down

Will you have some lunch?

LOMOV

No, thank you, I've already had lunch.

NATALYA

Won't you smoke? Here are some matches. It's a magnificent day, but yesterday it rained so hard that the men did nothing all day. How much hay did you manage to get in? Would you believe it, I was so set on getting it done that I had the whole meadow cut, and now I almost feel sorry—I'm afraid the hay may rot. It might have been better to wait. But what's all this? I believe you're wearing tails! This is something new! Are you going to a ball or something? By the way you've changed—you're better looking! But really why are you dressed up like this?

LOMOV

In agitation   You see, dear Natalya Stepanovna . . . The fact is that I've decided to ask you to . . . listen to

me. Naturally you'll be surprised, possibly even angry,
but I . . . *aside* How dreadfully cold it is!

NATALYA

What is it then? *pause* Well?

LOMOV

I'll try to be brief. You are aware, of course, my dear
Natalya Stepanovna, that I've had the honor of
knowing your family a long time—from my very
childhood in fact. My late aunt and her husband—from
whom, as you know, I inherited the estate—always
entertained a profound respect for your father and your
late mother. The family of the Lomovs and the family
of the Chubukovs have always been on the friendliest
and, one might almost say, on intimate terms. Besides,
as you are aware, my land is in close proximity to
yours. Perhaps you will recollect that my Volovi
meadows lie alongside your birch wood.

NATALYA

Excuse me, but I must interrupt you there. You say
"my" Volovi meadows. But are they really yours?

LOMOV

Yes, mine.

NATALYA

Well, what next! The Volovi meadows are ours, not
yours!

LOMOV

No, they're mine, dear Natalya Stepanovna.

NATALYA

That's news to me. How do they come to be yours?

LOMOV

What do you mean, how? I'm speaking of the Volovi
meadows that lie like a wedge between your birch
wood and the Burnt Swamp.

NATALYA

But yes, of course. They're ours.

THE
PROPOSAL

LOMOV

No, you're mistaken, my dear Natalya Stepanovna; they are mine.

NATALYA

Do come to your senses, Ivan Vasilievich! How long have they been yours?

LOMOV

What do you mean by "how long"? As long as I can remember—they've always been ours.

NATALYA

Well, there you must excuse me for disagreeing.

LOMOV

You can see it in the documents, my dear Natalya Stepanovna. It's true that the Volovi meadows were a matter of dispute at one time, but now everyone knows that they're mine. There's really no need to argue about it. If I may explain—my aunt's grandmother handed over those meadows to your great-grandfather's peasants for their use, rent free, for an indefinite period, in return for their firing her bricks. Your great-grandfather's peasants used the meadows rent free for forty years or so and got accustomed to looking upon them as their own, and then when the settlement was made after the emancipation . . .

NATALYA

But it wasn't at all as you say! Both my grandfather and my great-grandfather considered that their land reached to the Burnt Swamp—so the Volovi meadows must have been ours. So why argue about it? I can't understand you. It's really rather annoying!

LOMOV

I'll show you the documents, Natalya Stepanovna!

NATALYA

No, you must be just joking or trying to tease me. What a surprise indeed! We've owned the land for

something like three hundred years, and now suddenly
someone declares that the land isn't ours! Forgive me,
Ivan Vasilievich, but I just can't believe my own ears.
I set no value on those meadows. They're not more
than fifteen acres, and they're only worth about three
hundred rubles, but it's the injustice of it that disgusts
me! You can say what you like, but I can't tolerate
injustice.

LOMOV

Hear me out, I implore you! Your father's grandfather's
peasants, as I've already had the honor of telling you,
fired bricks for my aunt's grandmother. My aunt's
grandmother, wishing to do something for them . . .

NATALYA

Grandfather, grandmother, aunt . . . I don't understand
anything about it! The meadows are ours, that's all!

LOMOV

They're mine!

NATALYA

They're ours! You can go on trying to prove it for two
days, you can put on fifteen dress suits if you like, but
they're still ours, ours, ours! I don't want what's yours,
but I have no desire to lose what's mine. You can
please yourself!

LOMOV

I don't want the meadows, Natalya Stepanovna, but
it's a matter of principle. If you wish I'll give them to
you as a present.

NATALYA

But I'm the one who could make a present of them to
you—because they're mine! All this is very strange,
Ivan Vasilievich, to say the least of it! Till now we've
always regarded you as a good neighbor, a friend of
ours. Last year we lent you our threshing machine, and
because of that we had to finish threshing our own corn

in November. And now you're treating us as if we were gypsies! You're making me a present of my own land! Forgive me, but this isn't neighborly conduct! To my mind it's almost impertinent, if you want to know.

LOMOV

You mean to say then that I'm a usurper? I've never stolen other people's land, madam, and I won't allow anyone to accuse me of it. *goes rapidly to the decanter and drinks water* The Volovi meadows are mine!

NATALYA

That's not true; they're ours!

LOMOV

They're mine!

NATALYA

It isn't true! I'll prove it to you! I'll send my men to mow those meadows today.

LOMOV

What's that?

NATALYA

My men will be working there today!

LOMOV

I'll kick them out!

NATALYA

You wouldn't dare do that!

LOMOV

Clutches at his heart

The Volovi meadows are mine! Don't you understand that? Mine!

NATALYA

Don't shout, please! You can shout and choke with rage when you're at home, but please don't overstep the mark here!

LOMOV

If it weren't for these dreadful agonizing palpitations, madam, if it weren't for the throbbing in my temples,

I would speak to you very differently! *shouts* The
Volovi meadows are mine!

NATALYA

Ours!

LOMOV

Mine!

NATALYA

Ours!

LOMOV

Mine!

Enter Chubukov

CHUBUKOV

What's all this? What are you shouting about?

NATALYA

Papa, please explain to this gentleman to whom the
Volovi meadows belong—to him or to us.

CHUBUKOV

To Lomov The meadows are ours, my friend.

LOMOV

But forgive me, Stepan Stepanich, how do they come
to be yours? At least you might be reasonable! My
aunt's grandmother gave over the meadows to your
grandfather's peasants for temporary use without
payment. The peasants had the use of the land for forty
years and got accustomed to regarding it as their own.
But when the settlement was made . . .

CHUBUKOV

Pardon me, my dear friend. You forget that it was just
because there was a dispute and so on about these
meadows that the peasants didn't pay rent to your
grandmother, and all the rest of it. And now every dog
knows that they're ours—yes, really! You can't have
seen the plans!

LOMOV

But I'll prove to you that they're mine!

CHUBUKOV

You won't prove it, my dear man.

LOMOV

Yes, I will!

CHUBUKOV

But why shout, my dear boy? You won't prove any-thing by shouting! I don't want what is yours, but I've no intention of letting go of what's mine. Why should I? If it comes to that, my dear friend, if you're thinking of starting a dispute about the meadows and all the rest of it, I'd sooner make a present of them to the peasants than to you. So that's that!

LOMOV

I don't understand this! What right have you to give away someone else's property?

CHUBUKOV

Permit me to decide whether I have the right or not! And really, young man, I'm not used to being spoken to in that tone, and so forth. I'm twice your age, young man, and I beg you to speak to me without getting excited, and all that.

LOMOV

No, you're simply taking me for a fool and laughing at me! You call my land yours, and then you expect me to stay cool and talk to you in the ordinary way. Good neighbors don't behave in this way, Stepan Stepanich! You're not a neighbor; you're a usurper!

CHUBUKOV

What's that? What did you say?

NATALYA

Papa, send the men to mow the meadows at once!

CHUBUKOV

To Lomov What was it you said, sir?

The Volovi meadows are ours, and I won't give them
up! I won't, I won't!

LOMOV

We'll see about that! I'll prove to you in court that
they're mine.

CHUBUKOV

In court? You take it to court, sir, and all the rest of it!
You do it! I know you—you've really just been waiting
for a chance to go to law and all that. It comes natural
to you—this petty niggling. Your family always had
a weakness for litigation. All of them!

LOMOV

Please don't insult my family! The Lomovs have all
been honest men, and not one of them has ever been on
trial for embezzling money like your uncle!

CHUBUKOV

Every member of the Lomov family has been mad!

NATALYA

Every one of them—every one!

CHUBUKOV

Your grandfather was a dipsomaniac, and your
youngest aunt, Nastasya Mikhailovna—yes, it's a
fact—ran away with an architect, and all the rest of it.

LOMOV

And your mother was deformed! *clutches at his
heart* This shooting pain in my side! The blood's
gone to my head. . . . Holy Fathers! Water!

CHUBUKOV

Your father was a gambler and a glutton!

NATALYA

Your aunt was a scandalmonger—and a rare one at
that!

LOMOV

My left leg's paralyzed. . . . And you're a schemer. . . .

THE
PROPOSAL

Oh, my heart!... And it's an open secret that before the elections you... There are flashes in front of my eyes. Where's my hat?

NATALYA

It's mean! It's dishonest! It's perfectly vile!

CHUBUKOV

And you're just a malicious, two-faced, mean fellow! Yes, you are!

LOMOV

Here it is, my hat. My heart... Which way do I go? Where's the door? Oh! I believe I'm dying. I've lost the use of my leg. *walks to the door*

CHUBUKOV

Calling after him

I forbid you to set foot in my house again!

NATALYA

Take it to court! We'll see!

Lomov goes out staggering

CHUBUKOV

The devil take him! *walks about in agitation*

NATALYA

Have you ever seen such a cad? Trust good neighbors after that!

CHUBUKOV

The ridiculous scarecrow! The scoundrel!

NATALYA

The monster! Grabs other people's land, then dares to abuse them in the bargain!

CHUBUKOV

And this ridiculous freak, this eyesore—yes, he has the impertinence to come here and make a proposal, and all the rest of it! Would you believe it? A proposal!

ANTON
CHEKHOV

NATALYA

What proposal?

CHUBUKOV

Yes, just imagine! He came to propose to you.

NATALYA

To propose? To me? But why didn't you tell me that before?

CHUBUKOV

That's why he got himself up in his tailcoat. The sausage! The shrimp!

NATALYA

To me? A proposal? Oh! *drops into a chair and moans* Bring him back! Bring him back! Oh, bring him back!

CHUBUKOV

Bring back whom?

NATALYA

Be quick, be quick! I feel faint! Bring him back! *shrieks hysterically*

CHUBUKOV

What is it? What do you want? *clutches at his head* What misery! I'll shoot myself! I'll hang myself! They've worn me out!

NATALYA

I'm dying! Bring him back!

CHUBUKOV

Phew! Right away. Don't howl. *runs out*

NATALYA

Alone, moans What have we done! Bring him back! Bring him back!

CHUBUKOV

Runs in He's coming right away, and all the rest of it. Damn him! Ugh! You can talk to him yourself; I don't want to, and that's that!

NATALYA

Moans Bring him back!

THE
PROPOSAL

CHUBUKOV

Shouts   He's coming, I tell you! What a job it is,
O Lord, to be a grown-up daughter's father! I'll cut
my throat! Yes, indeed, I'll cut my throat! We've
abused the man, we've insulted him, we've kicked him
out, and it was all your doing—your doing!

NATALYA

No, it was yours!

CHUBUKOV

So now it's my fault! What next!

Enter Lomov

LOMOV

Exhausted   These dreadful palpitations. . . . My leg
feels numb. . . . A shooting pain in my side.

NATALYA

Forgive us, we were rather hasty, Ivan Vasilievich.
I remember now: the Volovi meadows really are yours.

LOMOV

My heart's going at a terrific rate. The meadows are
mine. Both my eyelids are twitching.

NATALYA

Yes, they're yours, yours. Sit down.   *they sit down*
We were wrong.

LOMOV

To me it's a matter of principle. I don't value the land,
but I value the principle.

NATALYA

That's it, the principle. Let's talk about something
else.

LOMOV

Especially since I have proof. My aunt's grandmother
gave over to your father's grandfather's peasants . . .

ANTON
CHEKHOV

NATALYA

Enough, enough about that.   *aside*   I don't know

how to begin.   *to him*   Will you soon be going shooting?

LOMOV

I expect to go grouse shooting after the harvest, dear Natalya Stepanovna. Oh, did you hear? Just imagine— what bad luck I've had! My Tryer—you know him— he's gone lame.

NATALYA

What a pity! What was the cause of it?

LOMOV

I don't know. He may have dislocated his paw, or he may have been bitten by other dogs.   *sighs*   My best dog, to say nothing of the money! You know, I paid Mironov a hundred and twenty-five rubles for him.

NATALYA

You paid too much, Ivan Vasilievich.

LOMOV

Well, I think it was very cheap. He's a marvelous dog!

NATALYA

Papa paid eighty-five rubles for his Flyer, and Flyer is better than your Tryer by far.

LOMOV

Flyer better than Tryer? Come, come!   *laughs*   Flyer better than Tryer!

NATALYA

Of course he's better! It's true that Flyer's young—he's hardly a full-grown dog yet—but for points and cleverness even Volchanetski hasn't got a better one.

LOMOV

Excuse me, Natalya Stepanovna, but you forget that he's got a pug jaw, and a dog with a pug jaw can never grip properly.

NATALYA

A pug jaw? That's the first I've heard of it.

THE
PROPOSAL

LOMOV

I assure you, his lower jaw is shorter than the upper one.

NATALYA

Why, did you measure it?

LOMOV

Yes. He's all right for coursing, of course, but when it comes to gripping, he's hardly good enough.

NATALYA

In the first place our Flyer is a pedigree dog—he's the son of Harness and Chisel—whereas your Tryer's coat has got such a mixture of colors that you'd never guess what kind he is. Then he's as old and ugly as an old hack.

LOMOV

He's old, but I wouldn't take five of your Flyers for him. I wouldn't think of it! Tryer is a real dog, but Flyer . . . It's absurd to go on arguing. Every sportsman has any number of dogs like your Flyer. Twenty-five rubles would be a lot to pay for him.

NATALYA

There's some demon of contradiction in you today, Ivan Vasilievich. First you pretend that the meadows are yours, and now you're saying that Tryer is better than Flyer. I don't like it when people say what they don't really believe. After all you know perfectly well that Flyer is a hundred times better than your . . . well, your stupid Tryer. So why say the opposite?

LOMOV

I can see, Natalya Stepanovna, that you think I'm either blind or a fool. Won't you understand that your Flyer has a pug jaw?

NATALYA

That isn't true.

ANTON
CHEKHOV

LOMOV

He has a pug jaw.

NATALYA

Shouts It's not true!

LOMOV

What are you shouting for, madam?

NATALYA

Why are you talking nonsense? This is quite revolting!
It's time your Tryer was shot, and you're comparing
him to Flyer!

LOMOV

Excuse me, I can't continue this argument. I have
palpitations.

NATALYA

I've noticed that the people who understand least about
shooting are the ones who argue most about it.

LOMOV

Madam, please be silent. My heart's bursting.   *shouts*
Be quiet!

NATALYA

I won't be quiet till you admit that Flyer is a hundred
times better than your Tryer.

LOMOV

He's a hundred times worse! It's time he was dead,
your Flyer! Oh, my head . . . my eyes . . . my shoulder!

NATALYA

As for your idiot Tryer—I don't need to wish him
dead; he's half-dead already!

LOMOV

Weeping Be quiet! My heart's going to burst.

NATALYA

I won't be quiet!

Enter Chubukov

CHUBUKOV

Now what is it?

THE
PROPOSAL

NATALYA

Papa, tell us frankly, on your honor: which dog's the better—our Flyer or his Tryer?

LOMOV

Stepan Stepanich, I implore you, tell us just one thing: has your Flyer got a pug jaw or hasn't he? Yes or no?

CHUBUKOV

Well, what if he has? As if it mattered! Anyway there's no better dog in the whole district, and all that.

LOMOV

But my Tryer is better, isn't he? On your honor!

CHUBUKOV

Don't get excited, my dear boy. Let me explain. Your Tryer, of course, has his good points. He's a good breed, he's got strong legs, he's well built, and all the rest of it. But if you really want to know, my dear friend, the dog has two serious faults: he's old and he's snub-nosed.

LOMOV

Excuse me, I've got palpitations. Let us look at the facts. Perhaps you'll remember that when we hunted in the Maruskin fields my Tryer kept up with the count's Spotter, while your Flyer was a good half mile behind.

CHUBUKOV

He dropped behind because the count's huntsman hit him with his whip.

LOMOV

He deserved it. All the other dogs were chasing the fox, but Flyer started worrying the sheep.

CHUBUKOV

That's not true! My dear friend, I lose my temper easily, so I do beg you, let's drop this argument. The man hit him because people are always jealous of other people's dogs. Yes, everyone hates the other man's dog! And you, sir, are not innocent of that either! Yes!

ANTON
CHEKHOV

For instance as soon as you notice that someone's dog
is better than your Tryer, you immediately start something or other, and all the rest of it. You see, I
remember everything!

LOMOV

So do I!

CHUBUKOV

Mimics him   So do I! And what is it you remember?

LOMOV

Palpitations . . . My leg's paralyzed. . . . I can't. . . .

NATALYA

Mimics him   Palpitations. What sort of a sportsman
are you? You ought to be lying on the stove in the
kitchen squashing cockroaches instead of hunting
foxes! Palpitations indeed!

CHUBUKOV

Yes, honestly, hunting's not your line at all! With your
palpitations and all that, you'd be better at home than
sitting on horseback being jolted around. It wouldn't
matter if you really hunted, but you only go out so that
you can argue or get in the way of other people's dogs,
and all the rest of it. I get angry easily, so let's stop
this conversation. You're just not a sportsman, and
that's all there is to it.

LOMOV

What about you—are you a sportsman? You only go
out hunting to make up to the count and scheme against
other people. . . . Oh, my heart! You're a schemer!

CHUBUKOV

What! I—a schemer?   *shouts*   Be silent!

LOMOV

Schemer!

CHUBUKOV

Milksop! Puppy!

LOMOV

You old rat! Hypocrite!

CHUBUKOV

Hold your tongue or I'll shoot you with a dirty gun like a partridge! Windbag!

LOMOV

Everyone knows—oh, my heart!—that your wife used to beat you!... My leg ... my head ... flashes in front of my eyes.... I'm going to fall down.... I'm falling.

CHUBUKOV

And your housekeeper has you under her thumb!

LOMOV

Oh, oh, oh!... My heart's burst! My shoulder's gone.... Where's my shoulder?... I'm dying! *drops into an armchair* A doctor! *faints*

CHUBUKOV

Milksop! Puppy! Windbag! I'm feeling faint. *drinks water* Faint!

NATALYA

A sportsman indeed! You don't even know how to sit on a horse! *to her father* Papa! What's the matter with him? Papa! Look, Papa! *shrieks* Ivan Vasilievich! He's dead!

CHUBUKOV

I feel faint!... I'm suffocating! Give me air!

NATALYA

He's dead! *shakes Lomov by the sleeve* Ivan Vasilich! Ivan Vasilich! What have we done! He's dead! *drops into an armchair* Doctor, doctor! *sobs and laughs hysterically*

CHUBUKOV

What now? What's the matter? What do you want?

ANTON
CHEKHOV

NATALYA

Moans He's dead! Dead!

Who's dead?   *glancing at Lomov*   He really is dead!
My God! Water! Doctor!   *holds a glass of water to
Lomov's lips*   Take a drink! No, he won't drink. So
he's dead and all that. What an unlucky man I am!
Why don't I put a bullet through my brain? Why
didn't I cut my throat long ago? What am I waiting
for? Give me a knife! Give me a gun!

Lomov makes a slight movement

I believe he's coming around. . . . Do have a drink of
water! That's right.

CHUBUKOV

LOMOV
Flashes before my eyes . . . a sort of mist. Where am I?

CHUBUKOV
You'd better get married as soon as possible and—go
to the devil. She consents.   *joins their hands*   She
consents, and all the rest of it. I give you my blessing,
and so forth. Only leave me alone!

LOMOV
Eh? What?   *getting up*   Who?

CHUBUKOV
She consents! Well? Kiss each other and . . . and the
devil take you!

NATALYA
Moans   He's alive. Yes, yes, I consent.

CHUBUKOV
Come now, kiss each other!

LOMOV
Eh? Who?   *kisses Natalya*   I am so pleased! . . .
Excuse me, what's it all about? Ah! Yes, I under-
stand. . . . My heart . . . flashes . . . I'm so happy,
Natalya Stepanovna.   *kisses her hand*   My leg's   THE
numb.   PROPOSAL

NATALYA

I . . . I'm happy too.

CHUBUKOV

What a load off my back! Ugh!

NATALYA

But . . . all the same, you must admit it now: Tryer
is not as good a dog as Flyer.

LOMOV

He's better!

NATALYA

He's worse!

CHUBUKOV

There! Family happiness has begun! Bring the champagne!

LOMOV

He's better!

NATALYA

He's worse, worse, worse!

CHUBUKOV

Trying to shout them down

Champagne! Bring the champagne!

CURTAIN

A JUBILEE

A JEST IN ONE ACT

THE
CHARACTERS

SHIPUCHIN, *Andrei Andreyevich, the middle-aged chairman of the Board of Directors of the* —— *Mutual Credit Society. Wears a monocle*

TATYANA ALEKSEEVNA (Tanyusha), *his wife, aged twenty-five*

KHIRIN, *Kuzma Nikolaevich, an elderly book-keeper at the bank*

MERCHUTKINA, *Nastasya Fëdorovna, an old woman. Wears an old-fashioned coat*

SHAREHOLDERS

EMPLOYEES *of the bank*

The action takes place at the offices of the
—— *Mutual Credit Society*

The office of the chairman of the Board of Directors.
At left a door leading to the main office of the bank.
There are two desks. The room is furnished to give an
impression of luxury: velvet-covered armchairs, flowers,
statuary, carpets, and a telephone. It is midday. Khirin
is alone; he is wearing felt boots.

KHIRIN
Shouts through the door
Will you send to the chemist's for four kopecks' worth
of valerian drops? And bring some fresh drinking water
to the chairman's office! Must I tell you a hundred
times? *goes over to one of the desks* I'm quite worn
out. I've been writing for three days now—I haven't
slept a wink—writing the whole day here and the
whole night at home. *coughs* And on top of all
that I'm feeling feverish all over. I'm shivering, I've
got a temperature and a cough, my legs ache, and I
keep seeing things like exclamation marks in front of
my eyes! *sits down* That scoundrel, that buffoon of
a chairman, is to read a report at our general meeting
today. It's to be called "Our bank, today and in the
future." He seems to fancy himself as a sort of Gam-

A
JUBILEE

betta! *writes* Two . . . one . . . one . . . zero . . . one . . . six . . . He's trying to throw dust in their eyes, so I've got to sit here working for him like a galley slave. All he did was to put a lot of imaginative nonsense into this report, that's all—the devil take him!— while I have to sit and click the counting beads all day long! *works with the beads on the abacus* I just hate it! *writes* Well, it comes to . . . one . . . three . . . seven . . . two . . . one . . . zero . . . He's promised to reward me for my work. If all goes well today and he succeeds in hoodwinking the audience, he's promised to give me a gold badge and a bonus of three hundred rubles. We'll see. *writes* But if my efforts are wasted, my friend, you mustn't complain if . . . I'm a hot-tempered man. When I'm roused I'm capable of committing a crime. Yes, indeed!

Noise and clapping offstage. Shipuchin's voice is heard saying, "Thank you! Thank you! I'm deeply touched!" Enter Shipuchin. He is in evening dress and a white tie and is holding an album with which he has just been presented

SHIPUCHIN
Standing in the doorway and speaking into the office My dear colleagues, I will cherish this gift till my dying day as a memento of the happiest occasion of my life! Yes, indeed, my dear friends! Thank you once again! *kisses his hand to the audience and goes toward Khirin* My dear, my most esteemed friend, Kuzma Nikolaevich!

While he remains on the stage employees come and go from time to time with papers for his signature

ANTON
CHEKHOV

KHIRIN
Getting up Andrei Andreyevich, may I have the

honor of congratulating you on the fifteenth anniversary of our bank and of wishing you . . .

SHIPUCHIN

Shaking his hand vigorously

Thank you, my dear friend. Thank you! We might
even kiss to celebrate this day—this very special day—
our jubilee! *they kiss* I'm so very, very glad! Thank
you for your services, for everything—thank you! If
I've done anything useful during the time I've had the
honor of being the chairman of this bank, I owe my
success in the first place to my colleagues. *sighs* Yes,
my friend, fifteen years! Fifteen years—that's a fact—
as true as my name is Shipuchin. *eagerly* Well,
how's my report? Getting on?

KHIRIN

Yes, I've only got five more pages to do.

SHIPUCHIN

That's fine. Then it'll be ready by three o'clock?

KHIRIN

If nothing prevents me I'll finish it by then. There's
only a trifle still to be done.

SHIPUCHIN

Excellent! Excellent! That's a fact—as true as my
name's Shipuchin! The general meeting is at four
o'clock. My friend, give me the first half; I'll go
through it. Give it to me quickly. *takes the report* I
pin my highest hopes on this report. This is my
profession de foi or, to put it more accurately, my
fireworks display! My fireworks display—that's a
fact, as true as my name's Shipuchin! *sits down and
reads the report to himself* I feel devilishly tired
though. I had an attack of gout last night and the
whole morning I've been fussing and running around.
Then all these ovations and the emotion and agita- A
tion. . . . I *am* tired! JUBILEE

Writes   Two . . . zero . . . zero . . . three . . . nine . . .
two . . . zero . . . Everything's going green in front of
my eyes with all these figures. . . . Three . . . one . . .
six . . . four . . . one . . . five . . .   *clicks the beads of the
abacus*

SHIPUCHIN

Then there was an unpleasant episode. This morning
your wife came to see me and complained about you
again. She told me that last night you'd been chasing
her with a knife—and your sister-in-law too. That sort
of thing won't do, Kuzma Nikolaich! It really won't
do at all!

KHIRIN

Sternly   Andrei Andreyevich, since this is our jubilee
day, may I take the liberty of making a request? I beg
you not to interfere with my family life, if only out of
consideration for the incredibly hard work I'm doing
here. Please don't!

SHIPUCHIN

Sighs   You're an impossible character, Kuzma
Nikolaich. You're a good man, really, quite a
respectable fellow, and yet with women you behave
like Jack the Ripper or someone of that sort. Really I
can't understand why you hate them so!

KHIRIN

And I can't understand why you love them so. . . .

SHIPUCHIN

After a pause

The employees have just presented me with an album
and I hear that the shareholders are going to present me
with an address and a silver tankard.   *plays with his
monocle*   That's fine! As true as my name's Shipuchin!
It won't do any harm! A certain amount of ceremony

ANTON
CHEKHOV

is necessary for the reputation of the bank, devil take it!
You're one of us, so you know all about it, of course.
I composed the address myself, and as for the silver
tankard—I bought that too. I also bought the cover for
the address—that cost me forty-five rubles, but it can't
be helped! They wouldn't have thought of it themselves. *looks around* What a fine set of furniture
though! What a collection! There! They say I pay too
much attention to trifles, that I only want the door
handles polished, the employees to wear smart ties,
and a fat porter to stand at the front door. But no, my
dear sirs! The door handles and the fat porter are not
trifles! I can be as much of a plebeian as I like at home,
I can eat and sleep like a pig, I can have my drinking
bouts . . .

KHIRIN

I beg you to refrain from making insinuations!

SHIPUCHIN

Oh, I'm not insinuating anything! What an impossible
character you are! I was just saying that at home I can
be a plebeian, a parvenu if I like—I can indulge my
habits—whereas here everything must be on the grand
scale. This is a bank. Here every detail must impress;
everything must have a solemn air, so to speak. *picks
up a scrap of paper from the floor and throws it into
the fireplace* My chief merit lies simply in this—I've
raised the reputation of the bank to a very high level!
It's the tone of the whole thing that matters so much!
That's a fact—as true as my name's Shipuchin! *looks
Khirin up and down* My dear fellow, the delegation
from the shareholders may be here at any moment—
and you're wearing felt boots and that scarf . . . and
your jacket's a simply incredible color. You might have
put on a frock coat or at least a black jacket.

A
JUBILEE

KHIRIN

My health is more important to me than all your shareholders. I've got a fever all over me.

SHIPUCHIN

Agitated But you must agree that this is out of place! You're spoiling the whole effect!

KHIRIN

I can hide if the delegation comes. As if it mattered! *writes* Seven . . . one . . . seven . . . two . . . one . . . five . . . zero . . . I don't like things being out of place myself! Seven . . . two . . . nine . . . *clicks the beads of the abacus* I simply can't stand things being out of place! You'd have done better not to invite ladies to the jubilee dinner today.

SHIPUCHIN

What nonsense!

KHIRIN

I know you'd like to fill the hall with them today just to show off, but you'd better watch out! They might mess up the whole thing for you! They cause nothing but trouble and disorder.

SHIPUCHIN

On the contrary, the society of women is elevating!

KHIRIN

Indeed! Take your wife for instance. She's supposed to be well educated, but last Monday she blurted something out—and it took me two days to get over it. All of a sudden she comes and asks me in the presence of strangers, "Is it true that my husband bought a lot of Dryashko-Pryashko shares for our bank, and then the price fell on the stock exchange? My husband is so worried!" And all that in the presence of strangers! I just can't understand why you confide in women! Do you want them to land you in court?

ANTON
CHEKHOV

That'll do, that'll do! This is all too gloomy for our
jubilee day. By the way you've just reminded me.
looks at his watch   My dear wife is due to arrive quite
soon. In fact I ought to have gone to the station to meet
her—poor little thing! But there's no time and . . . and
I feel too tired. To tell you the truth I'm not very
pleased that she's coming at all. I mean I am pleased,
but it would have been better still if she'd stayed at
her mother's a day or two longer. She'll insist on my
spending the whole evening with her, and we'd
planned a little expedition for tonight after dinner.
starts   You see, I'm beginning to tremble from sheer
nervousness. My nerves are so on edge that I feel a
mere trifle might make me burst into tears. No, no, I
must be strong . . . that's a fact—as true as my name's
Shipuchin!

*Enter Tatyana Alekseevna. She wears a raincoat and
has a traveling handbag on a strap over her shoulder*

Ah! We'd just been talking about you—and here you
are!

TATYANA

Darling!   *runs to her husband. A prolonged kiss*
SHIPUCHIN

Yes, we were just talking about you.   *looks at his
watch*

TATYANA

Breathlessly   Did you miss me? Are you well? I
haven't been home yet; I've come straight here from
the station. I've got such a lot to tell you, such a lot!
I can hardly wait. I won't take my things off; I'll only
stay a minute.   *to Khirin*   How do you do, Kuzma
Nikolaich?   *to her husband*   Is everything all right
at home?

A
JUBILEE

SHIPUCHIN

Yes, everything's all right. I believe you've gotten plumper and prettier during the week you've been away. Well, did you have a nice trip?

TATYANA

Excellent! Mamma and Katya send you their greetings. Vasili Andreyich told me to give you a kiss.   *kisses him*   Auntie sent you a pot of jam, and everyone's put out with you for not writing. Zina said I was to kiss you from her.   *kisses him*   Oh, if you only knew the things that have been happening! The things that have been happening! It makes me frightened even to speak of it! Such goings-on! But I see from your expression you're not really glad to have me back!

SHIPUCHIN

On the contrary! Darling!   *kisses her*

Khirin coughs angrily

TATYANA

Sighs   Poor dear Katya, the poor darling! I'm so sorry for her, so very sorry!

SHIPUCHIN

My dear, we're celebrating our jubilee today. A delegation from the shareholders may be here at any moment, and you're not properly dressed.

TATYANA

Of course—the jubilee! Congratulations, my friends! I wish you . . . So there's going to be a reception and a dinner! That's what I like! By the way, you remember that beautiful speech you've been composing for the shareholders—it took you such a time!—are they going to read it to you today?

ANTON
CHEKHOV

Khirin coughs angrily

Embarrassed   Darling, it isn't usual to talk about such
things. Really, you'd better go home.

TATYANA

In a moment, in a moment! It won't take me a minute
to tell you and then I'll go. I'll tell you everything from
the beginning. Well. . . . After you'd seen me off I sat
down beside that stout lady—you remember—and
began to read. I don't like talking on railway journeys.
So I kept on reading until we'd passed three stations
and didn't exchange a word with anybody. Then
evening came on and I began to have all sorts of depressing thoughts. A young man was sitting opposite
me—a fellow with dark hair, not at all bad-looking.
Well, we got talking. A naval man joined in, then a
sort of student.   *laughs*   I told them I wasn't
married. What a fuss they made over me! We chatted
right on till midnight. The dark-haired fellow was
telling screamingly funny stories, and the naval man
kept on singing. I laughed so much that my chest began
to ache. And when the navy man—oh, these sailors!—
when he found out that my name was Tatyana, do you
know what he started singing?   *sings in a bass voice*
          "Onegin, I cannot deny,
          I'll love Tatyana till I die"

Tatyana breaks into laughter; Khirin coughs angrily

SHIPUCHIN

All the same, Tanyusha, we're disturbing Kuzma
Nikolaich. Do go home, darling. You can tell me
afterward.

TATYANA

Never mind, never mind, let him hear it too. It's most   A
interesting. I won't be long telling you. Well, Serëzha   JUBILEE

met me at the station. Another young man turned up too—a tax inspector, I think—quite a nice-looking fellow, especially his eyes. Serëzha introduced us and we all took a cab. The weather was wonderful.

Voices offstage: "You mustn't go in there! It's not allowed. What do you want?" Enter Merchutkina

MERCHUTKINA
In the doorway, waving her arms at someone outside
You don't have to grab at me! What next! I want to see the chief.   *comes in; to Shipuchin*   May I have the honor of introducing myself, Your Excellency? I'm Nastasya Fëdorovna Merchutkina, a provincial secretary's wife.

SHIPUCHIN
What can I do for you?

MERCHUTKINA
If it please Your Excellency, it's like this: my husband, provincial secretary Merchutkin, has been ill five months, and while he was at home receiving treatment, they dismissed him from his job without any reason, Your Excellency. And when I went to get his pay, they'd gone and deducted twenty-four rubles, thirty-six kopecks if you please! Whatever for, I ask you? They told me he'd borrowed from the Mutual Aid Fund and other people had guaranteed the loan. But how could that have happened? As if he'd borrow anything without asking my permission first! They shouldn't have done it, Your Excellency. I'm a poor woman—I can only keep myself going by taking lodgers. I'm weak and defenseless. I have to put up with insults from everybody, and I never hear a kind word from anyone.

SHIPUCHIN
Excuse me.   *takes her petition from her and reads it standing up*

ANTON
CHEKHOV

TATYANA

To Khirin But I must begin at the beginning. Last
week I unexpectedly got a letter from mamma. She
wrote to tell me that a certain Grendilevski had made
a proposal of marriage to my sister Katya. A very nice,
modest young man, but entirely without means or any
definite position in life. And unfortunately—just
imagine it—Katya was rather attracted by him. What
was to be done? So mamma asked me to come at once
and use my influence with Katya.

KHIRIN

Sternly Excuse me, you've made me lose my place!
You—your mamma and Katya—and now I don't
know where I am and I'm all mixed up!

TATYANA

As if it mattered! You should listen when a lady is
talking to you! Why are you so grumpy today anyway?
Are you in love or what? *laughs*

SHIPUCHIN

To Merchutkina Excuse me, what's all this about?
I don't understand.

TATYANA

Are you in love? Ah-ah! You're blushing!

SHIPUCHIN

To his wife

Tanyusha, darling, please go into the office for a
minute. I won't be long.

TATYANA

Very well. *goes out*

SHIPUCHIN

I don't understand this at all. Obviously, madam,
you've come to the wrong place. In fact your business
has nothing whatever to do with us. You should apply
to the department where your husband used to be
employed.

A
JUBILEE

MERCHUTKINA

But sir, I've been to five different places already and they wouldn't even read my petition. I just couldn't think what else I could do. But my son-in-law, Boris Matveich—I'm grateful to him—he gave me the idea of coming to you. "Go to Mr. Shipuchin, mamma," he says, "he's an influential gentleman, he can do anything." Please, Your Excellency, help me!

SHIPUCHIN

Madam Merchutkina, we really can't do anything for you. Please understand: your husband, as far as I can make out, worked in the Medical Department of the War Office, whereas our institution here is a private one, a commercial concern, a bank. Can't you understand that?

MERCHUTKINA

As for my husband's illness, Your Excellency, I have the doctor's certificate to prove it. Here it is, if you'd be kind enough to look at it.

SHIPUCHIN

With irritation   That's excellent. I believe you, but I repeat—it doesn't concern us.

Tatyana's laughter is heard offstage; then a man's laughter

glancing at the door   She's interrupting the work of the clerks out there.   *to Merchutkina*   It's a queer business and even rather absurd. Doesn't your husband know where you have to apply?

MERCHUTKINA

My husband doesn't know anything, Your Excellency. All he keeps saying is, "It's not your business! Get out!" That's all.

SHIPUCHIN

I must repeat, madam; your husband was employed

at the Medical Department of the War Office, whereas
this is a bank, a private commercial institution.

MERCHUTKINA

Just so, just so. I understand, sir. So would you please
tell them to pay me just fifteen rubles, Your Excellency?
I don't mind not having all of it at once.

SHIPUCHIN

Sighs Ough!

KHIRIN

Andrei Andreyich, I'll never finish the report at this
rate!

SHIPUCHIN

Just a moment. *to Merchutkina* You don't seem to
be able to grasp it. Please try to understand that to
make a request like this from us is just as absurd as to
apply for a divorce at . . . let's say at a chemist's shop
or at the Assay Office.

*A knock on the door. Tatyana's voice offstage: "Andrei,
may I come in?"*

shouts Wait a bit, darling! In a minute! *to
Merchutkina* You weren't given his full pay, but
what has it got to do with us? Besides, madam, we're
having a jubilee today. We're busy, and someone
might come in here at any moment. Please excuse me.

MERCHUTKINA

Your Excellency, do have pity on an orphan woman!
I'm weak and defenseless. I feel so worn out, I might
just as well be dead. The things I have to do—taking
lodgers to court, running around on my husband's
affairs, looking after the house—and now my son-in-
law is out of a job too.

SHIPUCHIN

Madam Merchutkina, I . . . No, forgive me, I can't
talk to you! My head's going around and around.

You're disturbing us, and you're wasting your own time too. *sighs, apart* What an idiot! And that's a fact—as true as my name's Shipuchin! *to Khirin* Kuzma Nikolaich, please explain to Madam Merchutkina ... *makes a hopeless gesture and goes out into the office*

KHIRIN

Approaches Merchutkina, sternly
What is it you want?

MERCHUTKINA

I'm a weak, defenseless woman. I may look strong, but if you could take me apart and look at me properly, you'd see there isn't a single healthy bit in my body! I can hardly keep on my feet, and my appetite's all gone. I drank some coffee this morning and I didn't enjoy it a bit.

KHIRIN

I'm asking you a question: what is it you want?

MERCHUTKINA

Please, sir, just tell them to pay me fifteen rubles. I can wait a month or so for the rest.

KHIRIN

But surely you've just been told in plain language that this is a bank!

MERCHUTKINA

Of course, of course. And if necessary, I can show you the medical certificate.

KHIRIN

Have you or have you not got a head on your shoulders?

MERCHUTKINA

Kind sir, I'm only asking for what is legally due to me. I don't want anything that isn't mine.

KHIRIN

Madam, I'm asking you a simple question: have you a head on your shoulders or is it something else? Well,

devil take it, I haven't the time to talk to you! I'm busy!
shows her the door   Please!

MERCHUTKINA

Surprised   But what about the money?

KHIRIN

The fact is that you haven't got a head at all; you've
got this instead.   *taps the desk and then his forehead
with his finger*

MERCHUTKINA

Offended   What's that? You mind your own business!
You can do that sort of thing with your own wife, not
with me. I'm a government official's wife. You'd
better not take any liberties with me!

KHIRIN

Flaring up, in a low voice
If you don't go away this minute, I'll send for the hall
porter! Out with you!   *stamps his feet*

MERCHUTKINA

Steady, steady! I'm not scared of you! We've seen the
likes of you before. Pen-pusher!

KHIRIN

I don't believe I've ever seen anyone looking so
repulsive in my life! Ough! She makes me feel quite
dizzy with anger.   *breathes heavily*   I'll tell you once
more. D'you hear? If you don't go away from here,
I'll grind you to powder, you old witch! I've got such
a temper that I'm capable of making a cripple of you
for life! I'm capable of any crime!

MERCHUTKINA

Your bark's worse than your bite! I'm not afraid of you.
I've seen the likes of you before.

KHIRIN

In despair   I can't bear to look at her! I feel quite sick!   A
I can't stand it!   *goes to his desk and sits down*   He's   JUBILEE

filled the bank with petticoats. How can I get on with the report—I just can't!

MERCHUTKINA

I'm not asking for anything that's not mine; I'm asking for what belongs to me by law. You shameless fellow! Wearing felt boots in a place like this! You yokel!

Enter Shipuchin and Tatyana

TATYANA

Following her husband

Well, then we went to an evening party at the Berezhnitskis'. Katya was wearing a little blue taffeta dress trimmed with fine lace, with a low neck. It suits her so to have her hair done in a pile on top of her head, and I arranged it myself. When she was dressed and had her hair done, she looked simply enchanting!

SHIPUCHIN

He is suffering from a migraine

Quite so, quite so. Enchanting. Someone may be coming any moment now.

MERCHUTKINA

Your Excellency!

SHIPUCHIN

Dispirited   What now? What do you want?

MERCHUTKINA

Your Excellency!   *points at Khirin*   That man there. Yes, him. He tapped on the desk and then on his forehead. You told him to look into my case, but he's just being sarcastic and saying all sorts of things. I'm a weak, defenseless woman.

SHIPUCHIN

Very well, madam. I'll look into it and take the appropriate measures. Just go away now. Later on! *aside*   I've got an attack of gout coming on!

ANTON
CHEKHOV

Approaching Shipuchin, in a low voice
Andrei Andreyevich, allow me to send for the hall
porter and tell him to throw her out of here. This is
getting impossible!

SHIPUCHIN
Alarmed No, no! She'll start screaming; there are a
lot of private dwellings in this building!

MERCHUTKINA
Your Excellency!

KHIRIN
In a tearful voice
But I've got to write the report! I won't have time to
finish it! *returns to his desk* I just can't go on!

MERCHUTKINA
Your Excellency, when am I going to be paid the
money, please? I need it right now.

SHIPUCHIN
Aside, indignantly What an extraordinarily repulsive
woman! *to Merchutkina, in a gentle voice* Madam,
I have already informed you that this is a bank, a
private commercial concern.

MERCHUTKINA
Be kind to me, Your Excellency; be a father to an
orphan woman! If the medical certificate isn't enough,
I can get a paper from the police too. Tell them to pay
me the money!

SHIPUCHIN
Sighs heavily Ough!

TATYANA
To Merchutkina But granny, haven't they told you
that you're in the way here? You really are a strange
person!

A
JUBILEE

MERCHUTKINA

Madam, my beautiful lady, I've nobody to help me with my troubles. Eating and drinking don't mean a thing. I had coffee this morning, and I didn't enjoy it the least little bit.

SHIPUCHIN

At the end of his tether, to Merchutkina

How much is it you want?

MERCHUTKINA

Twenty-four rubles, thirty-six kopecks.

SHIPUCHIN

Very well! *takes a twenty-five ruble note out of his wallet and gives it to her* Here's twenty-five rubles for you. Take it and please go away!

Khirin coughs angrily

MERCHUTKINA

Thank you kindly, Your Excellency. *puts the money away*

TATYANA

Sits down beside her husband

I ought to be going home though. *looks at her watch* But I haven't quite finished telling you yet. I'll finish in a moment; then I'll go. The things that have been happening! Oh, the things that have been happening! Well, we went along to the party at the Berezhnitskis'. It was so-so, quite jolly, but not specially jolly. Katya's admirer, Grendilevski, was there too of course. Well, I had a talk with Katya, I cried a little, I used my influence with her, and she agreed to talk it over with Grendilevski there and then at the party, and she refused him. Now, I thought, everything's straightened out as well as anyone could wish. I've made mamma happy, I've saved Katya, and now I can relax a bit too. But what do you think? Just before supper Katya and I

ANTON
CHEKHOV

were taking a stroll in the garden and suddenly . . .
agitated And suddenly we heard a shot! No, I can't
speak of it calmly! *fans herself with her handkerchief*
I just can't!

SHIPUCHIN

Sighs Ough!

TATYANA

Weeping We ran to the summer house and there . . .
there lay poor Grendilevski . . . with a pistol in his
hand.

SHIPUCHIN

No, I just can't bear it! I can't bear it! *to Merchutkina*
Now what do you want?

MERCHUTKINA

Please, Your Excellency, could my husband have his
job back?

TATYANA

Weeping He'd shot straight at his heart, just there.
Katya dropped down in a dead faint, poor dear. And
he too was dreadfully scared. He just lay there and . . .
and begged us to send for the doctor. The doctor came
quite soon and saved the unfortunate young man.

MERCHUTKINA

Your Excellency, could my husband have his job back?

SHIPUCHIN

No! I can't bear this any longer! *weeps* I really
can't! *stretching both his arms toward Khirin, in
despair* Turn her out! Turn her out, I implore you!

KHIRIN

Coming up to Tatyana
Get out of here!

SHIPUCHIN

No, not her. That one . . . that horror. *pointing at*
Merchutkina That one!

KHIRIN

Not understanding him, to Tatyana

Get out of here! *stamps his feet* Get out I tell you!

TATYANA

What? What are you saying? Are you mad?

SHIPUCHIN

This is dreadful! How unfortunate I am! Make her
go away! Go on, turn her out!

KHIRIN

To Tatyana Out of here! I'll make a cripple of you!
I'll smash you to pieces. I'll commit a crime!

TATYANA

Runs away from him while he chases her

How dare you? You're being extremely impertinent!
Andrei! Save me! Andrei! *screams*

SHIPUCHIN

Running after them

Do stop this, I implore you! Be quiet! Spare my
reputation!

KHIRIN

Chases after Merchutkina

Get out of here! Catch her! Smash her to pulp! Make
mincemeat of her!

SHIPUCHIN

Shouts Stop, stop! I beg you! I implore you!

MERCHUTKINA

Holy Fathers! Saints! *screams* Holy Fathers!

TATYANA

Shouts Help! Save me! Oh! Oh! I feel faint! I'm
fainting! *jumps onto a chair, then falls down onto a
sofa and moans as if in a faint*

KHIRIN

ANTON
CHEKHOV

Chasing Merchutkina Smash her! Skin her alive!
Cut her to pieces!

Oh, oh! Holy Fathers! Everything's going black in
front of my eyes! Oh! *drops senseless into Shipuchin's
arms*

*A knock on the door. A voice offstage says, "The
delegation"*

SHIPUCHIN
Delegation . . . reputation . . . occupation . . .

KHIRIN
Stamping his feet
Get out! The devil take it! *pulls up his sleeves* Just
let me get hold of her! I could commit a crime!

*Enter a delegation of five men all dressed in frock coats.
One holds the address in a velvet cover, another the
silver tankard. Employees of the bank look in through the
open office door. Tatyana is on the sofa, Merchutkina
in Shipuchin's arms, both moaning softly*

A SHAREHOLDER
Reads in a loud voice
Our dear and most respected friend, Andrei
Andreyevich! As we cast a retrospective glance at the
past of our financial institution and survey in our
mind's eye the history of its gradual development, we
receive an impression that is, in the highest degree,
satisfactory and refreshing. It is no doubt true that in
its early stages the small dimensions of its original
capital, its failure to carry through any big financial
operations, and the indefinite character of its aims, set
before us in sharpest outline Hamlet's question: to be
or not to be? In fact at one time voices were raised
suggesting that the bank should be closed. But then
you put yourself at the head of our concern. Your   A
knowledge, your energy, your outstanding gift of tact—   JUBILEE

572 all these qualities brought about extraordinary success
and exceptional prosperity. The reputation of the
bank . . . *coughs* The reputation of the bank . . .

MERCHUTKINA
Groans Oh! Oh!

TATYANA
Moans Water! Water!

SHAREHOLDER
Continues The reputation . . . *coughs* the reputation of the bank has been raised by you to such
heights that our institution can now compete with the
best concerns abroad.

SHIPUCHIN
Delegation . . . reputation . . . occupation . . .

> "One night two friends went out for a walk
> And as they strolled they had an earnest talk.
> Oh, do not say your youthful life is ruined—
> That through my jealousy you suffered
> pains untold . . ."

SHAREHOLDER
Continues in embarrassment
Then as we cast a realistic glance at the present, our
dear and most respected friend, Andrei Andreyevich . . .
dropping his voice In the circumstances we'd better
postpone it. It will be better to postpone it. . . .

They go out in confusion

CURTAIN